In Search of the Next P.O.T.U.S.

(President of the United States)

One Woman's Quest to Fix Washington
A True Story

Judy Frankel

ISBN: 0996203206
ISBN-13: 978-0-9962032-0-3

DEDICATION

In memory of Aaron Swartz, hacker, writer, and activist,
whose brilliance was snuffed out too soon.

-and-

To my Bubala.

CONTENTS

ACKNOWLEDGMENTS

I wish to express my deepest appreciation to the following authors and critics who helped me become a better writer: Paula Reuben, Eddy Bay, Julie Brown, Jody Wilkinson, Mary Jo Hazard, Tom Mooney, Jean Shriver, Cat Spydell, Jeff Guenther, Gill Beall, Judy Bayer, Lorrie Kazan, Vangie Maynard, Cheri Newell, Lori Jones, David Freeman, Saquina Akanni, Tricia Hopper, Larry Andrews, Chris Lynch, Laura Porter, Al Kanauka, Rudy Whitcomb, Laura Hines-Jurgens, and Ildy Lee.

Thank you, Suzanne Kellner-Zinck for believing in me when I needed it most. For their constant support and encouragement, I am grateful for Sarojni Mehta-Lissak and Lizabeth Delfs. For his gardening acumen and humorous anecdotes, I appreciate James "Jimmy" McCollum. For her positive, upbeat thinking, thank you, Arely Posz.

Thanks to Naomi Carling, Naomi Janzen and Stephen Fearnley for lulling me back to sleep in the middle of the morning when I usually have "monkey mind."

Praises to Angela Houle for editing my manuscript. A special thank you to Roslyn Bodanis, for excellence as a proofreader and networker.

Regarding accuracy, I thank Don Chance for his comments on derivatives. Thanks to Peter James Bearse for his consistent guidance and support, and to Carmine Gorga for his advice on economics.

Manu Martinez deserves praise for his work linking Native Voice TV across the country. Perhaps he will also start the first big Citizens Congress with Peter Bearse.

To Money Out, Voters In (MOVI) members, and especially to Mary Beth Fielder and Michelle Sutter: thank you for all you do in the movement to get money out of politics. To Holly Mosher, producer and the dude, John Ennis, thank you for teaching us about voting problems.

For coming through at the last minute, Jim Montgomery deserves a heap of praise. To my sister, Janet Moyer, you know how much I love you.

And finally, thanks to my fellow Wolf PAC volunteers for being patient with me while I finished this book. A special acknowledgement goes to: Cenk Uygur, Alison Hartson, Kathy Orlinsky, Kit Cabello, Steve Geller, Kari Khoury, Will Yate, Jaime Garfield, Noah Neumark, Stephan Medcalf, Jerry Ryberg, Lucas Smalldon, Mary VanDerostyne, Elie Parham, Regina Marie, Samuel Fieldman, Michael Hughes, Vince Wallace, Jason Bonsall, Kayode Medugbon, Susan Singer, and Mike Monetta. There are too many Wolf PAC volunteers to do them all justice. Thanks to you, we have a fighting chance to turn the tide

AUTHOR'S NOTE

For the purpose of presenting a cleaner more readable text, the reader will not be burdened with endnote numbers. I have organized my research in a bibliography, arranged by chapter, at the end of the book.

Though the stories contained herein are true, I have taken the liberty to change certain names or inconsequential details to protect the privacy of specific individuals. When I write about a popular public figure, my account cleaves as closely to truth as one person's viewpoint allows. When using first and last name, I endeavor to be as factual as possible, especially regarding first-hand experiences. But for the fantasy interludes, all bets are off.

INTRODUCTION

I distrust countless politicians and I'm fed up with Congress, but the government plays a role in many aspects of my life. It dictates the food in the supermarkets, it decides upon access to the Internet, oversees loans for education and the budget for weapons of mass destruction. It takes a third or more of my income and what do I have to show for it?

Our government is broken. We no longer live in a country that represents the people who live here. In fact, Washington spends a lot of money and hurts us. If we were living in a system made "of the people, by the people, for the people," would we let Citicorp get away with inserting a special provision into the last-minute government funding bill in December, 2014, to make sure American taxpayers will bail them out the next time their banking practices threaten to crash the world's economy? Would we have gone to war with Iraq? Would we pass laws that protect the interests of monopolies that are squeezing out our savings?

Because our government is broken, many of us have dropped out. Since we aren't voting and participating in democracy, nothing is going to change.

Now is the critical moment for Americans to rise to the occasion. Together, we are going to make things better, and this is a handbook for making that happen. With the tools described herein, let's answer the question: if crony capitalism is horrid and socialism is frightening, what kind of government will work?

Imagine having a decent President to guide us during these

times. Someone with vision, someone inspiring. More Americans vote during Presidential elections than during midterm, congressional elections. It's fun to feel like a part of deciding who becomes the next "leader of the free world." Americans love to see a rags to riches story in business; wouldn't it be great to watch some relative unknown, a third option underdog, rocket to the top? Thanks to the Internet, the next POTUS (President of the United States) might rise up from a viral, populist movement.

However, this story isn't just about searching for the next POTUS. I'm also seeking a new Congress. Congress can fix the United States' problems, but not the Congress inhabiting Washington right now. How about electing trustworthy representatives who will protect our rights and repeal laws that have ruined our economy and our Constitution?

If you care about our country, our one and only home, then you're in the right place.

The following chapters are organized into four sections, with my personal story woven throughout to provide entertainment. The first section describes how I developed my electioneering website called Writeindependent.org that endeavors to remove the barriers between voters and candidates while making lobbyists obsolete.

The second section unpacks the problems as I see them, and yes, I'm concerned about who becomes our next President because that decision makes a huge difference.

The third section explores the humbling realities of trying to run a nonprofit political social welfare organization. My cautionary tales of setbacks will prevent those who follow from treading the same territory. However, through my activism and research, I identify a six-point plan for fixing Washington, an amalgam of solutions bubbling up from the "get-money-out-of-politics" communities. I pinpoint the movement that will restore our self-governance, whether Congress likes it or not.

Finally, the last section shares simple actions that make sense for the average person, for everyone who cares about this country. The reason I wrote this book? It's a call to action. America, your motherland, is being violated before your very eyes and she needs you, now more than ever.

SIX POINT PLAN
TO FIX WASHINGTON

The Six Point Plan for improving the U.S. government to make it more responsive to Americans:

1. Use a well-designed, interactive website to review candidates' platforms, ask them questions via debates, and engage in solutions.
2. Ask your representatives to sign the "Pledge for Honest Candidates" that promises to pass the American Anti-Corruption Act and if they refuse, then only vote for candidates who *will* sign it. For more information, see http://www.writeindependent.org/contentpage.php?id=19
3. Ask your state's legislature to demand a "convention of the states" to amend the Constitution (see Chapter 38 for details and descriptions of the type of amendments needed).
4. Make rigorous civics education in high school mandatory so that citizens learn how to be politically responsible.
5. Give every registered voter membership to a Citizen's Congress. (See Chapter 38 to learn how a Citizen's Congress is an effective means for citizen participation in power.)
6. Clean up the ballot box and vote-counting. Remove barriers to free and fair elections. (See Chapter 30.)

1
ANYTHING IS POSSIBLE

Something hit me very hard once, thinking about what one little man could do. Think of the Queen Elizabeth: the whole ship goes by and then comes the rudder. And there's a tiny thing on the edge of the rudder called a trim tab. It's a miniature rudder. Just moving that little trim tab builds a low pressure that pulls the rudder around. It takes almost no effort at all. So I said that the individual can be a trim tab.

Society thinks it's going right by you, that it's left you altogether. But if you're doing dynamic things mentally, the fact is that you can just put your foot out like that and the whole ship of state is going to turn around. So I said, 'call me Trim Tab.'
  – Buckminster Fuller, American designer
and inventor 1895-1983

This story about a new vision for America began in a garden. More specifically, it started with a juicy, red, ripe tomato.

I grew up on a farm, approximately 126 acres in Limerick, Pennsylvania, population 5,000. My dad was a pharmacist, not a farmer, and a Mennonite family across the way grew corn and soy on our fields. Dad had a little garden patch, 20 feet by 40 feet, next to the chicken coop. Treasures from its harvest conditioned my palate for extraordinary food: crunchy cucumbers, crisp green beans packed with real flavor, and sweet cantaloupe. Dad's tomatoes are etched into my memory—each luscious globe packed with sugar and a tinge of tomato-y tartness.

As a kid, I delighted in watching purple crocuses push their petals out of the thawing ground. Soon after, daffodils with their yellow faces reaching for the sun announced the arrival of spring. Clouds of lilac fragrance wafted up the path of rock steps from the driveway to the front door of our two hundred and fifty year old colonial farmhouse.

I spent much of my childhood alone, exploring our property and its riches. I plucked a hundred blossoms from the enormous banks of honeysuckle. With my thumbnail, I broke each flower's tender petal just above its green calyx at the base, but not all the way through. I placed the honeysuckle on my tongue and pulled the pistil to collect a drop of nectar, sucking its sweet moisture. I'd gather handfuls of wild violets and Johnny jump-ups for my mother, filling the kitchen with little bouquets. And life was good.

I hiked up through the forest, into rooms carpeted with dense fallen leaves. The branches above, moving softly in the wind, formed the roof of my cathedral. If my friends couldn't come to play in the boondocks, I had Hartenstein creek, the wildflowers, and wind swooshing through the canopy of dense trees to entertain me.

But my paradise was under attack. A nuclear power company threatened the break into Limerick's skyline with two massive cooling towers. My mother joined a ragtag group of activists to fight it. With her encouragement, at twelve years of age, I spoke in front of the Nuclear Regulatory Commission (NRC), asking them, "what are you going to do with the nuclear waste?"

The NRC only smiled at me from behind their table on the dais. They knew the citizens would not prevail; there was too much money involved.

Six years later, the worst nuclear power accident in U.S. history happened at Three Mile Island, only 80 miles to the west of us. The core of their second nuclear reactor partially melted down, and soon after, hypothyroidism doubled in newborns downwind of the power plant.

Mom marched on Washington at the big no nukes rally. She prepared me to become an activist while my Dad infused me with a passion for gardening.

At 30 years of age, I bought my first real estate in Long Beach, California. My condo didn't have a back yard in which to plant even a clump of thyme. I searched for a community garden and found one that put my name on their waiting list in 1996. I tried growing plants in pots on my balcony in the hopes of tasting the ultimate Dad-inspired tomato, without much success.

In 1998, I finally became the proud steward of a community garden plot. I had my first serious tussle with dirt through double-digging, applying biointensive, organic mini-farming methods I learned from a book by John Jeavons. I have fond memories of sowing each seed with tender loving care, ever mindful of its season, neighboring plants, and its sequence in the cycle of crop rotation.

One day, I asked the more experienced gardeners a question they could not answer. The founder of the community gardens suggested that I phone a master gardener (MG) through the Cooperative Extension program. What is a master gardener, I wondered? How does one earn that distinction? And can I get a baseball cap with an embroidered logo on it that says I'm a master gardener?

I called the MG hotline to ask my question. As a result of that conversation, I attended a ten-week course through the University of California Cooperative Extension Master Gardener Program. They taught me about the soil-food web, how to grow grapes, and what the letters N-P-K mean on a bag of fertilizer. They hoped I would impart that knowledge to low-income families, planting seeds throughout Los Angeles.

Fast forward to 2011. I was newly divorced and needed full-time employment. I have a little gardening business called Judy's Homegrown where I prune, train and fertilize fruit trees, grapevines, and rosebushes. It doesn't pay the bills yet. After being out of the workforce for a decade to focus on the special needs of my child, it's been difficult to get a running start on a career.

Fortunately, my daughter and I live in our house surrounded by a lush vegetable garden and rare fruit orchard. Without a reliable job, I couldn't qualify for a mortgage, so I paid for my home with my deceased mother's inheritance and proceeds of the sale of our family farm in Pennsylvania. Currently, I grow more than one hundred and fifty varieties of fruits, vegetables, and herbs on 6,500 square feet in my yard. This translates to a lower food bill, as about

90% of our produce comes directly from the garden. But I worry about losing this little farm if I can't cover the property taxes.

To meet my financial obligations, I started looking for a clue that would direct me not just to any job, but instead to a vocation. Sometimes signs don't come out of the ether; they grow like gallstones, over a long period. And then one day, it just hurts so badly you have to get the operation. That's how I discovered my calling.

Before I reveal the inciting event that pointed me in the direction I would take for the next 18 months, let me explain the build-up. I had been learning how food production, and especially nutritionally dense food, depends upon little organisms in the soil—microorganisms like bacteria and fungi that digest nutrients so that plants can absorb them.

A California Rare Fruit Grower friend named Jimmy had given me a package of granular mycorrhizae (my cor eye zuh). "Pure, fresh, alive!" the bag promised on its label. When sprinkled in the soil, the fungi attach to plants' root systems, increasing their surface area by one hundred fold. Mycorrhizae (literally "root fungi") looks like white filaments of thin silly string. Marijuana growers love the stuff, and add it to their hydroponic setups to get the most out of each individual weed.

What's great about fungi is that they synergistically turn regular plants into super plants, sucking up nutrients from thither and yon with the fungi's extended root-like system. These super plants then capture vast amounts of carbon with their bodacious leaf surfaces and transfer it into the soil.

From working with these special fungi, I was primed to have my mind blown when I read the book *The Organic Manifesto* by Maria Rodale. She connected the dots for me by explaining that these super plants, in concert with microorganisms, can combat climate change! Mycorrhizae is not only an elegant way to mitigate global warming, it is helpful for growing food in hostile weather.

Does the President of the United States know about this fungus? I wondered. At the same moment that I'm ready to write my congressman to ask if he would leverage this information to deal with climate change, Maria Rodale goes on to say that through chemical farming, we're messing with these organisms! She wrote that herbicides like RoundUp® have been wreaking havoc on beneficial bacteria and fungi.

Our current agriculture system sprays tons of the weed killer on our food, more than four pounds per person per year in the United States. Monsanto, a chemical company, was the first to patent glyphosate (gli fos ate), the active ingredient in RoundUp®. When farmers buy RoundUp Ready® seeds, they sign a contract to spray the resulting plants with RoundUp®, killing weeds while soaking the food Americans eat in glyphosate.

It's the one-two punch. Monsanto has been selling products that keep plants from acting as super carbon eradicators while impregnating our food with chemicals.

When I walk the aisles of a grocery store, I imagine a pink cast over the food packages that might have RoundUp® in it. Anything made from corn or soy. Anything with high fructose corn syrup, modified food starch, glutamate, malt syrup! Monsanto recommends "preharvest crop staging" of wheat and canola to control weeds, so anything with wheat or canola. The list of suspicious ingredients is so long, it's almost a guarantee that if it isn't labeled "certified organic," it's likely to have a glyphosate-soaked plant somewhere in its production life. About 80 to 90% of the processed foods in the supermarket are tainted by herbicide. Since I'm not one hundred percent certain that it's safe, I don't want to eat the "pink" food.

Monsanto's own studies show statistically significant decreases in viable fetuses and mean fetal body weight of the pregnant rats they dosed with glyphosate. Much later, I would find out about the physiological link between glyphosate and autism, Alzheimers, and Parkinsons. RoundUp's® proprietary chemical brew that makes the glyphosate absorb into the plant's tissues amps up that toxicity. And you can't wash it off.

The genesis of my personal mission to stand up to the agribusiness giants happened one day while running errands. Still in the state of mind that I had discovered the answer to climate change, my purpose in life announced itself as I dropped off a pair of pants at a self-professed "environmentally friendly" dry cleaner. The toothy but sour proprietor noticed the book I was carrying. "What are you reading?" he asked.

"*The Organic Manifesto*, by Maria Rodale," I answered. "She believes that if we switch to organic farming all over the world, it will hold off global warming." It was June of 2011.[1]

"It's too late," he said.

I stood there, stunned. Did this man, who claims to be my eco-buddy, really just say what I thought I heard? He punched his register and printed out my receipt as though he hadn't said anything significant.

His off-handed remark set off an explosion of my figurative gallstones sending a sharp pain to my head. What is he implying? That we're doomed? That we should give up? What is the point of being environmentally conscious?

He wanted to explain his comment, but it was moot. I cut him off and left his place as fast as I could. I felt like crying, but I was also angry. What kind of future will my daughter and other children have if the message they receive from us is that humans have no effect on our destiny?

I thrashed through the possible scenarios with existential angst. Are we passive visitors to this planet? Perhaps it wasn't meant to last, like a mass of uncivilized savages carelessly trudging from pump to parking space, from work to tomb. Maybe we each have a sick fascination for viewing large-scale catastrophes like outlandish weather patterns and watching mad lunatics march young soldiers or mercenaries into danger, knowing things are terribly wrong, but not doing anything to push the "stop" button.

Have you ever heard the question: if you could be assured of success, what would you do? I have taken that query to heart. I want to choose a career that somehow stops chemical-based agriculture and stops the insane practice of putting profits over

---

[1] In his book about global warming called *The Greatest Hoax: How the Global Warming Conspiracy Threatens Your Future*, U.S. Senator James Inhofe doesn't actually deny global warming. He does, however, take the same position as some of the scientists that Mr. Inhofe quotes in his book: that should a catastrophic scenario prove correct, the Kyoto protocol would not prevent it. Mr. Inhofe also explains that the blame for global warming can not be placed on human influence. I ask Mr. Inhofe: does it really matter if humans caused it, if our families and their children will have to be concerned about global warming's effects? Would Mr. Inhofe prefer that we do little or nothing to mitigate its effects? Reducing carbon is the main antidote to increases in atmospheric temperature. Should we continue to increase carbon, or decrease carbon?

health. But if I were going to be successful at whatever I chose, why end there? What good would it do for us to inherit a planet full of water unfit to drink and poisoned air, with so much free floating radiation and Chromium 6 that cancer touched everyone under thirty? I want to clean up the ecology of our home, to inspire a large-scale waste management program. How different would the world be if we all worked together to replace war-like aggression with agriculture, and replace the burning of fossil fuels with other safer technologies? In return for this adventure, I desire the comfort of knowing my daughter will live in this garden when we are done making the world safer and healthier.

We can alleviate our pain and suffering, before it gets worse.

Will you join me?

We are at a crisis point, a transition. When we stuff down our feelings of helplessness, we retreat rather than facing our problems. Our misguided government's oppression is overwhelming. We try to ignore it and hope someone else takes care of it. Yet, we're afraid that if we sit idly by, the world will spin out of control.

No! Don't give up. Join me. We shall restore the rule of law. We shall restore the American ideals of safety in our homes, privacy in our effects and communications, and freedom to speak and assemble peacefully, even when protesting our own government.

If we stand together as a force for good, we shall change what's going wrong. We will breathe again. We will feel like a weight has been lifted, and our spirits will soar. The question is: how will it happen?

The only way to make such ambitious changes is through politics. I thought about the President's role in influencing the world through his or her choices. And Congress holds the keys to setting policy.

An idea seized me for accomplishing this enormous task of healing America, forcing me to lie awake most nights. It was like I had fallen in love; I could barely think about anything else. Looking back, I realize that it was sheer naïveté that caused me to believe I had stumbled across the answer to our political quagmire. Sometimes the most powerful ideas are the simplest. This was the idea: why not advertise the names and platforms of all the candidates running for federal office online, so that anyone can campaign for office without having to spend half of each day raising a "bazillion" dollars? Then maybe we could get some fresh faces in Congress who are not beholden to corporate backers. Thus, Writeindependent.org was born and my journey to the New America took its first steps.

2
INSPIRATION STRUCK

Whatever you can do, or dream you can, begin it.
Boldness has genius, power and magic in it.
– Johann Wolfgang von Goethe, German writer and statesman
1749-1832

I searched the Internet to find a website like the one that was formulating in my brain. If designed well, it would show all the candidates running for Senate in each state with open seats and all the candidates competing for the House of Representatives in each of the federal congressional districts. It had to explain to regular folks how to run for office, should accept a new candidate's nomination, and most importantly, would give voters a way to communicate their solutions to the candidates.

The purpose of an electioneering and problem-solving website is to give Americans a way to directly participate in their own governance, based on the principles upon which our country was founded. As Robert Kennedy said, "In a democratic society, law is the form which free men give to justice. The glory of justice and the majesty of law are created not just by the Constitution—nor by the courts—nor by the officers of the law—nor by the lawyers— but by the men and women who constitute our society—who are the protectors of the law as they themselves are protected by the law." Citizens must be involved in creating and supporting the laws, or someone else will decide who gets what, and how the law is enforced, without regard for Americans' needs or pain.

If only voters could see all the choices laid out in one place, they could throw their support behind a particular person by clicking "thumbs up." And ultimately, it could be used to demand that the candidates show their position on specific bills or issues...*before* they get elected.

No more could voters use the excuses, "I had to choose so-and-so, because only the ones who have money can win," or "he was the lesser of two evils." With the power of online consensus and thoughtful, intelligent review of options, voters can convince one another that a particular man or woman has their best interests at heart. The electorate can give serious consideration to candidates who perhaps don't have the money to buy television ads, but who build support through meeting constituents face-to-face, debating the competition, and utilizing social media.

What I found through searching the web is that you have to visit several separate websites to collect information on the candidates. It's never an apples-to-apples comparison. Campaign websites often list a bunch of hollow promises and campaign rhetoric. What if we made candidates accountable to the public through questions and answers or a simple, uniform vetting process? And what if voters could begin a conversation about the solutions the people of each district most want to see promoted?

The original design for the website had six parts:

1. An easy-to-read platform for each federal candidate.

2. Forms for nominating someone (or one's self) to run for office. I encouraged unemployed visitors to "run for office" and "replace your congressman."[2]

3. An "ideas" section, organized by issue, where anybody or entity (group of people) could post their solutions. The ideas have a "thumbs up or down" feature, and message boards for comments from other users.

4. An educational component, teaching voters how to use their

---

[2] I focused on fixing the federal government only. Many folks have asked me to include state governments at Writeindependent.org. One can only imagine how huge a website would have to be to handle both state and federal governments in one place.

write-in voting power so that we can elect an independent President, even when she isn't listed on the ballot.

5. A "Presidential Appointments" section, where voters recommend excellent people to work at the President's behest in one of the 1,600+ positions appointed by a newly elected President.

6. A user profile page, showing whom you endorse, what solutions you posted or liked, and any communication you've written on the message boards.

A powerful feature of the website is that it enables the voter to promote an idea by writing a suggestion and getting his friends to give it an up or down vote. This function was inspired by *The Citizens Briefing Book*, part of Obama's transition website, Change.gov. Immediately after Obama won the 2008 election, I received an email with a link to this well-designed, sleek portal asking for my suggestions for the new administration. Everyone who visited the site was welcome to feel as though they had a straight line to the new President if their idea captured enough clicks.

A Minnesota-based company called Reside developed *Citizens Briefing Book* using Customer Relationship Management (CRM) software from Salesforce.com. The later company's CEO, Marc Benioff said, "with Salesforce CRM Ideas, government can transform a closed conversation into a collaborative dialogue that leverages the wisdom of the crowd." I felt I was reaching an important audience when I wrote my suggestion to "stop government subsidies to oil companies."

Did Obama listen to "the crowd" and what became of their ideas? The most popular suggestion that received 70,509 votes as of January 2009, was to legalize marijuana. In my opinion, the fact that pot is illegal is as ridiculous as the prohibition of alcohol. Marijuana users prove how much they are suffering from our laws every time they have a chance to rally. Unfortunately, because they came in first (and third) place with their agenda, the *Briefing Book* didn't get the attention I thought it deserves. It was criticized for appearing "embarrassing" because at a time when the country was reeling from the financial meltdown and two wars, pot smokers were the most vocal activists using the site.

The rest of the citizen-generated ideas were inspired, passionate pleas that came from a groundswell of needs that have not gone away. If our government listened to what the participants wrote in *The Citizens Briefing Book*, they would repeal the tax cuts on the wealthiest 1%, make reduced-scale farming profitable, replace government sponsored abstinence education with real sex education to prevent sexually transmitted diseases, build bullet trains and light rail, permanently close torture facilities, allow the terminally ill to choose their own path, construct national wireless service, debate and vote for/against bills online, make sure that sign-on bonuses aren't revoked from soldiers who are injured in the line of duty, end the war against American citizens, and stop the pay-to-play culture in Washington.

What happened to *The Citizens Briefing Book*? It was shut down shortly after January 2009 and replaced by a petition process on Whitehouse.gov. Obama didn't act on most of the *Book*'s recommendations. They took down the site and all the content along with it. I felt as though our comments were disposable to this administration.

Who used the site? Probably a lot of Democrats. Where were the Republican ideas? Were they asked for their participation? It's not fair to leave out half the country when you want to know the will of the people. A website that delivers open democracy is more powerful than partisan politics. It's time for the whole country to become involved in running our government. Not the other way around.

The best-kept secret in America is that it's not necessary for a presidential candidate to appear on the ballot in order to win. If people who were disgruntled about our government used this method to cast a protest vote, Mickey Mouse might have already won the Presidency. In most states, a write-in contender has a chance to win if enough people spell her name on paper or through the electronic voting booth's keypad.

What I like best about writing in a name is that it's much harder for other people to tamper with your vote. No hanging chads like Bush v Gore! No rigged voting machines flipping a switch, no black box issues. Your vote is your vote is your vote.

Presidential hopefuls have an uphill battle trying to get their name on the ballot in all 50 states. For example, in California, a contender must secure more than 150,000 signatures to have his name listed. Comparatively, to run for President as a write-in, candidates must file a declaration of intent in most states. This prevents a popular, much sought-after candidate such as Elizabeth Warren or Ron Paul from winning through a write-in voting campaign based on fans alone. If Senator Warren doesn't declare her intent to become President, there's not a lot her supporters can do. Some states, like North Carolina and Illinois, make it especially difficult to file a declaration of intent to run.

Where write-in votes are not accepted for the presidential race (as in Arkansas, Hawaii, Louisiana, Mississippi, Nevada, Oklahoma, and South Dakota) there's no point to filing as a write-in candidate. In Louisiana, the ballot is accessible to candidates without huge hurdles, so write-ins aren't necessary. Washington D.C., Oregon, New Jersey and Washington state only count write-ins when there are a significant number of write-in votes. In some states, there is a peculiar rule: if a candidate loses in the primary, they are barred from running as a write-in for the general election, but nothing is stopping a write-in candidate from skipping the primary and going straight for the general, November election.

Write-in voting notwithstanding, I couldn't find a website that had everything on my wish list. The League of Women's Voters invented SmartVoter.org and Vote411.org; both websites display who is running in your district and state, but won't let you add yourself as a candidate, and has no interactivity like the "ideas" section I envisioned. VoteSmart.org, a completely different organization, shows how the candidates stand on the issues if they have enough backbone to answer VoteSmart's "Political Courage" test. But it doesn't allow constituents to add their ideas or interact with those who are running for office.

Websites about issues, such as OnTheIssues.org, didn't list all the candidates, and those that listed all the candidates such as Politics1.com didn't show how they stood on the issues. Within five minutes, many websites revealed themselves as either right or left leaning, even when they aimed to shoot down the middle.

In the midst of the same old red vs blue, I found an interesting site called *Americans Elect* (AmericansElect.org). They sought to promote a presidential hopeful who didn't "belong" to the parties and who would qualify to debate through the Commission on

Presidential Debates. For backing, they had millions of dollars from founder hedge fund manager Peter Ackerman and other wealthy people. Our strategies differed in that my website would address Congress, not just the President of the United States (POTUS).

When I tried using Americans Elect's website, I found it to be very limiting, almost like the man behind the curtain didn't want me to see him. I couldn't talk to the people who ran their organization because they made themselves unapproachable. There was no contact information anywhere to be found.

It thrilled me to know that I wasn't the only one who wanted a third alternative. Perhaps Americans Elect were onto something, and a large percentage of Americans know just how horrible the two usual choices have become.

Let's build a movement to find a President who echoes our values and won't bow down to money. Let's create a citizen-run government because Congress is failing us! We need to organize. To do this, we can communicate online, before our net neutrality is gone. What shall we call this Internet portal that will organize everyday citizens into a powerful force for good?

3
AMERICAN BEAUTY

Naming can satisfy a need, it can shorten a conversation that otherwise might go on for hours.
– Nihad Sirees, Syrian writer

The hardest part of starting a business is coming up with a name that is memorable, easy to pronounce, describes the product, and will last forever.

I did everything wrong. I didn't have thousands upon thousands of dollars to spend on focus groups and weeks upon weeks to come up with a brand.

The first name I chose was "Writein2012.org" because I thought this was a temporary situation—we would only need to write in a POTUS for 2012, and then I could go back to being a gardener and a writer. That tells you how naïve I was about what it takes to reach Americans and then convince them to change their voting habits. If I hadn't been so trusting that good ideas rise to the top, I would have stopped bothering to try. Just like a teenager who has fallen in love, I couldn't see all the faults in my plan.

I announced my new endeavor to a friend in Connecticut who loved the idea of the website. She knew that I would need money to hire a web developer, so she referred me to a fundraiser named Susan from New York. A fundraiser! Maybe Susan could help me so that I could hire other people. This business was going to require a big staff. Susan and I could be the engine to create new jobs! And those employees would find funds from their friends, and so on, and so on.

I called Susan and explained what I was doing.

"Do you realize what this could be?" she asked.

"What?"

"You could make money off the information you're getting from voters!"

"What do you mean?"

"Polling information. You can sell valuable information to candidates for money!"

I hadn't thought about the site as a poll-taking tool, but she was right. If we had enough participants, we could make real money, not just ask for donations.

Susan helped shoot me, a willing cannonball, into my journey for the next year and half from conception to Election Day. Her enthusiasm gave me the hubris to think this new website would become successful. In my mind, I saw her as a sunflower, tall and loaded with big, obvious seeds. Susan the sunflower, radiating bright yellow energy.

Susan had an impressive resumé, having raised money for nonprofits such as New York University and Mount Sinai Medical Center in New York. She presented herself as logical, step-by-step oriented. The more we talked, the more excited we became about the possibility of real political change. When she expressed an interest in partnering with me, I felt like my power had immediately doubled. An experienced fundraiser could help start the website as a nonprofit entity and then as we gained popular support, we could start selling polling information. Susan convinced me to change the name to something timeless, removing the 2012 limit. Thus Writeindependent.org was born.

Both the words "write" and "independent" are essential to solving our two party system. Our founding fathers needed to *write* down their ideas and outline the main points of their fledgling government to secede from the United Kingdom and claim their *independence*. Likewise, I am gaining my own independence and writing the first draft of my new life as a free woman in a reinvented world. Parsing the name another way, we are Dependent upon a Write-in voting majority to break out of the duopoly represented by the two parties.

To design a logo with the intent of expressing my unique personality, I searched for a symbol the entire nation could latch onto. I chose a rose from my garden as the logo. Not just any rose, but one called American Beauty whose petals are a deep pink color. The remarkable traits of this rose give it spectacular advantages. Most rose bushes are constructed by grafting a scion (a tiny bit of the desired rose's stem) onto a vigorous rootstock called Dr. Huey. American Beauty stands on its own roots because it's a tough little bush and all the canes (stems) coming out of the ground produce the authentic rose. In contrast, Dr. Huey sends out new shoots from the ground and will take over and ruin the rose plant if you don't remove his suckers. (Choose your own metaphor for who Dr. Huey represents. Multinational corporations? The billionaires who've bought our government? The attorneys who write the trade bills?)

In addition, American Beauty is a repeat bloomer. It comes back over and over again, and its fragrance is heady and intoxicating. It's also rare. I have never met a rose grower besides myself who owns one. Only one nursery sells it, as far as I know. Grateful Dead aficionados will recognize the rose from its appearance in artwork that graces the album cover by the same name.

I likened the American Beauty to those caring folks whose roots go deeply into the soil, those tough-minded individuals who are proud to belong to a country that stands for something grand. The American Beauty rose became, for me, a powerful metaphor for any hearty citizen who cares about her home, who weathers each storm and comes back strong in the face of adversity. People trust her to be true.

I took a photograph of an American Beauty from my garden and used it as the logo on the first business cards for Writeindependent.org. It graced the left corner of the website's original banner. I envisioned that when visitors came to the home page, they could click and drag the rose logo to Washington D.C. on a map of the U.S., causing phantasmagorical fireworks to explode all over the screen.

At the bottom of the home page, I wrote: "This website is dedicated to my daughter. I am doing this for all my loved ones, but principally for you, because I want to leave this world a better place than before..."

I bought the domain name "Writeindependent.org" and posted a Craig's List ad: seeking web developer. Out of four self-proclaimed developers, one person refused to take the job, saying that the website would be too unwieldy and large for his talents. ("You're going to need a page for each state!") Another developer who met me wanted to run the whole site on Word Press, which seemed odd for such an ambitious endeavor.

The developer who impressed me the most was a creative designer named Ernesto, probably in his late 20's, who was interested in what I was doing and had a can-do attitude.

His previous online work had a youthful, energetic quality to it. I reasoned that his edgy designs coupled with my warm and fuzzy text would attract the social media-savvy demographic whose attention we desired.

Ernesto wore black rectangular glasses and product in his short spiky hair. He was shorter than I, dark skinned, thin and tattooed. He lived alone in Redondo Beach rather than with the mother of his child in San Francisco. He was hungry for work, motivated to prove to his girlfriend's family that he was worthy of her hand, and a sympathetic character. I wanted to support him, to help him fulfill his potential.

The day after hiring Ernesto, I had a huge anxiety attack.

4
ANXIETY ATTACK

We must all hang together, or most assuredly, we shall all hang separately.
– Benjamin Franklin, July 4, 1776

Even though I received spousal and child support from my ex, Roscoe, it didn't cover my monthly expenses. I stopped buying clothes, entertainment, ate out only once a week, and made sure to run errands all in one trip, so I could save on gas. I relinquished my Netflix account, reduced my cell phone to the bare minimum plan, and almost never used the drycleaner. I even stopped paying for haircuts. Luckily, a hairstylist neighbor accepted my tree pruning in trade for visits to her salon.

I thought my new business could eventually change my fortune. I put my savings on the line, first by giving a chunk to website developer Ernesto, so that I could start something important and valuable.

Then I had the big panic attack. It came on without any provocation. I was showering with my daughter Clarissa to rinse off the chlorine from a summer swim, washing her hair as she chattered on and on about how she didn't want to eat at the restaurant I was suggesting, because they didn't have pasta. She got stuck in a loop, repeating the same question over and over again: "What else do they have?"

While she demanded an answer from me, I imagined a scene of millions of Americans rallying people to invest in some specific energy system that replaced oil. There was enough money to actually get it done. And we all recognized that gasoline for cars was now a thing of the past. What if everyone saw this new investment opportunity as a way out of the recession? What if the people who had too much cash lying around (the job creators, tax evaders, hedge fund managers and the people who made out like bandits) finally knew what to do with it all? Many billions of dollars circulating in the economy again! No more recession! How would that look, dressing up the world that way?

The energy of these thoughts felt refreshingly euphoric, other-worldly, like heaven on earth. People working again! So many jobs, so many idle hands activated! Families thriving, happiness beyond measure, contentment for the masses, even those who had been used to living in fear or uncertainty! People saying, "tomorrow will be better!" and really meaning it. Those who had been holding their breaths breathing deeply again. Smiling again!

As Clarissa kept repeating, "What else do they have?" I kept going into this state of infinite possibilities. I was going to actually accomplish everything I wanted, though it might take several lifetimes to achieve whatever it was. My thoughts raced ahead several years, imagining that it had already come to pass. I suddenly had this indescribable feeling of losing myself, being one with the universe, and I almost felt like I was losing consciousness. My heart was pounding out of my chest and I couldn't pay attention to anything, although the smallest sliver of my awareness heard "What else do they have?"

In this expanded state, I couldn't see my daughter anymore. It was like I was blind and deaf, because I was in this black inattention tunnel. There were no hands, arms, feet or legs to feel. All was numb. I thought that I had passed into the space where people go when they die. My heartbeat was all that was left, and it was balancing on that precipice between being and not being. The beginning and the end of a life is this beat, this movement and the sound that goes with it. Sloosh clunk sloosh clunk. Sloosh clunk, as fast as possible.

The part that is me made an executive decision. *I want this life. I want to live.* This child, Clarissa, needs me. "What else do they have?" she was still asking. Then I saw the top of her head, her blond hair all wet, and I kissed her crown, and concentrated on the love I feel for her so that I could stay in my body. "I want to see you grow up, I want to see what happens to you," I said. My heart, though still pounding, returned to a more normal pace. My whole body shook from fear. I reminded myself that my heart is good. I have a strong heart, I can handle this gushing and clunking and stay alive.

I have a job to do here. I can't disappear now. It took probably ten minutes before the uncontrollable shaking and trembling went away.

It was a panic attack, pure and simple. I searched the Internet for a strategy to handle anxiety. I found an amazingly helpful tidbit through my research and subsequently wrote a blog post called "Change is Scary." In it, I share a cure from Dr. R. Reid Wilson, a leading expert in treating anxiety disorders, with a link that takes the reader to a YouTube called "Dr. Reid Wilson clip – How the Amygdala Learns." That one video was enough information for me to stop having panic attacks. His work also helps veterans with Post Traumatic Stress Disorder.

A couple days later, I had more anxiety about fear of death. It didn't last long because I assimilated two ideas. I have come to terms with the fact that I am living my path, no matter the outcome. If I die young, or before I finish all the things I feel are important, then so be it. Secondly, if I am going to die soon anyway, I might as well play and have as much fun as I can while I'm here. After I made these connections solid, I concluded that life is not that tenuous, that even people who glimpse the line between life and death don't just die because their mind goes to that existential place, or because their heart is beating out of their chest.

A week after hiring Ernesto, Susan the Sunflower broke the news that she couldn't be my partner. She said that starting a business required more hours than she was willing to put in, and she had small children, and her time was valuable. Her announcement only strengthened my resolve to stay the course.

Although I no longer suffered from tunnels of panic, I still felt anxiety. The pressure to make a living, the uncertainty of my business idea, and the fear of facing the unknown kept me awake at night. To endure the quiet hours of the morning, I'd sit up and write. I blogged about politics, our present culture of cynicism, how to adapt to change, about economics, trade bills, the debt of gratitude we owe our military families, and about happiness. All told, I amassed more than two hundred consecutive days' worth of posts, except for Thanksgiving and Christmas of 2011.

And I wrote more. While Ernesto was drafting the first version of the site, I was furiously writing the content for each page. The Home Page, About Us, the Mission Statement, how to run for Congress, how to cast a write-in vote, the Jobs page for people who wanted to work at Writeindependent.org, the Donate page, and each state's page showing the basic requirements for candidates with links to the 50 Secretary of State offices responsible for overseeing elections. My specific voice, the design of the pages and the flow of the website had a warmth, a liveliness that no one else could have created.

If I ever wanted to know for whom I was writing, all I had to do was remember the day I met myself on the concrete begging for money.

5

ROCKY ROAD

It is our duty now to begin to lay the plans and determine the strategy for the winning of a lasting peace and the establishment of an American standard of living higher than ever before known. We cannot be content, no matter how high that general standard of living may be, if some fraction of our people—whether it be one-third or one-fifth or one-tenth—is ill-fed, ill-clothed, ill-housed and insecure...

– Franklin D. Roosevelt, January 11, 1944

As I approached a post office in Orange County to mail a package, an appalling sight greeted me. A woman, whom I estimated to be in her 20's, sat flat-legged on the hard concrete with her back against a pillar. I didn't scrutinize her hair or clothing because I was too ashamed to stare. Apparently sober, she held a cardboard sign saying: "Single mother of three children. Need money for food. Please help." As if that weren't heartbreaking enough, the woman's three little kids fidgeted and played nearby.

One son, brown haired, wearing a dark blue sports shirt with red stripes on his short sleeves and a red number five on his chest looked to be about three years old. *What kind of adult would he be, not knowing the security of a home during his formative years?* I wondered. Flung about the streets at such a young age, would he be part of a new age of men and women, the desperados of the "New Silent Generation" named after the children who grew up during the Great Depression?

Since she claimed to be single, was she living with her parents, or did she live in her car with her children, like so many homeless Americans who lost their jobs and houses in the recession? *There but for the grace of God go I.*

I couldn't stop thinking about her. *How long would she sit there, and would she be back tomorrow and the next day?* If I gave her a dollar, it's unlikely to change her circumstances. How could I really help her?

I was overtired from working long days into the wee hours of the morning and unable to sleep properly for worrying about supporting myself. Partly because of fatigue, and partly because the desperate mother and her desperado children shocked me, my eyes welled up. Could I observe her plight dispassionately?

She represented one of the forty-five million people in the United States who are down on their luck with little chance for a break. Forty-nine million people, a third of them children, go hungry (or "food insecure" as the USDA calls it) at least half of each month. Is this the sign of a free and prosperous country?

As I waited at the Post Office, I dreamt that she and thousands like her would walk with me to the steps of the Capitol building and demand a redress of grievances. We would stand on a platform at the National Mall with a microphone to outline a New Deal of Relief, Recovery, and Reform. We would cut right to the core of corruption and restore the middle class values of fair employment for a fair wage, a good education, and yes, homeownership.

Before desperate moms and the desperado youth can stand with me, we need to know the history that brought us this broken and corrupt government. How is today's cycle of poverty and depression like the Depression, and what can we learn from it? How did we recover from the Great Depression?

6

THE NEW DEPRESSION

*Those seeking profits, were they given total freedom, would not be
the ones to trust to keep government pure and our rights secure.
Indeed, it has always been those seeking wealth who were the
source of corruption in government. No other depositories of
power have ever yet been found, which did not end in converting to
their own profit the earnings of those committed to their charge.*
– Thomas Jefferson

We are not free until we straighten out our economy. We can't
be free if we have to worry about having a place to call home, a job
that pays for food, and a future worth living for our children. True
freedom comes from exercising our political will to force Wall
Street to follow fair rules of commerce and investment. We are at
risk, the same as we were before the Great Depression when the
Federal Reserve gave the banks, in concert with securities, too
much latitude to create speculative bubbles. We shall regain our
freedom today when we understand how we came to this state of
affairs by examining our own history.

On my mother's father's side, I come from an Austro-
Hungarian family of tailors who emigrated to the United States in
the late 1800's. My maternal grandfather Irvin Stern was born
sometime around 1903. When I knew him, he had wild white hair,

bulging blue eyes, and the strength of a bear.

While my grandfather was a young boy, a small coterie of men did something momentous 16 years before the Great Depression started. They pushed through an amendment to the U.S. Constitution that allowed our federal government to tax individuals on their income, laying the groundwork for the Internal Revenue Service (IRS). In order to add such wording to the Constitution at that time, 36 states had to agree to the new amendment. On February 3, 1913, Secretary of State Philander Knox claimed the Sixteenth Amendment, that would make the IRS a legal entity, was ratified. Since the 1950's, the Anti-Tax Movement cited many reasons why Knox's announcement was made in error, but it's too late to do anything about income taxation. It's here to stay.

Simultaneously, a handful of wealthy bankers and businessmen crafted the Federal Reserve Act, enacted December 23, 1913. The Act allowed the new Federal Reserve[3] and its member banks to issue money and "loan" it to our government, simultaneously creating debt. Today, 40% of our national debt is in service to those private banks, run by a handful of powerful individuals. Ostensibly, the IRS, created by the same interests who were angling for a central bank, provided a method for putting the American taxpayers on the hook for the coterie's business dealings inside and outside the states. J.P. Morgan was perhaps the wiliest of the financial elite in making the U.S. his piggybank. "His financial perspective helped him to see the benefits of making monetary loans to governments and securing them with strong and reliable methods of tax collection," writes Robert L. Schulz, founder of We The People Foundation.

Woodrow Wilson, who signed the Act when the Fed was created, lamented that the United States was suffering under monopolistic rule. "We have, not one or two or three, but many, established and formidable monopolies in the United States...We have restricted credit, we have restricted opportunity, we have controlled development and we have come to be one of the worst ruled, one of the most completely controlled and dominated, governments in the civilized world—no longer a Government by

---

[3] The "Fed," so named to suggest that it is run by the government, is at best a quasi-government institution.

free opinion, no longer a Government by conviction and the vote of the majority, but a Government by the opinion and duress of small groups of dominant men."

Once the bankers cemented their centralized banking scheme to create currency, the Fed made money plentiful by keeping interest rates low. Money flowed in the Roaring Twenties, so easy and cheap to borrow, that people opened margin accounts to play the stock market. A speculative fever took hold, making Wall Street a kind of pyramid scheme, much like the derivatives market of today.

Meanwhile, the Fed was making money out of thin air. If you look at a dollar bill, you'll see the words "Federal Reserve Note. This note is legal tender for all debts, public and private," but it doesn't say anywhere that it's backed by gold. A dollar created in 1920 and loaned to our government at six percent interest, compounded yearly, becomes a debt of $13,781 by 2020. "The banks lent the dollar into existence but not the additional $13,780 needed to pay the loan off, forcing the public to go further and further into debt in search of the ephemeral interest due on their money-built-on-debt," writes Ellen Hodgson Brown in *Web of Debt*.

When the stock market crashed in 1929, and a run on the banks ensued, many lost their homes to foreclosure along with their savings. Consumer spending plummeted and industry laid off workers. As there was high unemployment, little money was available to buy goods, so more workers were laid off. Property that had been stewarded by farmers fell into the hands of the banks and financial elite.

In 1930, four million Americans were out of work. By the time my mother was born in 1931, six million people were unemployed. (By comparison, in February of 2015, the Bureau of Labor Statistics reported that 8.7 million Americans were unemployed.) My grandfather and his family had little money for food. He and his father went door to door in the greater Philadelphia area, asking to mend clothing or fit garments. My "Pop-Pop" could sew any suit to perfection, hiding the seam and customizing a jacket by taking in a waistline or adding a dart, even with a pocket in the way.

In the 1930's, when my mother was a little girl, my grandfather opened a formal wear rental shop and later a costume business with money borrowed not from a bank, but from his brothers-in-law, who owned a small chain of groceries. He worked hard to make a living. Because he had seen how people lost their homes and savings during the Great Depression, he didn't trust the banks or stocks. He kept his savings in the form of gold and silver coins and favored real estate as an investment over gambling in the stock market.

On April 5, 1933, Franklin D. Roosevelt issued Executive Order 6102 requiring Americans to relinquish all gold coins, bullion, and certificates to the U.S. Treasury, or else face huge fines and imprisonment. Fearing the confiscation of his wealth, my grandfather stashed his gold and silver coins in secret compartments of his house.

By June 5, 1933, the United States was unofficially off the gold standard. It meant that the Federal Reserve was no longer required to back our currency with gold. The powerful coterie of insiders could create as much money as they desired by government fiat, set interest rates, expand and contract our currency at will to meet their objectives.

The Great Depression lasted more than ten years. Recovery was slow, even when Franklin D. Roosevelt introduced a wealth tax: 75% on incomes over five million dollars. FDR started the largest public works project ever, the New Deal. From 1933 to 1938, a series of laws passed which funded social programs. The Depression prompted the implementation of unemployment insurance. Public works projects built tens of thousands of hospitals, schools, sanitation projects, and public buildings. Savings accounts were restored, farm and home foreclosures stopped. Workers were given the right to organize. Two Senators, named Carter Glass and Henry B. Steagall, set guidelines for the banking industry that would eventually bring back the public's trust in banks and securities. The Glass Steagall Act, passed June 16, 1933, did two important things: 1. It separated savings and loan (commercial) banks from speculative, (securities) investment type banks, and 2. It established the Federal Deposit Insurance Corporation (FDIC) insuring bank deposits up to a certain amount (then $2,500, currently $250,000). The goal was to protect the economy from bankers and financiers who were gaming the system and to prevent a run on the banks from ever happening again.

The New Deal wasn't sufficient to raise America from the ashes of the Great Depression. It wasn't until the Fed loosened its purse strings in 1939, and loaned money to our government for World War II, that jobs became plentiful. Military jobs. Weapons jobs. In today's parlance, we would call that military socialism.

Don't forget, Roosevelt didn't take care of the original sin. The Fed has the keys to the vault of the money supply. And what happened to the Glass Steagall Act? It eroded through decades of exceptions and workarounds by increasingly large degrees, until it was as though Glass Steagall had never been enacted. By the time Citicorp merged with Travelers, an action that would have been considered illegal in the late 1930's, they didn't even wait until the final repeal of Glass Steagall with the passage of the Gramm Leach Bliley (GLB) Act in 1999. The reason it should be illegal for such a merger to take place is that one company shouldn't be able to handle both ends of a mortgage transaction. First, the bank makes money by selling a mortgage and then the securities firm bets you're going to default on that mortgage, selling foreclosure insurance to people (or entities) who have nothing to do with the transaction. It's like selling life insurance on the terminally ill to unrelated parties, then causing them to die.

Who was policing the banks and securities underwriters anyway? The Federal Reserve? Our government officials? Hardly. Under the current deregulated structure, banks and securities firms are supposed to police themselves! Fancy that. Today, they still benefit from insider information, laughing all the way to work.

The Commodity Futures Modernization Act, signed into law in December, 2000, deregulated the highly speculative derivatives market. Under this law, credit default swaps, a type of derivative, is handled without oversight. "Two of the worst votes I ever made in this place was the Commodity [Futures] Modernization Act of 2000 that exempted all of these swaps from any regulation or any margins," said Collin Peterson, U.S. Representative of Minnesota's 7th district. "I didn't know any better. The other vote I made that was really bad is eliminating Glass-Steagall. We should have never done that, and I bought into that. You know, if we had Glass-Steagall back, this wouldn't be an issue here ... At the time we did the Modernization Act, there were $80 billion in swaps, in derivatives. We gave 'em legal certainty, we eliminated the regulation requirements, and it went to $700 trillion and it blew up on us. So just be careful: You can vote any way you want, but this could come back and haunt you."

I find it hard to believe that Gramm, Leach, and Bliley wanted their names on a bill that would bring down our financial system in the worst crisis since the Great Depression. That's essentially what this Act did. It trusted the bookies who had insider information to be honest and to turn themselves in whenever they did wrong. It took less than eight years for the Act to show us that not everyone in the financial industry can be trusted.

Had any President abolished the Fed and returned the creation of money back to the American people and our United States government, we might have insisted on the kind of transparency in the financial industry that keeps any one entity from taking advantage of our currency. It's up to us to monitor our money supply, for swindlers always abound.

FDR was correct when he warned: "We have come to a clear realization of the fact that true individual freedom cannot exist without economic security and independence. 'Necessitous men are not free men.'[4] People who are hungry and out of a job are the stuff of which dictatorships are made."

Every now and then, I run into folks who say we need to have a dictatorship. They're suggesting we have a benevolent dictator, an oxymoron. I disagree that we're headed toward dictatorship, although a President whose back is against the wall has no other choice but to use his executive privilege and the power of veto to fight with Congress. No, what's really going on behind the scenes is much more complex than the dictator/beleaguered President scenarios.

In the next chapter, I will explain why I am so disappointed in Obama and the reasons I began to search for a better POTUS in

---

[4] Paraphrased from *Vernon v Bethel*, 1762. English property case law. The original quote was: "...necessitous men are not, truly speaking, free men, but, to answer a present exigency, will submit to any terms that the crafty may impose upon them."

2012. If you're still angry about the way Wall Street, the huge insurance company American International Group (AIG), and the banks have undermined our monetary system, get ready for a gut-wrenching ride through the White House of Horrors.

7

CHIEF COMPLAINT

-or-

How Obama chose disappointing appointees, violated the Constitution, and missed his opportunity at the bully pulpit

I'm afraid, based on my own experience, that fascism will come to America in the name of national security.
–Jim Garrison, District Attorney of Orleans Parish, LA 1967

Full disclosure. I voted for Obama in 2008. I admit that I got misty-eyed because an African-American was elected to the highest post in the land. He sounded good behind the podium. He has a level-headed quality about him, a good vocabulary, and he makes statements with which I wholeheartedly agree. However, something isn't right. I can't tell if he's the ultimate diplomatic politician, flat-out lying, or if he's a puppet. All is not well.

I used to cringe every time he made, in my opinion, a flagrantly bad choice. *What's gotten into him? Has he lost his conscience?* In this chapter, I specify my disappointment in President Obama or any future President who keeps us on the same path.

The profound effect of money's influence on government isn't new to the Obama administration. If we keep voting for Republican or Democrat Presidents, we will continue to get a corporate-run, war-hawking government. It's not enough to put a woman in office. Changing the face of the President isn't going to make a difference if she's backed by the same powers that helped elect Obama, Bush, Clinton, and Bush. It's time both liberals and conservatives do something about this plutocracy, oligarchy, kleptocracy. Everybody seems to know what the problem is, so why aren't we changing our voting habits?

Harry Truman, POTUS from 1945 to 1953 complained of his position, "Well, all the President is, is a glorified public relations man who spends his time flattering, kissing and kicking people to get them to do what they are supposed to do anyway." It seems to me that the President doesn't take his cues from America proper, instead he listens to a few people who are protecting their interests at all costs. We need a leader who will stand up to people who have taken advantage of the Oval Office and halls of government for years, whether they are patronizing politicians with campaign funds or using the revolving door between the private sector and public service, seeking their own gain in the process.

To review Obama's presidency, I will briefly touch on three areas of concern: his presidential appointees to his cabinet and crucial administrative positions, violations of the Constitution, and missed opportunities at the bully pulpit. Some will argue that the bully pulpit no longer exists, but I consider any speech that the President gives in front of a large audience as an opportunity for Mr. Obama to tell the truth, to open discussion, to educate. Even if he has to explain complex subjects by breaking them into smaller parts, he should try to inform the public.

1. Presidential Appointments
Obama's presidential appointments have failed to inspire hope for me in three realms:
  1a. Economics.
  1b. Food.
  1c. Net neutrality.
2. Violations of the Constitution
Several bills violate the Constitution or our Constitutional rights:
  2a. The National Defense Authorization Act (NDAA).
  2b. The Authorization for Use of Military Force (AUMF) Act.
  2c. The Foreign Intelligence and Surveillance Act (FISA).

3. Neglect at the Bully Pulpit

I criticize the President for blowing his opportunity to educate from the bully pulpit on three of my "favorite" topics:

3a. The Trans Pacific Partnership and other disingenuous "free trade" agreements that give power and money to few while the rest of us are sleeping or staging our revolt.

3b. The prison population and how prisons have become big, bad businesses.

3c. Climate change.

1. Presidential Appointments

When a President is sworn in, his first order of business is choosing his cabinet and the people who will oversee each department. Like a team captain choosing his players, you want him to pick the best and brightest. In my garden, about 95% of the insects, birds, and animals are "beneficials" meaning they either do no harm, or they do a tremendous amount of good. The last five percent are the pests who create all the problems that ever were. It's almost as though Obama chose the gophers, a solitary beast that eats all the roots, leaving the plant sagging. Sometimes they pull the whole plant into their hole to gobble it up.

1a. Economics

Obama's former economic advisors Christina Romer, Larry Summers, and Peter Orszag crafted the $700+ billion bailout of the 2008-2009 financial crisis, without also making certain that those who took huge risks at the expense of the American taxpayer would stop their irresponsible behavior, both by putting them in jail and fixing the underlying causes. While Romer returned to academic life at Berkeley, Summers received $2.7 million for speaking engagements from the same firms that he helped bail out. Orszag took a high-paying job at Citicorp, one of the bailed out banks. Thanks to them, we have no idea where all the bailout money went. However, talking about where the money went doesn't address the real issue. Remember why the banks needed to be bailed out in the first place? And how can we prevent the banks from going bust again?

Most of the financial experts who oversaw the 2008 bust will be long gone when the next shoe drops. 74th and 75th U.S. Secretary

Treasurers Timothy Geithner and Hank Paulson and Chairman of the Federal Reserve Ben Bernanke will not be involved if loosely regulated derivatives[5] cause concern. Also gone is former Fed Chairman Alan Greenspan who testified in front of the House Oversight Committee, "I made a mistake in presuming that the self-interests of organizations, specifically banks and others, were … protecting their own shareholders and their equity in the firms," in reference to the deregulation of banks, securities, and exotic financial instruments like credit default swaps and synthetic derivatives.

To underscore just how dangerous poorly regulated derivatives are, the Financial Crisis Inquiry Commission concluded in their February, 2011 report that the passing of the Commodity Futures Modernization Act that affects federal and state regulation of derivatives "was a key turning point in the march toward the financial crisis."

If you've fallen asleep, this is the point where you need to wake up and pay attention, because our current derivatives market is like a sleeping dragon. From estimates provided by the Bank for International Settlements, the market value of outstanding derivatives is about $17 trillion, a significant figure by any standard. The notional amount[6] of derivatives is more than $700 trillion. A few unscrupulous hedge fund managers have the means with which to cause another crisis with 2008-recession type ripple effects throughout the world.

---

[5] Mayra Rodríguez Valladares, managing principal at MRV Associates, a capital markets and financial regulatory consulting firm, describes a derivative as "a contract between two parties whose value is determined by changes in the value of an underlying asset. Those assets could be bonds, equities, commodities or currencies. The majority of contracts are traded over the counter, where details about pricing, risk measurement and collateral, if any, are not available to the public." In layman's terms, it's a bet, where the trader is a bookie, and the bet can be almost anything that the imagination can dream up. The bookie gets paid no matter how the bet works out. Derivatives have been called "financial weapons of mass destruction" by Warren Buffett. (See http://www.fintools.com /docs/Warren Buffet on Derivatives.pdf)

[6] Notional value: The total value of a leveraged position's assets. This term is commonly used in the options, futures and currency markets because a very small amount of invested money can control a large position (and have a large consequence for the trader). Definition: Investopedia

"Blaming derivatives for crises is like blaming your word processor if you get caught plagiarizing," says derivatives expert Don Chance, author of *Introduction to Derivatives and Risk Management*. It isn't necessary to blame derivatives, per se, for the next financial collapse when there are plenty of people in the financial industry who, like plagiarizers on their word processors, use these tools to nefarious ends. They proved they could do so prior to 2008; they can do it again.

Obama's Wall Street cronies don't stop there. Obama appointed bank-friendly prosecutors like Mary Jo White at the Securities and Exchange Commission and Lanny Breuer as U.S. Department of Justice's Assistant Attorney General. Obama's Attorney General, Eric Holder started the "too big to fail, too big to jail" attitude with a memo he wrote in 1999 calling non-prosecution necessary, fearing it would hurt innocents who were employed by the big banks but not involved in the scams. That infamous "Holder memo" has made institutionalized crime go unpunished.

Holder and Breuer worked for a law firm that defended the same banks they were supposed to prosecute as government appointees. All you have to do is look at the client list of Covington and Burling to see where Holder and Breuer made their money. Mary Jo White has been criticized as having conflicts of interest for representing clients JP Morgan Chase, Bank of America, and Goldman Sachs prior to her appointment.

Bloomberg News reported that all told, the Fed gave out $1.2 trillion in bailout funds in late 2008 that weren't disclosed to Congress while taxpayers gave another $700 billion through the Troubled Asset Relief Program (TARP). Nobody went to jail, but more to the point, nobody fixed the underlying causes, allowing white-collar crime to continue without slapping one wrist of the most heinous, unethical criminals.

In other words, starting with Bush and continuing under Obama, Holder and his ilk got away with obliterating the rule of law.

1b. Food

When Obama chose former Monsanto's attorney Michael Taylor as Deputy Commissioner for Foods for the Food and Drug Administration (FDA), I could not have been more disappointed. The FDA has a long history of looking the other way as genetically engineered foods have entered our supermarkets. If the food industry had to clearly label "contains genetically engineered ingredients" right on the packaging, it would help those of us who want to know what we're putting in our bodies. Until independent, long-term studies have been conducted on humans ingesting genetically engineered food liberally sprayed with RoundUp®, I don't want to take my chances eating it.

Japan, much of Europe, Russia, even the military in China have banned genetically modified organisms (GMOs). However, our government is filled with friends of GMOs. Senator Roy Blunt of Missouri, in collaboration with Monsanto, injected words into the sequester bill to make it impossible to sue Monsanto if and when we find out that genetically engineered food is making us sick. Dubbed the 'Monsanto Protection Act,' it was slipped in when workers, whose paycheck depended upon the government not shutting down, were anxious to see a deal done. Obama signed it in 2013 with nary a squeak about how he's giving up our Constitutional right to use the court system to ensure safety of our food. In September of the same year, a massive public opposition movement stopped the Monsanto Protection Act from continuing.

The shelves in the grocery store hold boxes and packages of food I try to keep away from my daughter. Michelle Obama says she doesn't want her kids eating high fructose corn syrup (HFCS), however, corn subsidies produce cheap HFCS and corn sugars from Genetically Modified (GM) corn. I've been trying to avoid the foods that contain HFCS that sweetens soft drinks, bread, canned soup, yogurt, cereal, many processed foods. But without GMO labeling of genetically engineered ingredients, it's nearly impossible to know which foods might have been sprayed with RoundUp®. Republicans stood in the way every time Obama tried to reduce government subsidies that make HFCS. First he appoints a pro-genetic engineering industry insider who claims Monsanto's RoundUp Ready® corn is safe, then Obama complains when he can't have less corn syrup subsidies.

For Secretary of Agriculture, Obama appointed Tom Vilsack, an attorney, not an agriculture person. Tom Vilsack has always been a big supporter of biotech. When companies like Monsanto, Bayer, Dow chemical sell patented seeds and manipulate the food supply through trade agreements like the Trans Pacific Partnership, it helps them to have a friend like Mr. Vilsack at the United States Department of Agriculture (USDA). Oran B. Hesterman, former professor of crop and soil science, would have been an ideal candidate for the top position at the USDA. In his book, *Fair Food: Growing a Healthy, Sustainable Food System for All*, he gives witness to local food and farming operations producing healthy food while being environmentally responsible. Mr. Hesterman also proves that he's more than willing to work within corporate environments such as Costco and Kellogg.

1c. Net Neutrality

The Internet faces a constant threat to free speech that creates a barrier to democracy. What the average Internet user wants is 'net neutrality,' whereby information travels at a consistent rate of speed no matter what website he's visiting. The biggest case of an Internet Service Provider (ISP) mucking with users' download speeds was in 2007 when Comcast got caught throttling BitTorrent's peer to peer file sharing and paid $16 million to settle.

America has some of the slowest, most costly Internet service in the world. Under current laws, ISPs such as AT&T, Cox, Time Warner, Comcast, Sprint, T-Mobile and Verizon can mess with interconnectivity and can discriminate against certain applications, picking winners and losers. Without the FCC's true protection of net neutrality, ISP's can capitalize on five loopholes that the FCC neglected to close in February 2015 when they reclassified high speed Internet as a Title II utility service. The FCC has decided that they will regulate ISPs on a case-by-case basis, inching us toward losing equitable public access of our information highway.

If the big ISPs wanted to keep Writeindependent.org from becoming successful, all they would have to do is price me out. Make the website too expensive to run or visit, and it's finished. Losing net neutrality could effectively make it impossible for the little guy or the homebound mother to launch an important business over the Internet. No more free enterprise.

Here are a few solutions: one is to implement true net neutrality rules, as outlined by experts in the industry such as Barbara van Schewick, Professor of Law at Stanford University. A second solution is to break up the biggest providers so that competition can (theoretically) drive down prices and improve service. Last, and probably most effective, is to build open municipal-level fiber networks, city by city. They would be faster and cheaper, and protected by the citizens. Susan Crawford, author of *Captive Audience: The Telecom Industry and Monopoly Power in the Gilded Age*, writes: "According to Christopher Mitchell of the Institute for Local Self Reliance, a national expert on community networks, more than 400 towns and cities across America have installed or are planning networks." However, the big five ISPs have pushed through laws in 19 states making it nearly impossible for cities within their boundaries to construct their own fiber networks.

What does Obama have to do with all this? He appointed Tom Wheeler, a former top lobbyist for cable and wireless companies, to chair the FCC. That's like asking your alcoholic uncle to watch the bar. Obama's friend, David Cohen, Comcast's Executive VP, has generously supported his campaigns. Obama golfs with CEO of Comcast Brian Roberts. Comcast gave Obama nearly $300,000 to help him get re-elected, and spent $53 million in the past three election cycles to grease the necessary politicians. Might Obama have shaken hands, agreeing to support the merger of Time Warner/Comcast and to uphold loose FCC regulations? Why else would he appoint an industry insider to head the FCC?

One more thing before you argue that Obama defended net neutrality by urging Tom Wheeler and the FCC to classify the Internet as a public utility. Even though he talks a good game, he knows that the Trans Pacific Partnership (TPP) is poised to impose similar restrictions as SOPA (Stop Online Piracy Act) and PIPA (Protect IP Act) that was so bad for Internet freedom. While he's distracting you with net neutrality, he's working to push the TPP through. So is he really for a free Internet?

We profess to defend and promote democracy everywhere, but where will democracy go if net neutrality disappears? If monopolies clamp down on our access to information, say goodbye to free enterprise and democracy. Both depend upon the unrestricted flow of ideas, commerce, and information.

2. Violations of the Constitution

The second way that I'm reviewing Obama's presidency is by asking which Constitutional rights have slipped away? I can't blame Obama alone, but he would have to stand up to his own party to explain that Democrats are just as guilty as Republicans for passing laws that undermine our rights. We need a President who goes toe to toe with any party who's wrong.

2a. National Defense Authorization Act (NDAA)

The NDAA outlines the budget for the Department of Defense while giving the federal government unprecedented latitude to capture and detain those they deem as terrorists on American soil without due process. Obama reinforced provisions that Bush had signed earlier, but the new 2012 NDAA includes frightening wording in Section 1021 (b)(2) and Section 1021 (c)(1) providing "that any person who commits a 'belligerent act' against the country can be imprisoned indefinitely 'without trial' until the vaguely worded period of hostilities has come to an end," said Pete Sorenson, a Lane County, Oregon Commissioner. Mr. Sorenson urges Americans to put enough pressure on Congress to delete the unconstitutional provisions in the NDAA.

In its current wording, the NDAA violates the First (free speech), Fourth (unlawful search and seizure), Fifth (due process), Sixth (speedy trial), and Eighth (cruel and unusual punishment) Amendments. A bi-partisan group called People Against the NDAA (PANDA), started by concerned citizens from Bowling Green, Ohio are working to educate Americans about this threat to our Constitution. Their mission is to repeal the NDAA and urge people to participate in our government. Short of a complete repeal or change in the wording, PANDA offers support for individual states and counties to pass anti-NDAA legislation.

Congressional member Buck McKeon (R-CA) Chairman of the House Armed Services Committee inserted the Detainee Security Act into the NDAA, and Senators John McCain and Carl Levin tweaked it, violating our Constitution by codifying the indefinite detention provisions in the Military Detainee Procedures Improvement Act. Those who saw this addition as necessary to the protection of our country from terrorists argue that an enemy combatant should have different rights than a citizen of the U.S. once they cross a certain line. But this logic forgets the basic problem here. Who is a terrorist? Do they have to be militant? Do they have to belong to a group of outsiders? Or can they be Americans who disagree with the way our government functions? Would whistleblowers fit into that definition? Further, if we keep a prisoner for questioning without due process, how do we obtain evidence without skewing the process with our obvious bias of "guilty until proven innocent?"

Because a major provision in the bill effectively prevented Guantanamo from being shuttered, Obama must have signed with deep regrets, feeling pressured by the House and Senate to put his name to paper after he had many times threatened to veto it. The main reason he cited for signing was that the objectionable parts were outweighed by the urgency to fund $662 billion in defense.

Obama signed the NDAA "with reservations" and wrote a lengthy list of objections, most in regard to curtailing (his) executive functions. He wrote: "I want to clarify that *my* (italics mine) Administration will not authorize the indefinite military detention without trial of American citizens" referring to Section 1021 of the NDAA. However, that doesn't calm my fears of its violation of the Constitution. It's like saying, *I have a chair bolted to the floor of my basement and mounted with handcuffs, but I won't use it.* And there's no guarantee that the next President won't start detaining Americans who refuse to stay in line, whatever that line is.

2b. Authorization for Use of Military Force (AUMF)

I discovered that Obama signed a new AUMF, that makes drone warfare worse under his presidency than all others before him. With the AUMF, Obama is now able to make a "kill list" of terrorists that our military members murder using drones. There are no charges, no trial, and it's done without adhering to the same rules of engagement that apply during a war. The President has become judge, jury and executioner. Do drone murders prevent large-scale attacks of terrorism on Americans, or do they cause the kind of terror that begets more terrorism? How long before drones are used to spy on Americans, determine that they are terrorists, and then target us from a faraway console with a kill switch?

2c. Foreign Intelligence and Surveillance Act (FISA)

Regarding the National Security Administration (NSA), we Americans would have impeached President Nixon for the kind of activities this administration does with impunity. It uses provisions put in place by the FISA to wiretap Americans without their knowledge. The NSA violates the Fourth Amendment when they look at our emails without warrants. Whistleblowers Ed Snowden and Bill Binney revealed that the NSA is collecting massive data on us.

Section 215 of the USA Patriot Act greatly expanded the use of FISA subpoenas, forcing people to hand over anything the government wants in complete secrecy. The FBI can spy on a person because they don't like the books he reads, can demand he hand over "any tangible things," so long as the FBI specifies that the order is "for an authorized investigation . . . to protect against international terrorism or clandestine intelligence activities." Does the FBI have to show probable cause to obtain these items? No. According to the government's own document on the subject of Section 215, the FBI "does not have the authority to define 'probable cause' [because] it is a statutory and constitutional term." In other words, the Federal Bureau of Investigation (FBI) isn't filled with constitutional scholars, so give them a break! Meanwhile, your personal effects, computer information, emails, phone records, just about anything they want is theirs for the taking.

3. Missed Opportunities at the Bully Pulpit

If we had a President who told the truth and wasn't protecting his cronies from public scrutiny, the American people would have a reason to listen to him. Then we could get some real work done, because the public could get behind someone who spoke against monopolies, control of the media, legal entanglements and taxation that handcuffs small and medium-sized businesses.

3a. The Trans Pacific Partnership

I believe that the Trans Pacific Partnership will be *the* issue of the 2016 elections because it gives voters a simple way to know whether a candidate is pro-people or pro-corporate-backers. While most Americans don't know what it is, Obama has been trying to force it through by a process called "fast track promotion authority." Presidents use this maneuver when they don't want to allow Congress to filibuster or amend a bill.

The Trans Pacific Partnership, a so-called "free trade" bill, gives large special interest groups and monopolies even more power than they already have through longer patent protection (up to 120 years!). It allows corporations special privileges to sue governments, and then it specifies three attorneys (a "tribunal") who will oversee those lawsuits. In this kangaroo court, a corporation like Monsanto could sue our government if our laws stand in the way of their making a profit. For example, if we pass a law to ban RoundUp® because we need further study of its long-term health effects, Monsanto can sue federal and state governments and the lawsuit goes before the aforementioned tribunal who decide whether or not Monsanto should be paid a settlement. Then the taxpayers are on the hook for funding that amount. That's just one of the many provisions of the TPP. Public Citizen, a watchdog group of trade-savvy experts, warns how the TPP affects our civil liberties, access to medicines, and use of the Internet. I explain the Trans Pacific Partnership in more detail in Chapter 27 and Appendix 7.

The Trans Pacific Partnership bill has been crafted under stringent secrecy. Six hundred special advisors have access to its 29-chapter legislation, but the general public does not. In fact, even our own Congress has little to no access. Julian Assange, founder of Wikileaks, said: "The selective secrecy surrounding the TPP negotiations, which has let in a few cashed-up megacorps but excluded everyone else, reveals a telling fear of public scrutiny." I worry how many Congressional members have been promoted, perked, and funded to say yes to this Trojan Horse of a bill without even reading it. Remember the North American Free Trade Agreement (NAFTA) and General Agreement on Tariffs and Trade (GATT)? What did those so-called "free trade" bills ever do to spur economic growth in the USA?

3b. The Prison Industry

Obama hasn't talked about the prisons that now hold more than 2.3 million people, or one out of every 100 adult Americans. At least 37 states have legalized contracting of prison labor while the taxpayer foots the bill for their housing and food. One example of this is UNICOR, a for-profit organization that operates 110 factories out of 79 federal penitentiaries making military supplies totaling $583 million in sales.

Rather than discuss this as a problem, Obama offered more taxpayer money to incarcerate more people. His budget request for 2013 increased the amount given to federal prisons to $6.9 billion, up 4.2% from the previous year. Most sentencing in federal prisons are for drug offenders, not violent criminals.

"When prison contracts incentivize keeping prison beds filled, it exposes the hypocrisy of our elected leaders' public policy goals of reducing the prison population and increase efforts for inmate rehabilitation," writes Peter Choi, former candidate for state senator in California District 26. "Indeed, one for-profit prison company sent letters to their stockholders boasting of the high percentage of prisoners who returned to their prisons."

President Obama could have used his bully pulpit to have a conversation about how mass incarceration hurts our country, economy, taxpayers, and the inmates themselves. Instead, he's helping investors make money off companies using prisoners. I ask, facetiously, if prison labor is meant to be a deterrent to drug possession and dealing, why don't we videotape the treatment of prisoners so that our youth can see what happens to you if you deal, use, and carry drugs?

A country is only as strong as its moral character. How we treat the least among us teaches us about our society. If we stash them away and prefer not to look, it's like ignoring a festering wound. Covering it up doesn't negate the fact that it needs attention.

3c. Climate Change

Despite all his promises to address global warming, Obama hasn't shown much leadership with respect to energy policies and climate mitigation strategies. Countries like Germany and Sweden are doing a much better job of solving energy needs without fossil fuels.

Regarding climate mitigation, there has been much debate over a type of geoengineering called "Solar Radiation Management" (SRM). SRM consists of spraying a mantle of sulfur dioxide all over the world that would theoretically block the sun's rays and cool the earth. To implement SRM, high-flying jets would spray sulfate aerosols into the stratosphere. Say goodbye to blue skies.

In March, 2007, Obama's science advisor, John P. Holdren included geoengineering as a way to mitigate global warming in his keynote address, *The Energy Challenge and How to Meet It*. David Keith, Director of the Institute for Sustainable Energy, Environment and Economy, an educator who speaks about SRM and recipient of Bill Gates's patronage, says that one billion dollars of taxpayer money isn't a lot, in the scheme of things, to combat climate change.

No matter how scientific it sounds, tampering with the sun will affect weather patterns and our ability to grow food. Mainstream articles about SRM, such as those appearing in *Scientific American*, assuage our fears by claiming that such techno-fixes aren't a viable answer.

Though David Keith denies that this type of geoengineering is taking place right now, witnesses to jet "chemtrails" would argue differently. What are those long-lasting, whitish plumes coming out of airplanes? Residents of Mt. Shasta, California bombarded their Shasta County supervisors of District 1 with their concerns over what they assumed is the release of superfine particles of aluminum, barium, and strontium into the atmosphere that may end up on soil, in streams and drinking water. Although I remain unconvinced that SRM is taking place consistently, I have wondered about experimental flights and particulate release.

The most convincing testimony I found regarding application of SRM is Kristen Meghan's. For nine years, she was an embedded liaison for the military as an industrial engineer. Her job was tracking health hazards and looking at any time someone wanted to buy a chemical. She had to track that chemical from cradle to grave, using an Air Force Form 3952, Approval of Hazardous Materials. When orders for tons and tons of nano-particulate aluminum, barium, strontium, and forms of oxides and sulfates came across her computer, she needed to know what they would be used for. She denied many of the orders because she wasn't getting answers. Finally, when her supervisor put the heat on her to approve them, she did a little digging.

"Geoengineering is occurring, it's been occurring, it is not new, and your tax dollars are funding this. I one hundred percent know that the U.S. Air Force was involved." Her testimony is so compelling, I urge everyone to watch her on YouTube by typing in "chemtrails whistleblower" or Kristen Meghan before they take "Geoengineering Whistleblower ~ Ex-Military ~ Kristen Meghan, Hauppauge, NY, January 18th, 2014" down from the site. Decide for yourself if she is the real deal.

With regard to burning fossil fuels, Obama speaks about the benefits of fracking without educating us about its dangers. Fracking is the extraction of liquid natural gas by forcing water laced with a proprietary brew of chemicals into cracks and fissures underground. One of the largest drilling areas is in Marcellus shale, a huge rock formation located under western Pennsylvania, eastern Ohio and West Virginia.

In Pennsylvania, more than 7,100 wells have been built since 1996. As of this writing, there have been at least 3,880 violations worth $5.9 million in fines. In other words, frack now, pay fines and settlements after the damage has been wrought. Neighbors of the wells have brought class action lawsuits against gas companies. The lack of solid research, inspections, and investigation to prevent contamination problems, paint a picture of a rush to frack.

A 2011 study by Robert B. Jackson et al of the Duke University Nicholas School of the Environment and Earth Sciences warned that "during the first month of drilling and production alone, a single well can produce a million or more gallons of waste water that can contain pollutants in concentrations far exceeding those considered safe for drinking water and for release into the environment. These pollutants sometimes include formaldehyde, boric acid, methanol, hydrochloric acid, and isopropanol, which can damage the brain, eyes, skin, and nervous system on direct contact."

Jackson's study framed that it wasn't the actual fracking process that caused the escape of contaminates into local air and water. Rather it was: corroded well casings, spilled fracturing fluid at the drilling site, leaked wastewater, or direct movement of methane or water from deep underground.

Two years later, Jackson again measured fugitive gas concentrations in water near drilling sites. He verified that "homeowner's water has been harmed by drilling. In Texas, we even saw two homes go from clean to contaminated after our sampling began." Thomas Darrah, Assistant Professor of Earth Sciences at Ohio State, lead scientist and co-author of the 2013 study, said that leaks from poor casing and cementing "is relatively good news because it means that most of the issues we have identified can potentially be avoided by future improvements in well integrity."

But is it really good news? And how far into the future will we wait until the polluting stops? Gas companies have known about the causes of contamination since at least 2010 and have not resolved the issues. The New York State Department of

Environmental Conservation, concerned with the effects of fracking, thought it best to learn from the mistakes in Pennsylvania and published a paper called *Review of Selected Non-Routine Incidents in Pennsylvania*. They reported "numerous occurrences of methane migration into residential water wells during 2010 ...were attributed to the failure to properly case and cement wells." Residents in New York have successfully won a moratorium on fracking, albeit a temporary one.

In addition to problems of methane containment, I found this disturbing information in the NY study: "The discharge of fluid from the well pad was caused by the failure of stormwater controls due to extraordinary precipitation and other factors." In other words, when storm waters reach high levels, there is a much greater chance of chemicals from the drilling process leaching into our lakes, waterways, and drinking supply. A storm like Sandy, floods from heavy rains, and storm surges from extreme weather could permanently poison water in, around, and under fracked areas.

"Many of the leaks probably occur when natural gas travels up the outside of the borehole, potentially even thousands of feet, and is released directly into drinking-water aquifers," said Robert Poreda, Professor of Geochemistry at the University of Rochester, co-author of Darrah's study.

Victims of fracking have to purchase all their water for washing, cooking, and drinking. Homeowners near drilling sites have difficulty obtaining mortgages and property values have declined as buyers avoid houses with toxic water.

It's not enough to examine only water. Health experts cite air contamination from benzene, a cancer-causing chemical, to be among their greatest concerns. A five-state (AK, CO, OH, PA, WY) study of air samples collected near wells "identified eight volatile compounds at concentrations that exceeded... Environmental Protection Agency (EPA) Integrated Risk Information System (IRIS) cancer risk levels." Believe it or not, the samples were collected by local community members because "exemption of oil and gas operations from provisions of the Clean Air Act, Clean Water Act, Safe Drinking Water Act, Emergency Planning and Community Right-to-Know Act, and other statutes *limits* (italics mine) data collection on the impacts of oil and gas development."

Explosions at well pads have rocked towns in West Virginia, Pennsylvania, and Texas. In addition, fracking may be fomenting more earthquakes. "If you pump water in a fault, the fault can slip, causing an earthquake," says Cliff Frohlich, a geophysicist at the University of Texas at Austin.

Where is the federal government in reviewing all this activity? Former VP Cheney inserted a "Halliburton loophole" into the 2005 energy bill that stripped the Environmental Protection Agency of its authority to regulate fracking.

How "clean" is liquid natural gas as fuel anyway, since we're worried about climate change? When natural gas is burned, it still puts carbon dioxide in the air. While coal produces the most CO_2 at 228 lbs/million Btu's, natural gas (117 lbs/million Btu's) comes in slightly lower than gasoline (157 lbs/million Btu's).[7]

Obama waited until June of 2014, five and a half years into his presidency, to propose a 30% cut in carbon dioxide emissions from coal by 2030. My worry is that it's too little too late. What this country needs is a *major and immediate* overhaul of energy policy to have an impact on climate change, not just a 30% cut in coal emissions over the next 15 years.

"If enough of us stop looking away and decide that climate change is a crisis worthy of Marshall Plan levels of response, then it will become one, and the political class will have to respond, both by making resources available and by bending the free market rules that have proven so pliable when elite interests are in peril," writes Naomi Klein in her clarion call *This Changes Everything*. If everyone who was worried about losing their coal or oil jobs were employed within the year by another safer healthier industry, and if that system worked as well as fossil fuels, they would not complain about switching to cleaner energies. A government led by a President who is pro-people could make this happen.

Without political power, we feel helpless. This is why Americans must rally.

To me, it isn't important to have the perfect plan to fix these problems. What is important is taking laser-focused action rather

---

[7] A Btu or British thermal unit is the amount of energy it takes to heat or cool one gallon of water by one degree Fahrenheit.

than giving up and saying, "it's impossible." I forged ahead and developed a strategy that I thought would work.

8
THE STRATEGY

*If you have built castles in the air, your work need not be lost;
that is where they should be.
Now put the foundations under them.*
– Henry David Thoreau 1817-1862

Before I discovered the six-point plan outlined on page five of this book, I had my own strategy for fixing our government. It wasn't perfect, but it had teeth. First, we needed a website such as the one I was developing with Ernesto. Second, we had to make Americans aware of the website through a television infomercial. And third, we had to promote and vote for candidates who had signed a pledge to remove money from politics. To do all this, I needed to open a nonprofit entity.

A week before hiring Ernesto, I shot an email to an election attorney, asking to open a 501(c)(4), a nonprofit political corporation. The lawyer sent me an engagement letter and instructed me to file for a Federal Tax ID#, find board members, fill out forms for the proper agencies and review the corporate bylaws. I needed to open a checking account for the new business.

Two and a half weeks into his contract, Ernesto announced that he had the first images of the website. He came to my home office to show me the mockup in which he would eventually drop my text. I was beyond buzzed to see what he had dreamt up.

Across the banner of the home page, he had chosen an

interesting hand-written font for Writeindependent.org. The American Beauty rose looked slightly out of place to the left of it, being so pink, vulnerable, and well… flowery.

For the Presidential Page, where the Presidential candidates would be listed, Ernesto found a breathtaking picture of the White House with proud red flowers lined up around the huge fountain on the front lawn. A panoramic photograph of the massive Capitol Building, where Congress convenes, filled the banner above the Congressional pages. My heart soared looking at what we had created. The project felt bigger than me, as though it were taking on a life of its own.

When I thought to start breathing again, I decided to get a second opinion on the home page, which was not nearly as impressive as the images of Washington D.C.

The Small Business Administration offers a program that helps entrepreneurs launch ventures. They call it the SCORE (Service Corps of Retired Executives) program whereby experienced counselors volunteer their time to answer new business owners' questions.

Mary, the SCORE counselor, sat behind a large desk ensconced in the offices of the Palos Verdes' Chamber of Commerce. She wore no makeup, had a long thin face and pale skin, and smiled at me as though she couldn't wait to get started.

After showing her the website and a letter I wrote to raise funds, she began to scrutinize my logo on the home page.

"No, no, no!" she said. "What's this—a rose? What's a rose doing on a political website?"

"It's an American Beauty rose."

"Does it say American Beauty anywhere? How would I know it's an American Beauty?"

"It doesn't say."

She paused, but I could tell she was not happy. "You're trying to attract voters, right?"

I nodded in agreement.

"This rose is too feminine. It's going to turn men off. Get rid of it."

My trepidation over using the logo meant I was predisposed to letting it go. Getting rid of it made me sad, and I had already spent money on business cards with the flower. Ugh! What a waste.

I went home and replaced the American Beauty with an outline of the continental United States with the American flag inside. The new graphic was a far less interesting logo in my estimation, but it wasn't sentimental and couldn't be perceived as weak. Roses would attract only women, or so my SCORE counselor thought.

Mary advised me to remove all the flowers from my blog as well, since she was allergic to pollen and just looking at them made her want to sneeze. However, I refused to change the glorious photos of roses throughout my blog because they relaxed me, even when the posts had touched on a depressing reality.

Mary asked, "how will you reach your audience to let them know about this website?"

I handed her the first fundraising letter I had written and explained that I intended to shoot an infomercial prior to elections.

Her eyes peered directly into my skull. "Do you know how much money you'll need to buy national airtime?"

"It's easy enough to find out," I replied. "My ex is an infomercial guy."

9
SEDUCING MONEY

Martin Luther King didn't get up 50 years ago and say:
I have a budget and a plan!
– Alan Clayton, Scottish entrepreneur

I asked my ex, Roscoe, how much it would cost to do a national infomercial campaign, and he said I would need four million dollars. How would I get my hands on that kind of money?

As Ernesto neared his deadline for finishing the website, I was invited, via email, to attend a fundraising event for an animal rights organization called Compassion Over Killing. Perhaps I would learn how they raised money and apply the same methods.

At the event, as chance would have it, I sat next to a woman named Jeanne whose vocation was raising money for nonprofits.

A week later, I met with Jeanne and her colleague to discuss their proposal. They warned that it would take *a couple of years* before the money would start coming in. What? My spirits dropped to my feet. I didn't have enough savings to keep anyone on payroll for a couple years! It was the age-old problem of being undercapitalized. If I hadn't already committed myself to the website, this might have been the time to give up, but I'm not a quitter. I had to come up with other ways to raise money.

In the middle of one night, I had two brilliant ideas to spruce up the donation page of the website. One was to have something fun happen whenever a donor clicked on a radio button next to the amount they were donating. When a donor clicks on the circle next to one dollar, a big happy face appears. For $10, a cute little happy face throws his hands up with the words "Big hug!" in a bubble over his head. For $25, he blows a kiss and says "Thanks for the add!" At $50, he claps while the caption reads "Bravo!" For $100, the donor receives a special gift after happy man says "Cool!" with a big thumbs up. There is one final choice of "other," for donating any amount.

The gift for donors who gave more than $100 was my second bright idea, and it is truly priceless, in that I found out I could not buy one for all the money in the world. I had compiled a playlist for a "mixed CD" of music that was meant to accompany an as-yet unpublished book I wrote about my midlife crisis. Each track represented a synchronicity, a magical coincidence of meaning. Using some of the songs from that list, plus new songs that described my new political obsession phase, I compiled the "Soundtrack for Election 2012."[8]

I posted a gig on Craig's list, asking for someone who knows how to obtain the rights to this amazing soundtrack. Several people answered the ad, and each one wanted very much to help me clear the songs performed by classic artists such as Deep Purple, Sting, the Beatles, Stevie Ray Vaughan, Electric Light Orchestra. Each Craig's List person came back with the same answer. *It can't be done.* I just wanted people to be able to download the songs all at once; I didn't expect a cut. It was like selling the music *for* the artists, not taking anything from them.

Since it appeared impossible to clear all those wonderful titles, I did a workaround. I told donors that they would receive the list to the "Soundtrack for Election 2012" that they could then download themselves by painstakingly finding all the tracks. I hoped that someday, somehow, this soundtrack dream would materialize through providence.

Music or no music, the money wasn't flowing in. I had no expertise in fundraising, and no "Susan the Sunflower" to help me.

As a last resort, when I couldn't raise money for my nonprofit, I could approach investors to fund it as a for-profit enterprise. Something about "for-profit" didn't sit right with me. I thought

---

[8] See Appendix 2 for the list of the songs and the significance of each one.

that a website designed to change the way our government functions should belong to "the people," and as such, it should be nonprofit. Perhaps it could start out as a for-profit and switch over to non-profit once it was underway. It was time to finish the business plan and raise capital, but I needed help. Who would I hire?

10
INDEPENDENT CONTRACTORS

There is one thing in this world you must never forget to do.
If you forget everything else and not this, there is nothing to worry
about, but if you remember everything else and forget this, then
you will have done nothing in your life.
–Rumi, mystic poet 1207-1273

I thought that I could infect everyone who worked alongside me with zeal and passion because we were going to fulfill America's greatest need. How could we possibly fail?

I had been writing the bare bones of a business plan but I needed help so that I could focus on fundraising. I placed an ad on Craig's List for an MBA from a leading business school who had experience working at a website-based company. I wrote: "You will write descriptions of the competition and collect demographic data to support immediate fund raising and Venture Capital seeking endeavors."

"Why are you interviewing people at the house?" one friend asked. "You don't know these people! They could be dangerous!"

On paper, nobody who answered the ad looked like an ax murderer to me. The gentleman I invited for an interview had been to MIT graduate school, worked at Northrop Grumman and the U.S. Coast Guard. He had been a project manager and engineer since 1994, and had been a principal in starting a job referral website. Nothing about his resumé screamed trails of blood.

Thomas arrived in a beat-up, twenty year old car. He was either very hungry or a poor performer. Obviously, his money wasn't on his wheels. His calm voice and easy smile made him instantly likeable. Thomas had the early middle-aged spread from years of sitting.

"It looks from your resumé you're trying to get a website off the ground. Tell me what the challenges are," I asked.

"We had a great concept for matching engineers to jobs, but it wasn't the right timing." Just as the economy tanked.

Despite his masters degree from Rensselaer Poly Tech and studies at Massachusetts Institute of Technology (MIT) Sloan focused on entrepreneurship, he was unlucky. He had written the business plan for his current company and watched it take a dive as unemployment skyrocketed. He was a product of our times, an ambitious family man who wanted to be on the board of the next successful start-up. After the dot com bubble burst, it took a recession for dreamers to realize that the days of big breaks, loaded sign-on packages, fanciful initial public offerings, golden parachutes and soaring stock prices is over for most of us.

He showed me the business plan he had written. I trusted that this well-spoken, seemingly "can-do" employee would deliver quality prose. I hired him because of his impressive history, his education and because he was hungry for work.

Two is more powerful than one. Our grand experiment doubled its engine of creativity. We were grabbing onto the opportunity of a lifetime to formulate an agency that responded to the electorate!

Thomas sat at the desk in my office in front of his laptop. He wrote comparisons between similar websites and collected social media data to show investors. Assuming that web traffic flowed heavily from all the media coverage we would naturally, automatically, and generously receive for the work we were doing, Thomas could show that candidates would pay to be on our website. With 468 open seats in Congress every two years, and who knows how many candidates giving, say, a meager $25 each to post each month, he even showed reasons why the plan would be profitable.

I completed the financials and future projections with the help of an accountant friend, based on numbers Thomas conjured up in the perfect world of imagination, as any startup must do.

When I read the first page of his plan, it lacked any passion in its description of Writeindependent.org. With the fire of inspiration in my breast, I wrote the executive summary of my "Fix Congress Plan," the basis for Writeindependent.org. I defined the problem, the solution, the urgency, and how to act now![9]

The website was due to launch two days before Thomas's assignment would be over. Theoretically, Ernesto would finish by September 1, 2011. I had been checking on Ernesto's work all along. If the whole website was a house, he barely had the foundation and the frame. He slapped on a front wall, but behind the façade, the plumbing, electrical, even most of the rooms weren't finished.

When the website didn't launch as planned, the best I could do was give Thomas a pep talk about the future. I had a Los Angeles Venture Association (LAVA) event coming up and I wanted his participation and support.

I gave Thomas his final check. "You'll come with me to meet venture capitalists, right?"

"Sure," he said.

Later, I reflected on his contribution to my business plan. He used Facebook's popularity to show how social media rocked the world with its pervasive presence. A Facebook comes along once in a lifetime. It was a fluke, an anomaly that will never happen again. Using Facebook's statistics to explain what might happen for any new website is cheating.

After Ernesto and Thomas, the third person I hired came with a team. She was the owner of a public relations (PR) firm in Chicago. My ex, Roscoe, had used her company at his previous employer and had been satisfied with the results. I knew her personally and had been to her wedding.

The proposal her team sent me promised two huge phases of media outreach. When the time was right, they would draft byline articles and secure speaking engagements. I asked the team to begin in California. The west coast has a reputation for starting trends that travel eastward and I wanted to leverage my home base

---

[9] See Appendix 3, Executive Summary of Writeindependent.org

as much as possible. Wouldn't Los Angeles papers and magazines naturally want to write about a local business that aimed to fix Congress?

And oh, I had fantasies about the media coverage that would come later.

I am sitting, center stage, on a chair of a nationally televised talk show with Conan O'Brien, or the ladies of the View. "So what makes you think you can choose the next President of the United States?"

"People today are too busy to research and find out alternatives to the two choices foisted upon us. I felt it was time to find someone decent and honest, who isn't part of the political machine."

Conan counters, "Everybody wants to vote for a winner, and nobody is going to believe that a third choice can make it. Look at Ralph Nader; many think he ruined Gore's election."

"Yes, but it could work the other way. Republicans could decide to abscond and choose the best candidate rather than the one who follows the party line, which is getting too extreme on the right for many people. Look how hard it has been for the Republicans to find a likeable GOP (Grand Old Party) candidate."

"So you think you're going to call the middle for everybody?"

"Sure! I'll do it. I just won't do it until the day before the election, so nobody can smear the candidate with negative ads. I'll come back on your show in November and tell you who I found, and then let the country decide if she's better than the other two who are entrenched in the current system."

In my vision of a fortuitous future, I will phone in my favorite candidate from an undisclosed location wearing a bright floral print muumuu. The ladies of the USA will support the President I identify, the news will spread like wildfire, and she will surge ahead at the polls to secure her win.

Ernesto finished creating the form that candidates would use to summarize and post their platform on our website. It was so simple to fill out. The form asked them why they're running for office and five specific goals they planned to achieve once they won the election. I needed a day-to-day employee to populate the website with candidates. I found my fourth hire at the birthday party of a friend. Her name was Sharon, a bright, blonde haired, brown-eyed sparkplug.

Sharon's background was in sales and marketing for an educational bookseller. She had been looking for work after leaving a long-term job. She found it difficult to work in an office where a few co-workers smoked pot during their breaks. In contrast, I wouldn't offend her with plumes of smoke or the odor of weed-infused clothing every time I opened my office door. I don't do drugs.

"I appreciate your passions and am thrilled for you!" she wrote in an email before I hired her. "I am excited at the prospect of it myself and all of its possibilities."

Sharon tried to woo political bloggers to our site, hoping they would blog about us. She wrote letters to the trustees of causes like global warming, explaining that they now have an ally in Writeindependent.org because we could help them reach candidates and their constituents. She also pitched in where my PR company left off, because they only contacted each media outlet once. When she phoned or emailed journalists, radio personalities, and television shows, Sharon articulated our mission like a pro. She became my mutual admiration officer and cheerleader. She gave reality to my dreams.

When I reviewed Sharon's correspondence to see how she was presenting our company, she used an inordinate number of exclamation points! I asked her to remove some of them.

"I'm excited!" she said, fairly bouncing off her chair.

"Everyone can tell by what you're writing."

While Sharon was trying to popularize our website, I was focused on raising money. I would soon find an ally in a billionaire who was fed up with Congress.

11

MR. TALL

This is America,
This vast, confused beauty,
This staring, restless speed of loveliness,
Mighty, overwhelming, crude, of all forms,
Making grandeur out of profusion,
Afraid of no incongruities,
Sublime in its audacity,
Bizarre breaker of moulds,
Laughing with strength,
Charging down on the past,
Glorious and conquering,
Destroyer, builder,
Invincible pith and marrow of the world,
An old world remaking,
Whirling into the no-world of all-colored light.
– Amy Lowell
American poet 1874-1925

With my business plan finished, I was ready to show it around. I called it the "Fix Congress Plan" because I saw that as the Ace, which once uncovered, would allow all the other cards to fall into place. Make Congress respond to Americans' wishes and we wouldn't have so much war, pollution, abject poverty or rotting schools.

I thought it was time to get out of the house, shed my inhibitions about mingling in crowds, and seduce an investor. I had not proven that the website would actually Fix Congress, but nothing was going to stop me now that I had my mind set.

Back in August, 2011, I learned from an op-ed piece in the *New York Times* that Howard Schultz, CEO of Starbucks was fed up with the debt crisis and the inability of Congress to come up with a realistic budget. Mr. Schultz announced that he was pulling any further support in the way of campaign funds until they did the work necessary, and encouraged other CEOs to follow his lead.

Mr. Starbucks himself! Oh happy day! What could I accomplish with a man like that in my corner?

I immediately borrowed his autobiography *Pour Your Heart Into It: How Starbucks Built a Company One Cup at a Time* from my local library. I read about a key person who was instrumental in starting and building his company. A man who shoots hoops with Mr. Schultz, whom I will refer to as Mr. Tall.

Mr. Schultz met Mr. Tall in the gym for pickup basketball games and their workouts became a business association that spring-boarded the coffee company. Mr. Tall is an attorney from Seattle who helped write the documents necessary for Starbucks to make its initial stock offering.

All I cared about was that he was Mr. Schultz's friend, that he had this powerful man's ear, and that I could find Mr. Schultz through him, because it was doubtful I'd get the CEO of Starbucks' attention through a letter, though I tried:

Dear Mr. Schultz,

Do you want to sell more coffee?

How do you get people to feel confident enough in their future to start spending their discretionary funds toward a cup of premium coffee at Starbucks? They want to get back to their usual spending habits, but fear over the economy has hampered their mental outlook.

If you want to give Americans a way to feel more empowered about their futures, then give them the confidence that when they go out to vote, they will actually be taking charge over their representatives in Congress. Help them restore trust in their elected civil servants to pass legislation for the greater good.

Boosting the morale of this country is just one of the objectives of my website, Writeindependent.org. You and I have the same purpose—we both want to help Congress become a functional deliberative body.

Writeindependent.org is the most ambitious political website on the Internet today, because it promotes candidates for each state's federal elective offices. I designed it after Obama's transitional website called *The Citizen's Briefing Book*, an ingenious site that asked the American people for their solutions to every issue that mattered to them. I combined his organized idea-sharing method with a simple 50-state "introduction to the candidates" platform, to provide a comprehensive clearinghouse for voters to see a healthier political landscape laid out before them, one not run by special interests.[10]

Please help me plant the seeds of a new America and give me the opportunity to inspire the voting power of our people.

Go to Writeindependent.org and click on the DONATE tab or contact me directly, ###-###-####. I would be honored to speak with you. Alternatively, you may email me at xxx@writeindependent.org.

Sincerely,

Judy Frankel

P.S. I really believe this country is full of innovative, industrious, intelligent people who want to make this country a better place, and want to create a brighter future for their children.

I sent Mr. Schultz this letter after investigating No Labels, the organization he had joined to remediate Congress. Their strategy involves twelve steps that promise to make Congress work. The centerpiece of their plan is the "No budget, no pay" legislation that requires Congress to decide on a budget before they can collect their paychecks. I had to wonder, *why would they agree to punish themselves for not doing their jobs?*

I envisioned Mr. Schultz and Mr. Tall lacing their basketball shoes over a conversation about this passionate Jewish mother who wants to wallop the behinds of Congress with a little website.

---

[10] A "special interest" is a group of people or an organization seeking to receive special advantages via lobbying. Many of these groups use money and favors to obtain their goals.

But how would I get Mr. Tall on the phone? If I were able to manage such a feat, what would I say? I dove into the Internet to scrutinize him, surprised by his google deficiency. One paltry interview held in 2007 quoted the mystery man as saying that he likes to invest in products that have a "save the world" component.

I found a lone photo of Mr. Tall's smiling face on his law firm's website. Twenty-six years after drawing up the documents to begin Starbucks with Howard Schultz, he now has receding thin, blonde hair atop an egg shaped head with a pointed chin and boyish good looks, despite his age.

I left two voice mail messages for Mr. Tall over a period of nine days, pursuing him as a potential client. I would begin a conversation by asking which type of corporation I should open, a nonprofit 501(c)(4) or a for-profit. He didn't need to know that I was already in the process of finalizing my articles of incorporation. One of my neighbors, a close friend named Maria, signed on as president, and two other friends became treasurer and secretary. Each of Writeindependent.org's three corporate officers were registered differently: Democrat, Republican, and Independent.

As I waited for Mr. Tall's return phone call, I investigated two venture capital organizations: the MIT Enterprise Forum and LAVA, the Los Angeles Venture Association. Both are skillful at marketing to entrepreneurs, and soon I became inundated with emails inviting me to events for schmoozing Venture Capitalists. On September 13, 2011, LAVA would host a panel discussing public relations for startups at the Skirball Cultural Center in Los Angeles.

I entreated Thomas, the MIT graduate who had helped write my business plan, to come with me and speak to investors. If he wanted employment, it made sense for him to approach Venture Capitalists and solidify his position in our enterprise. However, Thomas had evaporated, and what I mean is that he stopped returning my phone calls, stopped emailing me, just completely wiped himself off the face of the planet. I wasn't willing to drive to his home address to confront him, so I gave up on him.

Despite this discouraging turn of events, I kept going. The LAVA event was in my sights.

I couldn't remember the last time I had seen so many men in

one place. It reminded me of my days as a wrestling manager for Penn State—probably twenty males for every female. Is it really that bad for us women that the higher we ascend in money and ideas, the less women there are? This has got to change.

For the LAVA event, I looked like the amount of money I wanted to raise. A million bucks! Standing on three-inch heels added to my five foot, six inch frame, I wore slim black pants and a long black bouclé jacket that came in at the waist. I felt powerful, sexy and tall.

In my ebullient "I-just-started-a-company" euphoria, I glided around the banquet room of almost a hundred suit and tie venture capitalists as though I were Cinderella in business attire. If yesterday, they had seen me wearing dark yellow, dirt-stained leather gardening gloves and rubber Muck Boots®, digging a hole in the ground for composting stinky vegetable scraps, I doubt they would have expected me to attend their soirée.

My unusual business opened up a rarely used door. I was talking about politics. I assumed that Americans generally don't discuss politics in any social context because it's bound to piss someone off. Instead, I found the men engaging and ready to toss out jokes to match the mood that our government inspires. By chance, or perhaps because of their interest in money, most of the men I spoke with immediately told me they were Libertarians. Everyone could agree that Congress is behaving badly and is in need of repair.

I pushed a Libertarian button. I told one of them that "the next car I'll buy has got to run on fuel cells."

One gentleman reacted, "Fuel cells? Aren't you talking about a car that runs on batteries?"

"Not just batteries. I want a car with a reformer on board, which turns petrol into hydrogen. The hydrogen would go through a fuel cell, create energy, and drive an electric motor."

"That's no fun!" said the Libertarian. "I want my car to make noise when I punch the accelerator!" It was the classic "vroom vroom" that he desired. If his car didn't catch people's attention, if it weren't going to turn heads, he didn't want it. Apparently, the earth can go to hell in that Libertarian's paradise.

I didn't make a connection at the LAVA event. I learned that I needed traffic to the website worth bragging about before I could seek venture capital. It's the classic Catch-22. You have to get business before you get money, but you need money before you can start business. Oh, how I longed for a donor like Howard Schultz! What I could do with a man like that in my corner! Why wasn't Mr. Tall calling me back?

Three days later, I sat at my computer, talking with Sharon, when the phone rang. "This could be Mr. Tall," I said, half joking. It was a Friday afternoon and I didn't expect anyone to have their business head on at such a time.

"Mr. Tall!" I said out loud so that Sharon knew I had achieved the amazing. I launched into my first question. "Have you looked at the website?"

Of course he had, he said, and it was interesting. He wanted to know how I found him. I explained how I'd read about Mr. Schultz's disgust with Congress in the *New York Times* and that I discovered Mr. Tall himself through Howard's autobiography.

"In my humble opinion, I think that No Labels' strategy won't work because they are handling Congress with kid gloves" I said. "Their plan falls apart because they're asking a recalcitrant group of people to change the rules on themselves." What Mr. Schultz should do instead, I told Mr. Tall, is educate the voting public about the depth of Congress' betrayal of our trust.

"Six weeks before the election," I said, "we will run an infomercial that reminds voters about the Financial Services Modernization Act of 1999, the final blow for bank and securities regulations, the resulting housing crisis of 2008, and the negligence of our Justice Department to hold those responsible to account. Voters have short memories. Did you know that 104 incumbents who agreed to the Act have been repeatedly reelected since 2000?"

Mr. Tall wanted to know how I came to create such a website, what was my story? As I explained my background, how all these pieces converged: the gardening experiences with mycorrhizae, about my fears of the agribusiness companies ruining our food supply, my frustration with Congress' willful inaction, I heard my voice become rich, full of inflection, infused with passion. I dug deep to reveal my truth as a human being. I told him that I am first and foremost a writer, after which I became a gardener, and then most importantly, a mother.

I thought *it's better to be real than to guess what he wants to hear as an attorney or an investor.* I tried to speak to his soul to seduce him with an idea because it was the most powerful thing I had.

"You can't start a corporation without three board members," I said. "Then why would you have a government with only two parties? There's no tiebreaker!"

"How do you expect to get the kind of attention you need to take on a project of this scope?"

I told him I had hired a PR firm, and that they were contacting all the media outlets on my behalf.

"You need a famous person to do something like this. Who are you?"

I felt the burning, flushed sensation of a sudden lack of self confidence. "I'm nobody." I admitted. "I know what you mean. If I were, say, Leonard DiCaprio, I could get attention immediately."

"Howard Schultz can get an article in the *New York Times* because he's Howard Schultz," Mr. Tall said.

"I don't know how it's going to happen, but no one cares about this the way I do." Negative thoughts flooded my brain. *I am nobody, I can't do this thing. Nobody will listen to a nobody.* My inner thoughts came with the sting of failure. I had to bounce back and this leapt out of my mouth: "Leonardo DiCaprio isn't going to start a website."

I asked him if he had read my blog. Surely then he would know that I had a lot to say, more than the typical famous person.

"Yes, I've read your blog and you don't seem nonpartisan to me. You say you're trying to create a website that's neither left nor right, and yet you have leaning views." He had an erudite voice and sharp mind, precise as an architectural etching. I felt intimidated.

"True, I'm concerned about the environment. But the website works the same for anyone. The website is open for all viewpoints, it's just my blog that's personal." I had no apologies for being who I am. The basis for all government rests on one thing—is the institution trustworthy? The same went for the website—if the people who oversaw it were honest people, it would work.

"How much money do you have behind you? How much have

you raised in donations?"

"I'm doing this with my own money so far," I said. "With so much of my own skin in the game, failure is not an option."

"I hope you have a good day job."

I regretted what I said next. It came out uncensored as I'm thinking *this is not good.* "My ex gives me just enough money to hang myself. He thinks I'm going to sit on my hands, and that's not who I am." The bitterness with which I said it made me regret my words.

Mr. Tall peppered me with questions, then advised me to stick with the nonprofit. He said one thing that really bothered me. "You don't sound like an entrepreneur." It was the death knell. I could only imagine what that meant. I didn't talk about money enough. No figures about traffic to the site, nor how much I expected to gross, or cost of acquiring a customer.

What he did not realize was that I had always been an entrepreneur, starting businesses since I left college. My longest venture was a physical therapy clinic, but I had also started a bicycle messenger service and an edible landscape consultancy. I had only done things I felt passionate about, and no, I wasn't a Howard Schultz raking in the dough, but I also hadn't compromised myself or sold my soul to make the big bucks. Maybe this is what made me undesirable to Mr. Tall. I didn't have that sharky, cocky attitude laser focused on money, money, money. Was that it?

If I didn't sound like an entrepreneur, what did I sound like? Was he trying to say that I should give up this endeavor? That I was the wrong person to run something I created myself?

Even though he didn't offer to help me, I felt triumphant for having a twenty-minute conversation with him. I wished I had been able to ask him if he were married, had kids, considered his life a blooming success, satisfied that he could purchase whatever he wanted, making the world a better place in the process. He had all his needs met, and then some. He could go to his grave satisfied.

I fantasized that Mr. Tall exemplified everything I longed for in a partner—he was more intelligent than most, had a rewarding career, good friends, probably a wonderful family. I wanted to meet a man like that in my circles, in my everyday life. What would that take? How could I do that?

A great sadness came over me pondering my options. After all, he said I didn't sound like an entrepreneur. I had to recover from our phone call by moving on, trying to stay positive. I framed our talk in the best possible light—*maybe he missed his opportunity to take an amazing journey with me, that it was the result of his limited thinking that kept him from seeing the broader picture. Life does not have to always run in the same direction.*

From our conversation, three words stood out against all the others, echoing into the future. "I am nobody." What business did I have trying to do the impossible? By turning me down and refusing to help, Mr. Tall was preparing me for what lay ahead.

12

BETRAYAL

If you remembered all your mistakes, it would kill you.

– Irvin Stern, grandfather of the author

I was frightened out of my mind. The web developer, Ernesto, had promised to have the website finished by September 1, 2011, and he was now three weeks past his deadline. With the election less than fourteen months away, I was afraid I'd lose everything if I didn't roll out my PR and marketing plans in a timely manner. Without a fully functional website to show anyone, I couldn't raise funds, market my "product" or save America from our lousy government.

I bargained with God, wondering what He had planned for me. I prayed that He wouldn't let things get worse. I ruminated about possible awful scenarios that might happen if the website made a late entry onto the political scene. *Please save me from losing my house and my garden. If I run out of money because I can't make a go of this fast enough, would I rent out my spare bedroom? I'd lose my privacy. What about all the damage they could inflict on my house? I could actually lose money by renting out a room to someone who set the house on fire or forgot to turn off the garden hose, causing a sinkhole.*

I could deflate myself into tears thinking this way, even while outside pruning rosebushes amongst the flowers. Maybe I have too many damn rosebushes! They always need me.

I had trusted Ernesto because he came to my house to work early on. He seemed to know how to solve every problem I gave him. I treated him to his favorite Peruvian restaurant where we talked about his future, his hopes and dreams, his current disappointments. After his girlfriend got pregnant she moved north, a six hour drive away, to live with Mom and Dad. He had to show them that he could support their daughter and new little grandchild, that his love for all of them would outlast any struggle it took for him to prove his worth.

Now, one month later, to my shock and complete surprise, Ernesto announced the bad news that he was incapable of completing the job I had hired him to do. He begged out, saying that it was far more than he had expected and that no amount of extra time or manpower would make it possible. He did offer to help me transition to another company, perhaps feeling somewhat sheepish for letting me down when, only a week earlier, he had been the recipient of my homemade chicken soup with matzo balls for his flu.

This new admission that he was inadequately prepared to code my gargantuan website was like a swift punch to my solar plexus. The website's pages were only one quarter finished! All he had done was enter text and graphics, but the functionality wasn't there.

For what I had paid him, he had very little to show. He was far from creating a user profile page such as Facebook's individualized home screen. No message boards, no forms to fill out, no donation page. I admit that I had loaded him up with requests for what Writeindependent.org had to do, but considering how it was supposed to replace Washington's over-bloated bureaucracy with a more democratic method of citizen-run governance, it was amazingly simple.

Ernesto had tried using Joomla, an "open source content management system," which means it had customizable plug and play segments. He admitted to being a novice at Joomla, so he had brought in another developer who was supposed to fill in Ernesto's gaps of knowledge. For all I knew, they were sitting in his apartment doing drugs with the money I gave him. All told, I had handed him eight thousand dollars.

I rushed to search for another website development company. I evaluated three options. Two American website development firms wanted $100 grand and $25 grand, and lastly, an Indian company came in with the lowest bid at eight grand. Out of desperation and frustration, I hired the web developer in India because my ex-husband, Roscoe had many years' experience working with him and sending him business, all customers who were satisfied. I simply didn't have the money to hire the more expensive American companies.

It bothered me on so many levels that a website as fresh-faced and American as mine would be coded by computer geeks in India. I had to stay up late many nights to have computer to computer video conversations with Sanjiv, the owner. There were the language difficulties. His accent was often hard for me to understand. He spoke cryptically on purpose to avoid answering difficult questions. I have emails from him that I still can't figure out for the life of me. Communication is paramount when creating a website, and this had to be a collaboration. Over and over, I wished I had studied the language of coding and php. Or was it HTML5? I constantly berated myself for starting a website without this knowledge.

It took weeks to firm up the scope of the job and get the quotes, and then the most horrible thing of all happened. Ernesto bailed completely. He stopped answering my emails, stopped communicating. Sanjiv was asking for passwords and source code that only Ernesto knew! I had to find him, or the Indians would be required to start building the website from scratch.

Ernesto said he was in the process of moving, but I had no idea it was because he was dodging me. Then all the pieces started to fit together. Craig's List (beware!), his having to use Joomla but not knowing Joomla, his hiring other people supposedly to fill in for his inexperience.

In a state of panic and disbelief at my bad luck, I drove to Ernesto's old apartment to beg in person for the answers to my new web developer's questions. Time and again, I had the creepy feeling that I had been here before. I started counting the déjà vu interludes. They were happening at a rate of over one per hour. Something surreal was happening.

I went to his apartment, looked through the window and it was stark empty. I drove to the new address he had given me as his forwarding address. The unit was in a security complex. I waited by the entrance until someone with a key opened the door. I ran in. I knocked at Ernesto's "new" apartment but no one came. I looked through the window and could see people walking around, but they refused to answer the door. I knocked, I rang. I knocked again. I knew they were avoiding me.

I asked the neighbor, "Has anyone moved in here recently? Has there been anyone carrying boxes into this apartment?"

"No. Those people have been there for a long time."

The new address was completely bogus.

I believe that déjà vu happens when you are going through the appropriate path in life. It's a reminder of what you chose before you were born, when you're in that limbo or "heaven" taking a look at the life to come. The déjà vu experiences helped me know that this thing I was going through, horrible though it was, just had to happen as part of the correct realization of my purpose in life. But the property tax man loomed in my subconscious.

I then hired my private investigator friend, Shammy to find him. I've known her since 1991, and counted her as one of my closest friends; we spent that much time together. She had done many remarkable things. As a Porsche mechanic and consultant, she owned an auto repair shop. She produced an action movie, ran a health food store and a catering business. Shammy looked up Ernesto's name in her databases and found one within one mile of the address he'd given me.

I sat shotgun in her black GMC Safari outfitted with dark windows, high tech surveillance gear and bags for storing urine on long stakeouts. We walked into the lobby and searched the names on the postal boxes. Another security building! We bounded back to the sidewalk and waited for a car to enter the garage, then dashed through before the gate shut.

When no one answered our knocks on the door, we actually laid in wait. I imagined this experience would go into my book "Websites for Dummies" where I am the dummy, and the chapter I'm writing is "What Not To Do."

Finally, someone walked up and placed a key into the door we were watching. My friend sprinted to the resident and asked if they knew our Ernesto. No luck.

The critical knowledge that he had taken with him were passwords and code so that almost the entire website had to be started from scratch. The only thing that remained were some stock graphics and fonts, and they weren't even original source files. I had to give up on Ernesto.

The website ran as Ernesto's old, botched job until Sanjiv had enough of a site going, which took two months to create. They required another three months' work to finally iron out all the intricacies and add each function I'd requested.

When I searched for a new website developer, I learned valuable information that would help me market the site in a new and exciting way. I had heard of QR codes, but didn't know what they were. QR stands for Quick Response, first developed in Japan to help catalog and inventory parts in the manufacture of automobiles. Instead of a bunch of lines in a row, like bar codes, the symbols are arranged in a square shape. A Smart Phone or iPad loaded with a scanning app can take same device directly to your website just by aiming it at the newfangled "bar" code.

I made a mock-up of a wearable pin showing Writeindependent.org's name, logo and QR code with the words "Tag My Flag" at the bottom. I bought the domain name TagMyFlag.us and asked my new web developer to design a mobile website that would load onto your phone when you scanned my code.

I was so excited by the pins, I thought that they would catch on the same way "I like Ike" buttons had driven Eisenhower's campaign in the early 1950's before he declared which party he would run under. At that time in history, the two parties weren't so far apart and both Republicans and Democrats voted for him.

If people would wear Writeindependent.org buttons, they might actually start a conversation.

"What's that about?" one unenlightened citizen would ask the wearer.

"Check this out. Does your phone have a QR code scanner?" Savvy Internet users don't even have to ask this question because they have the app on their phone already. The uninitiated would search on their browser for a "QR code scanner app" and download it.

"Just point your camera lens at this square on my button, and it will take you to the website that is trying to de-bug Washington," the button-wearer would say.

The buttons were a natural as a marketing freebie. I offered them as a "gift" to donors who sent $25 or more. And of course, this would set up a chain reaction of people who wore the button and those who scanned it, and so on...

In my blissfully unrealistic creative state, I imagined myself being interviewed by Stephen Colbert of the Colbert Report. I would wear a button with a huge QR code on a stunning silky olive dress, tacky as that appeared. No one ever wore a pin like mine on a talk show, I assumed. Viewers would scan their television screens to arrive at the website right from their sofa, lounge chair or loveseat. How would I get the Colbert Nation to notice me? I was as far from Stephen's show as I could possibly be, given the fact that a "Colbert Bump" is something you have to be invited to experience.

Then something happened that would change the course of history, and in the process, make the website even more likely to get attention.

13
OCCUPY

...the fundamental need of American democracy is the practical
exercise of democracy—a rebirth of citizen activism. That requires
not only a populist rebellion against the political and economic
inequalities of our divided nation, but a hopeful rebirth of
American idealism, a revival of the belief that ordinary people can,
in fact, make a difference and turn the tide.
– Hedrick Smith, *Who Stole the American Dream?*

You can't steal money from people and just expect them to accept it. They are bound to get mad, like chisel-cut, cleft-chinned, often fuming hot Dylan Ratigan, host of the former self-titled MSNBC show. He summed up the problem in a segment that went viral on August 9, 2011. "There's a refusal on both the Democratic and the Republican side of the aisle to acknowledge the mathematical problem, which is that the United States of America is being extracted. It's being extracted through banking, it's being extracted through trade, and it's being extracted through taxation! And there's not a single politician that has stepped forward to deal with this!"

On September 17, 2011, Occupy Wall Street began with one thousand protestors in the heart of New York's financial district, Zuccotti Park in Manhattan. The pimple of anger in this country over unfairness, greed and corruption was swelling.

Watching the protests on The Colbert Report, I started yelling at my television. "Let me help you!" However, I couldn't find a way to get to the protestors. Even if I could, would they know how to use Writeindependent.org to get what they want? And the website wasn't ready yet!

I was in a funk, waiting for Sanjiv to say it was done, wanting to have more exposure, but unable to get Dylan Ratigan's attention or anyone else who had the same mission as I. To keep my spirits up, I asked the career counselor at a local high school if she knew any student volunteers who were interested in politics. One junior from Palos Verdes High School agreed to an interview, and I met him at Starbucks because I didn't have a proper office.

The student, whom I will call Fred, arrived in a suit and tie—not the typical high school attire. Thick black hair radiated from his head like a porcupine's quills arranged in cowlicks. When I asked why he was interested in government, he contained his anger while recounting the misbehavior of adults running our financial industry and our country. His understanding of the broad strokes of Occupy fanned his nascent political activism, and he wanted badly to join a demonstration.

His mother kept the household television tuned to Fox. Perhaps the website's success would be an unintended consequence of Fox's not-so-subtle, subliminal messages that we need a more efficacious form of democracy. Fred saw Writeindependent.org as the wave of the future.

His youthful energy plus eagerness to learn were tremendously appealing. Visions of marching excited Fred's desire to be swept up in a noble cause. He informed me that an Occupy rally was scheduled for downtown Los Angeles a couple weeks away, and could we go?

Why not?

Occupy reaches the public through the Internet by listing events and rallies, marches, and educational opportunities, as well as conference calls (Occupy Cafe). After obtaining the necessary parental approval, I drove Fred to the streets of Los Angeles, both of us not really knowing what to expect.

When we arrived at the designated spot, a news van already at the curb, we found roughly thirty protesters scattered about. An organizer yelled, "We're marching to the bank, and then we have a few foreclosed homeowners who will speak out!"

We all filed into a disorderly line and marched, or rather, walked the three blocks to the bank. I struck up a conversation with a gentleman tromping near me. He wore black jeans, black jacket, Raiders cap, and a sour expression.

"This is peaceful," I said.

"Yeah, but eventually we're going to have to be more forceful. We're not making enough headway." He sounded angry.

"I would hope it doesn't have to get violent, if that's what you mean."

"I want it to get violent. That would be fine with me!"

"What about voting the people out of Congress who took away the regulations that would have prevented this sort of bad behavior by the banks?"

"Voting? Pfffttt! They don't count our votes right, anyway! The system is rigged."

Our Occupy crowd chanted, "We are the 99 percent!"

Walking against the flow, a woman in cosmopolitan clothes with a scarf swirled about her neck darted toward a wall of glass doors to a mall. I hurried toward her to ask, "What do you think of Occupy?"

"I'm part of the one percent," she said. She wanted to get away from us fast. "I'm going *shopping*."

"I'm the one percent too," I said, referring to the time when my husband made enough to fit into that category. I wanted her to know that we're not angry at the one percent because it's really just the top .000063 percent who are running our country and our world. (Just 136 people gave more than 60% of the campaign funds to run the 2012 elections, most of it in secret.)

Did she really belong to the one percent? Did she even know what it means to belong to the one percent? When I startled Suzie Shopper, I didn't know that the top one percent makes at least $1.3 million per year, plus owns assets worth about $31.5 million. These numbers keep changing as the tippy top of the one percent keeps accruing more wealth. To me, the 99% idea meant that we are the majority, so if our needs aren't our being met, we're not using our clout politically. The one percent has Washington by the balls.

When we reached the square in front of the towering bank, I

soaked in the crowd's vibe. I admired the activists' pluck and persistence. Protesting with signs, standing around for hours under the weather, and walking in crowds is exhausting, hard, unpaid work.

I recognized a few faces. *Where have I seen them before?*

Then I remembered attending a presentation by an esteemed eco-activist named Vendana Shiva at Loyola Marymount just two months earlier. She spoke to a packed audience about protecting our God-given seeds against the big agricultural chemical companies that seek to control our food supply through their patents on plants.

There is a face from her audience at this rally! I identified another gentleman from a symposium on bees that I had attended three years earlier.

Maybe I have been an activist-in-training without even realizing it.

Protests are for people who are so disenfranchised, whose voices are so muzzled, that they have to make a statement with their bodies. It's a communication tactic. The civil rights activists expressed their struggles using feet on the ground in the Million Man March to Washington. Today's problems requires troops of Baby Boomers, Millennials, and a large group of idealistic students to create a powerful movement. An assembled, ranting crowd is indispensable to liberty.

Many people took the mike that day, and I was no exception. Occupiers are egalitarian folks who give everyone a chance to speak up.

"We have the power, people!" I yelled to the crowd in my gentle, almost too-cute voice. "It's Washington that made the banks overly powerful! We need to return to regulating the banks! We need to make our congressmen and the heads of the banks accountable! We have to organize! That's why I created Writeindependent.org, a website that helps us exercise our power!"

"Yeah!" yelled one or two people from the crowd.

"How did this happen? I'll tell you what happened! Our Congress repealed the Glass Steagall Act!" I felt the words fall from my mouth, roll along the pavement and dissipate into the sewers, like a fog. I wasn't connecting to my audience. I continued anyway.

"That's what motivated the banks to sell sub-prime mortgages. They were betting on us foreclosing on our houses and then they collected the insurance money!" I could already see their eyes glazing over. Even these Occupiers, who knew that something was rotten, might not have known about the Glass Steagall protections put in place in 1933.

I tried to explain the Gramm Leach Bliley Act, but I felt like I was on the fifty-yard line shouting to an audience of ten people in the top of the stands of the Staples Center. Then I realized how hard this problem is to solve. How does anyone educate so many people on such a complex topic? How do I convince enough participants to make the laser-focused choices that will strike at the root of this problem?

After I gave my story and my mission to the crowd, I felt no farther along. None of these people were going to rush home to look up a website that they barely remembered.

Then the real business at hand got underway when the stars of the rally showed up. Faith Parker, a 78 year old retired nurse who was evicted from her home of 50 years, told her story. Jaime Perez, in his 60's, talked about facing foreclosure. Their bank refused to negotiate, to re-set the loans, to forgive any debt, yet banks got away with a $700 billion bailout on the backs of the taxpayers?

Matt Ward, who organized an Occupy event at a foreclosure auction, urged community members not to reward the banks by buying foreclosed properties. For people caught in the subprime scam, Mr. Ward recommended emailing olasavemyhome@gmail.com for help. Cheryl Aichele spoke against the power structure that lawlessly repossessed homes like Bertha Herrera's, a 63-year-old chaplain from Van Nuys, California.

As I heard more horrors about foreclosures from other speakers, it occurred to me that the twelve million families who had to leave their homes because of bad loans represent a tipping point, a number large enough to throw the balance of power to favor the people. If only they would vote for the candidates who pledge to fix the financial industry. How would they know whom to vote for? And without an address, how would they vote in states that require an identification card?

The answer to that question came from another experience with Occupy. While researching the Occupy movement so that I could write about them in my blog, I found out that someone had branched off, calling his website Occupy the Ballot. This was either competition or a blessing in disguise. If Occupy became organized enough to mobilize their voting power, they would be formidable. I called the person who was responsible for starting "Occupy the Ballot" to find out if he would work with me. His name is Zach, an intelligent thoughtful twenty-something. I asked him to explain how he started his website.

"People aren't just going to vote between the two bad choices they already have," he said on the phone. "We need to get new people and fresh ideas into office if we actually want to change things. So I started Occupy the Ballot."

"How did you get to head this up?"

"It's not like, endorsed by the movement or any of the general assemblies. Right now it's really just a website. We're going to flesh it out and then publicize it, focused [on trying] to get a candidate."

I explained what I was doing. "We both want the same things. We need to get candidates to get rid of the money in politics and that's going to be extremely difficult. I think people really understand that lobbyists are running the show. When your goal is only to make money, then everything else takes a back seat. I'm a big environmentalist. I don't know if you are."

I could sense that he was suspicious of me, like I was a salesperson trying to twist his arm. He reluctantly said "yep."

"We all have to work together, the 99% with the one percent, Kumbayah," I said. I paused, expecting him to say that it will never happen, but he let me go on. "We have to entice the one percent to stop hoarding their money by doing it the only way they know how, and that is to invest in our future. We have to make a very attractive alternative to what they're doing right now, which is just digging in their heels and thinking about buying islands and bunkers and bullet proof Humvees." I laughed. "I mean, that's no way to live either, right?"

"Yep."

"I think there's a way to bring everybody into the conversation. We're not going to make everyone happy, but at least we'll exercise what our founding fathers thought was a good matrix. The whole idea went completely awry when we let capitalism go to this extreme, where we forget about taking care of the planet and we say to hell with everything except making money."

"I disagree with you on a couple things. I have a more radical view, 'radical' meaning wanting to change the entire system instead of just reforms." I liked his pluck, his verve. Here's a guy who isn't just home sitting in front of the tube wondering what kind of toothpaste to buy or if those smiling babes in the beer commercials are going to go for him if he imbibes.

He continued, "Capitalism is bound to lead to extremes. It will always create this one percent, whoever they are. I don't see that there is something wrong with the system. I say that the system is wrong. It's not broken. This is how capitalism is supposed to work."

I argued, "But opening a lemonade stand is capitalism. What you are worried about is extreme capitalism, where monopolies make it impossible for the little guy to compete. That's the problem, not capitalism itself."

"If I had my ideal, we would all be living on a barter system, instead of money. You do something for me, I do something for you. You give me healthcare, I give you food."

"Wow. When I die, I want to live in your world," I told him. "That's not going to happen on this planet." I was genuinely sad to break the news to him, but he wasn't deterred.

"You do live in my world!" he insisted. "You just have to see things the same way."

"There is hope for the future, if you and all your neighbors think the way you do," I said. "The problem is that the bullies who want to gobble everything up will upset your collaborative system every time you think you've hit homeostasis. That's why we need government in the first place. Because people aren't always good at tithing to help the poor, and because someone has to set the rules."

I said, "Imagine if football didn't have any rules, or if the game were rigged. What if one team always got the best players, the healthiest food and training, the best coaches, equipment and athletic fields, but no other teams had access to these things? And what if the first team paid off the referees so that even the scoring was skewed? That's what we have now. What fun would that be? Nobody would want to go to that football game."

I had on the phone a perfect ambassador for my daughter's future. An idealistic dreamer, an arbiter of a new government and a steward of our planet. Today's students are tomorrow's bureaucrats. I saw the link between my generation, his, and my daughter's as one timeline of the American Dream evolving into something new and grand, perhaps stronger and more resilient than our forefathers had ever imagined. Much as I admire the people who founded America, they were sexist, racist landowners who were looking after their own interests and their immediate gain. The Occupy movement wants a more level playing field than those rich slave owners of almost three hundred years ago.

"What does the Occupy movement stand for?" I asked.[11]

"As I said, we think that capitalism is the problem. The other thing we stand for is that we have no leader. It's a level movement; no leaders, no followers, no hierarchy. Each individual is a microcosm of the whole, therefore it is impossible to attack just one person and bring the whole thing down."

I agreed. "That's great. Then again, a leader could provide vision, guide, inspire, and help organize. In your leaderless group, good ideas can bubble up from anywhere, but someone still has to start writing them down to get things accomplished."

We talked about our strategies, and his included getting candidates to agree to some sort of anti-corporate-rule pledge. I asked him how far he got toward crafting such a pledge, and he said that he hadn't put pen to paper yet.

"Is your website trying to promote a third party, like some sort of independent party?" he asked me.

"No. It's not about parties. It's about people, Americans, all working together."

"That's what the Tea Party said they were, but now they are part of the problem."

"The original Tea Partiers were about too much taxation, too much government, and government oppression. They and Occupy are talking about two sides of the same coin. Occupy thinks that corporate money is the problem, and Tea Partiers think big government is the problem, when actually it's both. The

---

[11] For a statement from the Occupy Movement, see their list of grievances in Appendix 4.

corporations who pay the least in taxes are creating a government run by themselves and not the people." I grabbed a glass of iced tea and continued. "It's when the Tea Party got co-opted by the Koch Brothers[12] and the Republican right that they morphed into the same money-run politics that controls our red versus blue fiasco. A true Tea Partier would have to quit as soon as he was elected if he really believed that too much government was the problem. He'd have to lay himself off, downsize himself."

After we ended our call, Zach put my link on his website and I wrote a blog post about Occupy the Ballot. Neither one of us was strong enough to make an impact on the 207 million eligible U.S. voters (give or take a million) we needed to reach. But my life isn't over yet and neither is my Occupy the Ballot friend's.

From that phone call, I leveraged the idea of asking candidates to promise something. My conversation with Zach inspired me to write the Pledge for Honest Candidates, (for its latest iteration, see Appendix 5) which would become the lynchpin for the website and the key to what I still believe will tidy up Congress.

Now that Writeindependent.org's high school volunteer, Fred, and I had our curiosity satisfied about Occupy, we were ready to move on to our next adventure. While Sharon was still populating the site with candidates, Fred offered me a fantastic idea. It was he who noticed what I could not. "Why not run presidential debates? You've got the candidates on your website already. Let's find out what they stand for!"

---

[12] Brothers David and Charles Koch are affiliated with Koch Industries, the second largest privately held company in the United States. Their fortunes are mostly from oil.

14
PRESIDENTIAL HOPEFULS

Every noble work is at first impossible.
– Thomas Carlyle, Scottish philosopher 1794-1881

To my surprise and delight, I received a $100 donation in January 2012. Things were happening! Who would donate that much money? I discovered that it came from a man named Harry Braun who was running a campaign to become President. He was my first contact with an ordinary citizen with extraordinary belief in his ability to change the status quo. We had nineteen other presidential candidates listed on Writeindependent.org! Before long, he would enter into the presidential debates that Fred suggested we host.

I called Mr. Braun at his home in Arizona. He's a retired scientist on the Advisory Board of the International Association for Hydrogen Energy. First, I thanked Mr. Braun profusely for the donation. He said that he was impressed with the website, that he felt it was about time for something like Writeindependent.org. Why elections aren't run over the Internet, he did not understand.

"Why are you running for President?"

"Because, Judy, if we don't turn this ship around fast, we're headed for a world of hurt! And Obama ..." he laughed as if to say that Obama had no clue what he was doing.

"Tell me why you're our guy, then."

"I'm being realistic. There's no chance I could ever win. But I want to do everything I can to draw attention to the dire situation we're in. I'm not a politician. I'm a scientist. When the National Academy of Sciences is stating that the earth is in the final throes of being made uninhabitable, I cannot sit idly by."

"As President, what would you do about global warming?"

"The answer, Judy, is to switch to a solar hydrogen economy with wartime speed. And it's not going to happen until we get the people to demand a Constitutional Convention according to Article V of the Constitution."

At my request, we switched from phone to Skype. Mr. Braun looked to be almost 70 years old and reminded me of a nearsighted Mr. Magoo except with white hair and a serious, urgent demeanor. I asked Mr. Braun if I could record the conversation so we could put it on YouTube, and he was only too happy to allow it.

Mr. Braun continued, "Everybody says our country is a democracy, but as I point out, we are not and have never been a democracy. We have always been a republic ruled by an oligarchy, the super rich people, in secret, with lobbyists. The Fed does everything in secret and our monetary policy's all done in secret, by private bankers. Who gave them that power? Well, the Congress did. And the Congress was bribed to do it.

"So Article V of the Constitution says you have to put the majority of citizens in charge of the federal government and the Congress, meaning anything the Congress does is not law until the majority of citizens say so. That is what we call the 'Democracy Amendment.' It would be the 28th Amendment to the Constitution."

Mr. Braun was way ahead of me. I had never heard of an Article V convention, and I wasn't sure what he meant about using it to amend the Constitution. I wasn't even sure if I had read the whole Constitution yet, even though a friend had given me a small book of its text. Later I would learn that our founders had given us a "get out of jail free" card in Article V that the American people can use if our Congress and Supreme Court goes rogue. (See Appendix 9 for the text of Article V.) It allows for the states to amend the Constitution so that a concerted effort by citizens can change the fundamental principles under which we are governed.

Harry went on, "...what you have done with your efforts on Writeindependent.org is exactly how we can make this

Constitutional Convention happen, perhaps before the next election. [We have] to get this on the national news, and do it online."

Harry Braun believed that the national news media would publish a story about citizens calling for an Amendment Convention simply because it's a good idea. However, the media and its owners know they might lose money and power if we passed a Direct Democracy Amendment.

I played devil's advocate. "The biggest pushback is that people say they're too busy to get involved and learn everything they need to know. They're too busy working, trying to put food on the table, they're struggling just to get by."

I posted the video of our conversation on YouTube. If anyone wants to see Harry, he is available to the masses. It was the first of more than 160 videos I would share on "Writein Dependent," the YouTube channel where I uploaded the presidential debates I would soon host.

How does one run a presidential debate? I watched DVD's of the debates since Bush v Gore that I had copied from my Tivo. I studied the format. And what I found online was far more interesting. The League of Women Voters had sponsored the debates thrice from 1976 to 1984 but stopped doing so, releasing this damning statement:

> "The League of Women Voters is withdrawing sponsorship of the presidential debates...because the demands of the two campaign organizations would perpetrate a fraud on the American voter. It has become clear to us that the candidates' organizations aim to add debates to their list of campaign-trail charades devoid of substance, spontaneity and answers to tough questions. The League has no intention of becoming an accessory to the hoodwinking of the American public."
> —League President Nancy M. Neuman, *LWV*
> *October 3, 1988*

I always wondered why the debates seemed so scripted, twisted, and unreal. Now I had my answer. They *were* scripted, twisted and unreal. I hoped to change all that. If I could get at least one more presidential candidate from the website to agree to a debate, we could have a spirited dialogue, with vigorous questions and real answers! What would that be like?

Only one thing excited me more than asking the tough questions. I wanted to find out who these presidential candidates were as people, as relationships. Were they egotists, intelligent, crazy, or attention-seekers? Did they have actual solutions in mind? Or were they completely off base? How would they fare internationally? What was their experience and backgrounds, and what made them think they could be POTUS? Were they educated about all the issues in every area that mattered?

I invited the twenty presidential candidates listed on Writeindependent.org including a front-runner from each of the established third parties, such as Peace and Freedom; Reform; Constitutional; Libertarian; and Green to discuss what's really going on in this country. I hosted one debate per month for the nine months prior to November 2012, covering the following topics:

Debate #1 February 13, 2012: Economy and Jobs
Debate #2 March 12, 2012: Energy
Debate #3 April 9, 2012: Campaign Reform and Civil Liberties
Debate #4 May 7, 2012: Immigration & Naturalization, Illegal
    Drugs
Debate #5 June 4, 2012: Education
Debate #6 July 2, 2012: Social Security & other civilian
    programs
Debate #7 July 30, 2012: Military/War
Debate #8 September 24, 2012: Healthcare/Drugs
Debate #9 October 22, 2012: Foreign Policy

I never gave out the questions ahead of time. The candidates were unscripted and spontaneous.

With great excitement, I "met" the second presidential candidate who agreed to debate (the first being Harry Braun). Mr. Andre Barnett, the frontrunner for the Reform Party, called me in response to my invitation.

On his website's video, the somber Andre Barnett in crisp white shirt and bald head sits on a bench outdoors as though he were next to the six-foot deep hole of America's gravesite. Did this beefcake-looking "sought-after fitness model" and body builder have anything unvarnished to say that would signify to me that he had what it takes to run the country, or did he suffer from delusions of grandeur?

Mr. Barnett lives in Poughkeepsie, New York. He was more than willing to participate in debates. He decried the difficulty of outlier parties getting any meaningful consideration.

"We need all the attention we can get," he said on the phone. "It's an uphill battle, and all of us should be working together to get the word out that more than just two candidates are running."

I liked his attitude, his can-do spirit. He said, "I am spending a lot of my own money to run my campaign. I'm not one hundred percent sure I'm the party's frontrunner yet, but I am the favorite to win the nomination."

"If you don't mind, how much have you spent?"

"So far about two hundred grand."

I gasped inside. At least I wasn't the only one spending my own money. "Wow, Andre. You're quite serious."

"That I am," he said in his deep tenor voice.

With Andre, I had the second debate candidate, and we were on!

Of the other eighteen candidates, I received quite a few yeses. I sent them a list of specific topics for the debate under the Economy: the national debt; jobs; taxes; financial instruments; the stock and bond markets; international trade; 'entitlement programs' such as tax havens, capital gains-type interest provisions for hedge fund managers, and offshore accounts; subsidies; the Fed; and government contractors.

I think I scared off a couple people, because we ended up with only three debaters.

The third person, J.L. Mealer, a civil engineer, developer, and automobile manufacturer was our comedy relief. He couldn't wait to take the law into his own hands to deliver punishments and jail time, using the presidency like "top cop." During our debates, he quipped about his receding hairline. He casually tossed off remarks about sending the bankers to Guantanamo and backing our money with nuclear waste. It was not always clear that he was joking, but I had a few good laughs.

J.L. lives in Arizona with his romance novelist wife and three kids. He invented a 75 mpg automobile engine that the government and General Motors allegedly squashed after he had already raised the funds to start production. "You can read the whole story by typing in 'Mealer vs GM' on Google," he said.

Americans Elect, the website who was searching for a third candidate to face off against Obama and Romney in the debates, asked visitors to compose questions for the three of them. I saw each question as an opportunity to educate viewers just how deep the problems go, touching on topics barely mentioned in the media. It took about a week to prepare for each debate. I spent hours on research, devising the questions, sending out email reminders to the candidates, setting up the computer equipment and finding a person to hold up colored cards at different time intervals. On average, I prepared fourteen questions, hoping to get through all of them.

On the day of the first debate, Fred acted as timer and technical assistant. Considering that it was the first presidential debate of its kind, that we were making history, I was jittery and amped up. I had arranged to have my hair styled by my next-door neighbor. She blow-dried my hair straight and ironed it, taking out all the curly-q corkscrews and giving me news anchor polish. As time drew nearer to the countdown, I outlined my lips with pencil, colored them in with lipstick, and checked myself in the mirror. Not a typical garden geek day.

We were supposed to start at 10:00 am PST, but technology would not cooperate. Andre Barnett's laptop kept losing video capability, and we all had serious audio feedback. I had to start the debates regardless of these difficulties, or we would run up against Andre Barnett's next appointment on the campaign trail.

After a few introductions, we were off to a running start. "Considering that price fluctuations in oil affects our entire economy, what is the President's ability to control the oil cartels? What will you do to secure our energy future, and thus the foundation of our economy?"

Harry Braun began: "My thrust, since I represent an international engineering society that's in forty five countries, has all been focused for more than one hundred years on shifting from an oil economy to a solar/hydrogen economy. That's how you create millions of jobs because you've got to modify everybody's existing car, truck, home, their appliances at home, all of the power plants. Instead of burning coal, we want them to burn hydrogen because it's pollution-free and never runs out. So what we're creating is trillions of dollars of new wealth and millions of new jobs. These aren't government jobs that you might think run the deficit up. These are government jobs that will create vast wealth for our country every year."

"Okay. So JL you have a minute to rebut," I said.

"The hydrogen economy is actually a solid solution, however we've got the problem with the Federal Reserve needing their tax base, and they will not allow their cash cow, which is [taxes from oil] to disappear. Unless they can tax hydrogen the same way. And that's still going to take a national security act, to consider Congress a threat to national security... However, with the hydrogen, I agree with Harry that is a good solid plan."

JL Mealer's idea to declare Congress a threat to our national security made it hard for me to take him seriously, but he certainly is more aggressive than the No Labels organization! Imagine charging Congress with sedition,[13] seizing their assets, and sending them to Gitmo for holding our government hostage. Instead of cocktails at the Pour House on Capitol Hill, how about Congressmen in indefinite detention, wearing orange jumpsuits?

"So you agree with Harry that a hydrogen economy is a possibility?"

"It is a possibility. Yes. If you recall, the Mealer automobile is based on the hydrogen fuel cell. The government will not allow that on the market."

"Andre you have a minute to rebut."

---

[13] Sedition is "If two or more persons in any State or Territory, or in any place subject to the jurisdiction of the United States, conspire... by force to prevent, hinder, or delay the execution of any law of the United States... they shall each be fined or imprisoned not more than 20 years, or both." MoveOn.org circulated a petition arguing that that "the House GOP leadership's use of the Hastert Rule and H. Res 368 to shut down the government and threaten the U.S. economy with default is an attempt to extort the United States government into altering or abolishing the Affordable Care Act, and thus, is self-evidently a seditious conspiracy."

"I'll be very quick. Number one, Harry, I agree that the hydrogen economy is something that's interesting. However, when you're talking about government jobs coming in, whether they're creating wealth or not, that wealth is going to belong to the government, not the American people. We have to make sure that privatized companies are actually heading and leading that frontier. If we don't, then we're going to minimize the job growth in private industry and it's all going to be government. That's where you get into a socialistic society and we can't allow that. We have to make sure that the private corporations have an incentive to come back to the U.S. And if the government is actually running that program, providing the jobs, what incentive do they have to come back to the U.S.? When are we going to grow the private sector? I agree with you on many fronts, but we have got to focus on the private sector creating these jobs."

"Harry, would you like to rebut, please?"

"Yes, I'd like. Why isn't the private sector, Andre, creating these jobs? Nobody's stopping them. Why don't they just go do it, if they're going to do it? They have twelve trillion dollars they're sitting on. Who's in their way?" Harry's face was bright red. He continued, "And by the way, why would you want to give all these trillions of dollars to oil companies instead of the American people, because ultimately the question was: How do we balance the budget? You do that with money, and you'd make a lot more money if we are producing the hydrogen ourselves than if we give it to oil companies. And [the oil companies] hardly pay taxes at all, in fact, they get massive billions of dollars in government subsidies."

Andre answered Harry. "I understand and I agree, but I never said let's give it to oil companies. What I said was 'private sector.' There are many small businesses right now that are trying to break into that field. If you look at China, they've already gone into that technology. They are producing the energy from hydrogen that you're talking about right now."

Granted, we weren't able to discuss how hydrogen works on our debate, or how far away we are from making it as ubiquitous as gas for cars and oil for heating, but at least we were discussing an energy paradigm that our children could be using, instead of expecting oil to last into their adulthood at the current rate we consume oil.

After I asked the three gentlemen their ten questions, I spent all day and night editing the footage and posting it on YouTube, CNN iReport and Vimeo. As I watched the video, I realized that I still hadn't found my next POTUS. Each of the candidates lacked the essential mixture of traits I was seeking. If they had a well-rounded understanding of the issues, perhaps they lacked depth in their solutions. If they had international experience, maybe they lacked business acumen. Though they had strong personalities, I couldn't feel the kind of charisma from them that I was looking for in a leader, an orator who knows how to inspire and activate a country. And though they each had heart, I detected inflexibility that negated their ability to be mediators. They were missing nuance and subtlety. My debates were functioning the way debates should, the way I wish Democrats and Republicans would discuss the real world, not some 'talking points' world. When we get candidates talking about actual issues in real time, answering bold questions that dig up the dirt that is going on behind the scenes, then we will see who can run this country with fervor and competence.

It would take four more months before I found enough presidential hopefuls to round out the field, making our conversations more engaging. I will go into more detail in Chapter 21.

Writeindependent.org's website and video channels were becoming a powerful body of information, but nobody was going to know about us until I could pay for advertising and marketing. I needed help, so I carried a long rod to the ocean to find the big fish.

15
THE LETTERS

Those who have the privilege to know have a duty to act.

– Albert Einstein 1879-1955

The fishermen of San Pedro, California taught me one thing. If you want to catch a marlin or sailfish, you have to go where the big fish are. You can't expect them to come looking for your baited hook.

I began a letter writing campaign that went straight to the top. I concocted a short list of wealthy people who had expressed an interest in reforming our government, even if it meant they themselves would have less political clout if they succeeded in leveling the playing field for ordinary, middle class folks.

The first person to whom I wrote a letter had been a third-party candidate for President himself, Ross Perot. Here is an excerpt from that letter:

Dear Mr. Perot,

One of the most successful strategies of your run for presidency in 1996 was the infomercials that educated many people about the national debt.

Your comments at the Bush-Perot-Clinton debates were prescient: you saw the dangers of GATT and NAFTA, and spoke out against outsourcing our country to death and lopsided trade agreements.

I have a little daughter, and I expect that things will get a whole lot worse if we don't do something bigger and better than what our politicians have been doing. I am absolutely certain that you will be heartened to know about the website I have created to address the corruption in our government. It is a ray of hope.

Around the same time I mailed the aforementioned letter to Perot, a Harvard Professor named Lawrence Lessig appeared on Jon Stewart's *Daily Show* talking about money in politics. Professor Lessig, with his large forehead and small eyes framed by glasses referred to Congress, "It's no surprise that when they live this life they become dependent on the funders as opposed to the people and that is the corruption." Mr. Lessig started the group called Rootstrikers in an effort to untangle the torturous, twisted way that money has bound our politicians. "The money is the root and unless we find root strikers who are willing to strike at that root, we're never going to fix this problem in Washington."

Jon Stewart asked, "Is there any way we can come up with something maybe sexier than 'Rootstriker'? Because I feel like, for people to fight this, they're going to want to sound more heroic. How about 'Batmen'?"

I purchased Lessig's book, *Republic Lost*. In easy to understand prose, he explains how lobbyists like Mark C. Brickell and Washington insiders Senator Phil Gramm, Treasury Secretary Robert E. Rubin and Larry Summers, Rubin's top deputy, used their power to prevent the Commodity Futures Trading Commission (CFTC) from regulatory oversight of derivatives. Lessig writes, "We had flipped from a presumptively public market of exchange to a market where only insiders knew anything real about how the market worked, or what the assets were worth. That was great for the insiders, giving them enormous power to leverage into extraordinary profits."

It was my fervent wish to have Prof. Lessig interviewed for my infomercial. For another high profile interview, I wanted renowned

Columbia professor and economist Jeffrey Sachs.[14] I read his book, *The Price of Civilization* and was pleased to see him on YouTube, rallying the Occupy movement at Zuccoti Park, saying "Both the Republicans and the Democratic party figured that if they cut taxes for the rich, the rich would give them campaign contributions and they could all live happily ever after."

The third expert I wanted in the infomercial is author Jacob Hacker, who, along with Paul Pierson, wrote *Winner Take All Politics: How Washington Made the Rich Richer—and Turned Its Back on the Middle Class.* He would elucidate the economic unfairness under which we suffer, the fleecing of taxpayers by the banks and financial elites.

If I could secure commitments from Lessig, Hacker and Jeffrey Sachs, raising the money to produce and air the infomercial would be easier. I started campaigning for their participation through emails to their assistants. Without their help, I felt like a tiny bee buzzing at the base of a mountain of problems. If they would say "yes," perhaps I'd have enough clout to rise up on an airfoil to the clouds and reach wise men like billionaire Warren Buffett, Chairman of Berkshire Hathaway.

A chain email was circulating around the country about Mr. Buffett's prescription for deep cleaning Congress. Legend had it that he recommended making it impossible for representatives to be reelected unless they balanced the budget. Both he and his friend/mentor Charles Munger, Sr. knew the dangers of an unregulated derivatives market, and perhaps they wanted to make sure another Black Friday wasn't threatening to implode when those derivatives matured.

I wrote a letter to Mr. Buffett, pleading: "We cannot afford two more years of a Congress that refuses to fix the underpinnings of

---

[14] I later found out that Jeffrey Sachs is the Director of the United Nations (U.N.) Sustainable Development Solutions Network. Senator James Inhofe (in his book about the global warming conspiracy) warns that the United Nations' Millennium Development Goals may override personal freedoms, including land ownership and use of limited resources. I agree with Mr. Inhofe that the U.N. "must remain open and transparent about all that it does." Mr. Inhofe believes that the conspiracy's main goal is to arouse fear about some future catastrophic event(s) in order to gain consensus so that the UN's "elites" may exert power over the world's division of resources.

our market. Our dollar will ultimately become devalued. We still have a lack of oversight of financial instruments such as derivatives, which become a self-fulfilling prophecy for failure."

Mr. Buffett heads two holding companies, Berkshire Hathaway A and B. I had been to Nebraska for a Berkshire Hathaway shareholders' meeting once, and know how folksy Mr. Buffett can be. I offered to "come to Omaha to discuss this in person, if necessary." I reasoned that he wouldn't help someone he had never met.

Little did I know at the time how mired Mr. Buffett is in the status quo. His holdings included companies like ConocoPhillips, National Oilwell, Goldman Sachs, Bank of America, Coca Cola and Walmart. The later two companies and their suppliers or subcontractors commit egregious human rights and worker violations.

However, getting the country to switch from petrol to hydrogen requires a POTUS, not a financial guru. I would soon learn that Harry Braun wasn't the only one thinking about hydrogen. So is actor George Clooney.

From the Palos Verdes Library, I rented the movie called Ides of March, directed and co-written by George Clooney. Ryan Gosling and Mr. Clooney star as campaign staffer and presidential candidate, respectively. It was almost a year since release in the theaters, and I couldn't understand why it didn't get more attention. The movie surprised me when Mr. Clooney's character mentioned hydrogen energy at the bully pulpit. I hand wrote a letter, burned a copy of my Election 2012 soundtrack, encased it along with the titles and artists, and mailed all to his production company. I felt a little embarrassed, being a 50+ year old and writing fan mail, but I thought—what the heck?

March 8, 2012
Dear George,

Thanks for making the movie Ides of March. I had to laugh when your character made the speech about replacing gasoline with hydrogen. It was peculiar because there is an actual, serious presidential candidate running on my website named Harry Braun who wants to do just that!

My goal this election year is to help replace a lot of

congressional incumbents with virgin politicians using the power of social media. I want the new people to attract voters because they pledged to enact real campaign reforms. Don't you think that removing special interest money from politics would improve our government? Wish me luck! It will take some kind of miracle.

Enjoy the "soundtrack" enclosed. It's meant to inspire. I offer it to people who donate $100 or more to my cause. Please accept it in appreciation for your art imitating life.
Sincerely,
Judy Frankel
P.S. Check out our nonpartisan presidential debate from the homepage: Writeindependent.org

Here's the reply I was waiting for:

Dear Judy,
Thanks for the note and the music. My goal this year is trying to keep people from getting killed in South Sudan, so my plate is full. In three more years, maybe I'll run for President and fix the whole mess, if Obama doesn't step up and get some balls.
Regards,
George

Only he wouldn't be so bold as to write those words. He didn't return my correspondence. No surprise there.

I mailed my letter just in time to reach him by March 15th, coincidentally the title of his movie. Mr. Clooney had other plans for the Ides of March. He was in Washington D.C. to make his case for South Sudan, perhaps choosing his date carefully or perhaps not realizing the synchronicity.

If he wanted, Mr. Clooney could run for President and would probably win because of his likeability. Rather than asking President Obama for a favor of some military assistance in holding back the North from committing one war crime after another on the South, he could be the one saying that the full force of the United States military is behind protecting Darfur.

Perhaps Mr. Clooney wouldn't want to be President. It's a

thankless job. The POTUS gets blamed for everything that goes wrong, and when things don't get better, he will be blamed for things not going right even when they aren't under his control. The position isn't for an ordinary human being; it's for someone who wants to "Be President" more than anything else. Why would Mr. Clooney want to give up his movie star life to be saddled to a four-year commitment, constantly hamstrung by Congress and a divided nation? And if he really wanted to do all the right things, he'd be shot for sure.

I wrote a letter to another powerful man named Edgar Bronfman Junior. Lawrence Lessig had mentioned in his book, *Republic Lost*, that Mr. Bronfman was interested in restoring democracy to our people.

Mr. Bronfman is the son of the wealthy family who owned Seagram's, once the largest alcohol distillery in the world. He divested himself of his family's legacy to participate in the entertainment industry, first through Polygram, then MCA, Universal Pictures, and Vivendi Universal, finally most notably purchasing Warner Music Group where he served as CEO and Chairman.

What I liked best about Mr. Bronfman was that he had removed himself from less savory businesses to follow his heart into the creative arenas, more risky ventures. He also chaired the Board of Directors of Endeavor, a nonprofit that nurtured high energy entrepreneurs on the global stage.

I sent him the following letter:

Dear Mr. Bronfman,

I have put my heart and soul into developing a strategy to improve the democratic process in our republic called The United States. We the people are wise enough to know our votes are being co-opted by the two-choice-only party system. We have felt helpless that our voices really make a difference when our leaders and representatives are "bought" by special interests during the campaign financing process...

I began to cross pollinate my efforts by sending tailored correspondence to two wealthy individuals at a time. Thus, Mr.

Schultz received a copy of the letter I had written to Mr. Buffett and vice versa. In my imagination, they would talk to each other about these issues, if they would just pick up the phone.

Even though I knew I had a bee's chance at a 30th story businessman's bouquet, it felt great to get the correspondence mailed out. It was important to stay optimistic to accomplish my goal, because life is filled with tiny moments. That's all it is. I practiced the habit of focusing my mind on being awash in buoyant emotions. Rather than get everything I wanted right away, I figured that if I experienced enough failure, eventually things would turn around. Not that I wanted to fail, but that I had an agenda that needed to be carried out, whether anyone was on board with me or not. I'm trying to change the world to make it a better place. If people aren't with me today, perhaps tomorrow they will be.

Out of about fifteen letters I sent to wealthy people who had expressed an interest in cleaning the corruption of government, only one gentleman, whom I will call "Mr. Money," sent me a hand-signed letter. He asked if I knew about Americans Elect and No Labels because we seem to be doing similar things and perhaps we should be working together. I answered his letter with this correspondence:

Dear Mr. Money,

Thank you for your thoughtful letter dated March 1st regarding the existence of Americans Elect and No Labels, and how we should all join forces. I have tried to work with No Labels, and they largely ignored me.

I have attached the letter to Peter Ackerman of Americans Elect. The two of us are running completely different programs. His focuses on bringing a third party to the presidential ballot across 50 states, and mine focuses on not just finding a new President, but also promoting anyone who wants to run for Congress.

As you know, the President can only get so much accomplished on his own. He/she needs a Congress that will work with him to further his vision. The Congress we have now is so dysfunctional, that no one, even a messiah, could twist their arms to improve our government.

I have a strategy in the works that is a game-changer. I've

written the draft of a Pledge for Honest Candidates that removes huge money from politics, and those who run on my website who sign it will garner votes. Trevor Potter, attorney at Caplin & Drysdale in DC, will be finalizing the pledge so that it can double as legislation, once the candidates win seats in Congress.

Then I will have a great story to tell to the press. If Americans for Tax Reform can deliver money (and thus votes) to their candidates, this Pledge for Honest Candidates can deliver votes to candidates who run on Writeindependent.org.

The other part of my plan is to broadcast six weeks of election "edutainment" that promotes these Honest Candidates. We have a first-rate production company called Anonymous poised and ready to begin marketing research in April.

No one is doing anything quite like Writeindependent.org across the country. That is why I am still asking for your help. Please donate at the website or call me at ###-###-####.

Sincerely,

Judy Frankel

P.S. I will keep you informed as to Peter Ackerman's response.

Before writing a letter to Americans Elect, I researched its main financial supporter, Peter Ackerman. He is founding chair of the International Center on Nonviolent Conflict, a family philanthropy that aims to educate oppressed peoples to use nonviolent methods for resolving conflict. The financier amassed a fortune allegedly selling junk bonds alongside Michael Milken. Though never formally convicted of criminal charges, Mr. Ackerman paid a sum of $73 million in a civil case brought against him by the FDIC and the Resolution Trust Corp.

His son, Elliot Ackerman, served as the spokesperson and Chief Operating Officer (COO) of Americans Elect. "We live in a world where we have infinite choice as consumers and as citizens in every other facet of our lives, why is it acceptable that in our political lives, we have to only choose between brand A and brand B?" Elliot asks interviewer Chris Yandek in September of 2011.

Critics lambasted Americans Elect (AE) for their fundraising, even when AE has no ideological ax to grind. On Hardball, Chris Matthews and guest David Corn wouldn't stop asking Elliot who AE's donors were, not allowing him to explain what Americans Elect was trying to accomplish. Another critic, Garret Quinn of Boston.com complained, "These guys stood for something a thousand times worse than the bitter hyper-partisanship they whined about—a wish-washy just do something attitude towards governance rooted in the pipe dreams of 'radical centrists.'" Quinn said that Americans Elect's $35 million operation was doomed from the beginning. Confidently, he made this announcement on the day they pulled out of the race.

AE eventually failed at holding "the first ever nonpartisan online presidential convention in 2012, where any registered voter can be a delegate to that convention." When I wrote my letter to Peter Ackerman, no one knew how far AE was going to go. I sent the following letter to both Mr. Ackerman and to Mr. Money on March 26, 2012:

Dear Mr. Ackerman,

Mr. Money suggested that I contact you.

Before I knew about Americans Elect, I started a website called Writeindependent.org. Once in development, I discovered your son's organization through my research.

We do not compete; we are complimentary programs.

The focus of Writeindependent.org is to serve as a clearinghouse for candidates to run for federal office, including Congress. Like you, I am disappointed at our government's reluctance to change the military budget and all that goes along with the military industrial complex. In my view, war never accomplished anything worthwhile, and trying to stop war is very difficult. I applaud your efforts in searching for nonviolent means to resolve conflict. My heart is with yours.

Since you have been so generous with your son's vision, I thought that you might not be interested in supporting what I am doing. Mr. Money insisted that "I think we must put groups together that are doing similar things," and this is what brought me to you.

I really feel that at this point, we must talk about our endeavors to compare and contrast them, and see where we might help each other. We already have fine people who insist that running for the Green, Libertarian or other parties is good enough because at least they are on the ticket. I disagree with all my soul.

It is not enough to put another party on the ballot. We must do more. We must educate, educate, educate our populace. I suggest that we run a six week campaign prior to November 6th that explains how our Congress has failed us (specifically economically) and how we need to remove big money from campaigns to fix the problem.

Elliot's strategy for choosing a new President is laudable, but short sighted. If any President reaches his/her office with the same dysfunctional Congress we have now, they still cannot hope to improve our government or its mounting debt. And a third party is even less likely to accomplish anything if the party leaders of the two party system have their way.

There is too much to write in one letter. If you strategize with me, our efforts together will more than double each other's accomplishments. I urge you to call me at ###-###-####.
Sincerely,
Judy Frankel

I wrote the letter because Mr. Money suggested that I should work together with the Americans Elect folks. Writing to Mr. Ackerman turned out to be an exercise in futility. Despite the lack of communication, I stayed abreast of the Ackermans' efforts, hoping that they would accomplish their goal of getting a third contender on the stage at the presidential debates.

Meanwhile, the lynchpin of the Writeindependent.org strategy, the "Pledge for Honest Candidates" deserved its day in the sun. If enough candidates sign the Pledge that removes money from politics, the website might attract media attention for that reason alone. The question begging for an answer—are there any honest politicians out there?

16

THE PLEDGE FOR HONEST CANDIDATES

The restraints on men, as well as their liberties, are to be reckoned among their rights.

– Edmund Burke, Irish statesman 1729-1797

To stay happy-go-lucky in a maelstrom of bad news, I watched *The Daily Show* and *The Colbert Report*. Instead of medication, I used a dose of humor to deal with horrible events. Stephen Colbert makes me giddy, and his writers make me laugh loud enough to wake up the neighbors.

Stephen started a Super PAC (Political Action Committee) called Americans for a Better Tomorrow Tomorrow in March of 2011. PACs are organizations that collect funds and use that money to promote their favorite politicians and legislative agenda. Mr. Colbert had been raising money for his PAC all the while that I was trying desperately to put together my non-profit "public welfare" 501(c)(4) and hoping to get enough attention to do what he was doing almost effortlessly.

On The Colbert Report, election attorney Trevor Potter advised Stephen to open up a 501(c)(4) only seventeen days after I had received my Articles of Incorporation from my election attorney.

Stephen Colbert did a fantastic job of explaining a U.S. Supreme Court decision called *Citizens United* which ruled that corporations are essentially "people" and as such, they have the right to free speech, and so they (the corporations) should be able to donate as much money as they want from their deep pockets to blast their candidate(s) all over television.

A special "social welfare" entity like a 501(c)(4) can accept donations without divulging its sources. For the purpose of illustration, let's say the 501(c)(4) is called "Grandma's Skirts." Big donors give Grandma's Skirts a lot of money, then Grandma's Skirts give that money to a SuperPAC. That SuperPAC only has to report that their money came from Grandma's Skirts, they don't have to say whom specifically funded Grandma's Skirts. It's a lot like money laundering. Many of these 501(c)(4)'s close up shop after election time but before filing with the IRS, so they never have to disclose their donors on record.

Colbert explained campaign finance by the big boys thusly: "You stick your money in the hole, the other person accepts your donation, and because it's happening anonymously, no one feels dirty!"

Grover Norquist, a political professional, had done an excellent job of using money to control bureaucrats with his "Taxpayer Protection Pledge." Congressmen and women who signed his pledge could expect monetary help to get them elected. In 2010 to 2012, his PAC (called Americans for Tax Reform) used almost three and a half million dollars to run ads against Democrats. And once they signed it, there was no getting out of it without foregoing future funding. According to the Center for Public Integrity and OpenSecrets.org, this money could account for the defeat of Ben Chandler (KY-6th), Lincoln Davis (TN-4th) and Joe Sestak (PA-7th) in re-election campaigns.

What better way to un-pollute Congress than borrow the same tactic as Grover, using a pledge that would attract voters to a good old fashioned anti-corrupt candidate? I began to wonder if anyone would sign a pledge that removed money from the game of running for Congress.

The next day, I emailed Stephen Colbert's attorney, Trevor Potter, asking him to help me craft the pledge that was brewing in my consciousness.

Dear Mr. Potter,

My name is Judy Frankel and I left a voice mail message asking if you would be interested in polishing up a "Norquistesque" pledge. I have attached a first draft of the pledge. My goal is to have candidates who are running on my website, Writeindependent.org, sign this pledge to garner votes from citizens who are ready to mandate campaign reform.

I am asking you how much you would charge to polish this brief, but succinct pledge that will also act as a bill once these candidates reach office. The wording of the document has to be so well done, that it avoids being too intimidating, but eradicates the ridiculousness we're seeing with *Citizens United*, PACs, super PACs, 501(c)(4)'s, 527's, lobbyists' favors, insider trading, and on and on.

There are already numerous candidates running on my website that open their remarks with: "I take no Special Interest money so I'm not beholden to special interests." If this has the effect on voters that I think it will, this could easily go viral.

Sincerely,

Judy Frankel

Thus began the Pledge for Honest Candidates, a way of differentiating a "bought" candidate[15] from a supposedly more honest civil servant-type of candidate.

I had been following Stephen Colbert's fund raising with a mixture of jealousy, admiration and merriment when one day, he announced his Super PAC Super Fun Pack. His staff designed a green cardboard box affixed with a sticky label saying "Colbert Super PAC." They threw in a collection of items to motivate donors to give $100 or more. The idea was for college students and other Colbert fans to run their own Super PACs from their dorm room, bedroom, or boardroom. Of course all the money would go to Stephen's ColbertPAC, whose motto is "Building a Better Tomorrow, Tomorrow" or his 501(c)(4) called Colbert Super PAC Shh Institute. When he announced the Fun Pack, I whirred into action and expedited forty-nine "Tag My Flag" buttons to the writers so that they could toss it into the Super Fun Pack box with

---

[15] "Bought" candidate: Any candidate who is supported by a special interest and whose loyalties to that special interest's interest is greater than their loyalty to their constituents.

their tube socks and tee shirts. Through Google Analytics, I was able to see that some activity did light up in the Manhattan area of New York City around the time of the pins' delivery. It never amounted to anything, but for one brief shining moment, I thought perhaps one of Colbert's comedy writers looked at the site!

The original draft of the "Pledge for Honest Candidates" (PHC) contained more strict campaign funding regulations than had ever been suggested on any bill. The most important part of the pledge required candidates who adopted it to support a law that had the same force and effect, leveling the playing field for everyone on the federal level.

The first time I wrote the PHC, I included provisions that stopped the revolving door. Ex-congressmen shouldn't be allowed to take high-paying jobs at lobbying firms who might have promised the job as a way to get their pet project through. The PHC limited campaign funding to $100 per donation, ended insider trading, and warned of the punishment for violating these things. Most importantly, it broadly stated that there shall be no conflict of interest. It is a conflict of interest to take huge sums of money and then try to make an impartial decision on a bill that involves the same entity that gave the money.

The Pledge for Honest Candidates went through many revisions, but its original draft looked like this:

> I, the undersigned hereby pledge:
> That neither I nor my associates will accept anything of value over $100 in any calendar year from any one person or entity to be used in an effort to obtain or maintain the office which I seek, unless that entity also promotes or advertises for any of my competitors to an equal and equitable degree.
> That all of my campaign efforts are a matter of public record.
> That neither I nor my associates will participate in anything that can be construed as a conflict of interest or insider trading while in federal office or during my lifetime.
> That while in office and for five years after leaving office, neither I nor my associates will accept

anything of value over $100 in any calendar year from any person or entity that may compromise the integrity of my decisions.

That if it can be shown that I have violated any of the provisions of this pledge, I will have 30 consecutive calendar days in which to remedy the violation, or I will immediately be removed from office or face criminal charges.

Signed_____Date_____

Associates, for the purpose of this document, include but are not limited to: my family, friends, acquaintances, anyone with whom I come in contact or who is at arms length, any person or entity who would represent me or whom I represent.

Trevor Potter once served as the commissioner and chairman of the Federal Election Commission. He recommended that I speak to Josh Silver or Nick Penniman from United Republic, a group that had contacted him to draw up a pledge similar to mine. This piqued my interest greatly, because if anyone else were interested in doing what I was doing, perhaps we could join forces. I placed several phone calls and sent emails to both men at United Republic and waited.

After two weeks, I finally received a call from Nick Penniman of United Republic. I stressed working together across a broad vision of making the Pledge for Honest Candidates a lynchpin for candidates running in the 2012 elections. Mr. Penniman could use the website as a vehicle for promoting those representatives who promised to get money out of politics.

"What numbers do you have?" Nick asked, referring to traffic to my site and people who had signed in.

"My numbers are low," I said, knowing that I had less than a hundred subscribers.

"What kind of capital do you have? Any big donors?"

"No; I'm doing this all on my savings right now…"

I knew he had about two hundred fifty thousand subscribers at the time, but what I didn't know is that most of them came from

Dylan Ratigan's following. He had interviewed Nick and Josh Silver, the founders of United Republic on his show. Mr. Ratigan's frequent MSNBC contributor Jimmy Williams had recently launched a "Get Money Out" campaign, drawing in those viewers who agree that money has too much of an influence on Washington. United Republic joined forces with Mr. Williams and Mr. Ratigan, absorbing the Get Money Out fans whose emails they had collected.

"We don't have the bandwidth to add your website to what we're doing," Mr. Penniman said.

"What does that mean?" I asked peevishly. "Bandwidth? Does that mean you don't have the time to work with me?"

"Something like that," he said.

"I don't care about me; I'll give it (the website) away, if you would just make it known. It should 'belong' to the people. Use the power of it to promote the Pledge for Honest Candidates! Or call it whatever you want. Change the name. I'm not attached to it. It's just a good idea!"

In that moment, I couldn't believe that I had almost given the website away. I rationalized that if they accepted it, promoted it, made it work by getting their members to use it, that would have been better than the website dying an anonymous death.

Then it struck me. If they took it and were successful, I could be left with nothing. They would have taken the website, all the work I'd put into it, everything I had written, all my research and my savings, and I'd be relegated to the level of employee. Later I'd be fired for insubordination. I would have died the anonymous death, the unknown creator of Writeindependent.org.

In the end Nick said, "I'm sorry, but we're going in a different direction."

I cried after that phone call. I was angry with myself for taking steps that weren't working. I felt the heavy despairing weight of helplessness. If I couldn't even get the people who agreed with me to accept my work, then the website was an obscure anomaly, and I was running in place, going nowhere.

The day after Nick Penniman turned me down, Mr. Potter's office declined to help me, saying that "you likely do not need to retain a lawyer to issue a pledge." This meant I was on my own, as usual.

I looked at the stacks of boxes of business cards, at the checkbooks with my company's logo on them, at the glossy folders that I had bought for my press kits. Would I have to throw it all away?

17

YOU CAN'T KEEP A GOOD WOMAN DOWN

Fortune does favor the bold and you'll
never know what you're capable of if you don't try.
– Sheryl Sandberg, *Lean In: Women, Work, and the Will to Lead*

I decided that I was lucky Nick Penniman didn't want the website. I still believed in its utility and held fast to my conviction that some day it would take off. If it's not going to happen this way, it will happen some other way. I prayed for God to give me strength, and put my faith in this project, the way an acolyte follows the path of the creator. I just had to be patient; building Rome took time. I was reminded of my goal as I washed dishes at the kitchen sink and looked at my clock engraved with the words, "When everyone works together, then success takes care of itself."

I am determined to overcome every obstacle until people join me to overhaul our corrupt government. If Americans aren't uniting yet and I'm feeling down, then I look to others for inspiration to improve my mood. Who out there overcame great odds? Who else has strong convictions and an undying love for her children? Who is doing amazing things even when the situation is most dire?

I discovered an important person, a woman whom I immediately held in high regard when I read her blog. Her name is

Cindy Sheehan, a mother of a soldier killed in Iraq and die-hard promoter of peace. I couldn't stay down long, inspired by a vocal woman like Ms. Sheehan. Cindy wrote a brazen article in 2007 called "Good Riddance Attention Whore" in which she railed against the two parties:

> ...I was the darling of the so-called left as long as I limited my protests to George Bush and the Republican Party. Of course, I was slandered and libeled by the right as a 'tool' of the Democratic Party...
>
> However, when I started to hold the Democratic Party to the same standards that I held the Republican Party, support for my cause started to erode and the 'left' started labeling me with the same slurs that the right used. I guess no one paid attention to me when I said that: *the issue of peace and people dying for no reason is not a matter of 'right or left,' but 'right and wrong.'*

Our views about the menace of the two-party system could not be more alike. I felt compelled to contact this mother whose life was so changed by the death of her son that she became an activist.

I fired off an email to her:

Dear Cindy,

I learned about you from a book by John R. MacArthur (Publisher of Harper's Magazine) called *You Can't Be President.* ...

I don't know how we'll end up working together, but I have a feeling we will somehow.

By the way, I am trying to entice Roseanne Barr to participate in our March 12th nonpartisan presidential debates. I've sent her my press kit and two emails (through her manager) and I'm waiting for a reply.

I cried when I saw what you were doing: just gushes of tears. You inspire me!

Like you, I am extremely passionate about what I'm doing. I write my blog almost every day, and a lot of it has to do with, well, corruption.

Here's the first nonpartisan presidential debates: http://www.youtube.com/watch?v=bTZrtm2EIO0 There

are three men in these debates, any of whom would be better than what we have now. I'm in the little tiny box at the bottom, asking the questions.
With love,
Judy Frankel

She answered back:
Thanks for your note and your work.
love
cindy
(who are these guys in the debate?)

And I replied:
Cindy,
    'These guys' are regular people who decided that they needed to set our country on a better course. Each one has his strength, in different areas. I wrote about them in my blog called: 'I Want All Three.'
    I want you to know how excited I am that you replied to me! First, I was worried that you were still in jail after being arrested, and second I honor your work and your dedication (beyond my ability to express my appreciation).
L,
Judy

Cindy had been arrested protesting at Vandenberg Air Force Base in California on February 25, 2012. I was so excited to receive a reply from someone of Cindy's stature. Here's a woman who has devoted her life to changing the status quo, who has thrown herself, mind body and soul, into protesting the war atrocities committed on a daily basis. Cindy would pop up again and again in various ways throughout my trials with Writeindependent.org.

Who do we want to follow—someone who would lead us into war or someone who would guide us toward peace?

In addition to searching outside for inspiration, I still had Sharon, my right-hand gal, calling and emailing congressional candidates, asking them to share their platforms on our website. When they turned her down, they cited reasons such as not having the time, the manpower or the inclination to fill out our form. Those who did post with us were more than happy to get some attention.

Regardless of the consistent rejection, Sharon and I were building momentum at my home office. We were reaching out to the press and the media, following up activity that my public relations company had started.

One Friday, Sharon yelled excitedly, "I have someone from the Bill Maher Show on the line!" She said into the phone, "I have the founder right here with me. You really need to talk to her about what we're doing!" and thrust the receiver in my direction.

I heard a male voice, asking what we were about. After I gave him a quick summation, he said "So pitch me your story. Give me your best shot."

I was nonplussed. We needed a sound bite of news, not just a website.

"You don't watch our show, do you?" he surmised.

"No," I admitted. I couldn't tell him that I don't have HBO because I won't spring for the extra television package from my cable company. I barely saw a few clips from *Politically Incorrect* years ago. I had never seen a whole episode of *Real Time with Bill Maher*.

"I could tell you don't watch," he said, "because today's Friday and we're taping in a couple hours. Pitch me your story quick."

"I don't have a pitch right now," I said. "I'll have to get back to you."

I blew it completely. My whole body ached with a shock of depression. A wave of self-doubt flooded me. *I can't do this.* I can't do any of this; it's never going to go anywhere. I can't be on television! I don't have that kind of oomph. I'm a quiet person, a writer, a behind-the-scenes nerdy type who should never have a microphone, let alone a camera pointed at her. I'm nobody. I should go dig a hole in the dirt, bury my kitchen scraps in the garden and forget about the whole website thing.

I always have a container on the kitchen counter for scraps of vegetables. Potato and cucumber peelings, tomato stems, squash ends, carrot tops, eggshells. I slipped on a pair of Muck Boots® and grabbed a long-handled shovel out of my tool shed. In less than a minute, I dug a hole about eighteen inches deep and just as wide, then threw in the compostable green waste and covered it with the soil. While I was doing this, I ruminated over what I should have said to the man at *Real Time with Bill Maher.*

I'm the only person in the country who is trying to disinfect Congress by providing a pledge for candidates to sign that gets money out of politics, I should have told him. He would have asked me how many people had signed such a pledge, and how many people knew about it. I had nothing. I was at the very beginning.

I'm interviewing people who are running for President with my 'nonpartisan presidential debates,' I tried on as another pitch opener. He would have asked me "who cares?" about the unknowns who would never win.

Congress has only a ten percent approval rating. I thought, offering a problem/solution sort of paradigm might get his attention. *We're offering an alternative to that.*

Who are you? he would have asked me. *Why do we want to hear what you have to say?* I had nothing. I was right not to pitch him that day. I wasn't ready.

I was digging in the dirt. I looked at the soil, friable with variegated browns. The only thing I have control over is this little patch of land that I have been feeding and making richer with green waste. Now it's soft and it digs up easily. If I plant a broccoli plant right there it'll grow like gangbusters; that's one success I can claim. I don't fit into the mold of a TV personality type. I'm just ordinary. I'm a gardener, a farmer. It's what I do when no one listens to me. I fall back on the mundane tasks of sowing seeds, potting up the little sprouts, transplanting them into the ground and watching them as time goes on. That way, I know I'll have food come summertime. I thought *maybe I'm too afraid to be on television and this is why it's not happening for me.*

I gazed across the blue ocean. Off in the distance I saw Catalina Island and floating above the horizon, white puffy clouds. At my feet, a cabbage plant caught my eye. The savoyed leaves arranged around a tender incandescent green head appeared more like a flower than a vegetable. *If not for me, no you,* I said in my head to the cabbage. Then I began to weep. Why am I in this beautiful place? What did I do to deserve such bounty?

I know why I'm here. Who is going to care about this place like I do? Who will take care of the garden, who knows how it needs healing? If not me, then who would care enough to make this world a better place? I can't stop now. I'm not going to waste my life by giving up the one thing that makes sense to me. Preserving the world as a garden.

I was fully committed. I had spent a great deal of my savings and my passion for this project wouldn't wane, no matter how many bad things were happening. I was determined to find a way onto Mr. Maher's show.

I lost Sharon, the one person who was working with me, because of lack of funds on my part. I was frightened that her leaving would start me on a downward spiral. When we were together we'd bounce ideas around. She would laugh at my jokes, she had my back, she was inspired by me and vice versa. Working alone on such a huge task was overwhelming.

I couldn't stay down for long. Even if I couldn't hire someone to work full-time, I could use the services of a consultant, someone whose ideas would help bring in donations. Through his work, maybe enough money would come in to cover the cost of his fees.

All roads led to hiring a Search Engine Optimization (SEO) expert. A person who knows how to raise a website's ranking in Google or other search engines based on key words and phrases. A good SEO expert will also help drive donors to your cause and make money rain.

A few months back, I had attended an Internet marketing seminar and picked up the card of one fellow whom I will refer to as Clif. He was affordable, and most importantly, he was excited about the website. Clif is a big man in his 50's with plentiful gray hair and a self-effacing demeanor. His heart is as big as the world, and he gives 110% effort to his clients' projects. I liked Clif's spirited interest in politics.

He turned out to be both a blessing and a curse. Prior to hiring him, Clif admitted to having Attention Deficit Disorder. I decided to stick with him because I have a daughter diagnosed with ADD and hope some day that someone will give her a chance. Clif often talked circles around a subject, but his disability never interfered with accomplishing his work.

At my request, Clif composed a "to do" list of SEO activities. Most of the items required that I write press releases, articles, or blog posts, or pay someone else to do it. I was already a prolific blogger, so Clif hired Kim and Wella, two women in the Philippines, to copy my blogs onto hidden website pages. In theory, the more content-rich my site, the higher the Google ranking. Sanjiv, my Indian website developer, had published my blog on a separate site called WordPress, so I was not benefiting from my wealth of written material. If Sanjiv had known anything about search engine optimization, he might have told me to post directly onto the website, but he wanted me to pay extra for advice from an SEO company he worked with.

Kim and Wella picked up where Sharon left off, but instead of needing $37/hour, they charged $3/hour.

Clif helped me re-style each page of the website and place key search words in strategic locations. He critiqued the home page and I revised, tweaked, and rewrote the copy, making it much clearer how the website worked. He improved the designs Sanjiv's company had done by a dozen magnitudes of value. It was too darn bad that no one visited the site; it was beautiful.

The reason we had no visitors was twofold. People aren't searching for the kind of keywords we specialized in, like *write-in, voting, candidates, Congress*. And secondly, we weren't on the tippy top of the first page of search results. When one series of efforts didn't work, I would look for another way to get traction. Watching the movie *The Social Network* about the creation of Facebook, it dawned on me that it wasn't necessary to ask candidates to post their own platforms. And if we had everyone listed on the website, it would be simple to show who agreed to the Pledge and who didn't.

I pulled a Mark Zuckerberg. I instructed Kim and Wella to add every candidate they could find running for office, the same way Mr. Zuckerberg added names of college students from student directories to get Facebook started. The candidates' profiles are in the public domain, already on the Internet, and we were collating them all in one easy-to-use format, organized by state and congressional district. I should have felt disgraced for not thinking of it sooner, but instead I was fired up, knowing that my database of candidates would soon be comprehensive.

Each time the women finished a geographic area, I blanketed those candidates with emails asking them to sign the Pledge for

Honest Candidates. Some jumped at the chance to sign it! They wanted to stand out from the pack by saying that they weren't taking favors from anyone and that they only listened to their constituents. We added a red star by their name if they agreed to the Pledge, making it easy for voters to identify the people who weren't beholden to special interests.

With the website thus operational, I had a new mission that would carry me through. I was determined to join forces with Common Cause.

18
STRANGE BEDFELLOWS

*We raised it [PAC money] on my show and used it to materially
influence the elections — in full accordance with the law. It's the
way our founding fathers would have wanted it, if they had
founded corporations instead of just a country.*
— Stephen Colbert

Since 1970, Common Cause has been the premier nonpartisan,
nonprofit organization fighting the undue influence of money in
politics and helping ordinary citizens make their voices heard in
the political process. If I could reach their 400,000 members, then
the website would take off, and I'd be that much closer to being on
Mr. Maher's show!

I felt Common Cause was stuck in a rut. Their website lacked
personality and pizzazz, they weren't effective at reaching out to
the public, and worst of all, people who might have been members
were starting their own groups. If Common Cause had been more
effective, the leaders who started Rootstrikers and United Republic
would have joined them instead of launching new organizations.

Common Cause was hosting an event in San Francisco called
Uncommon Heroes where they would honor some bigwigs in the
'get money out' world. I wondered if I could turn some heads at
this soirée by injecting a little femininity.

Interestingly, Molly Munger and Charles Munger Jr. were to be honored. The Mungers are the offspring of Charles Munger Sr., the investment tycoon who befriended Warren Buffet. Mr. Munger Sr., five years older than Mr. Buffett, had become Buffett's investing confidante well before he became a household name. Their friendship holds a certain legendary status among those who have followed Warren Buffet's trajectory.

In a strange and exciting way, Common Cause members had become my "peeps." The stage was set. I had a fully functional website, a public relations press kit, and the clothes, style, makeup, and looks to make an immediate impression. I had sent Common Cause's attorney, Stephen Spaulding, information about Writeindependent.org in the hopes of obtaining their endorsement and getting their help re-writing my first draft of the Pledge for Honest Candidates.

By March 19, Stephen sent me this email:

Hi Judy,

I will be at the event in San Francisco, so I look forward to speaking to you when you're there.

Unfortunately, Common Cause is not able to endorse WriteIndependent.org or engage on the voter pledge. I'm sorry that this is not the news you were hoping for. For a variety of reasons, Common Cause does not engage in this sort of electoral or candidate work. This is especially the case where your organization will be doing the "PR and advertising" for candidates, including write-in candidates.

Have you considered reaching out to an organization such as Americans Elect?

Our Voters First Pledge was related to support for full public financing of congressional elections.

In any event, I wish you the best of luck and I look forward to meeting you in person on Thursday in San Francisco.

Best,

Steve Spaulding

This news, though disheartening, did not dampen my enthusiasm for the event because I was not only going to meet, but speak to the person whom I always named as my favorite actor. I made it my mission to talk with Richard Dreyfuss, the final speaker of the evening, to ask him to do the voiceover on my infomercial. I didn't care if the whole lot of them didn't take me seriously, so long as I could secure the voice I wanted for this spot, the voice of the "Think Different" commercials that Steve Jobs had crafted. The voice that ushered in a new generation of cool and technology for Apple.

Richard said, "Here's to the crazy ones. The misfits. The rebels. The troublemakers. The round pegs in the square holes. To the ones who see things differently. They're not fond of rules. And they have no respect for the status quo. You can quote them, disagree with them, glorify or vilify them. About the only thing you can't do is ignore them. Because they change things. They push the human race forward. And while some may see them as the crazy ones, we see genius. Because people who are crazy enough to think they can change the world, are the ones who do."

Luckily, my brothers live in the San Jose area, so I could stay for free. San Francisco, here I come!

Common Cause hosted the event at the elegant Julie Morgan Ballroom in the Merchants Exchange Building. Every step I took required my concentration because I am not used to wearing high heels. I had forgotten how lopsided the men/women situation was at the Los Angeles Venture Association event. I chose a beer at the bar, and tried unsuccessfully to drum up interest in my endeavors with fervent banter about the Pledge for Honest Candidates.

Across the room, I caught a glance from a tall, striking man with blonde hair, probably in his early 50's. He looked like he had been raised in prep schools and had just stepped off a yacht. All that was missing was his ascot and a pipe. He carried an air of being the most handsome man in the room, and looked at me as though he expected me to find him attractive. Him, I wanted to avoid.

Instead, I looked for Bob Edgar, for Stephen Spaulding, and especially for Richard. Would I be able to keep my mouth shut about the crush I've had on him since I was a teenager?

The room was arranged so that cocktails and hors d'oeuvres were served in the back, standing out in the open. Rows of chairs occupied the rest of the room, fronted by an elevated platform and a podium for the speakers. Suddenly, Richard Dreyfuss appeared front and center. Well before the cocktail crowd had chosen seats, I made my way to the second row near the center aisle so that I could quickly leave my chair when necessary.

I sat down and waited while Mr. Dreyfuss listened to his admirers tell tales. When it was clear that Richard was trying to wrap things up, I darted out of my seat and touched his sleeve, saying "It is an honor to meet you."

He took my hand to shake and looked directly in my face, smiling as a man would toward a handsome woman, as a sexy man would an equally sexy woman.

"Please don't leave until you've talked to me," I said. "I may have some work for you."

"Oh, really?" Richard said, his voice rising lyrically. "I like work…" And with that, I had set up his expectations for later.

Thus the event began. Molly Munger took the podium to give her thanks. As she acknowledged her wonderful family, I realized I was sitting in a whole row of Mungers. Molly could afford her own ballot initiative; that's how much money the family has. She had donated $44 million to get Proposition 38, "State Income Tax Increase to Support Public Education" on every Californian's ballot. Too bad the voters didn't like it.

Another honoree, Dolores Huerta, took the stage. I recognized her strength of character and resolve, distinctive of a woman on a mission. As a leader for civil rights, she suffered attacks at the front lines of labor disputes. She co-founded the United Farm Workers with César Chávez. I admired her more than the other honorees because she used people power rather than money to move mountains.

When Mr. Dreyfuss took the podium, I learned that he had made it his goal in life to bring civics education to the broader public. He had learned that it was an uphill battle, because schools don't do a great job of teaching students how our government operates. Without a proper civics education, students become adults who are ill-equipped to participate in our democracy in a meaningful way.

Much as Richard wanted to make his presentation entertaining, he was discussing a serious matter, a life-in-the-balance matter that would affect the children of all the coming generations. His facial expressions were appropriately somber. I could not help but wonder how strange my life had become that we were both on this similar path.

When Richard finished his talk, a fawning crowd immediately mobbed him.

As I watched Richard, surrounded by other Common Causers, I stood on my spiked heels with my long legs and thought to myself *I'm a few inches taller than I should be to talk with Richard eye-to-eye. I'm going to have to ask him to sit down.*

The last admirer, an artsy dude, bent Richard's ear with his stories until they noticed me standing in their triangle. Strangely enough, the dude asked, "Are you two married?"

Mr. Dreyfuss looked at me. He didn't immediately say "no." Instead, he searched for his conspicuously absent wife, waiting for me to answer the question. I let the idea hang in the air, trying it on for a pregnant moment. "He's already married," I finally said.

When the dude walked away, I reintroduced myself to Mr. Dreyfuss and we were quickly interrupted by another man saying, "We're going to the steakhouse across the street, if you want to bring your wife and have something to eat before you leave tonight." Richard begged out, but I made a mental note. *Common Cause people at steakhouse afterwards.*

I did not need to ask Richard to sit down; we both walked toward the chairs naturally. I asked, "How are you spending your energies to get civics into schools?" because he had barely mentioned it in his talk.

"I have a foundation called the Dreyfuss Civics Initiative." He held his hands cupped on his lap. "We're working with teachers to involve their students in a theatrical production that brings the formation of our government to life. We're going to film it, and then put it on YouTube, and send out a capsule to all the schools across the country for their civics lessons." He lifted his hands, fingers open wide. "We're getting students to experience history as though they were involved in the creation of our country." He gave me the website address, theDreyfussInitiative.org. I reflected his ideas back to him, so that he knew I understood.

I felt the natural break in our conversation, so it was time for my elevator pitch. In less than a minute, I laid out the sticks and stones of my work, showing him my press kit along with a special letter tailored to Richard himself. He soaked it in swiftly, for this was his special area of interest, and I had organized Congress and elections into an elegant, easy format. I asked his opinion.

Richard pondered the materials, then laughed and said in an exuberant burst of energy, "You know, this is *crazy*!" He emphasized "crazy" as though a light pierced into a dark sad corner. "…But it just might work!"

His words cheered me beyond measure. Finally, someone got it! Someone important! Someone who understands the entire problem, and all the little pieces that got us here. Most importantly he grasped the simplicity of it, like a cure that solves a disease.

"Would you be the voice for the infomercial?" I asked.

"You'll have to call my agent," he said. I could have been crushed, because it meant that instead of helping me, he wanted the money.

I asked him to look over the materials on his way home. To my surprise, he gave me his personal email address, which I memorized posthaste.

We stood up to say our goodbyes, and as I floated from the room, I almost forgot to take home the beer bottle parting gift.

Driving through the quiet streets of San Francisco, every street light imbued with glowing hopefulness, my stomach growled at me. I'm hungry. I haven't had dinner.

Wait! What did someone say to Richard before we started talking? Something about a steakhouse across the street? Although I was already fifteen minutes away from the event, no cozy eatery looked inviting enough to stand out against dining with people who understand that money is ruining the way our government runs. I turned the car around to my next adventure, and it surpassed my wildest wishes and inchoate dreams.

I approached the doorman of the skyscraper, asking for a steakhouse. "Right there," he pointed. The restaurant was a hundred-dollar-a-plate affair. I noticed the heavy wood wainscoting, white linen tablecloths, and the clinking of alcoholic beverages. While one couple left the dining area, I saw about twenty people seated at a long table. Something wasn't right. I didn't belong.

The host asked if I were joining a party.

"I just finished attending the Common Cause event across the street, and there should be some people here, but I'm not on the reservation list," I said, expecting to be turned away.

"They have two place settings left, so let me ask if you can join them," he offered.

Before I could protest, afraid that they would say "no," he had darted away. I surveyed the long, rectangular table of people engaged in spirited discourse: man, woman, man, woman all the way down the line. It registered that this was a gathering of friends and family, that the two empty seats at the end had been meant for Richard Dreyfuss and his wife, and that I was plowing into their party.

"They said you may join them," the host said, to my utter amazement.

I felt like a Marx brother crashing a hoity toity banquet, except I'm no Harpo and I wasn't going to stay quiet.

I walked down the entire length of the table to the last place setting on the side, and took my seat.

I immediately recognized that I was going to dine with a renowned family, the closest one can come to America's royalty. Eight or nine siblings, highly educated and accomplished in their own right, sat beside their partners, and I next to one such spouse. He was a most handsome and refined man clearly out of my league, none other than Mr. Ascot Yacht himself!

The eldest brother's best friend, whom I will call Albert, faced me across the table. He smiled enthusiastically at me, and we made introductions. He had swarthy skin, receding hairline, perfect teeth and lively brown eyes. Next to him, his lovely wife, an elegant woman in her mid 40's, every hair in place, flawless complexion and impeccable attire. She held out her hand to shake mine. She was warm and confident, her language and diction as clear and sparkling as carbonated water.

Mr. Yacht's wife was so involved in the conversation at the rest of the table that her husband was delighted to have someone with whom to chat.

"And what do you do?" he asked me.

"I'm a master gardener and a writer, but I started a website whose goal is to clean up Congress."

Albert was intrigued. He laughed, "Then you should be very

busy! How do you propose to fix Congress?"

I explained the website and the Pledge for Honest Candidates, and told them that it would only be a matter of time before this idea caught on because it was ripe.

I asked Mr. Yacht about his vocation.

"I'm in energy."

"Oh, really?" I explained how I had just conducted a presidential debate about energy and it was fresh in my mind. "So tell me, what do you think of hydrogen as a carrier fuel?"

"Pffttt! That's at least 150 years away. It's not practical for today's use; there are too many problems with it."

"One hundred and fifty years?" I asked. "But Germany has already built a 240 kilometer hydrogen pipeline in Europe, and even China has been using hydrogen. The only reason we haven't done it is that we don't have the political will yet!"

"Even with the political will, hydrogen is much more expensive than current available sources."

"Yes, but the reason we must convert now is that it becomes more expensive the longer we wait. Maybe you just don't like hydrogen."

"Actually, when I was a kid in high school, I wrote a paper on hydrogen."

"Aha! So there is a part of you that wants hydrogen to work, eh?" I emphasized the word "wants" by bringing my hands to my heart and pronouncing it beseechingly.

Albert lit up with a wide smile. He seemed to be an environmentalist in the company of industrialists. He saw Mr. Yacht talking to someone who wants to buck the established system and who isn't afraid of a little fight. He wanted to watch us heat up.

"Yes, but I'm a realist," he said. "They haven't found a cheap way to extract hydrogen yet. It takes electricity to make hydrogen, so it's a zero sum game." He was insistent that I stay on concrete ground level, and not fly into the pie sky.

"Aha, but hydrogen is a carrier fuel and the electricity can come from renewable sources, such as wind or solar. We just have to think differently how we will convert water into hydrogen without fossil fuels."

"That's a very tricky problem."

"We won't solve it unless we get started, right? Remember when Kennedy said, 'We have to do these things, not because they are easy, but because they are hard!' He rallied an entire nation to go to the moon! And I say, this is more practical than moon travel. This involves how we will drive our cars, get off oil, possibly even stop the military efforts that support the oil regimes. Why don't we use the defense money and oil subsidies to build hydrogen energy generation plants?"

Albert fairly bounced out of his seat.

"That's a long way off," Mr. Yacht insisted.

"How far off can it be, if we already have the technology at Lawrence Livermore Labs that shows how to store hydrogen onboard a Prius that has a range of more than 300 miles with one fill-up?"

"It's at least 50 years away."

"We went from 150 to 50 in less than an hour. I'd say that's quite an improvement!"

"I just don't see us moving away from fossil fuels anytime soon. When you know that in China, villagers can pick coal from the countryside and burn it, the dirtiest kind of energy there is. How are we going to stop that? It's free, they need to heat their homes and cook their food."

"Yes, that's a big problem. So you're saying we shouldn't do the right thing, because so many people are doing the wrong thing?"

"It's a matter of economics. They can't do the right thing."

"All the more reason we need to be an example for the world. China might show us the range of energy use, from the worst to the kind of energy that's zero emission, but the U.S. has the reputation for being cutting edge, and we don't want to lose that esteem."

Albert piped up. "You said you're a master gardener. I grow tomato plants in my back yard and right now I have a lot of peas."

His wife added "We put peas in every meal. We find a way to work them into breakfast."

"They're in the omelets," Albert said. "You have any tips on tomatoes?"

"Tomatoes are my specialty, actually. I'd recommend putting a spoonful of Epsom salts in the planting hole, along with mycorrhizae." I explained the filamentous nature of the fungus, grabbing nutrients from thither and yon.

We talked about gardening for the balance of the night, as people are usually more interested in lovely tasty gardens than energy production.

Mr. Yacht's wife finally looked over at us. He introduced her to me, and a heavy negativity entered the air. She gave me the stink eye as if to say, "Who are *you*?"

A more awkward moment threatened to ensue. How was I going to pay for my dinner without standing up and asking the entire table, "Who's got the bill?" I didn't want to appear a moocher.

Luckily, the head waiter delivered the bill to Mr. Yacht. I touched his arm, "Please let me pay for myself. I didn't know anyone here, and I just wanted some company for dinner. I didn't want to impose."

"No, it's on me," he said with a flourish, proud of his stature. The bill must have been more than two thousand dollars.

I thanked him and walked to my car on clouds, fantasizing how I would leverage this experience to my best advantage.

When I returned home, I immediately went to work on follow-up, my forte. I crafted a hand-written note to Mr. Yacht as follows:

Dear Mr. Ascot Yacht,

Thank you for dinner with the ____ family last week. You made me feel welcome, even though I didn't know anyone at the table and just showed up hungry after the Uncommon Heroes ceremony.

I appreciated the warm company and interesting conversation. If we ever elect a President who is sweet on hydrogen like Harry Braun, you will be the first person we call to set energy policy, provided you speed up your timeline (50 years?!).

Again, I do not take for granted your gracious hospitality and generous nature. Thank you from the bottom of my heart.

Sincerely,

Judy Frankel

I giggled for days at the thought of Mr. Yacht opening the note and remembering me, how hopeful I felt and blissful against all opposition. Why not get him to laugh with me? Life is too brief for small thinking.

Mr. Dreyfuss's email took much longer to write. Before I sent it, I pinged his email address to make sure it worked. It went through!

Dear Richard,

Meeting you on Thursday was a highlight of my year, not only because I've always liked you but because we share a common passion: returning this country to greatness.

You have really hit upon the crux of the matter on your website: we need to educate, educate, educate. I am behind you 100%, and will do everything in my power to make your vision a reality, even if it takes me the rest of my life to do it. But we need to start NOW. Let's get out into the nation more. If you commit to doing the voice over on the educational broadcast I'm planning, then all the other pieces will fall into place. . .

If you say "yes" to any of the ways you could help me, you will be my first big break.

Sincerely,

Judy Frankel

How strange for me to be offering Mr. Dreyfuss my support ("I will do everything in my power") when he had the upper hand in this transaction.

I heard somewhere that Common Cause had amassed $15.5 million along the way. If I could have gotten my hands on that kind of money, I'd have pressure-washed that goddam Congress by now! The reason they haven't done it is they have a weak strategy. Their vision is to act as a lobbyist group for "the people." Why in hell aren't "the people" using their votes to get what they want? Because corporate money speaks louder than constituents. Common Cause wants to get money out, but hardly anybody knows about them and their cause for the common folks, and it's their own fault. No strategy, no success.

I reflected on the event for days. If Common Cause solved the problem of money in politics, there would be no need for them anymore. Those who are on the payroll make their livings off the cause, so rectifying it was antithetical to their livelihoods. As long as the corruption continues, they have jobs.

I came home to my earth and sky garden, the smell of

springtime, sweet and shining in the sun. God sparkled all around as I rubbed peaches off my trees once again. Nothing would ever stop those fuzzy packages of potential from reappearing year after year. I have faith in the mystery of life, that with regularity spring will return and signal a new beginning.

19
PUBLICITY AND POPULARITY

Without publicity there can be no public support and
without public support every nation must decay.
– Benjamin Disraeli, British politician 1804-1881

Nothing, not even all the money I spent on web development, compared with the boatload of cash I gave my public relations company. I might have generated more attention had I thrown ten dollars at a time over a bridge. It might have been a better choice to buy a full-page photo advertisement for Writeindependent.org in the LA Times with only the American flag covering lascivious bits of my naked body.

When we contacted the mighty media conglomerates with a story about a website that facilitates a more democratic form of governance, there was no response. They would have to crush my little website because it could supplant the current campaign process, making expensive campaign ads go away.

I would have gladly done any legal thing if I could be assured to amass two hundred thousand subscribers, Twitter followers or Facebook "likes." And you can't plan to make a viral video because there's no guarantee it will hit the big numbers. The press must have crazies always trying to out-stunt each other to grab the public's attention.

Conversely, anybody who gets significant traction has to die a thousand deaths through the media if she takes a strong position on a popular issue. All the news shows have to do is dig up some dirt or make up some negative association, give their "thumbs down" and television watchers start saying, "Judy Frankel: bad," like zombies.

This problem of limits to the public's attention works in favor of the cads who do horrible, unethical but nevertheless legal behaviors that should, if society were moral, be punished. Conversely, if anyone tries to do something worthy, it will lose out to a voluptuous poser, porn, vacuous "reality" actor who squishes cake and shrieks obscenities, or to a song and dance video asking "What does the fox say?"

And why would the media want to give airtime to swabbing the decks of Congress, when they could get more ratings with a Kardashian? Why would Americans want to think about politics when they can anesthetize themselves with entertainment?

My public relations company called every media outlet we had discussed that might be interested in a story of a "citizen politicker" who "creates a pledge to revolutionize campaign finance." From all their efforts, they found one radio blogger[16] named Mr. Erin Hazard who was willing to interview me on his program airing in San Francisco. Unfortunately, Mr. Hazard doesn't have a Wikipedia entry—he's another unknown, like me.

Erin's sexy, smoky voice introduced me as an "up and coming individual in the world of politics." He read a description of my mission right off the press release. I could hear the broadcast's opening background music through my phone.

"What inspired you to launch this website?" he asked.

"I have a daughter—she's almost eleven, and I want to see things turn around in this country and improve," I said into the phone, pacing through my house. "I was so discouraged by Obama. I voted for him, but like a lover scorned, I feel he didn't deliver. We need a mensch; we need somebody who's just decent and good." My voice trembled, and I could feel the tears coming to my eyes. "I decided to create this ..." my voice went up an octave,

---

[16] A radio blogger is someone who hosts audio shows online. Anyone can become a radio blogger from their computer using a platform like blogtalkradio.com. The blogger/radio personality sets the parameters of the show, whether interview, question and answer, or commentary.

"movement, really. Writeindependent.org is a movement. It's trying to get people to collaborate, and to solve problems."

Erin asked, "When do you feel a site like this... obviously it won't take hold in 2012. What is your long term vision?"

I couldn't sit down. "It depends. If it goes viral it could be a lot faster than you're thinking. But I have no guess as to how long it will take. There is that possibility we'll get the unusual PR like the Jon Stewart Show or Stephen Colbert Report."

"Yeah," Mr. Hazard affirmed. He sounded convinced by my conviction.

"Realistically, Erin, the only way this is going to work is if we get about a hundred million to not only notice the site, but go to it and look at the alternatives to the red/blue candidates."

"Right. It's definitely a pretty lofty goal."

"Huge undertaking. I need all the help I can get..."

He asked me my views on money and capitalism.

"I'm totally for money. Money is kind of like love," I said, smiling. "If you spend it wisely and it improves your life, this is all great. But if you start using it to manipulate people, or you're creating something that's polluting, that's no longer unconditional love." I opened the sliding glass door to my backyard and stepped onto the patio. "When you buy an iPod, it's because you love what Steve Jobs has created. But if you are pumping gas in your car because that's the only type of car that's available, and you hate doing it, that's your arm-twisted love. It's not even love anymore." I could feel myself ramping up to putting my foot in my mouth, but the racecar had left the starting line. "When love and sex go together, it's a great feeling. That's how money should be. When you buy something you feel good about, it's like orgasm, right?"

Erin laughed, not because I was splashing kaleidoscopic dream paints on his interview, but because he got it.

We exceeded the amount of time he originally promised me for the interview, then he asked me to come back again.

People who participate in Blog talk radio like Mr. Hazard don't get paid for their work. They feel passionate about what they are doing. Erin had to go back and edit our recording before he posted it online, which meant he volunteered hours of his time putting an interview together. I can understand why people give up their radio blogs after a while, which is what happened to Mr. Hazard. I never got to do another interview with him.

On a different color of the political spectrum, I co-hosted a radio blog with a Tea Partier activist named Sally Baptiste from Florida. I discovered Sally through a group called GOOOH (Get Out Of Our House!) a non-partisan website, founded by Tim Cox of Texas, that offers a process for vetting new candidates, hoping to offer alternatives to the money-driven ones we've been voting into office. Ms. Baptiste supports GOOOH's efforts, as do I. Sally self-describes as an American Statesman. She recognizes that patriotic citizens are responsible for electing congressmen who aren't serving our best interests, and patriotic citizens are responsible to boot them out. Ms. Baptiste complains bitterly against the GOP and the Democrats, saying that both have lost their way.

Though we don't see eye to eye on everything, Ms. Baptiste and I could agree that both parties have been bought by powerful moneyed interests. We could agree that our Constitution is in peril, that our rights are being eroded by groups that have asserted more and more of their power as Americans have been dropping out of the political process or, worse yet, supporting candidates who are part of the problem.

Blog talk radio works like an underground system. It's media that belongs to the people, and as such, it's not large or monopolistic. The upside is that it naturally curates its own audience. The downside is that the political ones aren't reaching the typical voter, and by that, I mean their number of listeners isn't huge.

If I couldn't make it on the national scene, why not try local media? A woman from my city's Chamber of Commerce suggested I contact the editor of a local magazine called *Peninsula People*. If I could get the full color, glossy front page cover, everyone in my neighborhood would know what I am doing! Without using my PR company, I called the woman who is in charge of the Palos Verdes Peninsula publication and amazingly, she assigned me a reporter.

I met journalist Edith Johnson at Martha's Grill on 22nd in Hermosa Beach, the kind of place the locals frequent for its California style, laid-back atmosphere. An attractive blonde in her late 20's, Ms. Johnson wore shape-flattering jeans and a white blouse with a bright smile to match. She clasped my hand firmly, and immediately launched into an apology for not knowing much about political science.

"That's okay. In fact, that might work to our advantage, since I am trying to reach people who wouldn't ordinarily pay any attention to politics." I told her I came to this vocation the same way a car crash causes a mother to join MADD or a survivor of some calamity finds a new mission in life.

We took a table inside, hoping to find a quieter spot than the sidewalk café area. Edith turned on her tape recorder and I spoke passionately about President Obama's lack of substantive leadership and my disappointment over Congress. "The worse Congress performs, the better the website should do," I told her, hoping it would get into the article.

When I had Ms. Johnson sufficiently whipped up by the possibility that things might get better, she brought me back down to the task at hand by asking questions related to write-in voting. I was sorry I used "write-in" to name the website because writing in a candidate's name is a long shot toward getting them elected.

"The President is just window dressing," I said. "It's really Congress we need to focus on, and we don't need to write in any names to change it." I looked down at my plate and realized I hadn't been eating. "We just need to vote for candidates who agree to pass the Pledge for Honest Candidates as law."

When we finished the interview, I wondered how Edith would handle writing about politics with little or no knowledge of the topic. If only she had read Howard Zinn's *A People's History of the United States*, or anything by Matt Taibbi or Michael Lewis, she might be more motivated to do something about our government and by extension our whole financial system.

A week later, a photographer from the magazine came to my house to shoot photos in my garden for the article. She sent me a handful of headshots and poses, one that was far better than all the others. In my fantasy, based on the merit of what I was trying to accomplish, the editor would have to choose me for the cover of *Peninsula People* magazine.

I was almost sick with anticipation when I drove to the local library to see what the editor had decided. Instead of my smiling face, the cover photo was devoted to a young surfer named Alex

Gray. His article had to be more important than saving the world. Turned out, it was. Alex's brother had been a heroin overdose casualty, and the surfer speaks at high schools about the dangers of drugs. If he saves just one soul from committing suicide at each event, then he has saved that person's whole world.

I leveraged the article as best I could by sending the magazine to the same people who were on my letter-writing campaign. Then I added a few famous and powerful people who weren't on my list, hoping to draw attention to a story about one woman against the odds. I never asked for anything. I just sent it out into the universe on a wing.

I mailed one *Peninsula People* magazine to *Titanic's* director, James Cameron, with two post-it notes attached. Referring to his acceptance speech for Best Picture, the top note asked a riddle. "Why are we lucky that the earth is shaped like a sphere?" The note underneath answered, "Because then we can each be on top of the world!"

I believe that each of us has the ability to push or pull reality in our direction. Wildly successful people like Mr. Cameron know this trick of creating his world. He went to the top and exclaimed this statement, now he's going to the depths of the sea, searching for new life forms, ways to predict tsunamis, and how to stop oil spills like British Petroleum's in the Gulf of Mexico.

Even if these letters would never amount to anything, it felt good to plant some seeds. You never know.

Having a successful online business requires getting a significant amount of hits. For a new idea to take off, there has to be buzz. I started to wonder, how does this buzz begin?

I found a YouTube channel called PewDiePie by accident that has a ridiculous number of views. Seven billion! How did the owner of the channel attract 36 million subscribers? Why do so many people view his videos?

I found out about PewDiePie when I watched a movie called *Reign Over Me* in which Adam Sandler's character plays a video game called "Shadow of Colossus." I wanted to see the game in action, so I searched on YouTube. By pure chance, I found a 24-minute video called LETS START AN ADVENTURE BROS!

Suddenly I'm entering the realm of a cute "bro" named PewDiePie (pronounced like Cutie Pie but with a P). He's a master

Playstation video gamer whose superimposed face appears in a little rectangle in the upper right corner, while the game fills the rest of the screen. As PewDiePie navigates through Shadow of Colossus, a game of amazing, almost three-dimensional stunning graphics, he gives play-by-play commentary. He sweeps his light brown bangs out of his unblinking, tired eyes.

"I'm a little hung over," he says. "I want to play something beautiful and chill."

Watching his videos is an addictive waste of time. But seven billion hits? PewDiePie is paid handsomely in advertising, an estimated $100K to $1 million per month.

For playing around and calling his viewers "bros," he had amassed enough worldwide subscribers to start a movement of some sort. Why was Mr. PewDiePie so important to me? For two reasons: 1. Through video games, he has reached a population that is larger than the tipping point that I am seeking and 2. Games could be used to fix government.

To reach the tipping point, some experts estimate that the website would have to be adopted by 10% of actual voters. The last presidential election brought in roughly 130 million votes. Is the actual tipping point 13 million, or could we start to change popular opinion with a lot less than that? Couldn't less voters throw any election into question?

The inroads to substantial change require major attention, Christ-like attention, the kind that only George Clooney gets these days. There are probably more people who know George Clooney in our day than who knew Christ in his day. Perhaps if someone were actually nailed to a cross here in the USA, we could get something good done. We could use a messiah...

20
A WOMAN FOR PRESIDENT

*More specifically, are they ready to throw their weight into the
tougher challenges facing the development community: structural
inequality, political capture, fragile states? Those challenges
require an explicit focus on governance, politics and power: ill-
governance must be challenged, politics must be directly engaged,
and power must be re-distributed ... from elites to communities
and social movements.*
– Chris Jochnick, Director of Oxfam America

I asked Fred, the volunteer student, why he wasn't coming
around so much anymore. He explained that he was headed in a
different direction. He had decided to enter the military, saying that
there was honor in it. He was following his stepbrother who had
been in the armed forces, but who, for whatever reason, sat at
home, unemployed, living on what little he received from the
government. His military brother was smoking a lot of pot, staying
in, watching television.

This news was a blow to me, because I saw Fred entering the
armed forces as "giving in" to the current messed-up structure.
Maybe the armed services would catapult him into a sort of hell.
He was giving up on his promise as a powerful force for
transformation to, instead, become a cog in someone else's
machine. Specifically, a machine that lacks virtue and integrity.

"No!" I cried out. Fred looked at me, confused at my reaction.

"What? It'll be cool!" He was already swept up in a romantic vision, oblivious to the harsh reality of war and how it would change him.

"I could have helped you see another way of life, to lift you up! If you do this, I'll lose you to another world. You'll lose yourself. When did this happen? Weren't you interested in Occupy? Didn't you understand how we were trying to make things better? How is this life you're choosing going to make the world better?" I sounded like my mother, who warned me that with my personality and independent streak, I should not enlist in the military. It might not have been right for me, but that didn't mean it was wrong for Fred.

"I don't know," he said. "I just don't have the choices you think I have. Look at my family."

There was nothing I could do. He had to learn things his way. Maybe he needed to learn about other countries from walking their soil and seeing their sights. Perhaps he would come home with a deeper understanding and would still be a force for good.

My heart sank. He had been a rib in my tent, holding up a space for young people. What a world.

All the more reason to remain idealistic. My quest to find a POTUS was a symbol of my desire for a leader who would guide us to a better, fairer, uncorrupted government. Months ago, when I learned the requirements to run for President, I had written the following text which appeared on the Presidential Page of the website:

Do you have the heart required to make the United States a better place? Let us find out about you.

You need to be at least 35 years old and have been born in the United States, Guam, Puerto Rico or the U.S. Virgin Islands. In addition, you need to have had residency in the United States or its unincorporated organized territories for 14 years.

You will need to win 270 out of 538 electoral colleges. This is not the same as the popular vote, counting one vote for each person. This means your constituents will have to really like what you stand for, especially considering they will be writing your name millions of times instead of throwing a lever or coloring in a dot, or touching a computer screen. Your people will need to demand the paper to write out your name when it is not abundantly clear in the voting booth where the write-in votes are written.

You do not need to be on the ballot to win.

You will need to file a letter of intent in most states. To learn how, refer to this link: http://writein2008.blogspot.com /search/label/Alabama

The following states do not allow write-in votes:

Arkansas, Hawaii, Louisiana, Mississippi, Nevada, Oklahoma, South Carolina, and South Dakota. This amounts to 48 electoral colleges, so the write-in votes in other states will have to make up for this discrepancy in order for a write-in candidate to win. Arkansas has counted write-in votes in the past, so 6 electoral colleges may be hotly contested if there are a significant number of write-ins.

If there is no clear winner with 270 electoral colleges, the House of Representatives conducts a contingent election whereby each state gets one vote among the top three contenders. See: http://electoralcollegehistory.com/electoral/cr s-congress.asp for more information. The Senate similarly votes for the Vice President, except that each Senator gets one vote.

I know what I am looking for in a President. First, I have to be able to trust him or her. The President doesn't have to be a woman, but I'd be thrilled if a female were the best person for the job. I want someone who is softer, kinder, not as jaded as the politicians we've seen whose names get bandied about. If she doesn't lie or change her rhetoric depending upon the group she's addressing, that would be refreshing. I want someone who hasn't played games to get where she is.

I am searching for a person who leads with her heart and soul. I don't want someone who would give the bankers a pass when they convinced homeowners that their loans were good without reading them the fine print. I don't want a President who gives no bid contracts to Halliburton and spends money on hired guns like Blackwater (now Academi). I knew what I didn't want, which is more of the same. I am ready for real change, not the kind that goes on a poster, a false promise, or a hollow echo from a puppet.

Ideally, the President should also be an excellent communicator, with the rare ability to really listen. I want someone who takes climate change seriously who will move us away from fossil fuels quickly, a leader who will say "No!" to the petroleum industry. It's dangerous to focus on finite resources and to avoid getting ready for the future because it will be costly now. We need to gear up immediately behind a President who insists on conservation and preparation. Our children and their children deserve clean, renewable and responsible sources of energy that must be established by this generation.

I want someone who isn't afraid to say there's too much collusion between government and industries, such as our banks and Wall Street, the prison industrial complex, the war machine, agribusiness, the petrol/gas industry and the car manufacturers, the medical establishment and our universities.

The only way a heart can survive the forces that insist on having their way is to stay true to a course, which means saying no to a lot of people who are used to getting their way. I want a President who can stand up to sociopaths and psychopaths, a fearless leader who shows his strength through vulnerability. Someone who knows how to ask for help from America's best and brightest minds, most creative thinkers, most noble advocates of health and integrity. He or she is a protector of the rule of law and the Constitution. One who points out conflict of interest and blows the whistle on unfairness, the unscrupulous treatment of our ecology, and the plunder of other nations' resources. The best candidate will be a true visionary, who engenders confidence and inspires peace. I want someone with great parenting skills, who is caring and compassionate, not just toward his own family but to everyone in the world, including those who are pissed off. And while I'm at it, I want her/him to be clean and free of drugs and alcohol, healthy as can be, and bulletproof.

Neither of the parties is offering a President with the aforementioned traits and capabilities.

And if I can't find all this in one person, I want to elect three people to operate as President, so that we can divide up the job properly. One gentleman, Jeff Block of Georgia, who was running for POTUS on Writeindependent.org had the right idea. His platform included increasing the number of Presidents and their length of term. Each of three Presidents would have a twelve-year term, and every four years a new President would be brought into the group, while the first would retire. This would make it harder for an assassination to upset the entire works, and more than two parties could be elected at any given time. It would force our leadership to collaborate and it would stop the game of one party always trying to sabotage the President to make him look bad.

It was May of 2012, and Americans Elect announced that they had not received the requisite ten thousand signatures for any one presidential hopeful to be drafted. Thus, they dropped out of the business of third party promotion. I thought this was a great victory for me because I still hadn't given up.

In preparation for my fifth presidential debate about education, I perused the photos and information of intelligent, hard-working and charismatic people listed with Americans Elect before they took down their site. I found a serious candidate who had risen to the top of Americans Elect on her own popularity, a woman named Michealene Risley.

Ms. Risley is an activist for women's rights and a documentary filmmaker. She started a 501c(3) that raises awareness about global issues. At a TEDx conference in 2011, she told her story of short imprisonment in Zimbabwe while trying to shoot the film *Tapestries of Hope.*

I called and was surprised to find Ms. Risley at home, accessible and friendly. She enlightened me about her experiences with Americans Elect, and it was nothing like I had expected. Instead of being completely unbiased and above board, from her viewpoint, Americans Elect chose to ignore her popularity and only focus on the men, as though she didn't exist. Yet Ms. Risley came in third in subscriber polls.

I expressed my interest in having a woman participate in the discussion, that an intelligent woman would provide a refreshing change from what we've seen on television. Any time a candidate speaks about the truth of the issues, it's a breath of fresh air. I was tired of the same old talking points from the Republicans, about how healthcare like "Medicare for all" is a bad idea, that women should not be able to get birth control pills through their insurance because the church is against it, that women should be required to have a trans-vaginal ultrasound if they're thinking about getting an abortion, and other attacks on women's rights by the conservative establishment, coined a "war on women" by former Republican Tanya Melich. I explained my theory that if women got out to vote for a third party, we could win the election for the candidate rather than just become a spoiler, splitting the vote and allowing the worst candidate to win. If a woman had that kind of traction, both parties would be up in arms about losing voters to the alternate choice.

If ever there were a time for smart Republican women and smart Democrat women to abandon their respective parties, it is now. "Please debate with us," I pleaded Risley.

She agreed to join the fifth debate. I was ebullient! However, she gave me this disclaimer. "It's only a tentative answer, because my mother is very sick at the moment. I have been really thinking about dropping out, after all I've been through with Americans Elect and my personal life, and with my responsibilities here at home."

I told her I understood, but kept my fingers crossed. What if we had a President like Risley who actually cared about people and not raising money for his/her campaign? How different would our world be?

In addition to Risley, I wanted Buddy Roemer to debate with us. I had seen him interviewed on the Colbert Report when he announced his candidacy for President. He had a full grasp of the corruption caused by money and talked about campaign reform as the focus of his platform. I wasn't enamored by his energy policy since it still relied heavily on fossil fuels, but I respected his experience as the Governor of Louisiana. In his lilting southern drawl, Buddy condemned the two dominant parties while still holding on to the same policies of drilling for oil, fracking, and wooing corporations with lower taxes, reminiscent of the Republican platform.

As chance would have it, Carlos Sierra, Buddy Roemer's campaign manager had found Writeindependent.org while searching for opportunities to work for independent candidates. Carlos called me and explained that Gov. Roemer had dropped out of the race the previous Thursday. He wanted to know if I could hire him but I had to turn him down, regretting that I didn't have the money to pay for the kind of help that his politically cultivated brain could give me. While I had him on the phone, I asked if Gov. Roemer would participate in the debates despite his withdrawal, to add cachet and hopefully bring the attention of his followers to our endeavors.

Mr. Sierra agreed to ask Buddy if he would enter the debate, and in less than a day, the answer was "no." I put out my usual request to the established third party candidates, including Rosanne Barr who was seeking the Green Party ticket, asking them to participate. Only Andre Barnett of the Reform Party agreed to participate in the Writeindependent.org debates.

Then tragedy struck. Michaelene Risley's mother passed away and she dropped out of the race entirely before I was able to ask her any questions in debate number five. That left only two women with party nominations still in the race: Jill Stein of the Green Party and Roseanne Barr who was seeking the Green Party nomination, but who would end up in the Peace and Freedom Party with Cindy Sheehan as her running mate.

Herein lies our dilemma: if we want a decent, honest President, we can't rely on the two parties. Yet, if we can't bridge the gap between the average voter and the busy third-party candidates who don't have enough time and resources to meet everyone, then how are we ever going to elect them?

Out of the blue, another important Presidential candidate found Writeindependent.org. He stepped up to the challenge of the debates, celebrated my endeavors and believed in me.

21
I BELIEVE IN SANTA CLAUS

The leader has to be practical and a realist yet must talk the language of the visionary and the idealist.
– Eric Hoffer, American philosopher 1902-1983

"Do you believe in Santa Claus?" Clarissa asked me.

Should I tell her that Santa Claus doesn't exist? My parents told my siblings and me that Santa Claus was nondenominational, so we were lucky Jewish kids with loads of presents he delivered on the first day of Hanukah.

I didn't want to take away her illusions. If anyone had told me that writing letters to famous people was like farting in the wind, perhaps I wouldn't have written anything, and then I would have nothing to show for all my passion. My whole cause is one great "what if?"

After hosting four presidential debates on Skype, I received a phone call from an independent candidate named Santa Claus, a monk living in Nevada. He had been a law enforcement administrator in New York; now he is a child advocate fighting for children's rights. Tom O'Connor had his name legally changed to Santa Claus seven years prior. He looks like a traditional Santa Claus: round ruddy face, pug nose, and long white beard.

"Is this Writeindependent?" he asked.

"Yes."

"My name is Santa Claus, and I'm running for President."

Although I had reservations about his name, I felt proud to be the kind of person who could take someone seriously who says, "I am running for President," and actually provide them a forum for doing so. I surmised from his voice that he was sober and determined. "How did you find out about the website?"

"I was looking for Independent Write-in Candidate information and you popped right up." I thought my SEO expert, Clif, would feel vindicated if he heard this.

I asked a few questions to find out if he were legitimate. What was his background and experience, why was he running, and how much traction had he been getting? The first time I researched his Facebook profile, I tried to "friend" Santa Claus, but he had reached his maximum limit of nearly 5,000 friends. His newer Facebook Page doesn't have limits, and as of this book's release, he has almost 300,000 followers.

He had little luck with the press or national news. He had meager money invested in running for office, and had not taken more than $100 per donation so as to remain untarnished.

"Why are you running for President?" I asked.

"Because our leaders have no heart anymore. Our country has lost its way. They only listen to the mighty dollar, and they've sold their souls."

I hadn't heard anything like this from any of the other candidates, and I was intrigued.

I explained that I was hosting a debate in a few days, would he be interested in participating?

"You bet!" he said.

I wanted to make it that easy to join our debates. I sent him the same invitation that other 'presidential hopefuls' received, and offered him a practice Skype call. He declined, saying he felt comfortable connecting the day of the event.

I had so many candidates wanting to debate that I had to split the group into two sessions, because I could only get three people on Skype at one time without running into technical problems. Debate #5 was stacking up: Harry Braun, who had become a regular, Don Cordell of California who had joined us starting with

Debate #4, James Prattas of Hawaii who joined us in Debate #5, and Santa Claus had all confirmed their participation. JL Mealer had health problems and Andre Barnett was busy on the campaign trail.

Only Harry Braun showed up for every debate. When I told Harry Braun that Santa Claus had joined our ranks, he called me to protest.

"Judy, I like the debates, but I have to tell you, I won't be made a fool of and this Santa Claus fellow is making a mockery of our operation. You're going to have to put him on another time slot, or you can forget about me debating with him."

"Wow." I was flabbergasted, but I understood the problem. I wanted the debates to be taken seriously as well. "If that's how you feel, Harry, I'll make sure to keep you and him on separate time slots."

Clif, the SEO expert I had hired to bring up our Google ranking, was also disappointed that Santa Claus would join us. "We're going to be a laughingstock," he said. He mirrored my concerns. If anyone really wants to be President, he or she should have an opportunity to share his values, lay out his qualifications, and promote his agenda on Writeindependent.org.

Another candidate named Don Cordell was willing to debate Santa Claus. Mr. Cordell, an octogenarian from California with scant hair on his head, a beak nose and gentle voice often spoke about the good old days. He held tough positions against immigrants and was intolerant to religious freedom, in that he didn't want Islam practiced in the United States. He warned about Sharia laws that overlay and sometimes undermine our established laws. He fears violent Muslims and thinks that our borders are too porous.

Mr. Cordell also spoke about the ravages of war, citing Post Traumatic Stress Disorder (PTSD) in veterans. "About one person a day is committing suicide in our military... Most of us have some religious feelings about the sanctity of life. Seeing children in the hospital that have been burned and their arms blown off, we just can't take that." If he could go back to "the day" when things were better, he would. I cringed every time he talked about culture and religion, however he seemed truly sympathetic to the veterans and their struggles.

James Prattas, a Vietnam veteran from Hawaii, attended three out of nine debates. Looking like Mr. Clean minus the oversized muscles, he greeted me on Skype with his big smile and bald head. His laid back style and "love speak" didn't stop him from having an almost Armageddon outlook.

Speaking about PTSD, Mr. Prattas recommended that Hawaii host "centers that have naturopaths, chiropractors, healers, everything in the medical field and the holistic health system. We need to talk to these veterans, put them in the water... the ocean of unconditional love, bring them back to nature, let them know that everything is okay, there really is a God within us all, it's in nature...it's the nameless one...and we need to bring these guys here, not give them all these chemical drugs and screw up their brains."

I asked Mr. Prattas for his view of our military action. "Why do we fight?" he repeated my question. "All of us are being misused, manipulated, and controlled ... and our votes aren't counted and the whole thing's a mess ... and we're heading into a collision course." He didn't offer a solution, just a bleak future.

Next, the new guy in the red tee shirt and glasses answered the question, "Why do we fight?" Mr. Claus answered, "I'd personally like to see the Sheehan Rule applied... She (Cindy Sheehan) would like to see whoever wants to go to war go to war. If the Congress, if the President declares war, then they should be the first ones drafted into that war and be required to serve. I think that would stop wars pretty quickly." He pushed his glasses up his nose. "The founding fathers actually did that. They went to war, they lost their assets, they lost a lot of things in the process. ... Part of my slogan is 'restoring America's heart and soul.' And we've pretty much lost it."

I asked the debating presidential hopefuls about the Bush Doctrine: "Would you wait for an aggressive event to happen to us before taking military action, or would you go into countries that have not asked for our help to be so-called 'liberators?'"

Mr. Claus answered "I think our intelligence community is certainly smart and experienced enough to give Congress and the President information to work with, should there be a credible, provable threat against the United States. Barring the overwhelming evidence to indicate there would be grounds for a preemptive strike, I think we should stay out of that particular business."

"Do you feel that the intelligence community is trustworthy?" This was before we learned the extent to which the National Security Administration (NSA) was collecting vast information such as phone records, email, texts.

Mr. Claus continued, "I think it can be trustworthy. I think depending upon what their motives are. You just have to ask the right questions. We have to be willing to share the information in an honest way with Congress and the President. Right now the oversight is kind of shaky. But I do trust most of the intelligence community to collect adequate information we can base decisions upon."

"I think you brought up a good point. Maybe there needs to be eternal vigilance in seeing if there's an ulterior motive to people that we have employed," I said.

"It's also a question of the State Department as well. The State Department has to stop lying. They lie a lot. And if we want to have genuine communications, trustworthy communications with other countries, we have to stop lying."

After the fifth debate was over, I received a call from Harry Braun.

"I watched the debates with Santa Claus."

I paused, standing in front of my kitchen counter.

"He's okay," Mr. Braun said. "He said some good things."

"I know. He's good."

"I like him. If you want to include him with me next time, that's okay," Harry said.

"I'm glad."

Harry Braun had been with me from the beginning. I considered him my stalwart, so if he said Santa Claus was okay, then he was okay.

Regarding my YouTube channel, the highest number of views for the debates was for my question about Radio Frequency Identification (RFID) chips with 302 views as of February, 2015, probably because I've got one of the few videos talking about the little chips that can be read from scanners far away. Those rare techies who know about RFID and who are curious if they are being used in humans can find their answer at Writein Dependent's channel.

The videos weren't as popular as Justin Bieber, but it's a beginning.

On a personal level, having these far-reaching discussions with presidential candidates was changing me. I could no longer see myself with a male companion who wasn't thinking globally, who didn't care about the community where we live and around the world, and who wasn't interested in changing the status quo. If I couldn't stop thinking about these critical issues, and if my partner couldn't be right alongside me, we wouldn't have anything in common.

The debates made me feel like someone of consequence, if not to the world, then at least to these men running for President who were so driven to make the world a better place. At the end of each session, I had energy to spare. I couldn't wait to edit the footage into segments and publish them. Each time I imagined how I'd answer the questions differently, and I started collecting what I thought were the best answers. The resulting list of solutions can be found in Appendix 11, for which I cannot take any credit because they are all excellent ideas available to anyone who is interested. Feel free to add your ideas.

I still needed media attention, a cable darling who would give me a chance. What about Bill Maher? Maybe I was ready because representatives on the website were signing the Pledge for Honest Candidates!

22
REAL TIME

Freedom is participation in power.

– Marcus Cicero, Roman philosopher 106 BC-43 BC

Mr. Maher had written, produced, and starred in a movie called *Religulous.* I rented it from the library to learn about this Bill Maher person. Based on comments on the Internet, it seemed that people either liked him or they hated him. There was no in-between.

Religulous begins with a montage of religious scenes and one shot of a factory spewing filth in the air. Mr. Maher's voiceover says, "When Revelations was written, only God had the capacity to end the world. But now, man does too, because unfortunately before man figured out how to be rational or peaceful, he figured out nuclear weapons and how to pollute on a catastrophic scale."

I hadn't expected Mr. Maher to grab me with his eco-conscious concerns. I thought this was supposed to be a screed against religion and the violence it causes. Instead, it started with a personal story about Maher's childhood, his influences, and his curiosity about the faithful who believe some pretty ridiculous stories taught through religion.

In the documentary, he traveled across the U.S. seeking faithful churchgoers and tried to stump them with questions about their beliefs. The scene that struck me most was of Maher sitting with his mother and sister, asking them questions about his upbringing. His mother was Jewish, his father Catholic. The children had been brought up Catholic, but by thirteen years of age, Maher's family stopped going to church. I could see that Maher has a loving, tender side, evident in the respect he gave his mom and sibling in person. He doesn't seem to be the misogynist so often portrayed by people who dislike him. In fact, I am sure that he likes women. A lot. The pubescent Maher would have belonged to a religion where he was "allowed to masturbate even more than I was masturbating or get a girl. That's a God I would have definitely worshipped." He doesn't sound like a woman hater to me.

I decided to become an audience member of his show, *Real Time with Bill Maher*.

When I told Clif, my SEO consultant, that I was going to see Maher in person, he wanted to join me. To prepare for the taping, I polished up my press kit, burnt a copy of my soundtrack called "Election 2012" and bought a spill-proof container for a single rose from my garden.

The day of the taping, I found one perfect gorgeous American Beauty just right for plucking and fragrant as all get out. I had read somewhere in my research that Mr. Maher is a big organic foodie, so I earmarked some of my homegrown peaches, hoping to bring them in the near future when I would be a guest on his show. They were ripening in huge numbers at the time.

I asked Clif to pilot his car, unaware that he had a talking-and-driving problem. In our excitement to make it to the show, we left early. Clif couldn't stop talking about politics and as his blathering grew to a fever pitch, he missed our exit. When he finally found the right street, he turned the wrong direction, landing us in bumper to bumper Los Angeles traffic. We arrived late – forty-five minutes late! As we ran up to CBS Studios, the crowd wrangler immediately told me I couldn't give my bag of goodies to the host. They don't accept gifts. I drew in one last fragrant breath of rose scent and rushed it back to the car. Clif and I sat in back of all the other audience members, owing to the fact that we were almost last in line. I should have driven!

Mr. Maher never knew how close he got to the authentic

American Beauty in his studio. He lost his chance to breathe in its intoxicating scent.

It was important to learn the format of his show. I discovered that his first guest sits in a chair opposite him for an informal question and answer period. This time the honor went to an activist named Lynn Henning, a farmer from Michigan, who has fought to eradicate the manure lagoons from Concentrated Animal Farming Operations (CAFOs) festering in her neighborhood. However, because most of the burger-eating public does not have contact with these foul smelling places, they are unaware of what pollution is going on, or they don't care because it's NIMBY. It's Not In My Back Yard, so it's okay, right?

Mr. Maher told Lynn that she was the first farmer he'd ever had on his show. *I hope she isn't the last,* I thought to myself.

Mr. Maher treated Henning with the respect she deserves for putting her neck out as an activist. When her interview ended, the magic of set change happened in seconds, as fast as a NASCAR pit stop. Cameras realign, pieces of the stage break and reform, guests walk in on cue and settle themselves as the crew leaves the area behind the façade. Three, two, one…

Mr. Maher's other guests were political analyst Thomas Frank, former Bush economist Todd Buchholz, and writer-turned-politician Chrystia Freeland. Ms. Freeland wore a fuchsia dress that hugged her every curve. On YouTube, I observed that most of *Real Time*'s panels consist of two men and one woman, no doubt because men still dominate the political scene.

While sitting in the audience, it seemed to me an impossibility to become a guest. The panelists are all famous or well-known, have impressive credentials, hardcover books or awards, and most of all, they have done this sort of thing before. Knowing all this didn't stop me from dreaming. Who was Ann Coulter before Bill Maher? Did anyone know about Christine O'Donnell before Mr. Maher asked her to be on *Politically Incorrect*? Obviously, he chose those women because their views differed from his. Perhaps he was seeking sensational guests rather than someone who wants to buck the system.

I'm suggesting that we take a serious look at a third option for President. Mr. Maher had already decided that we have to choose between two evils. There was no serious consideration of alternatives, and so was there a place for me? And if I managed the incredible feat of making it on his show, how would I get over my stage fright?

I may have thought it was all over with Mr. Maher, but I was wrong.

23
THE DREAM

She was beautiful, but not like those girls in the magazines.
She was beautiful, for the way she thought.
She was beautiful, for that sparkle in her eyes when she talked
about something she loved. She was beautiful, for her ability to
make other people smile even if she was sad.
No, she wasn't beautiful for something as temporary as her looks.
She was beautiful, deep down to her soul.
– F. Scott Fitzgerald, *The Beautiful and Damned* 1922

Almost two weeks after attending *Real Time*, I dreamt about Mr. Maher and recorded it in my diary. Removing the sexual undercurrent, the gist of my dream was that I believed *it's possible for a third party candidate to win the Presidency.* In that ether where anything goes, Mr. Maher started to see it as a possibility, too. I told him that he threw his money away by giving a million dollars to the Obama campaign. If I had that magnitude of cash, I would direct my efforts toward electing more "Honest Candidates" to Congress and to the Presidency.

I rustled up the name and email address of the contact person who secures guests for *Real Time with Bill Maher*. I sent her my information and a pitch via email, and shortly thereafter she wrote back: "Thanks, but I don't think that you are quite right for us at this point."

When a door shuts in my face, I use music to pry it open. Nothing gets through the way music does, nothing lifts the spirit or inspires the way a song can. If God has a voice, if a word has a soul, it is through music that we hear the ineffable sound. Somewhere between the notes lies a message that bounces from heaven to earth or in the case of metal, hell to earth.

I prepared another Election 2012 soundtrack with the artists and titles of the songs showing through the jewel case and my business card inside saying, simply "Please research me." I placed the CD in an envelope and wrote: "To Bill Maher ONLY" on the outside. Then I addressed a large manila envelope to Bill Maher in care of his manager, Marc Gurvitz, and placed the envelope with the CD inside.

Instead of sending the whole schmear via United States Postal Service, I thought I'd give the delivery a personal touch. When I was 26 years old, I started a bicycle messenger service called "Cycle Express" in Long Beach, California. On the back of a yellow windbreaker, I had an artist airbrush a picture of a winged bicycle wheel underlined with the name of my business set in a "whooshing" font. The left breast of my jacket proudly reads:

Judy
Cycle Express

I dressed in bike shorts, shoes, helmet and delivery jacket, all professional and official-like and threw my bike in the back of my SUV. I drove to Mr. Maher's manager's building, parked around the corner, and set up my bike. Within minutes, I was a bicycle messenger zipping up to the office structure where Mr. Gurvitz and other entertainment types do their Hollywood thing.

When I arrived at the third floor of Marc Gurvitz's building, I ran up to the receptionist in a big hurry. She told me to go down the hall to the mailroom. Drats! I wanted to place it right on Gurvitz's desk. Ah, well. I'm going to have to trust the mailroom staff. They won't fiddle around with the mail; it's a sacred trust. I handed the large manila envelope over, and dashed out like a woman on a mission.

Would Marc Gurvitz ever give the inside envelope to Mr. Maher, unopened? Or would he be too curious and want to know everything? Would he pretend to be careless and open it "by mistake?" Would he copy the music onto his iTunes before he gave it to his client? Or would he plop it into the CD player in his car because nobody would ever know?

It bothered me that I couldn't be absolutely certain this delivery was made correctly. So I took extraordinary measures. Almost two weeks later, I drove to Mr. Maher's attorney's office to make another bicycle messenger delivery. This time, I wasn't delivering the CD.

Mr. Maher's entertainment attorney is named John Frankenheimer. When I researched him, I found out that he had brokered the deal between Edgar Bronfman Jr. and other investors to purchase Warner Music Group. As I mentioned earlier, I had written Mr. Bronfman a letter asking for his donation. Coincidence or synchronicity?

I addressed an envelope "Personal and Confidential" to John Frankenheimer. Inside, I placed a tri-folded piece of 8 ½ by 11 with stickers on the ends to keep it closed with the words "Personal and Confidential" on the outside, addressed to Mr. Maher. Thanks to my daughter Clarissa, I had plenty of colorful adhesive choices, so I used red daisies. It was impossible for Mr. Frankenheimer to open it without ripping up the paper.

The delivery went differently than I had expected. Mr. Frankenheimer's building has security. I ran in with my yellow jacket, found an elevator, and pushed the button. The car wouldn't move.

I asked the lobby's attendant how I should arrive at my destination. He walked me to the elevator with a special key that allowed me up to the desired floor. Without questioning me in the least, and owing to my trustworthy, innocent countenance, he had no difficulty allowing me passage. Perhaps I was the only bicycle messenger he had seen in years.

I handed the envelope to a woman sitting at the desk just inside the law firm's large double doors. On my way home, I listened to the soundtrack again, thinking to myself that Mr. Maher would finally hear it with an ear toward understanding some of what inspired it.

The letter that Mr. Frankenheimer held for Mr. Maher read:

Dear Bill,

I appreciate your sense of humor like nobody's business.

There is one problem, though: your show rarely posits solutions to our serious, urgent problems. I want to help you in this regard.

Please invite me on your show so that I can explain how we will fix Congress on election day. It is so simple, yet so compelling, and I am certain your viewers will "get it" right away. It's sure to cause a big stir.

By the way, did Marc Gurvitz give you the CD I sent you of some kickass music?

Please contact me at ###-###-####.

Sincerely,

Judy Frankel

I called Mr. Frankenheimer to follow up, and their office called back. I told the woman on the line that I would send an email to Mr. Frankenheimer with a four-minute video on YouTube called "The Easiest Way to Fix Our Government" that explains what I'm doing. In the same email, I mentioned to Mr. Frankenheimer that I had already written a letter to Edgar Bronfman, Jr. and I would be happy to forward it to him so he can see what I'm doing to raise funds. Most importantly, I asked for a meeting.

If a man can broker a deal like Warner Music Group, he can probably get the rights to my Election 2012 soundtrack. He must have amazing connections in the music industry. He'd also know how to pair a kickass soundtrack with a book. This may be my dream come true!

With this rattling around in my head, I fantasized about asking an attorney who does billion dollar deals for help with my tiny project, because after all, I am trying to save the world. Wouldn't he want to leave a legacy like that? If he could lift the country out of a downward spiral, wouldn't he take that chance?

I did all the follow up that a reasonable person with persistence would be expected to do. I placed one final phone call after the email that was never returned. I put the project of getting attention into perspective. It would be a long-term endeavor, perhaps decades long.

What would it take to get a yes? Trying to restore the American dream is so overwhelming, so huge, yet I was taking the necessary steps. First, I had an idea for spit shining Washington. Then I had the strategy for making it well known. I contacted the people who could make it happen, and everyone who could really help me said 'no' or ignored me. What would it take before I could accomplish something? Media doesn't want to share my story, wealthy people don't want to use their money to make themselves *less* politically powerful, and thanks to spam and Facebook, nobody wants to sign up for new things or give out their personal information to yet another website.

The last avenue I hadn't tried was grass roots activism. It was time to get out of the house and meet face to face.

24
BULLETS AND DICTATORS

If you have come to help me, then you are wasting your time.
But if you have come because your liberation is bound up with
mine, then let us work together.
– Lilla Watson and Aboriginal activists group, Queensland, 1970s

How do you get one hundred million people to dream the impossible dream? Then, how do you convince them their impossible dream can come true?

I researched Occupy, watched presidential hopeful Ron Paul supporters' videos, and saw the movie *Thrive: What on Earth Will It Take?* that allegedly has had more than twenty two million viewers. Each group is looking at the same ailing elephant named USA lying on her side, hearing her moan in her pathetic voice, and each describes the problems differently. Still, she's sick and we all want to help.

For my first face to face with grass roots activists, I chose a training class, hosted by 99% Spring, at the suggestion of an anti-establishment friend. I had no idea who 99% Spring really was or how they were started. I assumed they had something to do with Occupy. I was wrong, but more about that later.

The training explained "Non Violent Direct Action." Researchers at Harvard found that protest and resistance tactics are twice as effective as violence. I would learn about actions like marches, boycotts, worker cooperatives, community policing, just to name a few.

I drove to a private loft in West Los Angeles. At the check-in table, we were each given a 60-page booklet called *The 99% Spring Training Guide*.

The hosts graciously opened their two-story space to about forty-five people who had come from all over southern California. We sat in folding chairs in a large airy room that served as the event's auditorium, though it usually functioned as a combination dining, living area and office for two young professionals.

I looked around at all the activists. Half were middle aged to elderly, teachers and working folks with weathered faces of concern and a caring softness. Half were young people, students, professionals and yuppies with the same seriousness as the older attendees.

A tall, pale-skinned, dark eyed gentleman in his early 40's named Vlad officiated the program. Standing next to a large easel upon which rested a huge pad of white paper, with a black sharpie he squeaked down the words *Tell your personal story*.

Speaking with a thick Romanian accent Vlad said, "This is the most powerful tool you have as an activist, so I'm going to tell you my story."

Vlad described his native country as a repressive communist dictatorship. His parents were independent thinkers, critical of the regime and eager to leave. He recounted his earliest memory of being politically aware when at six years of age, he tried to touch the radio and his parents slapped his hand away and scolded him severely. "A radio in our home was very carefully tuned to the frequency of Voice of America. Everything on TV and in the newspapers in Romania was censored and not to be trusted. That's how I first became aware something was wrong." As Vlad spoke, I was thinking America's voice can no longer be trusted, our news sources are no longer verified, and the media is often controlled by corporate fiefdoms.

Vlad's family lived a few blocks from the country's one and only television station in Romania's capitol, Bucharest. "One evening, my dad came home and said 'Son, I'd like to take you out so you can experience history in the making.'" Vlad recounted, "My dad put me on his shoulders and we started walking toward the television station. When we turned the corner, all of a sudden I found myself in a sea of people. It seemed like the earth was trembling. The murmur of the crowd seemed as if there was electricity in the air. I could cut a square in the air and capture this power around me."

He described the scene in December 1989: a TV station surrounded by a fence, the mob pressed up against it. "Nobody dared to step over the fence and walk toward the building. Soldiers stood with their weapons pointed at the crowd in front of semi-armored vehicles. My parents decided to go home and it was a good thing. That is the night when the shooting started in the capitol."

When he paused, I looked down at my notepad. No bullets in my story.

Vlad explained, "That's basically how I first understood what revolution means, what people power means, what people power can do."

"This revolution was hijacked by the second level elite. The dictator [Nicolae Ceausescu] and his entourage were executed and the second level stepped up. The intellectuals and the students at the capitol realized what was happening and they decided to occupy the center of the city."

I instantly thought about Zuccotti Park and the Occupy movement on Wall Street.

"This occupation lasted for two months and it was taken away in a very bloody way. The new president, [Ion Iliescu] who was an ex-communist, sent the secret police out into the countryside to come back with workers and miners who had been isolated from media and they were subtly manipulated. So trains of miners and other workers started streaming into the capitol. They brought their tools." Vlad swung his arms, as if waving a pick ax or a shovel.

"The secret police guided them to the center square, telling them these students and protesters are 'outsiders;' they're here to hijack the revolution and they're basically hooligans."

Hooligans. I've heard that word before. Seems like whenever an unpopular government faces an uprising, they label the dissenters *hooligans*.

Vlad quickly recounted the bloody scene that ensued. "So the miners, with the secret police, beat the demonstrators and basically removed them from the square. After that, they went to the headquarters of the opposition parties, and burned them down as well. Once my parents saw this, they realized things were not going to change in Romania anytime soon."

Wow. Maybe things have to get much worse in the USA before people take action, before they do something about it. What will it take to gain control over our government again?

Shortly after the Romanian Revolution in 1989, Vlad's family emigrated to the United States. I asked him what he thought of our government.

"My take on the government is it has allowed itself to be taken over by a fairly small elite."

Comparing his Romanian experience to today's problems in the U.S., he said, "I see how difficult it is for truth in news to come out. I see how you can have a regime that's very insulated and does not really sympathize with the majority of the people who may not have the financial power to make their voices heard. I see how we actually live in a surveillance state, not different from what I experienced in Romania."

Vlad was hard-wired from a young age to stick up for citizens' rights. He knew what suppression felt like. However, most of us don't have parents who teach us to be politically engaged.

If we attend protests, Vlad warned, we might be taken away in police handcuffs. He coached, "Be prepared to have a chain of phone calls...." Although he didn't use such colorful words, he implied: *Be prepared to call your loved ones from the tank.*

For me, the biggest takeaway from the training was that Rosa Parks, the civil rights activist, did not just decide to ride in the front of the bus one day. She had been trained in nonviolent direct action, and was supported by a whole community of activists who helped bring her act of civil disobedience to a wider audience. If no one knew she refused to be segregated to the back of the bus, her action would not have galvanized the entire movement as it did. No idea, no matter how good, will ever make a difference until it reaches a tipping point of notoriety.

What will it take? Maybe the only way the website idea could get out is through the black market, the underground, a cult following of sorts. How that would happen, or if it would ever happen, I did not know.

Before I went to the training, I thought the 99% Spring came from Occupiers. That's the whole reason I went. I found out later they are a front group for, well, the Democrats.

MoveOn.org, a liberal activism group co-opted by the Democratic Party, grabbed my information from the rosters of the 99% Spring. I should have known because they paid for the pamphlets and the video presentation, which weren't cheap to produce. In other words, I was taking materials from a group who supported Obama.

I had hoped some of MoveOn.org's eight million members shared my views of Obama, now that he had been in office for almost four years. Surely, they understand the role of money in politics and how easy it is to become corrupted. If we can't agree on everything, at least we can agree that *Citizens United* was a bad Supreme Court decision, right?

25
CITIZENS UNITED

The definition of puke politics is that if it must have government at all, the government should be purposefully ineffectual almost across the board in terms of the functions we usually ascribe to the state and really only competent in one area, and that's giving away taxpayer money in return for campaign contributions.
– Matt Taibbi, Griftopia

MoveOn.org is a progressive, liberal public policy advocacy group that often raises money for Democrats. They self-identify as a group of concerned citizens who want to "find their political voice in a system dominated by big money and powerful special interests." I was beginning to feel like they were trying to co-opt the Occupy movement, which never took sides, red or blue, with their message. It felt a little dirty that MoveOn took my name and information from a 99% Spring event.

A woman named Carol phoned, asking me to come to a MoveOn event at her house and we shared stories. When she learned that I was trying to find a third option for President, she told me that she had been a Ralph Nader supporter, but she would never do that again. The last time Nader ran for President was in 2008 as an Independent against then-Senator Barack Obama and Senator John McCain. She has surrendered to the idea that only a

Democrat or Republican frontrunner with a huge bank account can win. She read me the riot act about how important it was to vote for Obama in 2012, and I didn't want to throw away my vote, now did I?

Despite the fact that I refuse to vote for a President that I can't feel good about, I went to the meeting at her house. I knew we could agree upon the main focus of our group—getting money out of politics.

I arrived at her beautiful Hollywood Hills Mediterranean style home with a trickling fountain in front. She had prepared a tantalizing spread of appetizers and veggies, and I brought two baskets of ripe peaches plucked from my trees.

About ten of us sat around Carol's long dining room table to learn about a Supreme Court decision called *Citizens United*. The decision is named after a Political Action Committee (PAC) that sued the Federal Election Commission (*Citizens United v. FEC*) because they were prohibited from broadcasting their propaganda piece called *Hillary: the Movie*. Judges from a lower court decided it was against McCain-Feingold campaign finance restrictions, saying that it was essentially a 90-minute campaign ad, "susceptible of no other interpretation than to inform the electorate that Senator Clinton is unfit for office, that the United States would be a dangerous place in a President Hillary Clinton world, and that viewers should vote against her."

PACs often use warm and fuzzy names to lull the public into thinking they're fighting for noble causes. On their website, Citizens United claim to be "dedicated to restoring our government to citizens' control." Ironically, they were fighting not for the typical individual's right to buy media, but for the ability of non-profits (often with secretive, unknown donors) to produce video on demand. Citizens United asserted that the McCain-Feingold Act is unconstitutional on the grounds that it limits speech, a First Amendment right.

Instead of looking at the campaign finance law under the McCain-Feingold Act as a violation of First Amendment rights, the Supreme Court examined McCain-Feingold in its entirety for constitutionality. As soon as they did that, they were able to come up with three grounds for siding with Citizens United. We need to consider all three if we are to overturn this awful decision.

First, they decided that we can't treat "speakers" differently, even if the "speaker" is a corporation. The five justices who came up with this argument used a 1976 decision *Buckley v Valeo* as the basis, saying that spending money is a form of political speech. Speech is a human right, protected by the First Amendment, but with the *Buckley* decision, that right to speech was extended to a legal construct that is essentially a phantom—the corporation. Thus corporations could be protected under the First Amendment, as though they were people.

Many supporters of the *Citizens United* decision confirm these grounds with slogans like "money equals speech" and "corporations are people." In their absurdity, the Supreme Court justices twisted our Constitution so that corporations now have the same speech rights as human beings. They claim that if corporations or wealthy individuals aren't able to spend as much money as they want on "speaking" then we're tromping on their First Amendment rights to free speech. I say, either split your money between opposing viewpoints, or make an equal amount of airtime "free" for those on the other side who want to exercise their right to free speech. Using money to "talk" perverts the whole process of debate. It's not debate when a company is blanketing the airwaves with messages that could be true or false. Justice William J. Brennan argued that the spirit of the First Amendment is to protect public debate, not enhance a corporation or union's ability to convince television viewers that there is only one logical outcome.

There will be true freedom of speech when speech is free.

Second, five justices argued that corruption is defined as "quid pro quo" (literally something for something). Defining corruption this way leaves a lot of wiggle room, because anything less than a flat-out bribe (I'll give you money if you give me a specific result) doesn't qualify as corruption. And bribery is hard to prove. Anything less than all-out bribery is not corruption, according to five Supreme Court justices, so spending huge amounts of money to support a candidate's election is okay.

Last, the highest court in our land explicitly argues that "independent" expenditures can't be corrupting. If the candidate didn't coordinate with the giver, then how can that candidate know what position to take on a bill? And if they don't know who gave them money, how can they be corrupted? Thus, corporations, unions and PACs should be able to spend as much money as they want, because, after all, they can put together ads without talking to their candidate, right? How could that be corruption?

I picture a corporation as one huge corpus with billions of mouths. Let's call this blob of mouths "Mondosygilla," a multi-billion dollar monstrosity that gobbles up everything in its path. It wants to pass a bill that forbids small businesses from suing it, making it above the law so it can sell products without regard for the damage they cause. Mondosygilla gives enough campaign support to just enough congressmen behind the scenes, where neither you nor I have access. Their legislation passes through Congress. During election time, Mondosygilla spends $44 million in ads, using every mouth on its bloated blob to scream confusing messages at voters and drown out any and all else that believes differently. Is that democracy? Or a behemoth blob with billions of blaring portals run amok?

Until 1976, we could differentiate between corporations and human beings. But the Supreme Court has a long history of making things easier for businesses at the expense of human rights. Corporations don't suffer the same consequences that people do for bad behavior. They don't have feelings or a conscience. Corporations enjoy many of the benefits of human beings, without any of the liabilities. A corporation can't go to jail, can't die, won't feel guilty if it hurts someone, or remorse when it does something wrong, doesn't have compassion toward its neighbors or its country. It's not a team player. It's an enemy of "too much" government, squelching laws that make society civil. If it can take advantage over its competitors, it will do so at every turn until there are no competitors left. Once it reaches the pinnacle of power, it will maintain its position at all costs, even if it means making food, water, soil and sea unsafe for life. It is not a member of society, so it doesn't have a sense of duty or proportion. Its only mandate is to make money.

According to the Supreme Court, if a corporation (or labor union) wants to get things off its chest, it can spend its general treasury money to do so. For example, when Goldman Sachs wants to make sure that our derivatives market won't become transparent, they can "speak" by spending millions of dollars to convince lawmakers not to regulate the market. You or I can rattle the cages of our incumbents, but we are outsiders. We could have made a difference with our votes, but we agreed with the wealthy that they have all the control, and we vote for one of two parties that have the most money.

On their website, Citizens United Political Action Committee says they promote national sovereignty, free enterprise, and limited government. Yet the *Citizens United* decision allows multinational companies to influence elections through PACs. What are foreign corporations doing funding our elections and lobbying our Congress? The Center for Responsive Politics is a nonpartisan research group that studies the effects of money on politics by tracking the financing of federal elections using reports filed at the Federal Election Commission and the IRS. They publish a long list of foreign corporations that fund congressional races at OpenSecrets.org.

Much of Citizens United's funding came from the Koch Brothers, billionaire oil men. The Koch Brothers spent $400 million to influence the 2012 elections exclusively to promote Republican candidates and ostensibly to further their pro-oil agenda. They publicly announced that they will spend $899 million to influence the outcome of the 2016 elections.

Money in politics was a problem long before five Supreme Court judges ruled in favor of Citizens United. The astronomical amounts spent on mailers; television ads; and red, white, and blue balloons at the parties' national conventions has steadily increased; from $5.4 billion in 2008, to $6.3 billion in 2012, to an estimated $7 billion in 2016. What these numbers should remind us is that if we haven't given money to our politicians, someone else certainly has, and they wouldn't be spending so much if it didn't reap rewards.

For each of the following industries, imagine how your attention has been wooed to think, feel, and behave a certain way at the polls. These are the figures for how much had been spent in the 2012 elections:

Finance industry – $1.63 billion
Health insurance industry – $1.26 billion

Energy industry – $919 million
Transportation industry – $561 million
Pharmacology industry – $525 million
Oil and gas industry – $363 million
Agribusiness industry – $359 million
Lobbying and legal industry – $274 million
Education industry – $265 million
Cable industry – $133 million
Mining industry – $85.6 million
Mortgage industry – $33.5 million
Private prison industry – $4 million

With money like this, is it any wonder our representatives aren't listening to us?

At the dining room table of our activist host, after we listened to a gentleman explain in detail the legal rationale behind the Supreme Court's decision, one woman summed it up. "The problem is, if you ask the average person on the street, they don't even know what *Citizens United* is, much less what it means to our democracy."

I sat with my mouth shut but I was burning inside, waiting for everyone else to finish complaining. Finally, I felt a moment when the room turned quiet. "Let's face it," I said. "The only way we're going to get people to pay attention to *Citizens United* is if Beyonce wears the words '*Citizens United*' across her chest." The room erupted in laughter, but I was serious.

"How do we get Beyonce to wear it?" somebody asked.

Exactly. This issue needs attention. When we see *Citizens United* across the chest of a sexy star, instead of thinking about a bad Supreme Court decision, we should think about uniting the citizens to add an amendment to the Constitution that overturns *Citizens United*. Where are these citizens?

26
GRASS ROOTS

...when such a movement took hold in hundreds of thousands of places all over the country it would be impossible to suppress, because the very guards the system depends on to crush such a movement would be among the rebels... But because it would be a process over time, starting without delay, there would be the immediate satisfactions that people have always found in the affectionate ties of groups striving together for a common goal... The elite's weapons, money, control of information would be useless in the face of a determined population.
– Howard Zinn, *A People's History of the United States*

What can we do when our government isn't solving the problems that affect every day of our lives? How do we step in and save our country from an ineffective, recalcitrant Congress? Instead of waiting for Congress to start being responsive to our needs, we citizens need to organize and assert our power. Who is making significant inroads to change the paradigm?

Occupy had no long-term strategy for fixing government, but they had hit the nerve of the zeitgeist. Surely those who had protested for Occupy would be interested in asserting their power. What about all the people who maybe don't identify with Occupy, but who agree that Washington is in a more or less constant state of passive aggression? What are they doing about the problem?

Shortly after the MoveOn meeting, in my search for frameworks under which politically engaged people share ideas, I found an activist group based in Oakland, California called People's Congress.[17] John Mulkins, an artist whose medium is glass, founded the organization and its website, peoples congress.org.

Mr. Mulkins sought to inspire a huge gathering on the mall in Washington, D.C. to show solidarity for re-envisioning the way our government works. To overcome a frozen Congress he suggested that the electorate express its wishes through national referendums that we vote upon. Many representative democracies use this process, such as Switzerland, Australia, New Zealand, Iceland, Greece, and Ireland. Critics of the referendum process have called this form of governance the "Never-end-um," meaning that issues come up for a vote too often or take too long, tiring out the voters.

"As Apple and Microsoft have done, we need to update our national operating system," John said in a blog talk radio interview in June, 2012. "We can decide for ourselves how we want our politics to be carried out. Give us time to create the solutions together, because I don't think we're going to see those coming from our government."

People's Congress hosted weekly conference calls that I attended without fail. Mr. Mulkins cultivated a feeling of cooperation and kindness amongst the other strong personalities and revolutionaries on the line. He had built a following of about two thousand volunteers and activists who received his regular e-newsletters.

A volunteer by the name of Manu monitored the calls. When he spoke, measuring every word, the call slowed down to molasses. Manu wears a ponytail and glasses. He's always on his last dime because activism doesn't pay well. In his dogged devotion to make the world a better place for his grandchildren, he has given up creature comforts like an apartment to call his own and knowing where he will find his next meal.

---

[17] Throughout this book, I refer to both a People's Congress and a Citizen's Congress. The terms are used interchangeably.

Manu curated speakers for the weekly calls such as Richard Windfeathers, a Native American Spiritual Leader from the Picuris Pueblo & Isleta Reservation of New Mexico, and Mike Gravel, former Senator from Alaska. We spoke with Hordur Torfason, the inspirational figure who helped overthrow Iceland's government during the Pots 'n Pans Revolution in 2011. I asked Hordur how to conjure a large group of people to make such a change in America. He said that you and I have to reach out, one family at a time, as he did.

"You have to visit neighbors' homes, sit down at the kitchen table, and plainly explain what needs to be done," he said. Iceland's relatively small and culturally homogenous, so it was easier. America's size and cultural diversity hampers this process.

"How can one person do all that here? Or how can we? We have maybe five, maybe twelve people on a good week on these conference calls!"

"It takes a long time," he said. I felt crestfallen. *There is a huge job ahead of us.*

"But you never give up," Hordur said. Never give up.

It was difficult for me to get a word in edgewise on the conference calls. I spend most of my time waiting for my phone to get turned on. When I finally explained what I was doing with the website, it landed like a turd. Everybody was thinking about a people's congress, not about using the Internet to find out if their representatives had signed a Pledge for Honest Candidates.

Still, I warmed to the concept of a People's Congress. I wanted to explore this idea, even expand it beyond what Mr. Mulkins had envisioned with his referendum concept, because it brought activists closer to the government participation that we so craved. The danger was that it might override reason, rule by passion and cause a "tyranny of the majority" about which founding father James Madison had warned. But I hadn't given up on a People's Congress any more than I had given up on Writeindependent.org or other methods for outshining the deadbeats in Congress.

Besides grass roots activists, I tried one other method for reaching an audience for the website —networking groups. I liked that they weren't political, because the problem I wanted to tackle was the corruption and belligerence of Congress, something to which I thought nearly everyone could relate.

A friend referred me to a woman's networking organization called Heart Link. Its founder Dawn Billings, a clinical psychologist, designed the meetings to increase serotonin and oxytocin, the feel-good, bonding hormones.

Members identifying themselves as "leaders" host meetings at their homes. Luckily Lynn, my closest leader, lived right down the hill in Rancho Palos Verdes. A perky blonde in her mid-50's, she busied about, arranging appetizers on her kitchen nook table surrounded by windows soaked in the ocean view.

Each woman who arrived tumbled into the house, unloading and unwinding her thoughts. About fifteen of us moved into the dining room, sat down with our own business cards, catalogs, and freebies. Lynn laid out the rules for the three-minute presentation each of us would give to explain who we are and what we do.

Sara, every hair in place, has her own organizing business. Fastidiously attired, Nikki is a home stager and color consultant. Yoshi owns a skin care salon, Jodi sells natural spa products, and Lucia performs Reiki to relieve her clients' stress. Dana hosts wine tasting parties to sell fine wines. Myrna is a life coach and hypnotherapist, Leslie is a divorce attorney. Tina sells Pampered Chef, Nicole does interior design, Andrea is a wardrobe strategist. Irene does feng shui, Lauren is a realtor who happens to sell a health tonic.

Of course, no one showed up with a website that aimed to put congressmen in a huge claw-footed tub to sponge bathe the corruption off them and wash the greed out of their mouths with soap. Who would try such a thing? Though my pitch got everyone in the room excited, fourteen powerful women were all I would reach that day. How would I broaden my message to fourteen thousand, fourteen million?

Amazingly, the last woman to give her pitch had the best odds at answering my needs. When Marci Klein described her business, my eyes began to well up with tears. She left the world of television production to spend more time taking care of her kids and launched Klein Creative Media, a one-stop-shop for producing heirloom DVD's. Her videos usually feature the story of one individual and how that person has affected the lives of others.

Marci's forever-tan, muscled body from years of surfing makes her look young, and she's got an intense, springboard energy. Her quick intelligence mixed with self-deprecating humor impressed me immediately. She downplayed her Emmy, saying "everyone wins one eventually, if you work in television long enough."

At the time we met, I was an emotional mess. I was moved, thinking that providence had placed this powerhouse woman by my side. It was as though fate was telling me *get your infomercial made!*

I looked at my savings and realized if I went for it, I'd have to spend about eight thousand more than I had earmarked for this entire endeavor. The chance of the infomercial going viral was like winning a multi-million-dollar lottery, but it would serve as a record of what I had worked on all year, and that was greater than any resumé. Marci's storytelling style would explain the website to people, and it would last forever. For these reasons, I decided to hire Marci to produce, film and edit the infomercial.

When I returned from the Heart Link meeting, I found an email from a MoveOn member alerting me to a horrific thing our government is poised to do stealthily, the way GATT and NAFTA were introduced as "inevitable." She introduced me to the Trans Pacific Partnership, the biggest power grab of the elite yet conceived.

27
TRANS PACIFIC PARTNERSHIP = BAD

Only puny secrets need protection.
Big secrets are kept by public incredulity.
– Marshall McLuhan, Canadian philosopher 1911-1980

An activist named Linda sent me a short email message stating simply that there is something even worse than *Citizens United*. She wrote, "Corporations could rule supranationally with the Trans Pacific Partnership (TPP) trade pact." The Trans Pacific Partnership is an international trade agreement that hardly gets any press. Will the American people be consulted on this piece of legislation? Why aren't we in the loop?

International trade agreements intrigue me because my Mom always complained about them. Right before I started Writeindependent.org, I began to study the General Agreement on Tariffs and Trade (GATT) and the North American Free Trade Agreement (NAFTA) with determination because of her warnings. I found them to be bad for America, and actually quite bad for the other countries involved. When I was browsed through trade agreements' affect on our U.S. workforce, I found Public Citizen, a watchdog group that parses long trade bills into layman's terms. They spelled out the Trans Pacific Partnership clear as day for me. The TPP gives mega-corporations unbelievable rights and privileges at the expense of our freedoms, consumer protection, financial security, and the USA's sovereignty.

Lori Wallach, Founder and Director of Public Citizen's Global Trade Watch and attorney specializing in trade law, reviewed the only chapter that leaked from this secretive 29-chapter bill. She is one of the most outspoken experts warning Americans: don't let this bill become law! On a YouTube video, I saw her refer to the bill as "NAFTA on steroids." It affects 800 million people stretching from Vietnam to Chile (including the U.S.) and encompasses 40% of the global economy. The Electronic Frontier Foundation, a nonprofit that defends our rights to a free digital world writes, "the Intellectual Property (IP) chapter would have extensive negative ramifications for users' freedom of speech, right to privacy and due process, and would hinder people's abilities to innovate." Wording of the TPP is reminiscent of the Stop Online Piracy Act a.k.a "SOPA" that would have surrendered control of the Internet to federal agencies. When SOPA was defeated in Congress because of huge public outcry, the multinationals dodged and weaved, inserting their interests into the TPP.

Reading the summary of the TPP is like discovering the super villain's diabolical plan in a futuristic horror/action movie. (See Appendix 7 for details of the TPP.) But there will be no Batman or Superman to save us, and the bad guys are attorneys dressed in designer suits. They aren't wearing makeup and costumes, and they aren't played by actors who wouldn't harm a third world child.

"The TPP includes the very controversial 'investor state system' which empowers individual corporations to directly sue governments," Ms. Wallach explains. "Three corporate attorneys act as 'judges' and these guys rotate between being the judge and being the guys suing the government for the corporation. They are empowered to give unlimited cash damages from us, the taxpayers, to these corporations for any government action: a regulatory issue, environment, health, safety, that undermines the investors' expected future profits."

Wallach recommends a website called Expose the TPP.org that reports: "Tribunals have already ordered governments to pay over $3.5 billion in investor-state cases" and "more than $14.7 billion remain in pending claims under U.S. agreements." Even if the governments win against the corporation, we, the taxpayers, must pay an average of $8 million in legal fees and tribunal costs to fight these cases.

The complexity and size of trade agreements shield them from being explained to ordinary citizens. It's almost as though summarizing the TPP's long-term, far-reaching effects requires a degree in trade law. This obfuscation is intentional, for if it weren't, we would have an easy time writing a sound bite to explain it. Author and activist Michele Swenson gave it her best shot: "Some anticipated consequences of the TPP, and its sister European Transatlantic Free Trade Agreement (TAFTA), proposal: compromise of environmental and worker protections in virtually every developed nation; banks will become 'way too big to fail;' prescription medications will be more expensive; natural gas costs will rise as there will be open season on our lands for fracking in order to export natural gas to the highest bidder; decline of food quality standards will jeopardize health; Monsanto will have free reign for unregulated sale of unidentified GMO foods; and corporations like Nestle will easily corner the market on water as a saleable commodity, rather than a basic right."

The reason you almost never see anything mentioned about the TPP in the media is that it's a highly secretive document. Oregon Representative Ron Wyden, subcommittee chair on international trade, wrote a Statement for the Record to President Obama, complaining that "the majority of Congress is being kept in the dark as to the substance of the TPP negotiations, while representatives of U.S. Corporations – like Halliburton, Chevron, PHRMA, Comcast, and the Motion Picture Association of America – are being consulted and made privy to details of the agreement."

For something so secretive, Obama knows exactly who to appoint to key positions in trade agencies who would help push the TPP along. Michael Froman, Obama's current U.S. Trade Representative collected $4 million in bonuses from Citicorp before leaving to help assist adoption of the TPP. Stephan Selig, former Bank of America investment banker took in $9 million prior to his appointment as the Under Secretary of International Investment and Trade. Their interest in passing the TPP stems from the bank-friendly provisions that would prohibit limiting the size of financial institutions, (safeguards against 'too big to fail'), prohibitions against reinstating Glass Steagall type firewalls between financial institutions, prohibitions against banning the sale of toxic assets, and prohibitions against controlling how much money flows into and out of a country. Massachusetts Senator and advocate for the Consumer Financial Protection Bureau Elizabeth Warren, in response to the TPP, said it's "a chance for these banks to get something done quietly, out of sight, that they could not accomplish in a public place with the cameras rolling and the lights on."

Why did Obama say he would support it? He has been gunning for something called "trade promotion authority" whereby a President can fast track a huge trade bill through without allowing Congress's full review and discussion. If Obama is unsuccessful at making the TPP go through, the next Democrat or Republican President will have a crack at it. That's why we *must* ask both the Democrat and Republican frontrunners in 2016 whether or not they support the TPP. Then we will know if they are beholden to corporations who stand to benefit from this so-called "free" trade bill, unless of course, they lie.

In a September, 2013 visit to Japan to attend the G20 summit, Obama remarked "I know that Japanese Prime Minister Abe is committed, as we are, to completing this year's negotiations around the Trans-Pacific Partnership, which promises to open up markets and create the kind of high standards and trade agreements throughout the largest and most dynamic and fastest growing set of markets in the world." However, what "high standards" is he agreeing to? There are no standards. In fact, in order for member nations to meet binding provisions in the TPP, "each country shall insure the conformity of domestic laws regulations and procedures" to the trade agreements, and our U.S. laws can take a back seat.

The countries currently talking in secret about the TPP are: the U.S., Australia, Brunei, Canada, Chile, Japan, Mexico, New Zealand, Peru, Singapore, Malaysia and Vietnam, with China, Brazil, and Russia potentially joining later. Six hundred corporate advisors are allowed to review and comment on the 29 chapters of the TPP, while most members of Congress do not have copies of the text and are forbidden to read it. Public or civic involvement?

None. Can journalists review it? No!

Who make up the panel of corporate advisors to the attorneys writing this TPP legislation? I found, completely by accident, that a large number of them were appointed to the Agricultural Policy Advisory Committee (APAC) and six Agricultural Technical Advisory Committees (ATACs). A press release from the USDA dated Sept. 8, 2011, said that Agriculture Secretary Tom Vilsack and then-U.S. Trade Representative Ron Kirk gave 148 private-sector executives this rare ability to cherry-pick policy for their industries through the TPP. It's important to note that Vilsack is a supporter of biotech and genetic engineered crops. Of the 148 representatives to these illustrious government committees, I found that 124 of them are advisors for the TPP. Could it just be a coincidence that 124 government appointees also have a role in crafting the TPP?

Remember Howard Schultz's concern over Congress not passing a balanced budget? As it turns out, he's got an advisor named Sudip Jhaveri working to protect Starbucks through the TPP. Mr. Jhaveri was appointed to the Processed Foods Agricultural Technical Advisory Committee in 2011 to cement his insider position in the USDA. It seems everyone who's anyone wants to jump on the sinking ship called the U.S. Government to get their piece of memorabilia in the way of taxpayer guarantees. Et tu, Brute?

Imagine being a sole advisor out of 600 who decided that this bill shouldn't go through. Would that person have much impact? I contacted one advisor, Laura Batcha of the Organic Trade Association (OTA), to find out her views on the Trans Pacific Partnership. She sent me a link to the OTA's position on GMOs but we never talked about how she would stand up against the big agriculture advisers, though I tried twice to set up a phone call. She will likely be pressured to cave in to the other 599 advisors to get this bill done. I can't imagine how strong Laura would have to be to stand up for a non-bioengineered seed supply if she's the only one doing so. It's unlikely that she will be able to secure any wording in the final document that would protect non-patented foods from genetic contamination (via pollen drift) or assert our right to label GMOs.

We are left without a voice speaking for the American people.

If you and I aren't one of the 600 advisors on the panel, we don't belong to an elite group that writes a handsome dowry into their children's future. You're either in, or you're out.

The lawyers who drafted the Trans Pacific Partnership's 29-chapter agreement may change its name yet again to confuse and dodge unfavorable press. It has already gone by another name, the P3-CEP (the Pacific Three Closer Economic Partnership).

The TPP has a huge sister agreement called the Transatlantic Trade and Investment Partnership (TTIP) between the U.S. and Europe that works basically the same way. "...Food lobby group Food and Drink Europe, representing the largest food companies (Unilever, Kraft, Nestlé, etc.), welcomed the negotiations, one of their key demands being the facilitation of the low level presence of unapproved genetically modified crops," reports Corporate Europe Observatory, a research group that exposes corporate lobbying efforts. The TTIP bypasses European bans on GMOs by allowing biotech companies to sue governments when their anti-GMO laws prevent them from piling up profits.

I discovered a resolution written by Walter B. Jones, Republican Congressman from North Carolina, that outlines these problems with the TPP and calls for more transparency of the text of this behemoth legislation. (See Appendix 8.) Mr. Jones does an excellent job of summarizing his concerns over losing our sovereignty to companies and special interests.

Why isn't anything mentioned on television about the TPP? If it will add such sweeping changes to the way business operates, ask yourself: why aren't traditional news sources telling us about this "free" trade bill?

While researching the TPP, I found a Madison, Wisconsin radio host named Sly who had been talking about how bad it would be for our country. What a great guy! He was ahead of the curve! I shot him an email, saying how impressed I was that he would bring attention to this horrible agreement and asking to be a guest on his show.

Sly's producer whose nickname is "Captain" returned my email to arrange the phone call for a radio interview. I was excited to talk about the Pledge for Honest Candidates because two people running in two different districts in Wisconsin had signed it. More importantly, I thought we should talk about the TPP because when word gets out how bad this 29-chapter bill is, the public will be up in arms. The problem is, many bills that pass Congress never get publicity. The average person isn't paying attention, and is too busy running his own life to be bothered with what Congress, the Senate, and the President are passing into law in front of our backs.

I remember my mom making a big stink about GATT. She couldn't believe that such a huge bill would get so many yes votes without ever having been read by most of Congress. Did the congressmen really care what it said if their re-election campaigns had been funded by the companies who would benefit?

On the day of my radio interview, I printed out a list of the incumbents whom Wisconsinites have voted back into office over and over again since 1999, and I was shocked to find that Paul Ryan in District 1, Ron Kind of District 3, Jim Sensenbrenner of District 5, and Tom Petri of District 6 had all voted for the Financial Services Modernization Act of 1999 (a.k.a. the Gramm Leach Bliley Act). Sly's interview with me was a month before the announcement that Paul Ryan was Romney's running mate. I figured that anyone who signed the Act was either too naïve to know what effect it would have on our economy or knew just what scams would go on, and passed it anyway.

Captain and Sly interviewed me over the phone. They liked our segment so well, that they invited me back. "Maybe some day you'll come to Madison," Captain wrote, probably thinking it would never happen.

Completely by coincidence, Marci, the producer/cameraman/editor for the infomercial we were about to shoot, was headed to Wisconsin to attend her in-laws' 50th wedding anniversary. Wisconsin had been a hotbed of dissent because Governor Scott Walker passed a bill that eroded workers' collective bargaining rights. Rallied by public workers and protestors filling Wisconsin's State Capitol building in Madison, voters tried to unseat Governor Walker in a recall election. By June 5, 2012, the recall was deemed unsuccessful.

The protests and political engagement of Wisconsinites in 2011 and 2012 made it particularly attractive as a backdrop for the infomercial. Marci and I wanted to interview random people on the street, thinking their emotions might still be raw from the recall election's results.

On July 23rd, I sent an email to Sly's producer: "Remember how you said I should visit Wisconsin? Well, I'm coming sooner than you think! I'll be there on August 6th and I'd love to get together with both of you!"

Plus, I had to taste the cheese!

28
WISCONSIN

I'd like to know what's so progressive about a failing system of public education, an eroding manufacturing base, declining employment and wages, youth with no prospects, skills or work ethic, the alarmingly rapid expansion of the nanny state with its attendant encroachments on our liberties, the dizzying explosion of public and private debt, the utter destruction of private savings and an entire generation of asset poor boomers and gen Xers who will be utterly dependent on the state in retirement.
– John Fury
From comments under Megan McArdle's blog post called
"Why I think the GOP will have control in 2017"

The centerpiece of my strategy to fix Congress involved a 28-minute infomercial, buying national coverage, and running it for six weeks prior to election day. I intended to cut different versions—one for progressives and liberals, one for the Bible belt, and one for conservatives, the same way political pros tailor their ads.

I wanted two messages built into the infomercial: how the Pledge for Honest Candidates will save us, and that the problem with our economy is the hoarding of mass sums of cash by a few companies and individuals. Like independent presidential candidate Ross Perot used infomercials to educate the public about the national debt in 1996 and how NAFTA was a bad trade agreement for Americans, I want to show voters how their representatives did us a disservice by passing the Gramm Leach Bliley Act.

If we were all getting rich in the stock market, perhaps no one would pay attention to my infomercial. The facts have come in— 95% of the gains from 2009 to 2012 went to the top 1%. Americans have a reason to be mad, and I wanted to foment that anger with the infomercial, causing people to vote for a new game plan.

Marci, my producer, had a different idea for the infomercial. Let's tell a story. I respected her judgment because she's the expert. She imagined the opening voiceover: "America, the beautiful. The land of opportunity. A country of freedom, honor, dignity and justice for all. As parents, we want to leave a brighter future and a legacy of hope for our children. In America, anything is possible. But is the American dream still alive?" We were headed to the land of cheese to find out.

I arrived in Wisconsin on a hot, muggy day in August. It took fifteen minutes to drive from my hotel to Madison's center. All roads lead to the dominating white capitol building, whose beautiful dome is based on the District of Columbia's, and is the second largest in the country next to our U.S. Capitol's.

After I picked up Marci from her in-law's house, we zoomed back downtown to grab a bite. Before our food arrived, Marci had already whipped out her camera and asked a fellow patron if the American dream were still alive?

"I'm not a young man and I don't think the America that I live in is anything like the America I was [taught] to believe in," said the somber blue-eyed man in the restaurant. No matter what we said, he was glum.

When I asked if he had kids, he said "yes," he has children.

"Do you have hope for the future, that things will get better?" I asked.

"Yes, quite a bit, but a lot has to happen."

"Do you think getting money out of politics would be a step in the right direction?"

"Yes, I do. I'd be stunned to see it happen."

We couldn't leave him feeling down without any hope in sight, so I told him how the website would steer him toward the representatives who agreed to the Pledge for Honest Candidates, effectively taking money out of politics.

"Would you be more inclined to vote for somebody that signed the Pledge versus somebody who didn't?" I asked.

"Everything else being equal, I guess so. Yes I would."

The next day, we hurried to meet Sly in the Morning's John Sylvester, radio host at 6:15 am. Sly is a big man with a deep voice, an exhaustive knowledge of politics, and a sharp cynical wit.

Marci set up her tripod while I situated myself in Sly's guest chair. He sat in front of an enormous console with buttons galore and a huge pendulous microphone in front of his face. Sly tried to give me a hard time.

"Some might call you naïve, Judy."

"I'm the person who makes you feel that anything's possible."

"People are scared. Their 401Ks have been depleted, they're worried about their son or daughter finally moving out of the house now that they're 30, people are losing their jobs, they want to know how this relates to them." Sly swung his wrist around and pointed his index finger in my direction, cuing me.

I was oddly calm. "The most important thing is information. So if you want to know who's running in your district and who's signed this pledge to take money out of politics, you have to have somewhere to go. And what I'm recommending to people is: only vote for pledge-signers."

Sly wanted to know how many people I've reached through Writeindependent.org. I told him that I was lucky if ten thousand people heard me through my efforts and his radio show. Sly had an idea for getting me a lot of attention, quickly.

"Have you got a dog?" he asked.

"No."

"Aw. I was thinking if you had a dog, why don't you strap it on the roof of your car? That has done wonders for Mitt Romney. He has got more attention for strapping Seamus on the roof of that car. Do something crazy! I used to have LA stations on my satellite dish. Try to outrun the police. You will get every media outlet there...put something on the side of your car. Put

Writeindependent.org on the side of your car!"

As we left the studio, Marci said, "Judy, please don't do something crazy like start a police chase." She was afraid I was going to take Sly's advice.

"The temptation is there," I teased her.

"Don't do it." Then, just to make sure, she said, "I think you'll be successful without resorting to stunts."

God, I hope she's right.

All told, we conducted seventeen man-on-the-street interviews over a two-day period. The consensus was overwhelmingly that America has been sliding downhill, that it's harder to make ends meet or get ahead of the costs of living here, and the dream of retiring into a safe secure setting seems less obtainable than ever. Yet, if Americans grab onto a great idea, we willingly adopt it and promote it. We want to make life better; we look up to the sky and see no limit. It all starts with money, the engine for everything.

29
THE ECONOMICS OF FAIRNESS

Rothschild destroyed the predominance of land, by raising the system of state bonds to supreme power, thereby mobilising the property and income and at the same time endowing money with the previous privileges of the land. He thereby created a new aristocracy, it is true, but this, resting as it does on the most unreliable of elements, on money, can never play as enduringly regressive a role as the former aristocracy, which was rooted in the land, in the earth itself. For money is more fluid than water, more elusive than air, and one can gladly forgive the impertinences of the new nobility in consideration of its ephemerality. In the twinkling of an eye, it will dissolve and evaporate.
– Heinrich Heine, German Essayist 1797-1856

When we returned home, I had the enormous task of choosing a script from the hours of footage Marci shot. The thread of my message had changed to "anything is possible." For a brief moment, I considered paying for Richard Dreyfuss to voice the infomercial if he was not too expensive for an hour or two of work. I had heard that people who think positive have best outcomes. Was I being delusional? Did I fool myself into thinking I could be successful, when the chances of actually making a impact were so slim? I decided not to entertain the idea of hiring Richard Dreyfuss.

Instead, I needed an expert for the infomercial who would talk about the one thing that everybody in this country cares about— money. Polls showed that more voters listed the economy as their top hot button issue than anything else. To make Americans mad at the unfairness of our system, I thought an economist would hit the right notes. Who did I know that is an economist?

Wait! Hadn't I made friends with an economist during the conference calls with the People's Congress? When I first heard the frustration in his voice every Sunday, Mr. Peter Bearse came across as a cranky troublemaker. He kept asking John Mulkins for a clearer mission statement for our fledgling group of revolutionaries.

Peter is passionate about politics. If he had been alive at the time of the first revolution, he would have been one of America's founding fathers. Mr. Bearse cuts a tall, striking figure with kind, blue eyes, bushy grey eyebrows and white hair atop a freckled cranium. He lives in New Hampshire and ran for U.S. Congressional office three times, once as a Democrat, once as an Independent, and most recently as a Republican. An international economist and senior, Peter draws from his long experience working with government agencies and countries to carve out new economic policies. He and I made a strong connection through the conference calls because of his outspoken nature and his undaunted desire to move quickly on things. He wanted change yesterday!

When we finally spoke to each other rather than through the People's conference calls, it was like coming out of a hot car to breathe fresh air. Peter had looked at the website and saw its value. I was validated! *Here is an intelligent man, able to review my work with a critical eye, and he likes what I am doing.* I asked him to fly from his home in New Hampshire to southern California to be interviewed for the infomercial. He accepted.

Peter arrived during a week that I had Clarissa. That Monday, Clarissa fell ill with a fever. She had to stay home from school, and I had to ferry her to the doctor, to the pharmacy, to buy food so that I could make chicken soup. Normally, I love taking care of my daughter when she's sick. She stays home from school so infrequently, that it's a rare treat to have her close and docile for so many hours.

This week was different. I had an economist flying in, and my producer coming over, charging untold amounts per hour to film us doing an interview. I hadn't prepared the questions I wanted to ask

Mr. Bearse yet. My daughter lay on the couch, saying "I'm bored!" The whining got on my shredded nerves quickly. I was losing it.

"I can't get my work done!" I yelled to Clarissa. Peter was always within earshot, probably thinking I was a shrew. "If only you didn't get sick this week, I could get so much more done!"

I immediately felt awful for blaming Clarissa. She couldn't help that she was sick.

Marci set aside a chunk of her day to film us. What would I do with Clarissa so that she didn't speak up while we were recording?

I sent her to my bedroom with a whole catalog of home movies that she loves to watch over and over again.

Marci captured Peter's passion during his interview. Sitting in front of my home's stone fireplace he said, "Members of Congress do not walk in your shoes. They walk in Gucci loafers! Why do people count so little, is because big money has come to count so much. You've got the system dominated by what I call four Bigs and their close interactions with each other. Big Money, Big Government, Big Business and Big Media. Where is the little guy? Where is 'We the people,' the first three words of our Constitution?"

The infomercial showcased his anger and excitement over how to exterminate the infestation of corruption in Congress. Peter believes that a Citizen's Congress and campaign reform are the cure.

Marci and I tried to keep the infomercial under five minutes long because we didn't want to tax those Americans with short attention spans. Even three minutes of YouTube is pushing it, no matter how important the message might be. The finished video came out to seven minutes, ten seconds because we became wedded to the best clips. Now when I watch the infomercial, I wish it were much shorter and tighter.

We called it "Fix Congress: Get Money out of Politics – Original Version." When Marci gave me the final edit, I took it upon myself to tailor slight variations for each of the following groups: Green, Libertarian, Democrats, Republicans and Wealthiest People.

I made a list of all the incumbents who had voted for the Gramm Leach Bliley Act, organized them by state and district, and scrolled their names after the following statement:

Introducing
The incumbents who ruined our economy
The following incumbents voted to pass the Gramm Leach Bliley
Act, also known as the Financial Services Modernization Act of
1999. This bill essentially dismantled the last vestiges of the Glass
Steagall Act of 1933, the protective measures that kept banks and
securities honest and in check. The passage of Gramm Leach
Bliley paved the way for the 2008 economic crisis and the current
recession. Do you want to re-elect these people again?[18]

It wasn't enough to include the names of the people who helped pass this act. I needed to communicate to the different parties and factions with my secret weapon—music. I set the list of incumbents who ruined our economy to different tunes for each version.

I cut a "Wealthiest People" rendition of the infomercial using the track "Fill Her Up" by Sting. This is the most haunting message of all, because it asks for a reckoning. It starts out a little country, and ends with a beautiful gospel-like, ethereal walk through the woods where the main character greets his conscience. I thought this would work where God didn't, for the non-believers. Music can do amazing things when all else fails.

Getting the video out was my next hurdle. I sent it to everyone on my email list asking them to network it widely. One of my gardening friends sent me a great suggestion—see if I can get it on national television via public access stations.

I was wild for this idea. I quickly blasted emails to every station across the U.S., enlisting the help of the Filipinas, Wella and Kim, who had helped me post every candidate's platform on Writeindependent.org. I could just imagine the station managers who received the infomercial, the culmination of my work and prayers for the past year and a half, thinking that this is truly unique. I wasn't Occupy, with my fist in the air. I wasn't a Tea Partier, shouting against taxation. I was just a Mom, trying to put the screws to Congress to restore the American Dream.

---

[18] See Appendix 1 for the list of incumbents who signed the Gramm Leach Bliley Act.

The infomercial was well-received by the public access channels' personnel. A few stations couldn't air it. Most of the station managers requested that someone local submit it. A handful wanted me to sign up as a provider of content, requiring me to fill out forms, submit them, and wait for an answer. I just didn't have enough time to go through all the necessary machinations to accomplish my goal. All told, I was able to give my infomercial to about a dozen public access stations that would fit it into their lineup. I also sent the audio of the infomercial to radio stations, hoping they would take the audio file and run with it.

Before I was to find out how many hits the website would get from all this activity, I had to do one more thing to change the world as we know it and restore people power.

30
THE BLACK BOX

Citizens must read and think, or perish from the earth
as slaves to those who control money.
There is only one thing that matters more than money
in this world, and that is the vote.
– Robert Steele, in a review of
Noam Chomsky's book, *Profit Over People*

We have a serious democracy problem in our country. Maybe our troops should be fighting for democracy right here at home. Eligible voters have dropped out, refuse to vote, or feel ambivalent about voting. "What difference is it going to make?" many of my friends ask me. In the 2014 midterm elections, less than 37% of age-appropriate, registered Americans participated. We have a right to be concerned, because even when we are allowed to vote, are "they" counting our votes correctly? How can we be sure?

The topics highest on my list of concerns are:

1. Voter Suppression
2. Voter Intimidation
3. Computer Vote Tampering and Vote Counting Irregularities
4. The Electoral System
5. Lack of Representative Voting Systems, i.e. First Past The Post vs Instant Runoff Voting
6. "Top Two" Voting

1. Voter suppression

A simple way to stop voters from voting is to make it appear that voting isn't working. Whether it means Americans believe their parties no longer represent them, that the ballot box is rigged, or that Congress is whack and no amount of voting is going to change that fact, voter suppression is happening if people aren't showing up at the polls.

Voter suppression comes in many forms. In June 2013, the Supreme Court struck down Article 5 of the civil rights movement's hard-won Voting Rights Act of 1965. Article 5 required nine states (Alabama, Alaska, Arizona, Georgia, Louisiana, Mississippi, South Carolina, Texas and Virginia) to obtain federal pre-approval to enact or enforce voting laws.

States have been angling for their own laws to crack down on voting rights. Before 2006, no state required a government-issued photo ID in order to vote. Now, 30 states have some form of voter ID requirement.

One benefit of the Supreme Court ruling is that it allows states to more easily enact online registration, which twenty states have implemented. The Brennan Center for Justice, a nonpartisan law and policy institute seeking to improve our systems of democracy and justice, asserts that sixteen states now have better access to voting.

However, voter ID laws aren't part of that better access. The assumption is that ID's will prevent voter fraud. Brennan Center for Justice states in a 2006 fact sheet that it doesn't make sense for someone to pretend to be someone else. "Each act of voter fraud risks five years in prison and a $10,000 fine—but yields at most one incremental vote. The single vote is simply not worth the price. Because voter fraud is essentially irrational, it is not surprising that no credible evidence suggests a voter fraud epidemic." Despite repeated investigations into allegations of voter fraud, including a five-year examination by G.W. Bush Jr.'s Department of Justice, there is not enough evidence to say that it's as big a problem as the disenfranchisement of many people who would struggle to produce an ID where states now require them.

"In-person voter impersonation on Election Day, which prompted 37 state legislatures to enact or consider tough voter ID laws, is virtually non-existent," writes investigative journalists

Natasha Khan and Corbin Carson as part of their News21 report called "Who Can Vote?"

Why is it hard for voters to obtain the proper ID? Can't they just show their driver's license? There are many reasons why this logic breaks down. Families and students who have recently moved won't have the correct address on their driver's license, which disqualifies them from voting in states with strict ID laws. And many people don't drive, hard as that may seem to those of us who do.

If you don't drive, how do you get a government-approved photo ID? You have to present your birth certificate to the proper authorities. Elderly people have difficulty placing their hands on their birth certificates. In fact, people who were not born in a hospital often don't have birth certificates. For poor people, the cost of obtaining a government-approved ID is prohibitive, especially when combining the fee with transportation costs to the proper government building. And there's a catch 22—to obtain your birth certificate, you often need a photo ID, but to obtain the photo ID, you need a birth certificate. So if you were born at home with a midwife, or if you were born in a state that requires you to produce a photo ID to get your birth certificate, you may be out of luck.

How many people don't have photo ID's in this country? The numbers are significant. I'm referring to *Americans*. The Brennan Institute conducted a thorough study and found it to be around 11%, or 1 in 10 Americans for whom obtaining a photo ID is difficult or impossible. Their report "conclusively demonstrates that this promise of free voter ID is a mirage. In the real world, poor voters find shuttered offices, long trips without cars or with spotty or no bus service, and sometimes prohibitive costs."

The cost of voter restriction laws to our democracy is great. Voter ID laws disproportionately disenfranchise the elderly, the poor, non-drivers, and students—those who typically don't vote Republican. States with elections that could have been swayed by discouraged voters in 2014 were: North Carolina's state senate, Kansas's governor, Virginia's U.S. Senate, and Florida's governor.

In Virginia's 2014 election, strict ID laws prevented 198,000 "active Virginia voters," who did not have acceptable identification according to the Virginia Board of Elections, from exercising a basic right as a U.S. citizen. To give you an idea how close these elections were, Senator Mark Warner bested challenger Ed Gillespie by only 12,000 votes, a lot less than those disenfranchised by ID laws.

In Florida, incumbent Governor Rick Scott squeaked by Charlie Crist with a 1.2% margin. Writes Wendy Weiser, Director of the Democracy Program at the Brennan Center for Justice at NYU School of Law, "Perhaps the most significant for this election was a decision by Scott and his clemency board to make it virtually impossible for the more than 1.3 million Floridians who were formerly convicted of crimes but have done their time and paid their debt to society to have their voting rights restored."

Another voter suppression tactic are laws that make it difficult for volunteers to help eligible citizens register to vote. Florida's House Bill 1355 for elections (not to be confused with HB 1355 Purchase of Firearms by Mentally Ill Persons) became effective in May of 2011. The voting-rights-restrictive HB 1355, that Governor Scott signed, sets forth crazy requirements for any group wanting to register new voters. The League of Women Voters (LWV) whose 91-year history of volunteering without any problems were so discouraged by Scott's law that they stopped helping citizens register in Florida. The new rules required that LWV members pre-register with the state, sign an affidavit under penalty of perjury listing all criminal penalties for any false registration, and run each registration form over to a county official within 48 hours. Oh, and each registrant had to carefully note the time they signed their form so that the county official could make sure the LWV worker got it there before the 48 hour buzzer rang. If the LWV volunteer messed up, she could personally face a $5,000 fine, third degree felony, and up to five years in prison!

Florida is not an isolated case. Ohio's Secretary of State Ken Blackwell instituted rules that make it "extremely difficult for small churches and other nonprofit organizations to hire and train voter registration workers—and they expose voter registration workers to felony charges for making mistakes."

Six weeks after the Supreme Court's decision to strike down Article 5, North Carolina passed some of the most restrictive voter laws in the country. It banned same-day registration, pre-registration for young voters, eliminated out-of-precinct provisional ballots, shortened the early voting period by one week, and disallowed extending polling place hours in case there were long lines. North Carolina's new laws will also require an ID as of 2016.

These requirements violate the Constitution because they are considered a poll tax. ID's cost time and money to obtain, and the poorer the citizen, the less time and/or money they have to search for an ID.

Who knows if Republican Thom Tillis would have defeated incumbent Democrat Kay Hagen in 2014's U.S. Senate race in North Carolina without all these restrictions? Rev. William Barber, the preacher credited for the "Moral Monday" movement, rallied a couple hundred activists in Greensboro, North Carolina's Government Square to get out the vote. As Barber explains, "for us the right to vote is not just a constitutional matter, but a right born out of struggle, out of sacrifice and a gift from the God of justice." The election ended with only a two percent spread, but the Republican prevailed despite Barber's Moral Monday activists whose efforts increased black voter turnout 45% over 2010 numbers.

2. Voter Intimidation

Incumbent Mitch McConnell sent out warnings to Kentucky voters that read: ELECTION VIOLATION NOTICE. You are at risk of acting on fraudulent information that has been targeted for citizens living in County_____." If you read further, you find that, "This document serves as a notification that you, as a resident of Kentucky and a registered voter in the aforementioned Commonwealth of fraudulent information that is being deliberately spread to voters in your area," then goes on to list the pack of lies his opponent, Alison Lundergan Grimes purportedly said. However, the piece of mail doesn't look like your typical ad. It reads like a warning.

Lundergan Grimes filed charges against McConnell on two counts of felony. McConnell may have violated Kentucky state law KRS 516.030 for Forgery in the Second Degree, intent to deceive with falsely designated "official" documents, and KRS 119.115, unlawfully attempting to intimidate voters.

Kentuckian college newspaper, *Berea Citizen*, published an ad warning students that if they were improperly registered, they could "face significant penalties" and have their right to vote challenged. Jonah Cabiles, campus organizer for the grassroots organization that filed a complaint with the Attorney General said that the words chosen sounded like "this really heavy legal term to intimidate student voters, especially those who ...aren't really specific with the Kentucky Revised Statute."

That's soft core intimidation compared with the "Wisconsin Poll Watcher Militia" who proudly advertised on Facebook that they will carry guns to the 2014 polls in search of citizens who might have warrants for dodging taxes. "Some will be headed to some of Milwaukee, Racine, and Beloit's worst areas," read one Facebook post. "We will be armed with a list of people to look for at each location." Radio host Rush Limbaugh gave a nod to the group, tying the tax evaders to the liberals who wanted to oust Governor Scott Walker. Another post at the militia's page said, "We can assure you that we will be targeting all democrats, not just the black ones. If you think we meant blacks only it is because you are a racist who thinks the only people with warrants are black. We know better because we have a nice list of people who are wanted democrat activist types. Most are actually white. We will target everyone."

The Facebook page for the militia has been taken down, because all I could find is a page called "Watching the 'Wisconsin Poll Watcher Militia.'" However, the sentiments written by the group were well documented online by other sources.

3. Computer Vote Tampering and Vote Counting Irregularities

The 2014 midterm election results may have been a complete farce. All it takes is one insider who knows how to flip a switch and the outcome changes. When it comes to voting, should we trust our votes to a computer that doesn't even spit out a receipt for confirmation? Do you trust your voting machine manufacturer?

Private companies like ES&S, Dominion (previously of Diebold or Sequoia), Smartmatic, and Hart Intercivic make most of the electronic voting machines. Three of five board members at Hart Intercivic are board members at HIG Capital, a global private equity firm that made a significant investment in the voting machine company. The Washington Post reported that "HIG employees as a whole have donated $338,000 to the Romney campaign this year, according to Open Secrets." Hart supplied the electronic voting machines that were used in the 2012 elections in precincts in Ohio, Texas, Oklahoma, Washington, Colorado and many other states.

These connections between candidates and voting machines are too close for my comfort. But it isn't just the cozy relationship that matters. It's important to know who has their hands on the ballots and the votes. In study after study, electronic machines have proven incredibly easy to rig. At Princeton University, researchers found that in less than one minute, a criminal could bypass the lock using a simple tool and replace the memory card with one containing malicious code. It's so easy to open the box that the researchers show how it is done in a video. "Any desired algorithm can be used to determine which votes to steal and to which candidate or candidates to transfer the stolen votes."

The abstract of the Princeton study goes on: "Malicious software running on a single voting machine can steal votes with very little risk of detection. The malicious software can modify all of the records, audit logs, and counter kept by the voting machine so that even careful forensic examination … will find nothing amiss." One machine can be rigged within less than a minute and then it goes viral. "An attacker could infect a large population of machines while only having temporary access to a single machine or memory card." And bear in mind, if you work for the elections office, you don't even need a key.

It really comes down to this: do you trust the people counting your ballot? "In more than 3,000 counties, parishes and independent cities, voter registration and precinct polling places are still controlled by party functionaries…whose loyalty resides with the leaders of their particular faction, rather than with the people" writes John R. MacArthur, author of *You Can't Be President: The Outrageous Barriers to Democracy in America*.

Besides computer rigging, there is the problem of absentee ballots. My precinct does "polling place voting" where the poll workers have a long list of neighbors they check off as each warm body takes a ballot. This system assures that each person is who they say they are and each voter casts only one vote. By comparison, Oregon and Washington mail out ballots whether you ask for them or not. Washington state has become the first to have nearly all mail-in voting. In both states, to verify that the voter is authentic, human counters compare signatures on the registration form to the ballot.

A voter with a legitimate reason to use an absentee ballot, but who forgets to include a copy of their photo ID when mailing it in, may have their vote tossed out unless they hand carry their paperwork to the proper authorities. To prevent these problems, visit http://www.longdistancevoter.org/forms to find out about absentee ballots.

In 2012, one in five Americans (27 million people), voted by absentee ballot. Of those, 258,000 absentee ballots were thrown out for arriving late in the mail, not having valid signatures, not having a matching signature, or "other."

If a voter forgets to bring his ID to the polls, shows up at the wrong precinct, or his name isn't listed on the roll, he can receive a *provisional ballot* and has a few days to clear up the problem. However, many poll workers don't know how to instruct voters to use their provisional ballot, and sometimes they don't offer them. Project Vote reports that in the 2006 general election, fifteen states rejected more than 50% of their provisional ballots, Kentucky counting less than 7%. Voters who are experiencing difficulties at the poll can call 866-OUR-VOTE for help.

After the 2014 midterms, Jim Allen, a spokesperson for the Chicago Board of Elections, said, "We did have a rocky start in a number of polling places where we had insufficient judges and/or equipment issues," citing that 2,000 election judges didn't show up as planned. It may have been a result of a "new dirty trick" whereby robocalls placed specifically to the judges instructed them to go to training sessions and told them how to vote. "You're telling people how to vote in a federal election and implying that it has to do with their employment."

Voting expert Bev Harris, author of *Black Box Voting: Ballot Tampering in the 21st Century*, describes the black box as "any voting system in which the mechanisms for recording and/or tabulating the vote are hidden from the voter, and/or the mechanism lacks a tangible record of the vote cast."

In her book, Ms. Harris recommends a method for

authenticating our votes. She writes, "In the U.S., we complain that our citizens don't think their vote matters. Here's a concept: Let people *see* their vote. Not a video representation of a vote hiding in a black box, but the *actual vote*. Count votes before they leave the neighborhood. Invite people in to watch the counting. And add a 21st century twist: install a web camera, so citizens can watch the vote-counting live, on the Internet."

I made friends at the League of Women Voters and asked the President of the Los Angeles chapter for help organizing a voter veracity program throughout the League. He referred me to a woman named Judy Alter who, since 2003, has dedicated her life to making sure our votes are counted accurately. Judy works with the Election Defense Alliance and Protectcaliforniaballots.org. She said, "ten thousand people [who fight for accurate vote counting] can't stop the computer insiders who rig the elections, but we can demand a return to paper ballots. 78% of the world's democracies use paper ballots."

Judy recommended using Poll Tape Capture to compare the actual count at each precinct against the reported count. It's up to us, the voters who want to track the ballots, to do the counting. Those who want to perform this important public service can find instructions in Appendix 10, Poll Tape Capture Instructions for Volunteers. In 2012, my friends at the League and I couldn't supply enough manpower or collective will to conduct an organized effort to ensure voter veracity. Perhaps 2016 will be different.

4. The Electoral College

Article II Section 1 of the Constitution describes the strange process of electors choosing the President. Presently, three hurdles must be overcome if we are to vote in a third party, and it's absolutely necessary to understand who these "electors" are and how they are chosen before we can strategize.

The legislature of each State appoints the same quantity of electors as the number of Congressmen (House Representatives plus Senators) in the manner the State see fit. Since there are 435 members in the House and 100 Senators, plus three electors from D.C., the total number of electors is 538. Generally, the electors are party leaders, persons who have ties with the presidential candidates or State elected officials. Theoretically, Americans are supposed to be choosing the electors, but have you ever been asked to select an elector to represent all the voters in your area? Hurdle number one is that the elector is already hand-picked by one or the other party.

In a perfect world, electors vote based on the majority's wishes for their geographical area. However, thanks to gerrymandering, the process whereby district borders have been carved out so that it's guaranteed to swing either Republican or Democrat, many voters feel as though they'll never be represented. Hurdle number two is that electors' districts have been rigged to favor a specific party.

And the last hurdle is the "faithless elector." That's the elector who refuses to vote for the people's preferred candidate, regardless of the majority winner. If an elector sees that the third option won but the vote is close, will he choose the people's candidate, or his party's candidate?

Finally, after all the electors have cast their ballot, if there is no clear winner with at least 270 electoral votes, a scary scenario may happen. It's called a "contingent election," the details of which are found in the 12th Amendment. If the electoral votes are split three ways, then the House of Representatives chooses our next President. Each State casts one vote for President (and the winner is the one who receives at least 26 votes). For Vice President, each Senator votes for one of the top two VP electoral vote getters, with the winner decided by obtaining at least 51 votes.

The 12th Amendment does not specify whether it's the outgoing House or the newly elected House that determines the President. However, the contingent election is likely to be held on January 6th, after the new members take (or return to) their offices. If the present Congress is called upon to conduct the vote, our past will come back to haunt us because the citizens who voted in 2014's midterms, the smallest percentage of voters since 1942, who selected today's GOP-led Congress, have a crack at disappointing the majority of citizens by choosing the next President for us.

Ultimately, we need to use our people power to abolish the electoral college and replace it with direct popular election of the President. Until that happens, Americans need to organize their support to back a third option. The third option needs to be so popular, the winner so undeniable, that the electors must give the people who they want for President!

5. Lack of Representative Voting Systems
Or How Votes are Calculated

Before I developed Writeindependent.org, I didn't understand First Past The Post (also called winner-take-all), Instant Runoff Voting (IRV), Ranked Choice, or Range Voting. I just assumed that my vote got handled like all votes do: one person, one vote.

The nomination process and the way our votes are calculated influences the outcome so much that it's hardly democratic at all. William Poundstone, author of *Gaming the Vote: Why Elections Aren't Fair and What We Can Do About It*, wrote "The smart operators who run the show know how easily it's rigged. Every 'paradox' of voting is an opportunity for insiders to force the outcome they desire."

Right now, we have First Past The Post. That means the winner is the person with the highest number of votes. But, is that person always who the majority wanted? No! A member of Congress can win with only a small 15% of the total number of votes, if everyone else just gets a little less. First Past The Post systems end up with just two parties in control; they mathematically devolve into a lesser of two evils situation. What's worse, once the two-party system is firmly in place, it creates a spoiler effect, where the third party who tries to get a toe-hold is demonized for making the worst evil win by taking votes away from the lesser evil.

So what's a better way of choosing a winner?

Ranked Choice Voting, also called Alternative Voting or Instant Runoff Voting (IRV) gives you a chance to rank the candidates from your most favored to your least, leaving blank the candidates you don't like at all. When the votes are counted, the candidate who gets the least 1st place votes is eliminated. Those who voted for the eliminated candidate give their vote to their 2nd choice. The candidate with the least votes is eliminated. And so on. Once a candidate reaches a majority of votes, they win. With Ranked Choice Voting, we have the ability to more accurately show our preferences, and it releases us from choosing the lesser of two evils or causing a spoiler effect. San Francisco began using IRV voting in 2004, but changed the name from "Instant Runoff" to "Ranked Choice" because, rather than being instantaneous, it took days to calculate the vote.

The last system that I'll cover is the one you're probably familiar with, because you use it every time you rate a book or a movie on the Internet. It's called "Range Voting," the method recommended by Poundstone. You may have seen five- and ten-star rating systems on Amazon and IMDb (Internet Movie Database). Voters' rankings are totaled and averaged out, so a movie might have a score of 7.3 (if they're good) or 2.4 (if they're not). To use the range voting system, you would see a ballot on election day that looks like this:

Names	1	2	3	4	5	6	7	8	9	10
Candidate A						X				
Candidate B										X
Candidate C	X									

Range voting eliminates spoilers and splitting the vote between two good candidates. It gives voters a chance to show how much they dislike someone, rather than just being silent. For these reasons, Range Voting is superior to Instant Runoff Voting, in my humble opinion.

6. Top Two System

Three states have a "Top Two" system for federal candidates whereby only the Top Two vote-getters advance to the general election, irrespective of party affiliation: California, Washington, and Louisiana. I'm drawing your attention to Top Two because the same forces who are trying to suppress, manipulate, and frustrate the process of voting may also be in the process of getting Top Two passed in *your* state.

I don't like Top Two because it:
a. restricts the number of candidates running for office.
b. reduces the amount of issues and solutions that tend to be discussed during debates.
c. allows the moneyed interests to bathe each opponent in cash, concentrating their influence on fewer candidates in the run-up to the general election.

d. confuses voters because it allows the candidate to change his party affiliation in the middle of the race. (A Republican can say he's a Democrat, if only to pick up the liberal vote.)

e. favors the person raising the most money the earliest.

f. Has all the problems that First Past The Post has, but does so on steroids because it cements those problems into place for the entire general election period:
   - favors incumbents
   - makes gerrymandering work easier
   - tends to promote the worst candidates through vote-splitting and the spoiler effect during the primary

Don't believe the hype if "Open Primaries" or Top Two comes to your state. They will try to convince you that it improves the democratic experience, but it's just the opposite.

Even if we take on these voting issues, several other problems stand in the way of effective representation. Gerrymandering, the media, polling, and the parties' nomination process each have negative impacts on our democracy.

States that have been gerrymandered to death cannot possibly reflect the voters' wishes, as district lines are drawn to purposely "purify" a geographic area to assure one party's victory. Maryland, North Carolina, Louisiana, West Virginia, and Illinois head the list of the most rigged districts, according to a study done by Azavea, my favorite mapping and data mining company. U.S. District Judge Paul Niemeyer said of Maryland's 3rd District that it resembled "a broken-winged pterodactyl, lying prostrate." The shameful shapes of gerrymandered districts make it obvious that political operatives draw the lines to control voting outcomes. Christopher Ingraham, a Washington Post blogger, conducted his own analysis of the least compact, most tortured-looking districts and concluded that "the Democrats are under-represented by about 18 seats in the House, relative to their vote share in the 2012 election."

Besides passing legislation to smooth out district lines and apportioning them according to the Constitution (that says districts must be drawn up as "contiguous and compact territory and containing as nearly as practicable an equal number of inhabitants"), communities experiencing difficulties should bring suit against redistricting based on its violation of Section 2 of the Voting Rights Act of 1965.

Finally, to overcome the misinformation of the media and polls discouraging voters from choosing outlier candidates, local efforts must be made to conduct debates earlier in the election season, before the primaries. And don't let the political pros set the discussion topics and questions. If your district is concerned about the rise of the military state, fracking, or storm preparation and remediation, conduct your own debates online. If you're worried about the Trans Pacific Partnership, find out where they stand before you vote for them. If you want to know if they've signed a pledge to support a 28th Amendment to overturn *Citizens United v. FEC* and the American Anti-Corruption Act, now is the time to nail them! Not after the elections; then it's too late. Get to know the people you're voting for. Don't let them railroad you.

Will you join me in getting rid of the black box and making elections meaningful? Let's bring back paper ballots, tally them in public view on election night at the precincts where the votes are cast, and videotape the proceedings. We must make voting accessible to every citizen who wants to participate, and use the Internet to rally political support for the best candidates and solutions via a website like Writeindependent.org.

In the meantime, "high [voter] turnout can overcome the margin of manipulation," says Greg Palast, author of *Billionaires and Ballot Bandits*. The more the public participates politically, the better able we are to protect our children from harmful practices such as lopsided trade agreements, subsidies for the rich, and environmental mayhem.

Please vote during this coming election. As Eugene Debs, the activist who fought for people's rights said, "It's better to vote for what you want and not get it than to vote for what you don't want and get it." Only one thing stands in the way of a collective belief that someone other than a Republican or a Democrat can take the highest office in the land. But it's also potentially a powerful tool for convincing voters that it can be done. Television.

31
TELEVISION TIME

I've been struggling now for years, to tell the American public
what's been going on. I haven't gotten through, because this
[financial] group has bought up the press and has been spreading
disinformation systematically. That undermines the whole point of
a democracy. How can voters vote without an informed opinion,
without the information that they're entitled to? So this strangle-
hold on information is going to end in very short order.
– Karen Hudes, former attorney at the World Bank

"Television is democracy at its ugliest," wrote Paddy Chayefksy, author of the movie *Network*. The problem is that the media tries to persuade you to believe the messages that the monopolies want you to believe, even if that information goes against your own best interests.

TVP, a non-profit trade association for the U.S. commercial television industry, reported "television is by far the largest segment of political media spending. On top of this continued dominance, TV stations' total political revenue has been growing at an extremely high rate: $1.5 billion in 2008, $2.1 billion in 2010 (+40%) and $2.9 billion in 2012 (+38%)" This is why media moguls and empires will assiduously oppose campaign reform and re-regulation of their industry. They've benefited from legislation such as the Telecommunications Reform Act of 1996 that allowed media companies to consolidate and grow into huge monsters covering our cities and rural areas, spanning the mountains, valleys, and farms. They've monopolized our geography, thus blanketing the USA with their messages. To fight back, we need to write new legislation that reigns in superpowers of media.

Let's turn this around. Don't we, the people, own our broadcast airwaves and regulate them ourselves through the FCC? How can people power use television time to inject some sanity into government?

During a People's Congress phone conference, guest speaker Duane Elgin, author of *Promise Ahead: A Vision of Hope and Action for Humanity's Future*, told his amazing story of obtaining an hour of prime time television in 1985. Mr. Elgin looks and sounds like an old mountain man, with white beard and soft voice. He spoke about citizens' legal rights to the airwaves, saying that broadcasters are obligated "to serve the 'public interest, convenience, and necessity' before their own profits."

The 1969 Supreme Court case that supports this concept can be found in the opinion on *Red Lion Broadcasting Co., Inc. V. Federal Communications Commission*, delivered by Mr. Justice White:

> No one has a First Amendment right to a license or to monopolize a radio [or television] frequency; to deny a station license because "the public interest" requires it "is not a denial of free speech."
>
> By the same token, as far as the First Amendment is concerned, those who are licensed stand no better than those to whom licenses are refused. A license permits broadcasting, but the licensee has no constitutional right to be the one who holds the license or to monopolize a radio [television] frequency to the exclusion of his fellow citizens. There is nothing in the First Amendment which prevents the Government from requiring a licensee to share his frequency with others and to conduct himself as a proxy or fiduciary with obligations to present those views and voices which are representative of his community and which would otherwise, by necessity, be barred from the airwaves.

In 1985, the Cold War had been going on for decades and Elgin wondered if the press had been reporting material that was representative of the community in which they lived. Elgin and his activist friends gathered enough support in the greater San Francisco area to obtain an hour of prime time television so that a sampling of citizens could broadcast their views about the Soviet Union and the Cold War. The resultant town hall style meeting aired on ABC. Their television audience was finally able to see that the attitudes of the reporters and commentators on TV did not represent those of the public, despite war propaganda.

Mr. Elgin compiled a "how to" kit for obtaining that hour of prime time, the community involvement necessary and legal arguments that lay out citizens' rights. He writes, "When a society enters an era of change and people don't know what their fellow citizens think and feel about critical choices, then neither the public nor the politicians know what is possible." He recommends Electronic Town Meetings (ETMs) to solve this problem.

Elgin suggests three steps toward developing dialogue between community members and federal policy makers. First, create an independent, non-profit "Community Voice" organization in each municipality so that Town Hall participants work under one umbrella. Second, "make a legal request for prime-time from local television broadcasters (ABC, CBS, NBC, and FOX) for a series of ongoing Electronic Town Meetings" and third, work in cooperation with local broadcasters to produce ETMs with real-time conference calling and web interaction, opening the conversation to the public. The goal is to make the ETM as close as possible to an in-person Town Hall Meeting. It would necessitate deliberation in relatively small groups. The ultimate point of a meeting is to share viewpoints and offer solutions.

Criticism of this type of communication comes from those who haven't tried it and who wish to keep the status quo. Haven't we suffered enough political ads that bash the opposite party's candidate? Aren't we tired of the same old talking points without hearing a discussion regarding the electorate's top concerns? Why haven't we seen any of the news networks deconstruct the Trans Pacific Partnership into its parts to explain it?

I see this as the great hope for our democracy. Most importantly, we would have the basis for a People's and Citizen's Congress, linking all the Electronic Town Meetings across the country, forming a new arm of government run by our grass roots.

At no time is the message of the media more important than during the presidential debates when the candidates are laying out their vision for your future. There are two choices and that's it, or so the public is led to believe.

Election day was fast approaching, and I still hadn't decided whom I wanted for President. Suddenly, I found another independent presidential debate online that could not be missed.

32
THE INTERNET SAVES DEMOCRACY

Every time you are tempted to react in the same old way,
ask if you want to be a prisoner
of the past or a pioneer of the future.
— Deepak Chopra

The Democrat versus Republican debates are hosted by a private organization called the Commission on Presidential Debates that has excluded everyone running for President except two people. In order to qualify for their debates, a participant must gain ballot access in enough states to achieve the 270 electoral votes necessary to win *and* demonstrate "a level of support of at least 15 percent of the national electorate, as determined by five selected national public opinion polling organizations, using the average of those organizations' most recent publicly-reported results." They set the bar so high, it's nearly impossible for anyone but the two parties' hand-selected poster candidates to make it.

Who made the Commission on Presidential Debates God?

After they winnow out all but two presumed choices, the Commission on Presidential Debates narrows down the areas of discussion as well. None of the questions asked of Obama nor Romney in the 2012 debates used the words "global warming" or "climate change" fearing it would disenchant voters. They completely ignored the issues of trade bills, GMOs, poverty and the failed war on drugs.

When all the other candidates get snubbed enough, we don't have to settle for somebody else's idea of a debate. We can start our own conversation, the way we did at Writeindependent.org. The Greens, Libertarians, Constitutional Party, Justice Party, etc. weren't taking advantage of my forum. *Where were the third parties debating,* I wondered?

I found my answer in an email from Santa Claus. "Here's a bit more on the 'Democracy Now!' debates," he wrote four days before they were scheduled to begin. "Democracy Now!" is a non-profit, viewer and listener-sponsored independent global newscast where host Amy Goodman focuses on stories that don't get reported in the mainstream media. On October 23rd, just after I finished my ninth presidential debate, Free And Equal Elections Foundation held third party debates in Chicago. It was moderated by *Larry King Live's* Larry King and Christina Tobin, elections activist and CEO of Free and Equal. *Democracy Now!* broadcast the event through television, Internet, radio, satellite and cable TV to an audience of tens of millions.

I called Ms. Tobin to ask how they selected their participants. She said to meet Free and Equal Elections Foundation's criteria, candidates had to obtain ballot access in at least 35 states (enough to qualify for an electoral college win) and receive one percent support in a national poll. Four presidential hopefuls qualified for the debate: Virgil Goode of the Constitution Party, Gary Johnson of the Libertarian Party, Rocky Anderson of the Justice Party, and Dr. Jill Stein of the Green Party.

Rocky Anderson spoke about income disparity and poverty; Jill Stein said we must repeal the Patriot Act and put an end to FISA and the Military Use of Force Act's overbearing powers. The more conservative candidates Virgil Goode and Gary Johnson wanted to reduce military expenditures to balance the budget. Of the six questions asked at Free & Equal's debate, five were submitted by social media such as Facebook, Reddit, Twitter, and Tout. They asked questions about illegal drugs, defense spending and the role of the military, college funding, and the National Defense Authorization Act's indefinite detention of Americans (Section 1021) and the Top Two system of ruling out candidates. I can't imagine the Commission on Presidential Debates allowing these topics in their forum!

In my opinion, Free and Equal's debates were too little, too late. Their final debate was on November 5, 2012, the day before the election. I expect that 2016 will be different because this country is poised for a frenzy of activism. When I asked Ms. Tobin about 2016, she said she believes many more candidates will qualify for the next debates because "more voters are ready for real change than ever before."

But we need to start *earlier*. If we started asking questions of presidential candidates one or even two years prior to November, it is possible that before long before the election, we will already know who we want for President. We need to edit the debates down to one video per question, so that voters can seek out answers to their specific concerns.

With existing technology, the electorate can ask the candidates a question from their cell phone, computer in the kitchen or laptop at Starbucks. On a well-designed website, voters will find their area of interest and type in a new question if it hasn't already been framed by someone else. Let's get to know the people who want to be President on a personal level, and watch them emerge from the general public through Internet debates, electronic town hall meetings, or their platform posted online. A leader can be brought to the forefront by our citizens, like cream rising. We won't need four million dollars to promote candidates when the debates go viral.

But a good leader plugged into a huge corrupt system is going to be infected by the corruption. Just replacing the war-torn stars and stripes top-hat on Uncle Sam's poor wretched head doesn't cure his systemic illness. I still had my sights set on Congress, and I wasn't giving up on my dream to replace those soulless, stubborn tools of the über wealthy.

33
THE FUNDRAISER

*The question here is not just about one of the numerous individual
cases in the struggle between a truth powerless to act and a power
that has become the enemy of truth. It is really a question of the
absolutely concrete demonstration of the point at which this
struggle at any moment becomes man's duty as man...*
– Martin Buber, Israeli philosopher 1878-1965

From the start, I knew Writeindependent.org needed money to
operate and advertise. In January of 2012, I began dreaming of a
huge outdoor fundraiser concert. I set my sights on Terranea, a
four-star seaside resort in my hometown of beautiful Palos Verdes.
Meaning 'new earth' Terranea's name hints at their eco-friendly
conservation practices. With its red-tiled roofs and Mediterranean
architecture sitting atop dramatic cliffs dropping into the beautiful
blue ocean, it would attract A-listers all the way from Beverly
Hills. In my fantasy:

*On the lawns of Terranea, a large stage with a public address
system faces the Pacific. Champagne fountains and fine crystal
flutes are neatly arranged on white linen tablecloths inside huge
white tents flanking the audience up and down the sides of the
field. Enormous arrangements of rich red, long stemmed roses
with white sprays of baby's breath and blueberry greens decorate*

the tabletops.

The event is reminiscent of the rock festival fundraiser Bonnaroo, but with a dash of panache and the haughtiness of Bohemian Grove. To match the size and scope of our mission's ambition, thousands of smiling guests fill the wide venue, seized with the power to transform our country. People over profits! An ocean of patriotic devotion. We aren't going to ask Congress "pretty please behave yourselves." Instead of asking permission, we're demanding transition!

Philanthropic artists bring guitars, instruments and painted canvases for auction. Hollywood's most celebrated directors and producers edited together a trailer featuring scenes from upcoming movies that have a "save the world" theme. The guests fly in from distant points, arriving in stretch limos.

Our master of ceremonies, Stephen Colbert, introduces the first guest, P!nk, with her number "Let's Get This Party Started!" She runs on stage pumping her fist, yelling "'Bout time we did something to rock the You S of A! Watch us"! Then she bounces on her heels three times, and the drum's beats reverberate through the ground, almost lifting everyone off the grass.

P!nk's trademark confidence and boldness proudly rallies the crowd into a frenzy. After her uplifting, party-inducing number, she announces the second musical group. They take the stage like troopers, honored to speak out about an issue that our government is mucking up.

Other artists, well-known for their activism, each take their turn. U2, The Clash, Sting, Radiohead, Bob Dylan, Coldplay, Peter Gabriel, Bruce Springsteen, Rage Against the Machine! We webcast the event, making everyone in the USA feel like a participant in real time. The webcast drives a fundraiser in the cloud in addition to the one on the ground. As the musicians sip champagne, make toasts, and clink their glasses on the field, computers allow fans to Skype the party.

In just one evening we raised four million dollars! Enough to do the six-week media blitz I had planned over a year ago!

It is possible to do such a thing because the stakes are so great. We're reclaiming our government, the engine that runs commerce, decides just how free we are, and how our economy shall play out. It all makes sense.

I needed help to carry out this endeavor. I enlisted my neighbor, Britta Wichers, an event planner extraordinaire with the same kind of upbeat attitude that I have. She's a feisty, buxom blonde with an infectious smile and a bold, raucous laugh. Before she became a suburban mother of two boys, she worked for bands Aerosmith, Guns & Roses, and KISS as a Production Coordinator. We met at her house way back in January, in the early stages of the website, to hatch our plans.

Britta recommended two things: that I assign a chairperson who would be the "rainmaker" type with a list of friends and guests to invite, and that I find silent auction items.

My neighbor and the president of my nonprofit corporation, Maria, said that she wouldn't have time to be my chairperson, but she had a list of friends whom she could invite. She also suggested that I list the fundraiser with Code Pink, an anti-war charity that works to redirect war funding into healthcare, education, green jobs and other life-affirming activities.

I met Maria for coffee at Terranea to imbue her with my vision. When I related my exploits to her, she listened and encouraged me. Through brainstorming and laughter, she gave her heartfelt support.

I wrote a letter to P!nk, asking if she would headline the event and bring in other performers to raise money against corruption in Washington. I was inspired to write to her because of an anti-war song she performed with her Dad called "I Have Seen The Rain."

P!nk didn't respond to my letter, and time was running out. November's election loomed around the corner, and my business had to gain traction.

Even with the encouragement of Maria and Britta, I didn't think I could host a fundraiser because the job of finding silent auction items was more than I could handle.

I had all but given up on the idea of a charity event until a volunteer offered his help through Jeanne, the nonprofit fundraiser consultant from Chapter 9. Jeanne found Rodney, a financial advisor for retirees and seniors, and suggested that I call him.

I met Rodney at the Torrance Marriot to find out how motivated he was as a volunteer. What was his story? Why would he stop a full-time job and look for unpaid work?

A middle-aged man with a charming disposition, Rodney sat at a crossroads. He saw how politics had changed his entire life. The Gramm Leach Bliley Act had directly affected how his clients fared financially, and it wasn't good. He unwittingly became an actor in selling toxic mortgages. He remembers his bank pushing these loans, hyping him up with fat commissions. He wasn't thinking that it was in any way similar to the dot com bubble. Life was great while the Ponzi scheme ripped through the country. People were buying houses, he was paid wads of money, everyone was stimulated to dream big, spend big.

Much like a cocaine addict, Rodney was living high and then came the crash of withdrawal. He had been laid off by the very industry that defined the housing crisis. He couldn't make money the same way and he felt remorse over what he had done. His life was in review, and his new choices had to be scrupulous, purposeful. He sought redemption, and he liked what I was doing, aiming directly at the top, where the problems originated.

When he agreed to sign on, my shoulder muscles relaxed, as though he had just cut the weight of the world in two. Rodney gave me the boost I needed to commit to running full steam into this next foray. Rodney's eagerness to right the wrongs in his life was the compelling reason I needed to stay the course.

When I called Terranea to choose a date, the event host and I discussed cost, and it was out of this world. The deposit alone would have been enough to stop me from living a normal life. We had to scale back and find a smaller venue, which took a week of driving around and searching. With Britta's suggestion, I settled on a bar in the centrally located town of Manhattan Beach.

Britta introduced me to a friend named Windy who makes invitations. She showed me some samples and suggested that she would stamp each individual piece of paper with a leaf design in red ink, to give it a handcrafted look.

The invitations read:

PEACEFUL REVOLUTION
A Visionary Fundraiser
Host: Writeindependent.org
Join Writeindependent.org for an evening in the seaside town
of Manhattan Beach to end corruption in Washington.

At the fundraiser, you will:

- Find out how the Pledge for Honest Candidates stops bribery in Congress
- Learn about emerging technologies in the new economy that will shape our future
- Talk with congressional challengers who have signed the Pledge
- Watch the "infomercial" that will change the course of history wherein voters connect the dots between our corrupt government and today's economy
- And *much more*

My invitation list included my close friends, acquaintances, famous people and artists, activists, politicians, comedians and wealthy individuals who displayed a strong interest in politics, the environment or changing the status quo. They had to be local, reachable. I used Contact Any Celebrities, a website listing service, to obtain mailing addresses to agents, managers, publicist or attorney. I chose about one hundred such people, none who knew me personally.

When it was time to address the other 400 invitations, Maria with the long list of friends emailed to say that misfortune had visited her house. Medical problems, family issues, and exhaustion conspired to make it impossible for her to help me. I asked for the list anyway, but she said it was too much to hand over, in that she had to personally go through each contact and she didn't have the time or energy to do so. I tried to be gracious by telling her that it was okay, that I had a list of my own invitees already. I didn't want her to feel bad for disappointing me, yet I knew this was a horrible omen.

You may be disappointed if you fail, but you are certain to be disappointed if you never try were the words at the top of the page in a manuscript book I'd been using as my diary. I was grasping at straws to keep my optimism afloat.

I called my private investigator friend who had helped me look for Ernesto, the website designer who blew me off. When I told her I was organizing a fundraiser, she blurted "That's a stupid idea. You're going to invite all these people and no one's going to come."

Okay, so I won't send you an invitation. My friend hadn't gotten the memo that I was going to remain positive throughout the rest of my life. Nevertheless, her comment stabbed my heart and when I hung up the phone, the corners of my eyes turned into faucets. What if she were right? Then I would lose rather than raise money.

It was already too late, and besides, I had to do everything in my power to make a go of this website. I was living my purpose, pursuing the most important work of my life. I was "all in." Somehow, I would get help. People would come out to pitch in.

34
FRIGHTENING DONORS

*The future of human freedom and the future of human existence
will be determined by what we do with seed and food.
Never before has human freedom been so threatened as it is
being threatened today.*
--Vendana Shiva, food and water activist

In late August of 2012, with the fundraiser only two weeks away, Marci, my video producer, and I were putting the final touches on our infomercial called *Fix Congress: Get Money Out of Politics.* When I told her I booked a venue in Manhattan Beach near her home for the event, she wanted to help me find guests.

Marci gave me the phone number of a local socialite, let's say her name was Barbie, who throws successful parties for her politician husband. The way Marci described her, I would have to give over my masters of ceremonies position to Barbie. *I would gladly do so for a rainmaker like her.* I already admired her for being popular, something I'd never enjoyed. Without ever meeting Barbie, I envied her.

Talking to this well-connected woman got me excited because she immediately understood the merit of what I was trying to do. Barbie was all ready to get behind me one hundred percent! Her schedule was tight, but she was determined to make it along with a handful of wealthy, politically savvy friends.

The Manhattan Beach venue had a big-screen setup where I would run my "show" consisting of the infomercial, a comedy skit, my PowerPoint presentation, and a talk by a Search Engine Optimization expert who was flying all the way from Pennsylvania. His name is Tim Daly, and according to Roscoe, if I could raise enough money to hire him, his marketing genius would turn the whole shebang around.

Mr. Daly loves to hate politics. He berated the two parties, Democrats and Republicans, for creating a battleground that makes America weaker. He warned me, "People still aren't ready for change. I know you think things are pretty bad, but I think things have to get even worse before people will wake up."

I pondered *how much worse do things have to get? Haven't we suffered enough?* I remembered the desperate mother in front of the post office from Chapter 5. Were things getting better for her?

I called the fundraiser "A Peaceful Revolution," but the presentation I was planning should have been called "Please join me or we're all going to hell." Between stories of what I had done, I was going to scare the shit out of my audience so they wouldn't hesitate to donate money.

The four parts of my PowerPoint presentation were: 1. Why I started the website, 2. The scary part, designed to convince donors to part with their money, 3. My experiences running debates for presidential contenders, and 4. The solutions portion.

For part one, to illustrate my story, I planned on showing photos of the seed-starting labs I taught at a nearby Palos Verdes elementary school, of my garden and my connection to the soil. I found photos of fungi so I could explain how it can be used to capture carbon, coaxing it underground indefinitely. I would speak about my run-in with the dry cleaner who almost made me cry when he said it's too late to respond to the consequences of climate change.

Then came the photos of doom.

I collated pictures of farmers' fields of dried corn, drought-parched soil, graphs about severe weather, and airplanes drenching crops in weed killer. I warned about the top five seed companies' wish to control all the seed they possibly can, and how controlling food and thereby human life is the consequence of a monopolistic market system paired with the biotech industry.

Rodney, the volunteer who was supposed to be finding silent auction items, had jazzed me up for nothing. Only an earthquake might have inched one of his toes toward his car to drive in the direction of a donor. He had run out of money and was facing eviction at the time. He returned to the same old racket he had done for years—financial services. Lately, he works for Covered California, helping uninsured people enroll for Obamacare.

A week before the actual date of the fundraiser, I had only about a dozen RSVPs. Britta, my event planner, called to ask if I wanted to cancel.

Cancel? The thought hadn't even occurred to me.

"No. I think if we go for it, we might break even, but if we don't do it, I'll lose money. Let's call everyone on the guest list. Maybe another dozen or so will show up. If we can get twenty people, we'll break even."

A few days before the event, I again solicited Barbie, the politician's darling, to ascertain how many of her friends were coming. She regretfully told me she couldn't make it, and there was no use inviting all her wealthy political friends if she couldn't be there. *Oh no. No, no. This can't be happening!*

No additional guests had replied "yes," but I had already put a deposit on the venue. Despite the low turnout, I wanted to do everything in my power to make a go of the website. I had to be able to look back and say, "I gave it my all!"

On the day of the event, I wish I could say that everything went without a hitch, but it didn't. Only ten people showed up and two of them were Marci and her husband. The buff body builder proprietor of the Manhattan Beach venue who looked like he belonged in a gym and not a restaurant, was angry with me. He said, "If I'd known how few people were coming to this thing, I'd have told you don't bother." He buzzed with the manic energy of someone on speed. "I might have filled up this room with real customers," he hissed at me, his eyes glowering.

"I paid your minimum," I replied sternly. "We'll do just fine."

He complained loudly and stomped out of the restaurant. Never to return. He neglected to give me the code to his wifi, which we needed to run a bit by standup comic Louis Black that I expected would put the crowd in a jovial mood.

Even with every nerve of my body on edge, I remained composed by thinking *I have to get through this, and if I do, I will never have to run another fundraiser again.*

Fortunately my event planner, Britta, remembered the wifi code and saved the day. After Tim Daly, the search engine optimization guru, gave his presentation, it was my turn.

I looked at my friends and neighbors and suddenly felt powerful. I squared my shoulders and imagined roots coming out the bottom of my feet, roots buried deep into the earth beneath, helping me stand anchored in my soul's purpose. It didn't matter how few attended. Finally, I had the opportunity to release my passionate story that had been fueling up inside me for the past year and a half. Maybe my words would open new doors.

"While you've been going to work or living your life day in and day out, I've been trying to make a difference by running presidential debates right out of my house," I said.

I pursed my lips to feel the gloss I recently applied, to make sure it was still fresh. I paraphrased Kissinger with his ominous prediction. "Who controls the food supply controls the people; who controls the energy can control whole continents; who controls money can control the world."

To prove that Monsanto is one such seed supplier that would like to control the food supply, I pointed to Canadian Percy Schmeiser, one of the best known of the small farmers who mounted an expensive legal battle against the giant chemical company. While my PowerPoint presentation showed a photo of farmer Percy sitting on a truck with grain running through his fingers, I said, "In 1998 Monsanto sued Percy Schmeiser, saying that he infringed on their patents because pollen from a neighboring farm using RoundUp Ready® canola had blown onto his canola. More than 844 family farms have been sued by, or paid settlements to Monsanto since the mid-90's.[19]

"My heart goes out to farmers all over the world who are trying to save their own seed but who have to contend with pollen contamination from Genetically Engineered plants."

If Monsanto were interested in feeding the world as they claim, then why don't they spend some of the $2.47 billion in profits they

---

[19] Though Monsanto won the lawsuit against Schmeiser, the court reduced the damages to zero. However, Schmeiser's legal fees totaled an estimated $153,000. The toll on his family, farm and his time can not be easily measured.

made in 2013 toward that end? How many starving people could they feed with, say, 10% of each year's net? Instead, Monsanto's own annual report shows how they spend their money to swallow up more biotech companies, not "feed the world." If that were their mission, they've failed miserably.

"Biotech companies are allowed to patent seeds. Pollen spreads that patent in the wind, as far as eight miles for sugar beets. What we have now is a handful of large companies who litigate us into submission with their patents. Don't listen to what they say; instead, watch what they are doing. Monsanto, DuPont, Syngenta—they're all chemical companies. They sell chemicals. How much is enough? And how much is too much?"

I looked at my friend and neighbor, Maria Elena, and I could tell she had no idea this was going on. "How far do their royalties extend into the food system? Some genetically modified seeds have a 'terminator' function, producing sterile offspring. This way, they can sell more seed next year, creating dependency on biotech seeds."

My toes were squished into the tips of my high heels, but somehow I forgot about them.

"In 2012, genetically engineered crops were used in 94% of soy and 88% of corn crops." I showed photos of ears of corn and yellow tortillas and asked my audience if they thought Michael Taylor, former attorney for Monsanto, now working as deputy commissioner for foods at the Food and Drug Administration (FDA) should maintain the following policy: "no safety studies on GMOs are required. Monsanto and other producers determine if their foods are safe." Quoting from Monsanto's own website, "There are not currently any human clinical trials used to test the safety of GM crops."

The next PowerPoint slide showed a plane flying over fields of food, dumping a thick spray of weed killer. "But it's not just ingesting GMOs that I'm worried about."

I looked over at Britta, and her arms were folded in front of her body, almost trying to steel herself against another tidbit of uncomfortable information.

"It's also ingesting the herbicides that are liberally sprayed on genetically engineered crops. The whole point to genetic engineering is killing weeds and pests, to make farming easier and more productive." Guests at the bar were oblivious, wrapped up in their own conversations.

"But it's not working, because as the weeds have developed a resistance to RoundUp®, they've become 'superweeds' upon which farmers are using even scarier herbicides, like dicamba and 2,4-D, both linked to cancer and reproductive problems."

My guests were hanging in there, despite my gloomy subject. Their rapt attention was focused on the big screen, where I showed the amount of herbicide used yearly. Maria Elena's husband shifted in his seat. Maybe he had just sprayed some weeds in the cracks of his sidewalk earlier that day?

"Toxic effects of RoundUp® include birth defects of the skull, face, midline, developing brain and spinal cord. The surfactant, polyethoxylated tallow amine, that makes RoundUp® absorb into plant tissues may be more harmful than the actual glyphosate and it's not tested by Monsanto for toxicity, since it's exempt from the Toxic Substances Control Act.

"Residues of glyphosate have been found in a variety of fruits and vegetables. This is because it readily moves into all parts of a plant. As it is inside the plant tissues, it cannot be washed off." I quoted Andre Leu, an Australian researcher on RoundUp® and its effects.

"Millions of acreage of what used to be pristine farmland and waterways is now funkified. The United States Geological Survey found RoundUp® in rivers and streams all over the country." (Later, in March, 2015, 17 experts from 11 countries analyzed the effect of glyphosate at the International Agency for Research on Cancer and concluded that it's probably carcinogenic. The World Health Organization issued a report based on their conclusions.)

"While RoundUp and GMOs have invaded the air, water, earth, and food, we are participating in a massive science experiment for the biotech and pesticide industries," I said. "And that's why we have to straighten out the USDA and the FDA." I wanted my guests to know that I intend to put an end to this, if not in my lifetime, then by pointing future generations in a healthy direction.

When I finished part two, the scary weed killer speech, I had built up my argument that we had better do something quick or we're doomed. I was supposed to do my customary pitch for donations, but I couldn't. I looked around at the expectant faces of my friends and said, "This was the time I was going to make my 'big ask' for money, but since you're all my friends, I'm not going to do that." The fundraiser was over, and I knew it. I wasn't going to raise enough money from ten people to put the infomercial on television.

The last part of my presentation, the "solutions" portion didn't get the attention it needed. Maybe if I'd had the kind of Terranea fundraiser of my fantasies, the suggestions of specific businesses that will usher us into the next generation would inspire investment. It's only by making firm commitments to innovation that we will ever get out of our downward spiral. A charismatic and credible leader could compel financial planners to start placing their bets on all the new colts and fillies who haven't come out of the gate yet. We still need that dynamic individual, buttressed by all the political will of the people, to put her clout behind the technologies of our new age and ring the starting bell!

Even though the fundraiser wasn't successful, I realized how much I had actually accomplished. Nobody else in this country had done what I had in the past year. Nobody else had organized and hosted presidential debates, asking 151 tough questions. Nobody had authored a Pledge for Honest Candidates and then found 54 candidates to sign it! Nobody had written almost three hundred blog posts and was crazy enough to write letters to wealthy individuals asking for money. And nobody else had risked a large percentage of what they owned, without a Plan B, without the financial support of family and friends, and with so much to lose.

I was that nobody. *Damn You, God! for making me trust You so idealistically!* Was I a romantic fool or a hopeful believer?

Would I have done it all again, knowing what I know today? Of course I would. I had to do it. I might have put all that money into a masters' degree, but instead I bought a once-in-a-lifetime experience.

I didn't realize it before, but standing there it suddenly became as plain as the pain in my toes caused by my high heel shoes. I have a story to tell! I will turn this hopeless experiment around. Folks must know what I learned, and if we join together, we can make a difference. Not me, working by myself, and not just my few closest friends helping me. This message needs to spread by word of mouth, the way a mother talks to her family in the kitchen or a father advises his children at the dinner table. Or a real friend tells another friend his life choices are killing him. I will write something worthy of being heard across the country, scrutinized by critics and book clubs, discussed at church socials, peddled at flea markets and farmers markets, shared at parent teacher organizations and in meeting rooms and accountants offices. I promise not to let this story die, even though I had temporarily failed at the business of cleaning up Washington.

If only we would start a peaceful revolution. A quiet, underground change that happens without anyone having to orchestrate it. Is it really an oxymoronic situation: a peaceful revolution? Is it a paradox? Even so, that's what I'm asking for. Revolt without violence!

35
THE PIT OF DESPAIR

*The most common way people give up their power is by
thinking they don't have any.*
– Alice Walker, American author and activist

I had hit the lowest of the low points of the past eighteen
months. The fundraiser had been a failure, and I self-identified
with that failure.

I could really understand why people want to end it all. That's
how badly I felt—like nobody really cares about me except who
I'm paying to work with me. Nobody wants me to run a website
like the one I'm running. Nobody asked me to do these things for
them. Few people want to vote for alternative candidates. The
public always had them available and didn't want them before.
Why would they now?

The anguish dug into the marrow of my bones. The
meaninglessness of it all, the feeling that no purpose in life is good
enough to feel purposeful. I was deep, deep in the pit of despair,
dragging a shovel out to the garden with barely enough energy to
scoop out a hole for the kitchen scraps. Had I more verve, I should
dig a lot deeper and wider and throw myself in there, and rest in
eternity.

I'd worn a hole in the toe of my Muck boots, and how was I
going to buy new ones? My chattering mind raced. *Nothing I am*

doing is working out. I will have spent all this money, more than seventy grand, and for what? It all sank in what a foolish experiment this has been.

I was bound to fail, even if I had every possible convenience, all the help I needed, money to play the infomercial, and hundreds of thousands of supporters. It wasn't just the timing wasn't right, or I was the wrong person to do such a thing. Any effort like this will fail because few people *really* want to change. That would require sustained effort, contending with the unknown, the fear of uncertainty, the seriousness of work, the delay of gratification for long-term gains. We Americans are too impatient to work toward results that might be down the line ten years. We want it now, or it's no good.

I talked to a Green Party congressional candidate and wow, was she dismal. She said only twenty percent of the population cares about our environment, and that it's too late to solve global warming, and because of that, why bother? I wasn't sure if she meant that *she* thought that way, or most people think that way. To her, "life is random and it's only by a fluke that we are even here. We should see the world as paradise and treat it accordingly." We seem to be in a big hurry to turn it into one hill with fracking and tar sands and burning fossil fuels, hot as hell, dry to a crisp, flooded everywhere else. Hot as hell!

I felt the need to sleep. Oh, the agony. When would things start to feel better?

My Dad had suffered from lethal depression. I am my Dad's daughter and like him, I think in these grand terms of life versus death or success versus failure. I do think of death as a release from all this. I understand the temptation and fascination people have for it, like a lover who never disappoints and lasts forever. I know, logically, life isn't about two opposing ideas. Life is filled with options and opportunities, with the chance to start fresh even when things seem most miserable. What self-respecting gardener would allow her field to lie fallow in perpetuity? This long and exasperating apprenticeship in activism must be building to a climax that only time will reveal.

This life isn't a joke, it's for real. It's a test of your strength and character. Don't give up.

If I gave it my best shot and I still couldn't realize my desires or any part of them, then how will Disney reconcile this failure? Their business model depends upon stories of people who prevailed against all the odds. Disney, who wants the Trans Pacific Partnership to pass, would have to give up the TPP for my wish to come true. Which is more important: the message that anything is possible, or bare naked ambition to amass money regardless of the cost to humanity and our dreams of a better future? Should we throw away the American Dream for the unbridled corporate takeover?

There were only four weeks before election day. I couldn't stop working. I had created something and I'd be damned if I wasn't going to use it to its maximum capacity. Remember the Pledge for Honest Candidates? It was about to get a second life.

36
THE PLEDGE REDUX

*As the Internet breaks down the last justifications for a
professional class of politicians, it also builds up the tools for
replacing them.*
– Aaron Swartz, hacker, writer, and activist (1986-2013)

Good ideas don't die just because you have no money. They
have a life of their own, and I was still in service to those ideas: the
website, the infomercial and the Pledge to get money out of
politics.

The Pledge for Honest Candidates was undergoing a serious
face-lift under a new name. The nonprofit United Republic (now
called Represent.us) hired Trevor Potter, Stephen Colbert's
election attorney and former chairman and commissioner of the
Federal Election Commission to craft a bill that makes it illegal for
our representatives to take huge favors or money from lobbyists
and PACs. Founders Josh Silver and Nick Penniman dubbed it the
American Anti-Corruption Act, the most stringent campaign
finance reform I've encountered.

Represent.us had a different strategy than my website. Instead
of waiting for most Americans to wake up and vote for people who
pledged to turn the bill into law, they sought to have more than one
million Americans *demand* that Congress pass such legislation.
Represent.us would find a few good representatives to walk it onto

the floor of the House saying, "this is what the people of America want," backed by a million signatures of Americans who are tired of having their voices unheard.

Represent.us found its first quarter of a million members by absorbing all the people who liked Dylan Ratigan and his "Get Money Out" campaign. Mr. Ratigan had amassed roughly 275,000 mad-as-hell followers while discussing politics and the economy from June 2009 to June 2012 on MSNBC. About two months after Nick Penniman told me he didn't have the bandwidth to work with Writeindependent.org, Dylan hosted his last TV program. Mr. Ratigan dropped out of the media's carnival show to lead a meaningful life.[20]

Unbeknownst to the folks at Represent.us, I was still working hard, trying to get more politicians to Pledge to pass what was essentially the American Anti-Corruption Act. Manu, the ponytailed moderator of the People's Congress volunteered to help me call as many candidates as possible. We placed a list of more than 1,400 candidates on a Google doc spreadsheet that anyone could access and change in real time, showing whether or not candidates had agreed to the Pledge. Manu tried to recruit others to make a few calls here and there.

With activities like these, I had no time to stay in the pit of despair. Instead, I shot a video of myself making phone calls asking candidates to sign the Pledge. I sat at my kitchen desk wearing a tie-dye shirt and my reading glasses, asking "Would you be interested in getting money out of politics?"

I posted it on YouTube, titled "Call your candidate: get money out of politics today!" showing how I successfully convinced someone to sign the Pledge. Pledge-signers got a red star next to their name on the website so that voters could easily find them. I sent all the candidates a link to the infomercial, so they could see how the red star would increase their chances that the money-out-of-politics crowd would vote for them.

---

[20] After handing over his Get Money Out mission to the folks at Represent.us, Mr. Ratigan now devotes his time to helping people grow food with less water, hydroponically. He co-founded Veteran Job Corps with Major General Melvin Spiese to teach veterans new skills and give them employment opportunities that build communities.

Ever since the Pledge began, I had been emailing candidates, repetitively asking them to sign. I changed the title of the document to "Agreement for Honest Candidates"[21] because "pledge" had gotten a bad reputation thanks to Grover Norquist, the mastermind behind the "Taxpayer Protection Pledge." Picture a man with money stuffed in his pockets, offering re-election campaign funds to those who promise to never ever, ever increase taxes. His Pledge works so well, and so many Congressmen have signed it, that the majority of Congress still won't budge on this issue.

Politicians who were running against incumbents were often eager to sign my Pledge because they needed every advantage possible to unseat their opponent. So far, I had found 54 Pledge signers, working my way to 61 before election day.[22] One candidate complained "You're making it seem like I'm not honest if I don't sign it!" to which I replied, "Oh, well!"

Those who refused to Pledge frequently gave the excuse that it crimped their ability to compete prior to passing it as law, because the current system was so lopsidedly stacked in favor of those who raised the most money.

Regarding the infomercial, I talked with as many public access stations as I could to have it aired. I was able to secure the commitment of a dozen stations to fit it into their schedules.

I made one last ditch effort to get some help. My public relations company told me that the sixteen thousand dollars I gave them had been used up, but their results had been less than stellar. After several calls and phone messages to the owner of the PR firm, I sent a persuasive email and she called me back. I made a compelling plea for her to help me, to assign someone to call the media outlets with an updated press release bragging about 54 pledge signers and the infomercial. After much arm-twisting, she finally agreed to help.

One of the employees at my PR company spent about three days on phone calls. As a result, Arianna Huffington, mother of Huffington Post, sent him an email saying "I'd love to have Judy's voice on the site about campaign finance reform or any other topic

---

[21] See Appendix 5.
[22] See Appendix 13.

that interests. I'm cc'ing our blog editor Erin to follow up. All the best, Arianna." This was the best news I'd received all year.

My heart sang with excitement over this achievement. I had a photo and a by-line with a well-known media outlet for the first time in my life! I was thrilled to be able to say I was a blogger for Huff Po. It was the sweetest success I achieved all year. And to have an email from Arianna herself, heaven!

On October 3, 2012, I watched the Obama versus Romney debates with a unique appreciation for what is missing from their donkey and elephant spectacle. Jim Lehrer's toothless questions stayed away from anything controversial by repeating "What's the difference between you two?" With a mixture of disgust and disbelief, I saw him hand over his balls to the people who whitewash the debates. They turn a blind eye to poverty, racism, our broke treasury, and the military aggression that causes us to ruin our chances of positive foreign relations in certain countries.

I jumped up and down. I threw Clarissa's Nerf football at the television. *You have no balls, Jim Lehrer!* It's not his fault; he's just following orders and he'd be out of a job tomorrow if he asked the questions I had. Candy Crowley moderated Obama and Romney's second presidential debate. She was better than Jim Lehrer, but couldn't get as deeply into the issues as I had. She would lose her job, too. I have nothing to lose.

For 2016, let's ask the questions listed in Appendix 6 because almost all the problems I touched upon are still going on.

The last four weeks before the election, I looked back on my exploits and regarded my experience with a mixture of frustration and subdued sadness. I entered the voting booth and cast my tiny vote for a candidate who would barely register a blip in the national tally. I didn't vote for Obama and I didn't vote for Romney, and enough said. I'll never vote for someone I can't trust, ever again.

The total hits on the website from all my hard work? Under 700 views at its highest point—three days before the election. This was the end of my grand experiment with a website that would revamp Washington. Too little. Magnificent insignificance.

I wasn't ready to dive back into the soil just yet. I had to meet the very people with whom I had been traveling in parallel.

37
YOU ARE NOT ALONE

Your great mistake is to act the drama as if you were alone.
Put down the weight of your aloneness and ease into
the conversation. The kettle is singing
even as it pours you a drink, the cooking pots
have left their arrogant aloofness and
seen the good in you at last. All the birds
and creatures of the world are unutterably
themselves. Everything is waiting for you.

– David Whyte, English poet[23]

Josh Silver of Represent.us invited me via mass email to a conference sponsored by Money Out, Voters In (MOVI) at UCLA's Law School on November 17, 2012. Many of the movers and shakers in the 'Get Money Out' world explained the problem, our options for solving it, and the legal mumbo jumbo that we have to go through to accomplish our goals.

As I watched one of the organizers of the UCLA event, Mary Beth Fielder, take the podium, I wondered why I had never met her before. She spoke passionately about her success spearheading the effort to have Los Angeles' City Council "officially endorse amending the United States Constitution to state that only human beings, not corporations, are entitled to Constitutional rights and

---

[23] Printed with permission from Many Rivers Press, www.davidwhyte.com

that spending money is not a form of free speech."

Money Out, Voters In (MOVI) consists of a hearty corps of volunteers who have been working to restore Proposition 49, the Overturn Citizens United Act, to the 2016 California ballot. Their objective is to shine California's overwhelming urgency to get money out of politics as a beacon for the rest of the country.

Mary Beth, co-founder of MOVI, worked with an organization called Move to Amend that won't stop until we amend the Constitution. I admired her clout, the fact that she commanded the room and had the ability to bring all the big cheese from across the country to this conference. She introduced another co-founder of MOVI, Michele Sutter, a strong woman who, along with Chip Travis, has been at the forefront of the California movement. Stephen Colbert's attorney, Trevor Potter presented at the conference along with my hero, Lawrence Lessig.

For the keynote address, Professor Lessig gave his sleek well-rehearsed presentation. He's one of my favorite speakers on the subject, and arguably the leading educator in the country for explaining how big money controls our government.

After lunch, I shook Professor Lessig's hand to thank him for his work. I told him that I had purchased his book, *Republic Lost*, but he couldn't autograph it because it was an e-book on my iPad. He laughed. His hands are thin, his fingers long, and he grasps exactly like I do. I found no point in telling him who I was or what I had done. It would take an entire book to explain, and I thought he might not be interested unless I had more than 200,000 Twitter followers.

At the UCLA event, I learned how much had already been done to pick up where the Federal Election Commission has failed. Campaigns should have all the donors clearly labeled on ads, but they aren't. The DISCLOSE (Democracy is Strengthened by Casting Light on Spending in Elections) Act takes care of this. In California, we have yet to pass our own DISCLOSE Act, SB 52 that requires political ads to show who their top three donors are. Our Congress has failed to pass laws forcing SuperPACs and 501(c)(4)'s to disclose their funding sources and why would they be so inclined? Dark money pays for those issue ads that use thirty seconds to bend the ill-informed public's vote. For example, Proposition 37 in California, a GMO-labeling law, was defeated even though most folks would like their food labeled. This was a result of big corporations and special interest groups pooling $45 million to spend on a deluge of misleading advertising. If a DISCLOSE act is on the ballot, just vote for it!

Regarding public financing of elections, Lawrence Lessig recommends that each voter receive a $50 voucher to support a specific politician or to fund elections administration. I will not give the subject its full treatment here, because I feel that Writeindependent.org or a similar website could provide most of the functions necessary for candidates to campaign for a lot less money. That said, California has a Clean Money Campaign (AB 583) that wishes to institute public financing, following the examples of Arizona and Maine. According to AB 583, candidates who raise at least 7,500 individual donations of $5.00 each would qualify to receive a million dollars in public financing. "Clean Money has lowered overall campaign spending, freed candidates from fundraising, increased turnout, and encouraged more qualified people to run including women and minorities," says the CA Clean Money website. Public Campaign, a nonpartisan non-profit outlines the list of states and municipalities that have passed Clean Elections initiatives—Maine, Vermont, Arizona, Massachusetts, North Carolina, New Mexico, New Jersey, Connecticut, Wisconsin, West Virginia, and Hawaii; Portland, OR; Albuquerque, NM; Chapel Hill, NC; and Santa Fe, NM. I would support a less expensive public financing program than the one offered by California's AB 583.

Most of the UCLA conference focused on a 28th Amendment to overturn *Citizens United*. Discussing the need for an amendment, nobody speaks better than New Jersey homeboy Cenk Uygur (pronounced Jenk You-grrrr), an attorney-turned news anchor for *The Young Turks*, an online political commentary show. His Internet audience is more than three million strong as of the publication of this book. When he decided to become an activist, he started an organization called Wolf PAC to train volunteers how to push through a 28th Amendment to end corruption.

Mr. Uygur punctuated each italicized word with his entire being. "*Sixty-seven* percent of Americans said politicians need to do something about climate change; they need to take legislative action. If we had a functioning democracy, there would be *immediate* action on that! But in reality, not a peep. Not from the Republican candidate, [not] by the *Democratic* candidate, and very importantly, [not] the people that profit the *most* from this corrupt system—television stations. Where does all that money go? A great majority of it goes to TV ads, so then are you surprised that there were no questions about corruption in *any* of the debates? There were no questions about climate change."

The MOVI (Money Out, Voters In) seminar helped me understand the need to amend the Constitution before we can truly remove money as a corrupting influence in Washington. If we did everything possible to pass the American Anti-Corruption Act but five judges on the Supreme Court say it's "unconstitutional" then our efforts will have been in vain.

There are two routes we can take on our way to amending the Constitution. One, we could pass resolutions asking Congress to amend the Constitution. The second way is to demand the amendment, because the act of asking gives Congress the opportunity to say no.

Move to Amend is, so far, *asking* Congress "pretty please give us this amendment so we can crack down on your corruption by money." They are giving members of Congress a chance to show us they are decent people who will do what is right by making it possible to put an end to big money ruling our government.

Perhaps, on our way to amending the Constitution, Congress members who don't want this amendment will put up a good fight, trying to convince us that money should do the talking in this country. It goes along with the ethos of our current state of affairs: money is king. Whoever raises the most money for his campaign wins.

This fact of elections (whoever has the most money wins) is why the vast majority of Americans don't believe in politics anymore. They want representatives who listen to them, not to money.

If your Congressman's job depended upon taking the campaign cash, would he not take it? If your Congressman has been buying expensive suits and shoes, enjoying lavish golf vacations to Ireland, flying in their funder's jets, using their insider information to pay for their kid's college, why would they give all that up? There are Congressmen who don't care about these perks, but the temptation is great. The ones who give in to the seductive life are not motivated to change the funding paradigm because they count on it to secure their next election win. Watch who fights this amendment to see who is gaming the system the most.

I believe we can't expect Congress to amend the Constitution even with all of us making demands. That's why Wolf PAC chose a strong mascot. They aren't going to ask "pretty please" of Congress. And neither will I.

As a result of the UCLA conference, I decided to become a volunteer for Wolf PAC.

I chose them for four reasons: 1. Mr. Uygur articulates the problem well, 2. The Wolf PAC team has built an easy-to-use program for volunteers, 3. Their volunteers are effective at rallying the public and explaining why we need a convention of the states (I believe we must trigger such a convention which I will explain in the following chapter), and 4. Mr. Uygur gives feedback to the volunteers through his broadcasts. When Wolf PAC wants to celebrate a victory in passing resolutions that call for a convention of the states, Mr. Uygur congratulates the state representatives, their staff, and the volunteers who helped pass that resolution. He gives the proper people credit for their hard work. Videos posted on his YouTube channel are positively inspiring.

Whenever I get depressed that "there's nothing we can do" to address the bickering between the two parties, I go to the Wolf PAC Google group and read the volunteer comments. I stop feeling so alone, and start having faith in Americans who haven't lost hope. Here's a sample of the passion pouring out of the Wolf PAC volunteers written on the threads of our Google group:

"Wolf PAC won't stop moving forward, even if Congress in Washington D.C. tries to slow us down by passing a weaksauce and watered-down campaign finance reform bill masquerading as a solution (or concession) which will, by their own design, fail to achieve exactly what's necessary to restore our Representative Democracy and save the Republic." –Stephan Medcalf, Wolf PAC State Organizer

"If Congress is thinking about merely rolling us back to the McCain-Feingold Era, they've got another thing coming. We don't want the future to at all borrow from or resemble the past. The situation was broken even in those days and all these rulings did was take an already messy situation and pour gasoline all over the fire." –Paul Tidwell

"I suspect the U.S. Congress, seeing that a States Amendments Convention is coming will attempt to short-circuit that effort by passing some watered-down thing that attempts to make them look like they've 'solved' the problem, but in actuality will create little effective change.

"My hope is that if Congress actually does pass something that is unacceptable before we can convene a States Amendments Convention, we will keep on coming and convene the States Convention anyway to further amend the constitution by changing or amending what Congress had passed." –Paul Keleher

Alison Hartson, Wolf PAC's California State Director, traveled to Sacramento to tell our state senate on June 23, 2014, "We've had enough. We're not going to cross our fingers and hope everything will get better. We need an amendment because we've already passed laws at the state and federal level that the Supreme Court has overturned. We are counting on you to do the morally correct thing and vote in favor of the people by voting yes on AJR1." Joining Alison at the senate committee hearing were 70 Wolf PAC members and 99Rise.org's March for Democracy activists who hoofed nearly 500 miles from LA to Sacramento to make their demands known. For thirteen minutes, citizen after citizen walked to the microphone in our Capitol's building and urged our California senators to vote yes. The resolution to call for a convention of the states passed by a vote of 5 to 2.

The most impactful work I've done for Wolf PAC was calling citizens in Illinois, asking them to call their state representatives and ask them to vote "yes" on the same resolution. This is how Illinois became the third state to pass a resolution through their state senate asking for a convention to propose a Constitutional amendment, and then New Jersey followed. Was it right for me, a Californian, to talk to an Illinoisian about an amendment for our Constitution? Yes! It's an issue of national importance!

The last time our Constitution was amended happened in 1992, when the states finally ratified the 27th amendment allowing Congress to change their salaries. Prior to that, the 26th amendment passed in 1971, lowering the voting age from 21 to 18. This proves that it can be done.

Amending the Constitution is a big job. We cannot work alone. I implore you, take responsibility as an American and cause a miracle to happen by joining Wolf PAC or talking to your representative about the need for an amendment. Things will get better when we take charge of our own country and stop the corruption. Next, I will explore the specific historic actions you can take to amend the Constitution.

38
HERE'S A SOLUTION:
AMEND THE CONSTITUTION

Power concedes nothing without a demand.

– Frederick Douglass, African American statesman 1818-1895

Amending the Constitution is a lot like holding an intervention for cousin Dave (Congress) who's just spent the last eighteen months pissing off everyone in the family. Except in this case, Dave knows we're planning to corral him and make him clean up his act.

The founding fathers must have realized that if Congress goes rogue and stops listening to their constituents, we must have checks and balances, a release valve we can use before we implode. That release is found in Article V of our Constitution, the instructions for amending the Constitution *without the need for Congress.*

If Congress cared about what we wanted, they could propose and pass an amendment themselves. Then 38 states must ratify that amendment for it to become part of our Constitution. If Congress refuses to propose the amendment that is brewing all across the country, or they can't come up with the requisite two-thirds majority in both House and Senate to pass such an amendment, then we need 34 states' legislatures to apply for an Article V "convention to propose amendments." Delegates from each state convene at a location specified by Congress.

Retired Chief Justice Warren Burger has warned "A new convention could plunge our Nation into constitutional confusion and confrontation at every turn, with no assurance that focus would be on the subjects needing attention." Personally, I feel his concerns are overstated. By the time the states convene, the amendment will be well crafted and thoroughly considered by constitutional scholars, the leaders of our movement, and the hundreds of thousands people who have made their desires clear to their state legislators. To me, it is insulting that a former Supreme Court Justice thinks we aren't wise enough or organized enough to hold a civilized convention.

In contrast, retired Chief Justice John Paul Stevens went on record to say that an amendment is needed to correct what he views as an "error" in campaign finance jurisprudence. "Elections are contests between rival candidates for public office," he said. "Like rules that govern athletic contests or adversary litigation, those rules should create a level playing field."

Alarmists will warn you that if we apply for such a convention, it could become a "runaway" Constitutional Convention. That's like saying when you light a candle on your dining room table, the whole house will go up in flames. To dispel this myth, refer to the actual text of Article V (see Appendix 9). It never says anything about a Constitutional Convention. It says "Convention for proposing Amendments." Conspiracy theorists try to frighten people by saying there will be a runaway convention, by which they mean the convention will scrap the whole Bill of Rights and start from scratch. Nowhere in Article V does it say that all previous amendments are up for grabs when a convention is called.

In reality, a convention of the states can only address one specific issue to amend the Constitution. It doesn't remove all previous Amendments. The National Conference of State Legislatures (NCSL), a bipartisan non-governmental agency, presents a paper called "Amending the U.S. Constitution by State-Led Convention" wherein the State of Indiana specifically explains why a runaway convention is impossible.

Mark Levin, author of *The Liberty Amendments: Restoring the American Republic* wrote, "Whether the product of Congress or a convention, a proposed amendment has no effect at all unless 'ratified by the legislatures of three fourths of the several States or by Conventions in three fourths thereof....' This should extinguish anxiety that the state convention process could hijack the Constitution."

Larry Greenley, journalist for *The New American*, argues that the Declaration of Independence offered one more release valve whereby citizens could scrap the entire government and start afresh:

"We hold these truths to be self-evident, that all men are created equal, that they are endowed by their Creator with certain unalienable Rights, that among these are Life, Liberty and the pursuit of Happiness. — That to secure these rights, Governments are instituted among Men, deriving their just powers from the consent of the governed, — *That whenever any Form of Government becomes destructive of these ends, it is the Right of the People to alter or to abolish it, and to institute new Government, laying its foundation on such principles and organizing its powers in such form, as to them shall seem most likely to effect their Safety and Happiness.*" (emphasis mine)

Mr. Greenley writes "As discussed above, the extra-constitutional 'right of the people to alter or to abolish' our government whenever it fails to secure our rights, as proclaimed by the Declaration of Independence, would certainly encompass altering the method of ratification for any new amendments that might result from an Article V constitutional convention." Mr. Greenley would have you believe that an angry mob will descend on Washington arguing to throw away the whole Constitution and start over. As an example he says (I'm paraphrasing here) that through a convention, we're going to write a new amendment into our Constitution to make it easy as apple pie to amend the Constitution in broad swaths. On the other hand, Mr. Greenley suggests that we not modify the Constitution because it's perfect. He's assuming that the Supreme Court always gets it right, whereas 38 states' citizens aren't educated enough to determine what is (or should be) constitutional. Mr. Greenley suggests that we should educate everyone so we can hold our government to the current Constitution, and *that* is the way to solve our problems.

We didn't get into this situation because citizens don't understand the Constitution. We are suffering because five justices of the Supreme Court decided that money is speech and corporations should have the same rights as people. If they hadn't given money so much power to influence elections, and if Congress were a functioning body, we wouldn't need to amend the Constitution. This is our only resort to come up against the Supreme Court when they make lousy decisions.

"We're stuck with these Supreme Court rulings allowing unlimited anonymous influence over our elections," said Timothy Smith, New Hampshire Representative, during his impassioned testimony prior to their House vote passing HCR 2, a resolution to hold a convention. "Conservatives call it crony capitalism; liberals call it legalized bribery...96% of the voters don't want *anyone* buying our elections...The political machine at the federal level has become completely invested in this institutional corruption. They have a vested financial interest in doing *nothing* about these national issues because their elections are completely dependent on the money.

"Asking Congress to fix Congress is like asking cancer to cure cancer! Thankfully, in their wisdom, the founding fathers foresaw the possibility that one day, Congress itself might become corrupt and might become the problem. They gave us, here in the states, a method of redress. Article V allows us to hold a convention to propose amendments."

In Illinois, during a legislative session to discuss their resolution to apply for a convention of the states, Representative Chapa Lavia explained why a runaway convention is a fiction: "There exists over 700 state applications on a variety of issues including those from 49 states previously passing resolutions and 45 states with current applications. Only conventions called on the same issues are counted together which is how we know that the convention's scope will be limited to a single issue once convened. There have been over 233 state conventions to amend and adopt state constitutions with zero runaway conventions, which is just a conspiracy theory."

The resolutions being passed in the states now are for one specific 28th amendment that will make it constitutional to pass campaign finance laws. First, I will touch on the gist of that amendment, and then I will offer a backup plan if the 28th amendment is not effective enough to eradicate corruption.

Besides Vermont, California, Illinois, New Jersey, and New Hampshire, other states have made amazing progress with the help of grassroots groups like Money Out, Voters In; Move to Amend; Common Cause; Wolf PAC; Public Citizen; and Lawrence Lessig's Rootstrikers. I believe that we will summon 34 states to apply for and trigger a convention, but only if we spread the word to our friends and neighbors about what needs to be done. Grass roots activists will have a huge job ahead of us to counteract the media's stronghold on citizens who do not read or are illiterate, but who nevertheless vote against their own interests. That's why "kitchen table," neighborhood political engagement plays an important role.

On September 11, 2014, the federal Senate did vote on an amendment to our Constitution called House Judiciary Resolution 119 (H.J.R. 119, dubbed the Democracy for All Amendment) that gives Congress and the states the power to regulate the raising and spending of money in federal and state elections. It is not exactly what we need. Luckily, it didn't pass, for if it had, we still might have Supreme Court dissent when trying to enforce the American Anti-Corruption Act, which outlines more aggressive bribery busting than H.J.R. 119 because it targets lobbyists.

Since the Bill of Rights, the states have never convened to pass an amendment to the Constitution. Congress has been petitioned more than 400 times to hold a national convention though none of these efforts forced Congress to comply. The 17th Amendment got pretty close but at the eleventh hour, just one state shy of triggering a convention, Congress decided to give in to the populace's wishes. It finally conceded by adding the 17th Amendment, which allows citizens to directly vote for their U.S. Senators.

We must have our best Constitutional legal minds craft an iron-clad amendment. The text has to be written so that it overturns *Citizens United v. FEC, Buckley v. Valeo, SpeechNow.org v. FEC, McCutcheon v. FEC* and related cases, while giving stringent campaign finance laws the ability to stand up against judicial challenges. To pass muster, our Constitutional scholars should compare the Renew Democracy Amendment[24] and Move to Amend's version called H.J. Resolution 29, the We the People Amendment.[25] The later expressly restricts corporations' rights, the former amendment addresses corruption. This is a work in progress, and if we need to add or change the wording, we should do it now before the states convene.

After reading these amendments and others,[26] in my opinion the Renew Democracy Amendment (RDA), crafted by volunteers in Montana covers the territory best. "Montana is about as red a state as you can get, and yet 75% of the folks realized that there's too much corporate influence and spending," said Craig Clevidence, Director of Renew Democracy. The RDA specifically addresses lobbying to erase any doubt that the American Anti-Corruption Act is constitutional. It identifies that only the voters should be funding campaigns, not wealthy candidates, unions, nor corporations. It gives Congress the ability to clamp down on "soft money," the kind that comes from Super PACs, unions, and other groups. And best of all, it gets rid of the electoral college. One-person-one-vote decides who wins the Presidency.

I cannot stress this enough: the amendment must have strong bipartisan state support or it runs the tragic risk of getting all the way to convention only to lose in the ratification process. And remember, if your legislators can be bought, or if the media can propagandize enough voters, you run the risk of losing the ratification right up to the end. Or the opposite could happen. "The chink in Wolf PAC's plan," said Michele Sutter of MOVI, "is that they aren't prepared for the complete *absence* of the media on this issue." Ms. Sutter worries that we will lose momentum as the amendment gets closer to becoming reality because most of the electorate won't know events on the national level when their news outlets aren't covering them.

Let's say we achieve the miracle of passing a 28th Amendment.

---

[24] See Appendix 14

[25] See Appendix 15

[26] Other amendments, each one missing a vital element, were written by Representatives Schiff, Edwards, Baucus, McGovern, Udall, and Sanders/Deutch as well as Jimmy Williams of Get Money Out (formerly Dylan Ratigan's group) and Wolf PAC.

What happens after winning that victory? Theoretically, if we institute ironclad campaign finance reform, Congress will represent us, not their funders. They will start to care about what we Americans want. They will repeal the laws that don't serve us, balance the budget, and pass laws that get rid of gerrymandering. They will return us to paper ballots that are hand-counted in public. That is the theory.

Let's say we prevail and the states amend the Constitution. What happens if things keep getting worse because our money-out program isn't able to overcome the gerrymandered districts, the delegates who refuse to vote outside of party lines, and the hoodwinked voters who live in a fog of media propaganda? When the ethics committees are paid off, when the corruption creeps back in because money always finds a way, we'll be forced to pass a 29th amendment. Remember back to Chapter 14, when presidential candidate Harry Braun suggested we pass a Direct Democracy Amendment? Mr. Braun said that Switzerland's direct democracy has been in place since 1291, and if they can do democracy, so can we.

This is Mr. Braun's proposed amendment: "We the People, hereby empower the majority of American Citizens to approve [revoke or veto] all laws, federal legislation, presidential executive orders and judicial decisions that impact the majority of citizens." I added the words "revoke or veto." In Switzerland, if 50,000 Swiss sign a form demanding a referendum to veto a bill, and a majority of the national electorate vote yes on that referendum, the bill is killed. In the United States, if we had that system, we might not have gone to war with Iraq or allowed our government to bail out the banks. At the very least it would encourage great debate.

Mr. Braun's suggestion may look like the best way to straighten out a totally corrupt, gerrymandered-to-death, black box voting, media-controlled system. Or is it?

If you give the voters a pure democracy, wouldn't "majority rule" become a problem in itself? Couldn't one faction grow so large or persistent that it eclipsed other reasonable interests? James Madison, fourth President of the United States, described a faction as "a number of citizens, whether amounting to a majority or a minority of the whole, who are united and actuated by some common impulse of passion, or of interest, adversed [sic] to the rights of other citizens, or to the permanent and aggregate interests of the community." Parties, special interests, unions, corporations, religious zealots are all factions vying for power. How does one mitigate this problem of factions?

Right now, we have corruption by money, the faction with the traction. In a pure democracy, we would have a government of the people potentially ruled by factions that outnumber or out-maneuver the rest, where the common good is overrun by greed, power, or ideological righteousness. How can we protect the common good against a majority rising that means to do harm to a small indefensible target or take rights away from them? Being Jewish, I worry that a large enough group of citizens with political cunning could begin another repression of a smaller group of citizens.

Madison assumed that our country was too large to be overrun by one or another faction, especially if we remained a republic. If he were alive today, I wonder if he would like to revise his opinion? Getting back to the original question, how does a country protect itself against a faction that would harm those with less clout?

First, can we agree that the United States is in the grip of a minority with too much control right now? Were it a truly representational government, we would participate in voting in greater numbers and we would have no reason to rise up and fix our political process. If the 28th "get-money-out" amendment isn't enough to remediate the influence of money and the media on our governance, then the *next* amendment must eliminate the chokehold of those in any branch of government who are acting as obstructionists or dictator, stopping us from achieving the common good. It must give ordinary folks the ability to have real influence in Washington.

How do we include the voters so that they count, yet avoid the pitfalls of direct democracy's potentially powerful factions?

We are likely not ready or willing to become the kind of nation Harry Braun's amendment would create. I believe his heart is in the right place, however, we need an amendment that makes each citizen realize his responsibility to maintain the rule of law and a civil society.

No discussion of direct democracy amendments would be

complete without former Alaskan Senator Mike Gravel's proposal. I first heard Mr. Gravel's voice on the People's Congress conference calls. He has been working on a direct democracy act and amendment for twenty-five years. In a symposium held in 2002, constitutional experts and attorneys, law professors, political science professors, and experts in direct democracy discussed and vetted Mr. Gravel's Citizens Amendment.[27] It overturns *Citizens United* while also giving Americans a vote on every bill that comes before the U.S. Congress.

Unfortunately, Section 3 of Mr. Gravel's amendment creates a hierarchy by appointing a Board of Trustees and a Director to a "Citizens Trust." I don't think a hierarchy will improve our situation. What method is there for people with different ideas to share their viewpoints without having to create a Directorship? Is there another system organized enough to effect political change on the federal level? Allow me to re-introduce a Citizen's Congress.

Each American should be educated in civics so that by age 18, she or he has the ability to participate in their own governance through a People's or Citizen's Congress. For the purpose of this book, I have chosen to call this congress a Citizen's Congress.

A Citizen's Congress could be given the right to participate in federal governance through a 29th amendment. The wording of this "Citizen's Congress amendment" should outline how registered voters will participate in three ways:

1. The U.S. Congress (legislative branch of government) only counts toward 50% of a vote to pass a bill into law; the other 50% has to come from a majority of the Citizen's Congress.

2. The U.S. Congress votes and can pass a bill, but the bill cannot become law if a majority of citizens disagrees with it. (Similar to the veto power of the Swiss.) –or–

3. A bill may be written by the Citizen's Congress, pass a majority, then the U.S. Congress goes through their normal process without changing the wording and must do so in a timely fashion. Our representatives have an opportunity to discuss the bill with the Citizen's

---

[27] See Appendix 16

Congress and advise accordingly. The U.S. Congress can veto the bill, but must do so against the wishes of the majority for the reasons Madison warned against: that the new law might be "adversed [sic] to the rights of other citizens."

A Citizen's Congress would help the voters of the United States energize the U.S. Congress. It will be much easier for ordinary citizens to petition Congress, to enact necessary legislation when Congress hasn't been proactive, to lobby members of Congress while a bill is in committee. And if the factions get too big, the U.S. Congress has a chance to step up and reason with the Citizen's Congress to convince voters when a bill is a bad idea. Perhaps the new bill goes against a smoothly-running law that is already on the books. Perhaps it violates a basic right of free people. Maybe it violates the Constitution. I believe this is one reason why a representative government was chosen by our founders and why a Harry Braun type of democracy would not succeed.

Under this type of Amendment, fewer bills will be introduced, and they need to be short and concise. It also requires putting a stop to last minute revisions, addendums and pork if the Citizen's Congress says *this is it, guys*. Don't mess with our legislation and play games by adding sanctions on Iran and loopholes for Citibank at the last minute.

How would the Citizen's Congress work? One way is by using tools such as E-Democracy.org where neighbors "build online public space in the heart of real democracy and community." E-Democracy's mission is to harness the power of the Internet "to support participation in public life, strengthen communities, and build democracy." E-Democracy has successfully hosted fifty local forums in seventeen communities across three countries: the United States, the United Kingdom and New Zealand.

From a site like E-Democracy, our local communities will in turn organize and share information at a general (or national) assembly meeting. Remember Duane Elgin who described how to use public airtime on television to hold meetings in Chapter 31? We will vote on bills online so long as voters don't mind making their vote public. With complete transparency, all voices can be counted properly.

We may not be able to prevent money from seeping into the election process and stop harmful media propaganda, but we can prevent Congress from passing laws like the Trans Pacific Partnership with a well-educated Citizen's Congress.

Peter Bearse, the economist who was featured in my infomercial, started a new Citizen's Congress by opening a 501(c)(4). Even if we don't pass a 29th Amendment to fix our government, it's important for Americans to have their collective voices heard. We can take the bull, the donkey and the elephant by their heads and join the Citizen's Congress now, without waiting.

And now for the actions you can take!

For those who ask me *what can I do right now,* may I suggest that you watch a video called *Interview With Wolf PAC leaders – Money Out Voters In!* in which ordinary citizens like you explain how they called their state legislators (for free!) to get a resolution started that calls for an Article V Convention. Visit Wolf PAC here: WolfPAC.com to get involved. If there's only one patriotic action you take in your entire life, this is it. If you've never voted because you feel like our government is broken, this is the first step toward fixing it.

The second step is for all of us to keep the pressure on our state assembly members, state legislators and federal Congressional representatives to support amending our Constitution. Phone calls to your public servants make a huge impact. If they are running for office, make them commit to applying for a convention of the states and the American Anti-Corruption Act and then hold them to it if they win their seat.

Without a Citizen's Congress to deliberate on the bills coming up for a vote, it might be difficult to get people to participate in the process. On average, about four to nine thousand bills come before Congress each year. Out of those, however, only a fraction get from committee to the House floor. Two websites that already disseminate information about pending bills: govtrack.us and opencongress.org are great resources for our Citizen's Congress.

An amendment that engages a Citizen's Congress will turn our representatives into advisers, experts at drafting legislation that culminates from a peer review process. Our government will be run through collective intelligence. No more backbiting, grandstanding, stonewalling, corruption and political shenanigans.

Right now, it's just a dream. Are we going to give up, or will we stay the course?

39
HOW TO GET TO HEAVEN

A loving person lives in a
loving world. A hostile person lives
in a hostile world. Everyone you meet
is your mirror.[28]
– Ken Keyes Jr., American author 1921-1995

If you could be assured of success, what would you do?

I remember asking myself this question before deciding to go on this quest. "Do the one thing you think you cannot do. Fail at it. Try again. Do better the second time. The only people who never tumble are the ones who never mount the high wire. This is your moment. Own it." Oprah Winfrey said.

Shortly after the election, the pre-payment for another year of webhosting came due. My web developer housed the site on a hard drive that he rents from a U.S. company, but he wanted to charge me $900 per year for the privilege of keeping it going. Considering how little I would have needed to use his services, it didn't seem right.

I raged inside, and wept about the unfairness of it all. I knew it was over, because I couldn't spend that kind of money to keep something going that nobody was visiting or using. I cried a lot. I could tell what kind of day it was by how many crumpled-up

---

[28] Reprinted from *Handbook To Higher Consciousness* by Ken Keyes Jr., Fifth Edition, Copyright 1975 by Living Love Center, 1730 La Loma Avenue, Berkeley, California 94709

tissues sat on my bed stand or the coffee table in my family room.

I decided to move the website to a smaller, less expensive host. My web developer wasn't happy about it, but he agreed to send all the information I needed to migrate the site. He warned that he couldn't help me anymore unless I paid him the nine hundred.

In the migration, the site got corrupted. It felt like all the blood left my body. I couldn't find any of the pages besides the home page, all the congressional districts were gone, even my blog had disappeared. The menu bar across the top and bottom didn't work. I was beside myself.

No matter what I did, I could not get the site to work properly. I implored Manu to help me and even paid him a few hundred bucks, but he was unable to find the line of code that would have straightened it all out. I lost the website, my blog, and all the work the Filipinas had done to list the candidates on the site.

Attempting to get Writeindependent.org going again became a nightmare that lasted four months, trying but failing repeatedly. I used up boxes of tissues, sobbing about the loss of my baby and I still didn't have a job to support me. I could forget about buying clothes for a very long time.

The president of my 501(c)(4) recommended I see her tax preparer so I could find out how to file my taxes for a non-profit. Within minutes of sitting down with the accountant and glumly going over the tens of thousands of dollars I spent, she told me that there were three ways to go with the business:

1. I could pay about $2,000 to an attorney before she prepared my taxes. She would charge me another $1,200 to help me file them. She warned me that I would need at least $2,000 per year for activities that would keep the non-profit open.

2. I could close up the non-profit with the help of an attorney.

3. I could find another organization that would take over my corporate shell.

I left her office crying. I didn't want to deal with it and I certainly didn't want to spend more money, throwing good after bad. Spectacular. Failure.

The most important thing I learned is that people are frequently wrong. They give terrible advice. I figured out how to file my own taxes as an exempt organization, filed electronically online, and I didn't have to pay a thing. It costs me about $25 every two years to keep the corporate shell going, and I can handle that.

I reminded myself to be grateful for being healthy, for being alive, and for having a wonderful daughter with luxurious blonde hair. Everything would work out if I let it. So what if I didn't approach things right? No one told me *not* to spend my money. It was all: *Yes! Spend it! Yes!* Now that it's gone, I can say *Don't ask me for any money. It's gone.* There's relief in that.

I made the executive decision that the only way I would run the website again is if people asked me to reinstate it, to duplicate it, or to start fresh and re-design it, and only if those people came with anonymous donations. I am done crying about it.

I still have my Writeindependent.org YouTube channel and all the videos I posted of the presidential debates I hosted. Above all, I had the experience of running something I was proud to create. I gave people employment and I affected the lives of those around me in a positive way.

Worrying about Writeindependent.org and wanting to get my message out en masse seems like a lifetime ago. Instead, now I lead a subdued, pastoral life with the birds singing in the fruit trees and little green plants, and that isn't such a bad thing. Writing and gardening, I can handle that. It's quiet and peaceful.

I revel in the ordinariness of being a nobody. Nobody bothers me. My phone doesn't ring much. It's quiet here – beautiful sunsets. I go outside in the dark with a flashlight to pick a gh for my bud vase and never get scared. I'm invisible, I think. No one reads my blog, nobody cares about me since my Mom died except Clarissa. Or so I thought.

I spent many hours in the garden, having I missed it so much. I wanted to work a solid week out there. The spiders were big and fat, frighteningly fat. I had two big mommas and I knew exactly where they hung out, so I wouldn't scare myself running into them.

The sky blazed red and pink and orange in streaks, reaching in fan shape above the sun, lighting the puffy clouds that moved ever so slowly. For half an hour it was a wonder to behold – like God saying "Yes! I am here!" Everywhere, glory across the sky. Life is good, robust, throbbing.

Behind my house, behind the fence, is a part of my property I call "the back forty." The phrase is a take-away from my farm days, growing up with acreage around the house. The back forty are the edges of a property, the damp lowlands, the forest and stream, the dense clumps of weeds.

When I moved to California, I planted fruit trees on my back forty behind the fence. Oro blanco grapefruit, the apple tree I received for winning the local apple pie contest, a kaffir lime, a Minneola tangelo, an Eversweet pomegranate, a Wonderful pomegranate, and a dwarf nectarine. But there's one huge, intractable problem. Ivy grows up the hillside and it threatens to take over the trees and choke them.

In running the website, I had neglected this area for more than a year and the ivy was a thick, tangled mass of roots below all the weed-cloth, cardboard boxes, and straw I had piled on to smother it. Ivy will stop at nothing; it grows three feet underground. On the first day, I attacked it with a pick ax mattock. I immediately saw it as a round-the-year project. As soon as I thought I'd finished the entire area, the ivy grew back where I started.

I dug so deeply that I feared I would lose my hill to erosion. I will have to fill a trench with cement someday, to separate the ivy from the "orchard" and I will have to carry the bags of concrete.

Within a few hours, I was crying at the enormity of the job. It overwhelmed me. I can't hire gardeners to help me. They wouldn't remove every last piece of root that could generate a new ivy plant. I would have to painstakingly attack it myself. When would I ever find the time for all that and for starting a new career?

Day after day, I returned to the top of my hillside. I worked out a system for it. I had two green waste cans, one for the old straw I would keep, and the other for the scraggly, ripped-out roots. I shoveled soil into a five-gallon bucket, meticulously removing pieces of root and digging even deeper. I poured the contents of the bucket into an area I'd already dug up. Every week, I filled two to three enormous green waste cans with more ivy. Month after month, I was making a little headway.

"Why am I doing this, God?" I asked. "Why is this my fate?"

It is because I am a steward. I can't just leave it alone, I have to tend it. It has to be clean and neat, abundant and lovely. I have to create the optimal growing environment for the fruit trees. And the fruit has to be sweet and dear, reverently grown, maximally expressed the way a tree would want its gifts to be. I can't be any other way. God put me in this garden and I will do this kind of work, until it is done.

Then I thought of Lawrence Lessig and his Rootstrikers, and I laughed. He has no idea what I'm doing on this side of the country! I'm hacking at the roots. I'm your rootstriker!

I will never give up.

This life is a test. It's testing to see if you live passionately, not listening to what everyone else says, but to your own inimitable heart. If you do this one thing, you get to heaven in this life on earth and in any future afterlife. We are given good hearts at the beginning, and feelings to guide us, and even when our parents behave badly, we have a choice to harden or soften those hearts.

The hard heart goes against the kernel of goodness and the soft heart listens to the goodness and bends to it and fights for it. The hardened heart loses its pliability and builds scars, and blocks out possibilities. All of creation is in the possibilities, so the hardened heart loses its vitality, the sense of itself as decent, good and dignified. The hardened heart has to lie to itself, say to itself *I am not that goodness. I hide myself from myself. I cannot fulfill what my kernel intended.*

There is a division – each choice is a division – and some choose goodness and others not, and that is as close to a description of heaven and hell as ever there was on this earth.

Next to your health, value a good conscience above all else.

40
VISITING THE HEARTLAND

Any intelligent fool can make things bigger, more complex,
and more violent. It takes a touch of genius — and a lot of courage
to move in the opposite direction.
– E.F. Schumacher, British economist (1911-1977)

At Lockheed Martin facility at Bethesda, Maryland, the entire workforce of more than ten thousand employees stands in a stadium-sized hanger. The new Commander in Chief walks onto a platform, followed by four-star General Ray Odierno, economist Jeremy Rifkin and Secretary of State Andrew Bacevich.

The 45th POTUS shakes hands with Marillyn Hewson, President and CEO of Lockheed Martin and Bruce Tanner, Chief Financial Officer. The new President of the United States places her notes carefully on the Lucite podium and checks the teleprompter for her first words.

"Hello, Lockheed Martin. Thank you, Ms. Hewson and Mr. Tanner for this opportunity to speak with the engineers, planners, and scientists at this great company, one of the largest defense contractors in our country." The room erupts in applause.

"First, I want you all to know that everyone here is keeping his or her job." A few scattered laughs relieve tension in the crowd. "That is my number-one priority. However, the focus of your company is about to change. You must always remember that as the taxpayers fund a substantial part of your wages, so must we answer to the ultimate stakeholders: the men and women who share in your vision to keep us safe while being a leader in scientific innovation."

The President pauses, allowing her words to sink in. She punctuates each sentence with enough silence to allow her audience to grasp the full measure of importance, the high level of urgency in her message.

"By electing me, you have handed me a mandate to utilize our human capital toward securing our country, not by violence, but by building relationships between us and the global community. We all agree on the basic premise that we have only one home, one earth and we must keep it healthy in order for us to thrive in the coming age. We must work together now, more than ever, if humanity is to prove that extinction is not our genetic, evolutionary or religious destiny.

"A lot of naysayers will tell you that it isn't time to decrease our dependence on fossil fuels today, but I want you to know that it's already happening. We need to secure the future for our children by capturing energy using cutting edge technology that we've already seen at Lawrence Livermore Labs, at Ballard Power and at Arizona State University. Your role is to build the infrastructure to support our new energy paradigm. So, of course you have jobs. In fact, this company is where America begins to get back on its feet, morally and ethically.

"The truth is, we cannot afford *not* to do this work. If we, who live and work near the nation's capitol, don't use our skills and abilities to make this change, more agile and aggressive companies will jump at the chance to fulfill these needs.

"That's why we're devoted to bringing your skill set up to the 21st century with job retraining over the next 18 months. You will learn everything you need to know to manage crews of technicians across the country who will install the electron-based infrastructure to replace the current oil-based containment systems and pipelines."

The POTUS takes a deep breath, because she knows that she's going to drop a big bomb.

"Everyone honors your dedication to building the F-35, and we would not be here today were it not for the legislators and supporters who made it possible to spend more than four hundred billion dollars over twelve years on this project. We also know that we cannot afford to produce something that will not fly, forgive the pun. I hereby grant you the awesome responsibility to start work that defines you as a positive force for good. Indeed, it is the only purpose in life worth fulfilling.

"Our greatest challenge in the coming decade will be preparing for the damaging effects of severe weather patterns caused by global warming. It is a greater threat than any other. Greater than terrorism, greater than any enemies we've ever faced.

"Our experts have been warning us for years that we can expect more droughts, floods, wildfires, and tornadoes. In this lifetime, without the proper energy sources, without proper water management, we will be living without air conditioning and heating, without fresh water, and without healthy food for our children. This is the grave consequence of the overuse of fossil fuels and the government's neglect, the deferred maintenance and lack of respect for the health of our waterways, soil, oceans and air.

"Life doesn't end just because we are struggling. If anything, life presents us with the imperative to cooperate and coordinate on a massive scale. I am here for you, to help you become leaders in your own communities, to stay civil in the face of adversity. You can, and together we will, make the adjustments necessary to counter the effects of climate change.

"We have a decision. Do we want to remain peaceful? Or do we want to become a society that says 'every man for himself'? I think you know where I stand on this issue. You didn't vote for me because I'd be an aggressive, dictatorial 'decider' for everyone else. You elected me because I'm going to listen to you make up your own mind how this country shall proceed."

41
CALLING ALL AMERICANS

It is not the critic who counts; not the man who points out how the strong man stumbles, or where the doer of deeds could have done them better. The credit belongs to the man who is actually in the arena, whose face is marred by dust and sweat and blood; who strives valiantly; who errs, who comes short again and again, because there is no effort without error and shortcoming; but who does actually strive to do the deeds; who knows great enthusiasms, the great devotions; who spends himself in a worthy cause; who at the best knows in the end the triumph of high achievement, and who at the worst, if he fails, at least fails while daring greatly, so that his place shall never be with those cold and timid souls who neither know victory nor defeat.
– Theodore Roosevelt (1858-1919)

I love the scene in *Mr. Smith Goes to Washington* where Jimmy Stewart looks at all the telegrams asking him to stop his filibuster, and he glances up at the Speaker of the House. The Speaker smiles at him. A knowing smile slides across Stewart's face as he realizes the truth. He had the public's support behind him all along because of his decency and old-fashioned rightness. I think in that moment, Stewart won. The message that he uttered with his hoarse voice: "love thy neighbor."

It doesn't take a whole nation to fix Washington. It only takes one person—you. If you give up, then you are giving up on your dream, the future of this great country, and your legacy. If you care, if you have a heart, then there is hope for all of us.

I'm going to march on Washington. I'll be there on November 2nd through 7th, 2016. If you're going to join me, please send me a line at judy@writeindependent.org. Together, we'll figure out a way to make this country strong again. All you have to do is show up.

—End—

AFTERWORD

Small Victories that Set Precedents

The spirit of the Pledge for Honest Candidates lives on as the American Anti-Corruption Act. You don't have to wait for Congress to pass a law that clamps down on campaign funding bribery. You can place a referendum or initiative on the ballot in your municipality, the same way Tallahassee, Florida successfully did so. Using the American Anti-Corruption Act as their model, a multi-partisan committee crafted a referendum for the November 4, 2014 election. Tallahassee was the first to pass a city-wide anti-corruption act in the USA 67% of the voters agreed to establish:

- an anti-corruption policy
- a code of ethics
- an independent ethics board with broad powers
- an ethics office and ethics officer
- a $250 limit per contributor
- refunds for citizens who donate small amounts to their favorite candidates

Tallahassee proved that you don't have to wait for the U.S. Congress to pass campaign finance reforms on themselves! Represent.us will help you pass an anti-corruption act in your town. Check them out.

Wolf PAC and Move to Amend are using a similar resolution/initiative model to amend the federal Constitution. To find the text of the resolution, visit Wolf PAC's website, go to the Toolbox and click on "Our resolution language" or find this link: http://bit.ly/19Xf49D

Barring any unforeseen circumstances, I will continue to host Presidential Debates via Skype every four years.

The success of this book's objectives rests with you, the reader. Please tell your friends to read this, and above all, review this book online, to increase its chances of benefitting from Amazon's algorithms. Every positive review increases our chances of reaching a larger audience.

Regarding Writeindependent.org, the website is resurrected as a work in progress. With the necessary support, the goal is to make it the standard-bearer as an egalitarian platform for electioneering and idea-sharing, giving voice to our collective desires. To see it reach its full potential, please visit: www.writeindependent.org /donation. Thank you!

APPENDIX 1

Incumbents who voted for the Gramm Leach Bliley Act

The following incumbents voted to pass the Gramm Leach Bliley Act,
also known as the Financial Modernization Act of 1999. This bill
essentially dismantled the last vestiges of the Glass Steagall Act of 1933,
the protective measures that kept banks and securities honest and in
check. The passage of Gramm Leach Bliley paved the way for the 2008
economic crisis and the current recession.
Do you want tpeople?

ALABAMA
Robert Aderholt – District 4 (R)
Spencer Bachus – District 6 (R)
ALASKA
Don Young – At-large (R)
ARIZONA
Ed Pastor – District 7 (D)
CALIFORNIA
Mike Thompson – District 5 (D)
Howard Berman – District 28 (D)
Brad Sherman – District 30 (D)
Gary Miller – District 31 (R)
Grace Napolitano – District 32 (D)
Xavier Becerra – District 34 (D)
Mary Bono – District 36 (R)
Ed Royce – District 39 (R)
Ken Calvert – District 42 (R)
Loretta Sanchez – District 46(D)
Dana Rohrabacher – District 48(R)
Duncan Hunter – District 50 (R)
Brian Bilbray – District 52(R)
CONNECTICUT
John Larson – District 1 (D)
FLORIDA
Connie Mack – Senate (R)
Corrine Brown – District 5 (D)
Bill Young – District 13 (R)
Alcee Hastings – District 20 (D)

Ileana Ros-Lehtinen – District 27 (R)
GEORGIA
Jack Kingston – District 1 (R)
Sanford Bishop – District 2 (D)
IDAHO
Michael K. Simpson – District 2 (R)
ILLINOIS
Bobby Rush – District 1 (D)
Luis Gutierrez – District 4 (D)
Danny K. Davis – District 7(D)
Judy Biggert – District 11(R)
John Shimkus – District 15(R)
INDIANA
Pete Visclosky – District 1(D)
IOWA
Leonard Boswell – District 3 (D)
KENTUCKY
Ed Whitfield – District 1 (R)
Hal Rogers – District 5 (R)
MARYLAND
Ben Cardin – Senate (D)
Steny Hoyer – District 5 (D)
Roscoe Bartlett – District 6 (R)
MASSACHUSSETS
Richard Neal – District 1 (D)
Jim McGovern – District 2 (D)
MICHIGAN
Debbie Stabenow – Senate (D)
David Lee Camp – District 4 (R)
Fred Upton – District 6 (R)
Sander Levin – District 9 (D)
MISSISSIPPI
Roger Wicker – Senate (R)
Bennie Thompson – District 2 (D)
MISSOURI
Jo Ann Emerson – District 8 (R)
NEBRASKA
Lee Terry – District 2 (R)
NEVADA
Shelley Berkley – District 1 (D)
NEW HAMPSHIRE
Charlie Bass – District 2 (R)

NEW JERSEY
Bob Menendez – Senate (D)
Rob Andrews – District 1 (D)
Frank LoBiondo – District 2 (R)
Chris Smith – District 4 (R)
Frank Pallone – District 6 (D)
Bill Pascrell, Jr. – District 9 (D)
Rodney Frelinghuysen – District 11 (R)
Rush D. Holt, Jr. – District 12 (D)
NEW YORK
Peter T. King – District 2 (R)
Carolyn McCarthy – District 4(D)
Gregory W. Meeks – District 5(D)
Nydia Velázquez – District 7(D)
Carolyn B. Maloney – District 12 (D)
Charles Rangel – District 13(D)
Joseph Crowley District 14 (D)
Eliot L. Engel – District 16 (D)
Nita Lowey – District 17 (D)
Louise McIntosh Slaughter – District 25 (D)
NORTH CAROLINA
Walter B. Jones – District 3 (R)
David Price – District 4 (D)
Howard Coble – District 6 (R)
Mike McIntyre – District 7 (D)
Mel Watt – District 12 (D)
OHIO
Mike DeWine – Attorney General (R)
Steve Chabot – District 1 (R)
John Boehner – District 8 (R)
OKLAHOMA
Frank Lucas – District 3 (R)
OREGON
Greg Walden – District 2 (R)
Earl Blumenauer – District 3 (D)
PENNSYLVANIA
Michael F. Doyle – District 14 (D)
Joseph R. Pitts – District 16 (R)
SOUTH CAROLINA
Jim Clyburn – District 6 (D)
TENNESSEE
John Duncan – District 2 (R)

TEXAS
Sam Johnson – District 3 (R)
Ralph Hall – District 4 (D)
Rubén Hinojosa – District 15 (D)
Sheila Jackson-Lee – District 18 (D)
Lamar S. Smith – District 21 (R)
Pete Sessions – District 32 (R)
Lloyd Doggett – District 35 (D)
UTAH
Orrin G. Hatch – Senate (R)
VIRGINIA
Robert C. Scott – District 3 (D)
Bob Goodlatte – District 6 (R)
Jim Moran – District 8 (D)
Frank Wolf – District 10 (R)
WASHINGTON
Doc Hastings – District 4 (R)
Adam Smith – District 9 (D)
WEST VIRGINIA
Nick Rahall – District 3 (D)
WISCONSIN
Paul Ryan – District 1 (R)
Ron Kind – District 3 (D)
Jim Sensenbrenner – District 5 (R)
Tom Petri – District 6 (R)

Note: These were seated House members during 2012. Whether they ran for re-election or ran for a different post, as Paul Ryan did in his bid for the Vice Presidency in 2012, I thought it was important for voters to know what their sitting representatives had done in 1999 and 2000.

APPENDIX 2

Soundtrack for Election 2012

1. I'm Alive by Electric Light Orchestra: When Nietzsche said that "God is dead," he might have meant that the church institutionalized religion and spirituality, removing it from the natural world. Or that the person who doesn't "believe" in God stopped noticing God all around him. When I first heard this song, it gave me an ebullient feeling and I didn't have any notion that God was involved. A few years later, I realized that this song could be a sign that God is very much alive, and that each person feels God in his heart. No religion necessary.

2. Hush by Deep Purple: This was one of my mother's favorite songs. It begins with a wolf howling in the background. I liken the wolf to the wildness of nature; that we all come from wilderness, and that we must respect the wild, whether animal or nature, before we begin to tame it in socially constructive ways. That respect should remain, even as we channel our baser instincts into sacred action.

3. Mojo Boogie by Johnny Winter: When this song first chose me by happenstance, the Gulf Coast was still reeling from Katrina's effects. I often think that God communicates through music. Maybe this is the Great Spirit's way of apologizing for the suffering people have to endure as climate crises raise the water levels on our cities, farms, and graveyards. Notice how uplifting this song is regarding New Orleans.

4. I Don't Know Why by Shawn Colvin: I chose this song for my daughter, to express how I feel about her.

5. Guilty by Matthew Ryan: This song has themes of war, eternity, and being saved from one's own demons, as well as those imposed upon us by others. I talked with Mr. Ryan about writing the lyrics to this song, and he denied trying to make a specific point. He thinks art can be translated any number of ways, and each person will arrive at his own conclusions.

6. Come To The River by The Jayhawks: I love this band, and it is difficult to choose one specific song when there are so many excellent ones. To me, this song is about falling in love and the price one has to pay when it happens to you.

7. Mary Had A Little Lamb by Stevie Ray Vaughan: This song is featured in a scene I wrote for my screenplay called "Needles," which became the midlife crisis book entitled "Seeds: An Incredible Love Story." I first heard the song while shopping at Costco, but I used it as the dance music for a scene I wrote about grocery shopping

at a small market in Needham called Roche Bros.

8. Hear Me (Tears Into Wine) by Jim Brickman, sung by Michael Bolton. I heard this by chance while I was gardening and listening to a friend's iPod. When I came across this treasure, I thought it expressed how someone feels when they are hitting a low point and want to reach out to God, or a loved one, or to the world.

9. When You Wish Upon A Star by Michael Crawford: This song captures the innocence of a person who has hopes and dreams. As a child, the whimsy of this song is simple to inhabit, but as one gets older, it's harder to sustain the suspension of disbelief that dreams can come true. Music helps us get there.

10. I Believe In You by Bob Dylan: This is my favorite Dylan song of all time. To me, there's no question this song is about God, but it's written so that lovers could argue that it's about a romantic love interest.

11. Si Paloma by Sun Kil Moon: Mark Kozelek, who wrote this piece, is one of my favorite composers for guitar. Here, he features both guitar and mandolin in circular, lilting melodies. It's uplifting without the use of words.

12. Nueva York by Santana: I bought Santana's album *Shangó* when I was in college and it never gets old. This song celebrates the heterogeneity of New York City while giving it a nod as the apple of our country.

13. Let My Love Open the Door by Pete Townshend: I can't help but remember why this song ended up in my first book: it's because a friend sang it to me while working in my garden.

14. Jainy by Five for Fighting: I named the character in my first book "Jainy" because I liked the sound of the name. The end of this song is meaningful for someone who isn't sure she will be okay. Wouldn't it be ironic if marijuana users end up helping us get Writeindependent.org going when I don't condone the drug's use?

15. Orion In The Sky by Shawn Colvin: I chose to use this track at the end of the Green Party's infomercial. These poignant lyrics speak about our mishandling of the environment: Because we've broken down the wilderness / And we've blackened up the skies / And we cry 'cause we've got no vision left / While the smoke gets in our eyes/ And there's no more time / And the dream is dying…

16. Here Comes The Sun by The Beatles: I was writing something poignant in my diary, and just when I was wasted from all the crying and energy expenditure caused by a catharsis, this song came on. I used this song as the background music to the Republican version of my infomercial, hoping to inspire the faithful by its religious

connotations or the atheists by its suggestion of solar power, depending upon how you look at it.

17. Fill Her Up by Sting, featured by James Taylor and written by Earl Scruggs: When I was looking for songs for my infomercial to play in the background of the scrolling list of incumbents who voted for the Gramm Leach Bliley Act, I thought this one would speak to the conscience of those who benefited from gaming the system. So what if it were legal? Was it ethical?

18. Highway Star by Deep Purple: This is a nod to the Libertarian at the LAVA meeting who wanted his car to make the "vroom vroom" sound. The more I listen to "Highway Star," the more I think it epitomizes how Libertarians want to feel: the freedom of a fast car on the road, nobody's gonna take it, it's got everything, big fat tires and driving power, nobody's gonna take my head, I got speed inside my brain.

19. Waist Deep In The Big Muddy by Pete Seeger: I wanted to use 'Get Up Offa That Thing' by James Brown for the Democrat version of the infomercial, but the infomercial hadn't touched on the hoarding of money that Democrats were supposed to "get up offa." So I had to choose something else that would make sense. I changed the song to "Waist Deep In the Big Muddy" by Pete Seeger because I felt that now we're following the General into waters over our head, and if we don't turn around, it will be too late for us. The war theme matched Obama's militaristic policies that are all too similar to Bush Junior's.

APPENDIX 3

Executive Summary of Writeindependent.org

Problem:

Media dictates politics today. The public expects advertising to help them choose a candidate. The only campaign method that reaches critical mass is expensive media on the national scene. Campaign funding has reached an all-time high, with no roof in sight. Citizens United, PACs, Super PACs, 501(c)(4)s, bundling, and lobbyists have paved the way for undue influence in Washington. It has got to stop.

Solution:

Writeindependent.org is a game changer to the 'politics as usual' morass by offering federal candidates a way to collectively campaign on television and through the media to compete against the special interests. By giving voters a clearinghouse for finding non-special-interest funded candidates (or becoming candidates themselves with very little money), Writeindependent.org focuses on giving people true democracy without all the backbiting, bickering, and ineffective drama of the two party system.

Writeindependent.org meets this need by providing the following capabilities:

- ❖ Social network community for subscribers and candidates.
- ❖ Showcase state and national issues in an organized way.
- ❖ Streamline grass roots momentum to resolve top political issues.
- ❖ Identify candidates for Congress and President most aligned with subscriber profile.

Strategy:

- ❖ Offer our candidates to sign a CAMPAIGN REFORM PLEDGE to act as the foundation of their platform which will deliver votes.
- ❖ Produce a half-hour "infomercial" to educate the public about economics and alternate choices for Congress and run media during the six weeks prior to the election.
- ❖ Utilize a public relations and advertising campaign to blast the country's airwaves, print media, billboards, and Internet.
- ❖ Use social media, SEO, YouTube videos and Google Ad Words, Facebook, Twitter, and the like to exponentially network the site.

Urgency:

To meet the challenges of the coming century, people from the sciences, technology, engineering, agriculture and medicine need to populate our Congress, rather than politicians with a law degree. Unlike any other time in history, the convergence of

❖ High Internet usage.
❖ 90% dissatisfaction of Congress among those polled.
❖ Progressive and Occupy movements gaining traction.
❖ Young voters ready for action.
❖ High unemployment.

Restlessness of the 99% who feel disenfranchised sets the stage for breakout change in election processes. That time is now and we must act.

APPENDIX 4

Occupy List of Grievances

The following document was accepted by the NYC General Assembly on September 29, 2011. It can be found at: http://www.nycga.net/resources/documents/declaration/

Declaration of the Occupation of New York City

As we gather together in solidarity to express a feeling of mass injustice, we must not lose sight of what brought us together. We write so that all people who feel wronged by the corporate forces of the world can know that we are your allies.

As one people, united, we acknowledge the reality: that the future of the human race requires the cooperation of its members; that our system must protect our rights, and upon corruption of that system, it is up to the individuals to protect their own rights, and those of their neighbors; that a democratic government derives its just power from the people, but corporations do not seek consent to extract wealth from the people and the Earth; and that no true democracy is attainable when the process is determined by economic power. We come to you at a time when corporations, which place profit over people, self-interest over justice, and oppression over equality, run our governments. We have peaceably assembled here, as is our right, to let these facts be known.

They have taken our houses through an illegal foreclosure process, despite not having the original mortgage.

They have taken bailouts from taxpayers with impunity, and continue to give Executives exorbitant bonuses.

They have perpetuated inequality and discrimination in the workplace based on age, the color of one's skin, sex, gender identity and sexual orientation.

They have poisoned the food supply through negligence, and undermined the farming system through monopolization.

They have profited off of the torture, confinement, and cruel treatment of countless animals, and actively hide these practices.

They have continuously sought to strip employees of the right to negotiate for better pay and safer working conditions.

They have held students hostage with tens of thousands of dollars of debt on education, which is itself a human right.

They have consistently outsourced labor and used that outsourcing as leverage to cut workers' healthcare and pay.

They have influenced the courts to achieve the same rights as people, with none of the culpability or responsibility.

They have spent millions of dollars on legal teams that look for ways to get them out of contracts in regards to health insurance.

They have sold our privacy as a commodity.

They have used the military and police force to prevent freedom of the press.

They have deliberately declined to recall faulty products endangering lives in pursuit of profit.

They determine economic policy, despite the catastrophic failures their policies have produced and continue to produce.

They have donated large sums of money to politicians, who are responsible for regulating them.

They continue to block alternate forms of energy to keep us dependent on oil.

They continue to block generic forms of medicine that could save people's lives or provide relief in order to protect investments that have already turned a substantial profit.

They have purposely covered up oil spills, accidents, faulty bookkeeping, and inactive ingredients in pursuit of profit.

They purposefully keep people misinformed and fearful through their control of the media.

They have accepted private contracts to murder prisoners even when presented with serious doubts about their guilt.

They have perpetuated colonialism at home and abroad.

They have participated in the torture and murder of innocent civilians overseas.

They continue to create weapons of mass destruction in order to receive government contracts.*

To the people of the world,

We, the New York City General Assembly occupying Wall Street in Liberty Square, urge you to assert your power.

Exercise your right to peaceably assemble; occupy public space; create a process to address the problems we face, and generate solutions accessible to everyone.

To all communities that take action and form groups in the spirit of direct democracy, we offer support, documentation, and all of the resources at our disposal.

Join us and make your voices heard!

*These grievances are not all-inclusive.

APPENDIX 5

Pledge (Agreement) for Honest Candidates
for 2016

I, the undersigned, hereby pledge that, if elected to serve as a member of the Senate or House of Representatives of the United States Congress, I will:

1. Enact the American Anti-Corruption Act in its entirety, without modification. To read the American Anti-Corruption Act, visit: http://anticorruptionact.org/full-text/.

2. Give my full support to an Amendment to the Constitution in the spirit of the drafts outlined in the Renew Democracy Amendment and/or the amendment suggested by Move to Amend.

3. Enact legislation that:

- Standardizes voting so that all states must use paper ballots and receipts showing the selection made.
- Counts ballots in public, open and accessible to being videotaped.
- Institutes range voting for all elected officials on the federal level, including President of the United States. This abolishes the electoral college.
- Changes the congressional district lines to adopt a "shortest splitline algorithm" and abolish gerrymandering.

Signed:_____Date:_____

APPENDIX 6

Presidential Debate Questions
from the Writeindependent.org Debates

Debate 1: The Economy
Debate 2: Energy
Debate 3: Civil Liberties and Campaign Reform
Debate 4: Immigration & Naturalization, Illegal Drugs
Debate 5: Education
Debate 6: Social Security and Other Civilian Programs
Debate 7: Military/War
Debate 8: Healthcare, Drugs
Debate 9: Foreign Policy

Debate 1: The Economy

1. Economy – Obama's budget, though closing the gap on debt, still remains $1.3 trillion short of being balanced in 2012. Rather than imagine the dire consequences of what might happen if the U.S. were unable to borrow money from other countries to pay its bills, what would you recommend to balance the budget?

2. Price of Oil – Considering that price fluctuations in oil affects our entire economy, what is the President's ability to control the oil cartels? What will you do to secure our energy future, and thus the foundation of our economy?

3. Free Market – Do we really have a free market today? Is the market truly free, or is it controlled by a few large corporations who lobby and write burdensome legislation that protects their interests, while stifling emerging, competitive technology and creativity? What would you do to help bring back a truly free market?

4. Entitlement Programs – Individuals and companies are using offshore accounts as tax havens. A practice called "transfer pricing" shifts corporate profits out of the U.S., hence bypassing taxation. Another example [of entitlements] is an obscure IRS rule that says that besides salary and bonuses, a hedge fund manager is taxed at only 15% for her share of the profit earnings on the assets she manages. These entitlements rob our government of tens of billions of dollars each year, according to a study by the Congressional Research Service. What would you do about these entitlement "programs?"

5. Self Regulating Businesses – Do you believe that businesses can be trusted to regulate themselves? After witnessing the activities in the

banking sector with sub-prime mortgages, credit default swaps and asset backed securities, with the effects of the Gramm Leach Bliley Act and the Commodity Futures Modernization Act, how do we know our future is in good hands? When companies would rather pollute and later pay attorneys fees for class action suits than deal with the cost of providing an environmentally sound process, can we trust businesses to do what is in the best interest of our people? And if not, what is government's role in making these companies do what is right?

6. Infrastructure & Energy Spending – Do you propose that spending money on infrastructure will alleviate our economy, or will it just put off our problems by adding to the debt? On what infrastructure programs would you spend our money?

7. Alternative Energy Spending – How do you propose our government be involved in funding alternative energy? What other funding sources could there be for kick starting an alternative energy program?

8. Trade Agreements – In 1993, President Clinton signed NAFTA into law, making it easier for trade between Mexico and the U.S.. GATT, under the supervision of the World Trade Organization systematically broke down trade barriers between the U.S. and most other countries. The FTAA (Free Trade Area of the Americas) threatens to extend this to 13 more countries. All these laws make it easier for American manufacturing companies to seek cheaper labor in countries where human rights violations are not punished and laws protecting the environment are lax or completely absent. How would you change these trade agreements to stimulate American companies to keep manufacturing jobs in America? Or would you keep the status quo?

9. Subsidy Programs – What government subsidy programs are necessary, and which ones need to be curtailed or cut, or thoroughly reviewed?

10. Top Executives Salaries – There is an expectation today for the top tier executives to collect astronomically high salaries, while squeezing costs at every juncture: demanding lower corporate taxes, low-cost labor with less benefits and more work hours or sending jobs overseas where there are few labor standards. These same executives expect no tax on importing or exporting, and cheap materials for manufacturing. With executives like these, changing trade agreements and taxation for imports and exports might drive up the cost of goods for our citizens. Could our consumers absorb that cost, or would you expect the companies directors salaries to bear the brunt of that cost, rather than seeing their stock prices decline?

Debate 2: Energy

1. Energy Plan – What is your energy plan for 2013 and beyond, and what is your timeline for implementation? How do you expect your energy plan to get funded? Will the government get involved or not?

2. Fracking – What is your position on fracking, the practice of forcing pressurized fluids, commonly into shale, to extract natural gas?

3. Oil Speculation – On April 21, 2011, the Department of Justice created the Oil and Gas Price Fraud Working Group whose mission it was to "root out manipulation of the oil market and gouging of consumers at the gas pump." The fraud working group has not found anything "illegal." However, financial speculators who never take delivery of oil make up about 65% of the trading in oil futures markets. Historically, speculation has hovered around 30%, setting a premium on oil even when there is ample supply. Regulators are trying to pass legislation to prevent excessive market speculation, but Wall Street is suing the Commodity Futures Trading Commission to make sure it doesn't get regulated and can therefore rise above 65%. As President, will you allow Wall Street to jack up the price of oil, or will you put pressure on Congress not to bow down again to Wall Street?

4. Energy Policy – Our government has not had an open energy policy since the Energy Task Force, officially the National Energy Policy Development Group, created by then-President George Bush in 2001 during his second week in office. Instead, it has arranged its energy policies behind closed doors with hand-chosen representatives from specific energy providers. How would you set your energy policy, and do you think it needs to be done in secret?

5. Distributed Energy – Distributed generation, also called on-site generation, dispersed generation, decentralized generation, decentralized energy or distributed energy generates electricity from many small energy sources. For example, SMUD (the Sacramento Municipal Utilities District) is the largest distributed utility solar energy system in the world. Distributed generation collects energy from many sources and may lower the impact on the environment while improving security of supply. Are you aware of successful blueprints of this method, and would you expand on this model or encourage it community by community?

6. Cap and Trade – Please explain cap and trade. Then tell us whether you would re-visit this program or not, and why?

7. Oil Exploration – What is your stance on oil exploration in the U.S. and abroad? Specify which areas are most logical for exploration and which areas should be avoided, in your opinion.

8. Nuclear Power – Japan is still reeling from the tsunami that caused

three reactor meltdowns at the Fukushima nuclear power plant. The "measurement movement" is reflected in the large number of citizens buying their own Geiger counters and checking for radioactivity in their food. Only two of the nation's 54 nuclear reactors are still operating, and the former Prime Minister Kan now says Japan needs to reduce its reliance on atomic energy. In light of these facts, what is your outlook for nuclear energy?

9. Solyndra – Obama has been criticized for his support of Solyndra because it was a failure. What did he do wrong, and how would you do things differently?

10. Fuel Cells in the Automotive Industry – Our auto industry is lagging behind Japanese auto manufacturers in developing fuel cells. Do you think fuel cells should be explored, or, since Japanese manufacturers have most of the patents on automotive use of fuel cells, thanks to Clinton and Bush's underfunded technological development to any significant degree during its infancy, should we now rely on other systems for car propulsion?

Debate 3: Civil Liberties and Campaign Reform
1. Voter Rights – Eight states this year passed voter suppression laws, part of an effort to make voting difficult for five million Americans. Suppression tactics include: voter identification laws, restrictions on early voting and absentee voting, restrictions on voter registration and registration drives. If people have trouble voting this year, what do you recommend they do to assure that their voices are heard?

2. Campaign Finance Reform – Members of Congress often promise to enact campaign reform, but they have not done anything to discourage K-Street or corporations from funding their campaigns. With the Supreme Court decision [*Citizens United*] that corporations are people, more money has funneled into campaign efforts than ever before, estimated to reach eight billion for the November 6th elections. How do you expect to change the system, when Congress will resist such change at every step?

3. Free Speech Comcast NBC Merger – This next question has to do with free speech. With the January 2011 merger of Comcast and NBC, one company has unprecedented control over media and the Internet. According to Josh Silver of United Republic, it "sets the table for Comcast to turn the Internet into cable television, where it has the ability to speed up its content, slow down or block its competitors such as Netflix, and hike the rates for its programming and services. We'll all end up paying more – whether you're a Comcast subscriber or not." Do you have any intention to bring more diversity and competition back into

the media mix and if so, how?

4. *Citizens United* Decision – The Move to Amend campaign seeks a new constitutional amendment which overturns the *Citizens United* Supreme Court ruling by stating that only people are people. Twenty four states already have laws that prohibit corporations from making independent expenditures from their general treasury. Do you think it necessary for people to fight for Constitutional amendments every time the Supreme Court makes an unpopular decision?

5. Public Financing of Elections – Americans for Campaign Reform recommends a Fair Elections Act, the centerpiece of which is public financing. According to their fact sheet, a candidate must raise $50,000 and win her party's nomination before qualifying for public financing of $4 matching funds for each $1 raised through constituents. In addition, it promises reduced media rates. Is this another example of government promising money it doesn't have to politicians? What is your take on public financing, and specifically this program?

6. Lobbying and Bribery – Even if public financing were a viable option, how do we handle the scourge to our democracy that is K-street and lobbying?

7. NDAA Indefinite Detention – The National Defense Appropriations Act (NDAA) reaffirms and expands the AUMF: Authorized Use of Military Force resolution which granted the President the authority to use all "necessary and appropriate force" against those whom he determined "planned, authorized, committed or aided" the September 11th attacks, or who harbored said persons or groups. The American Civil Liberties Union (ACLU) criticized the detention provisions, concerned that prisoners who may be held indefinitely could include U.S. citizens arrested on American soil. The liberal wording of the NDAA includes those who commit a "belligerent act" against the U.S. in the aid of enemy forces, and allows indefinite detention "without trial, until the end of the hostilities." Do you feel that the President needs this amount of authority, and does it violate habeas corpus? What will you do about this portion of the NDAA?

8. Habeas Corpus – According to Article One of the Constitution, the right to a writ of habeas corpus can only be suspended "in cases of rebellion or invasion the public safety may require it." Do you still think that the NDAA violates habeas corpus?

9. How To Trust Government Again – How much of the concern for our civil rights being violated relates to a general mistrust of our government, and how shall our government regain the trust of its people?

10. RFID chip – The RFID (Radio Frequency ID) chip is a tiny chip that is embedded in products, pets, or people that can be scanned from

yards away. It is helpful in tracking inventory or shipped items, can be used to check out at a check stand, and help police officers find your information quickly without having to ask you to pull out your license. Do you have any concerns that this technology violates privacy? Is this a slippery slope, and how so?

11. Patriot Act – Many scholars have noted that the Patriot Act violates our constitutional rights, in particular the 4th Amendment: "The right of the people to be secure in their person, houses, papers, and effects, against unreasonable searches and seizures, shall not be violated, and no warrants shall issue, but upon probable cause, supported by oath or affirmation, and particularly describing the place to be searched, and the persons or things to be seized." Specifically, the Patriot Act allows wiretaps on electronic devices, search without prior warrant, even for minor crimes, and "guilt by association," even when persons are unaware they are giving advice to a potential terrorist. On the other hand, the Patriot Act allowed authorities to use new technology to locate the people involved in the murder of Wall Street Journal reporter Daniel Pearl. Does the Patriot Act do more to protect citizens, or to violate their rights? What would you like to do about it?

Debate 4: Immigration and Illegal Drugs
1. Immigrant Rights – In your opinion, should immigrants have human rights equal to Americans?
2. Building a Wall – What do you think of building a wall at the border? Who should pay for the wall—all Americans or just the border states that want a wall? Who will build the wall? If we want to keep costs down, should we use Mexican labor? Should we build a similar wall between Canada and the USA? Do walls really keep people out of the country?
3. The Dream Act – The DREAM Act stands for: Development, Relief and Education for Alien Minors. Many children come to this country with their illegal alien parents, grow up here learning English, obtaining an education, often going to college. If it is found out that they have not obtained citizenship because their parents have not naturalized, they can be deported to a land foreign to them, without being given a choice to stay. The DREAM Act provides fast-track naturalization for alien minors who serve in the military or attend college for two years, so long as they arrived in the states prior to their sixteenth birthday. Would you support this initiative if and when it arrives on your desk for approval?
4. Deportation – The Department of Homeland Security is prioritizing deportation of undocumented immigrants who have committed crimes,

have recently crossed the border, or have re-crossed the border after being previously deported. Would you increase the deportation of immigrants to include other classes of individuals too? Which ones?

5. Arizona SB 1070 – Arizona law SB 1070 parts 6 a through d suggests police officers verify residence, confirm identity, determine immigration status, and find out compliance to federal registration laws. All of this could take hours, beyond what Part 2 of the law suggests (which requires police to check the immigration status of all persons they stop or arrest if "reasonable suspicion" exists that they are in the country illegally.) The law threatens to make racists distinctions or create an environment of harassment. What is your position on SB 1070?

6. Immigrants Taking Jobs – There is an assumption that illegal aliens take jobs away from Americans and use valuable social services not available in their native countries. But undocumented workers also create demand that leads to new jobs. They buy food, cars and cell phones, they get haircuts and go to restaurants. On average, there is close to no net impact on the unemployment rate. If undocumented workers pay taxes, should they be allowed to use social services like food stamps and Medi-Cal/Medicaid?

7. Detention Facilities – Despite numerous studies proving that immigrants are less likely to commit crimes than native-born Americans, Texas Representative Lamar Smith introduced the "Keep Our Communities Safe Act of 2011" (H.R. 1932) which proposes the expansion of an existing immigration lock-up system that would waste millions of taxpayer dollars and violate our constitutional ethos of individual liberty and due process. Many current detainees have no criminal record whatsoever and are held for months to years, without even a bond hearing. Our government's 2012 budget request for immigration detention already totals more than $2 billion, representing a 6.3 percent increase over FY 2011. Besides the fact that this is cruel treatment of human beings, could it be possible that these detention centers are no more than "big business" trying to make a buck with federal funds while simultaneously reinforcing the stereotype that immigrants are dangerous criminals?

8. Tex-Mex Border, Drug Cartels – In Texas, ranchers and farmers on the border see violence from drug cartels so consistently, that they post videos on a website called protectyourtexasborder.com, run by the Texan Department of Agriculture. The problem of drugs and violence in Mexico is well documented in a book by journalist Ioan (Yo an) Grillo called *El Narco: Inside Mexico's Criminal Insurgency*. A January, 2012 CNN report, citing Grillo's book summarizes the problem thus: "Wars occur because people cannot feed their families. They happen because

groups of people feel unimportant, disenfranchised, angry and broke. It only takes a few people with particularly hollow morals, capable of shutting off or suppressing guilt, to convince many that killing and dying in spectacular ways is tantamount to glory." Texans beg federal agencies to have a stronger impact on the problem of border violence and drug trafficking. 48,000 people have been killed in the last five years as a result of drug activity in and near Mexico, a formidable form of terrorism. What will you do about our border with Mexico where drug cartels are involved?

9. Legalization of Marijuana – Before we talk about legalizing drugs, I need you to make a clarification. If you are recommending decriminalization of drugs, you need to specify when it will no longer be a felony (requiring, for example, 1 year or more in jail) or a misdemeanor (requiring, for example less than one year plus a fine.) In October of last year, a Gallup poll showed that 50% of Americans think marijuana should be legalized. Currently, 16 states and D.C. have legalized the sale of marijuana for medicinal purposes. Should the federal government look the other way and allow states to regulate the use of marijuana?

10. Fear of Increased Drug Use – One of the greatest fears the population has for legalization of drugs is that it will cause drug use to rise, especially for young people. I have found data to support both sides: one showing no increase when legalized, others showing increases. If you suggest decriminalizing drug possession or use, what do you say to parents or people who do not want to see drugs use out in the open? Will decriminalization condone drug use?

11. Economic Effects of Legalizing Drugs – There is an assumption that legalizing drugs would be a boon to the economy in two ways: it would pave the way for regulated, American-made product, rather than importing questionable substances from other countries, and taxation of drugs would improve our debt situation. What do you think of these economic effects?

12. Portugal Legalized Drugs – In 2001, Portugal became the first European country to officially remove criminal penalties for possession of drugs, including marijuana, cocaine, methamphetamine and heroin. Addicts found possessing small amounts of drugs are sent to a panel consisting of a psychologist, social worker and legal adviser for appropriate treatment (which may be refused without criminal punishment). The theory was that jail time forced people to hide their habit, making it more difficult and shameful to seek help, and therapy is a lot less expensive than incarceration. Now, 10 years after adopting these policies, Portugal has the lowest rate of marijuana use in people

over 15 years of age in the entire European Union, and the U.S. has a higher percentage of cocaine users than Portugal has marijuana users. Could this program be adopted state by state, or do you think the country should adopt it all at once on a federal level?

13. Who Will Sell Drugs – Proponents of legalization say that it will end the drug trafficking cartels, though that is doubtful considering the fact that the Mexican drug trade is worth $39 billion in revenues. Even if the USA legalized drugs, who would distribute them? Walgreens? The local supermarket? Starbucks? What company would want the liability for selling a product as harmful as cocaine or heroin?

Debate 5: Education

1. Poverty and Education – The number one factor that correlates with poor educational outcomes is poverty. Our country is suffering from the highest poverty rate in 52 years. 22% of children live in poverty, 39% if African American and 35% if Hispanic. It's a vicious cycle. Poor education leads to more poverty, poverty to poor education. What is the answer?

2. Special Education – A large portion of the federal education budget is funding for special needs programs. Being the parent of a special needs child, I know from experience how we had to fight to obtain services for our child, partly because the school districts are loathe to give up the state funding that a warm body means to their bottom line. The school and we parents spent too much time and money on evaluations, attorneys and Individualized Education Program meetings (IEP's) – over 3 years – to finally convince the district that she needed prevention and intervention. Why not just do the prevention and intervention instead of agonizing over whether to do it or not for three years? Did you know that often schools make it so difficult to help our children reach their potential?

3. Student Loan Rates – Students graduating from college are drowning in loan debt, yet unable to find jobs with a livable wage. Many young people still live with their parents or under the poverty line. Yet Congress insists that in order to keep student loans at a reasonable rate, certain women's health care should go unfunded. If you presided over today's Congress, what would you tell them about student loan rates?

4. Autism Spectrum – According to the Centers for Disease Control, a recent study confirmed that autism and related disorders in the USA nearly doubled from ten years ago, so that now we are seeing a prevalence of one in 252 girls and one in 54 boys. Parents of these children are enormously impacted by the needs of these children, and their health takes a toll on our federal budget in the way of healthcare

and education costs. It behooves us to find out the causes and stamp them out. Will you support research in this area, and if it is found that environmental toxins are causing these problems, what will you do to the industries that put these toxins into our air, water, and soil?

5. Civics Education – One of the most important subjects missing in a quality education is civics, or how our government works and how civilians can participate in their government. Shouldn't civics lessons be a basic right and responsibility for all U.S. citizens? If so, would you consider adding that to the Common Core curriculum offered by Obama as the national standard, which [now] only covers math and reading?

6. Food Education – Growing Great is a curriculum-based program dedicated to inspiring children and adults to adopt healthy eating habits, teaching where our food comes from and how food impacts our longevity and wellbeing. Would you adopt this most basic curriculum into a national standard, or do you think there should be no national standards for learning about food?

7. Education and Defense – According to budget numbers, for every one dollar our government spends on education, $9.75 are spent on defense and manufacturing weapons of mass destruction. (We spend ten times the budget on defense as on education.) Does this proportion express your value system? What ratio of education to defense do you want to see?

8. State and Federal Funding – What should be the role of the local, state, and federal funding?

9. Teacher's Unions – What should be the role of unions in education?

10. National Standards – Obama's program for primary education focuses on national curriculum standards, called Common Core State Standards, which only address math and reading. Common Core standards are voluntary for each state to adopt or not as they see fit. Do you agree with providing national standards, or should each state set their own? If you agree with setting a national standard, what subjects besides math and language arts should be included?

11. Harlem Children's Zone – Geoffrey Canada of the Harlem Children's Zone in Harlem NY has been extremely effective in lifting children out of poverty by following the academic careers of his community's children. His program is largely funded by private sources and philanthropists. Under your administration, how would you support education in poverty-stricken areas?

12. Student Loan Debt – We have a student loan debt problem that mirrors the housing bubble: loans given out freely for a supposed good investment, are now going un-repaid. Obama's Band-Aid solution only

mildly benefits current students, not the unemployed graduates who have free time to protest in Occupy rallies. If we were lied to about "job creators" who still aren't stimulating the economy regardless of the fact that their tax breaks were extended, how do you propose to fix this problem of unemployment that so impacts our educational system? If the student loan bubble bursts, do you think lenders will strangle student loans much the same way banks are tight with home loans?

13. No Child Left Behind (NCLB) – The No Child Left Behind Act required testing of all students, regardless of their test-taking ability. The effect of this mandate is that some teachers taught to the test, or spent much instructional time focused on math and language arts, taking away time from more creative teaching and flexibility, in addition to important subjects such as the arts, physical education, etc. Would you include No Child Left Behind in your policies, or scrap the program?

14. Homework – Parents say they are used to seeing their children do two to four hours of homework per night. Competition for grades is fierce. In such an environment of pressure, people do not function creatively. For innovation to flourish, people need down time to dream, make unlikely connections between disparate ideas, and rest for their brains. Do you consider yourself creative, and what is your process? Please speak to your thoughts about homework: should it be a short review of the day's lesson, or long assignments?

Debate 6: Social Security and other Civilian Programs

1. Privatize Social Security – Would you support privatizing social security? Why or why not?

2. Sovereignty and TPP – Under the Trans Pacific Partnership, which both Obama and Romney support, a foreign corporation would be able to sue our government for standing in the way of their profit making agenda. An international tribunal, made up of three attorneys can rule in favor of the corporation, thus making American taxpayers liable for damages. Wouldn't the TPP effectively overrule our highest court in the land by agreeing to abide by this tribunal's decisions? Doesn't the President give away our country's sovereignty by signing the TPP?

3. Food Stamps and Jobs – According to a report by the U.S. Department of Agriculture, in 2010 almost half (47%) of all Americans who receive food stamps are children, 8% are elderly, and 20% are disabled. For the 25% who are left, or roughly ten million Americans, do you think the "job creators" could step up and offer them jobs so that they and their children could get off food stamps, instead of sending the jobs overseas where labor is cheap and items can be shipped here without tariffs?

4. TPP & SOPA – According to the Trans Pacific Partnership, which both Obama and Romney support, the agreement requires criminal enforcement for copyright infringement that goes beyond the Digital Millennium Copyright Act, causing the same constraints as SOPA, the Stop Online Piracy Act. Did you support SOPA, or were you concerned about it, and should we be concerned about TPP having the same effect? And by the way, Ron Kirk, U.S. Trade Representative denies that there are any similarities between SOPA and TPP, yet the TPP is consistent with all the trade documents we've seen in the last twenty years. In fact, Ron Kirk insists that these trade agreements should be discussed in secrecy and outside the public's purview. Your thoughts?

5. TANF – One of the purposes of TANF, Temporary Assistance for Needy Families is to provide monetary assistance to families with children, disabled, or elderly folks so that the able-bodied caretaker can obtain job training and get off of welfare. In fact, in order to receive TANF, a single head of household must work thirty hours per week to receive benefits. Could you improve on this program, and how?

6. Stimulus Plan of 2009 – Part of the American Recovery and Reinvestment Act of 2009 provides extended unemployment benefits, increases in food stamp benefits, a one-time payment to recipients of SSI and social security and veterans receiving disability and pensions. To fund this, our government is borrowing from our children's future. The wealthiest .1% of the population removed huge sums from circulation in the form of the bailout, yet seem oblivious to how their actions have resulted in a sluggish economy. How do you intend to fix this problem?

7. Trans Pacific Partnership Secrecy – The Trans Pacific Partnership (TPP) is a trade agreement, drafted in secret by 600 corporations without consulting Congress. Obama supports negotiations to pass the TPP and Romney wants it passed right away. Would you ratify the agreement if our Congress voted yes to any or all of the agreement's 29 chapters?

8. Affordable Care Act – What do you think of the Supreme Court's decision that the Affordable Care Act (ACA) is constitutional? Is there anything about the healthcare bill that you disagree with?

9. Medicaid – In a study recently conducted in Cook County Illinois, sixty-six percent of those who said they had Medicaid-CHIP (Children's Health Insurance Program) were denied appointments, compared with 11% who said they had private insurance, according to an article published Thursday in The New England Journal of Medicine. It is a sad fact that people with Medicaid are often turned down by medical providers, being told "we don't take Medicaid." Yet the Obama administration plans to use the program to cover more and more people as part of the ACA. In my experience, I have found that the Medicaid

clinics are rife with abuses by the administering facilities in both billing and lack of actual care. Knowing that this is a problem, what would you do to improve medical access and care?

Debate 7: Military/War

1. Executive Privilege Wars – Ever since Reagan, our Presidents have taken it upon themselves to decide whether or not to go to war. This is a violation of the law. In times of dire situations, that decision is supposed to be made by Congress. Reagan and every President since Reagan has exercised undue executive privilege in engaging our military, mostly in secrecy, illegally, and without Congressional approval. Once in office, would you stop this practice that Obama continues to perpetrate? (Joint Resolution 114, passed on Oct 10, 2002 granted the President the right to use force against Iraq at his discretion. This paved the way for war to be more easily entered into, without the deliberation of 535 members of Congress.)

2. PTSD – There is a grave disconnect between the values of an ordinary person and the act of killing another human being. In order to do a thing like that, you have to split yourself in two, or disassociate yourself from the act of killing. The backlash of killing another human being or multiple beings can be handled one of two ways: you can stuff those negative feelings down and ignore them, completely denying they exist, or you can have overwhelming feelings of regret, guilt, sometimes hopelessness to the point of depression. What would you do to support our men and women with Post Traumatic Stress Disorder?

3. Military for Defense – The original reason for creating a strong defense was to *defend* against invasion, against an enemy killing you. How far away have we gotten from a military that defends, and instead, have a military that makes bombs, airplanes, and drones for the sake of profit motives?

4. Profit Motive for War – Do our children really understand why we go to war? If they knew it was a business, and motivated by money, would they be so inclined to fight? What if our military's focus returned to a defensive mode, and we only used it sparingly, and only when absolutely necessary? In such a paradigm, many people who work in the defense industry would need to find other employment. What is your solution?

5. Military Suicides – Suicides in the military outnumber the death toll of casualties at war. Many of those who commit suicide do so because they cannot adjust to civilian life between deployments. Nobody is telling these men that what they have been doing in other countries feels wrong because in many cases, it is wrong. We are so far from just

providing the defense of our country that as a result, our soldiers can't make sense of their actions. Military officers often get angry at men who don't feel right about what they are doing. You are right to feel the way you feel, and now it is time to heal and the best way to do that is to learn how to handle anxiety. One of the best approaches is through Dr. R. Reid Wilson. Visit my blog on the website and type in "anxiety" to read my post called "change is scary" for specific information. And then make a pledge, to only partake in military efforts that provide for the defense of our country, and not to listen to rhetoric that says "freedom isn't free" or that we're fighting "for democracy." We thank you for your blind trust in our country's leadership that led you to where you are, because we would not be the United States without you. We, the people, want to provide you with leadership you can trust, who will not send you in harm's way unless absolutely necessary. Candidates, what would you like to say to the psyches of our military men and women to give them a sense of hope and that help is on the way?

6. Nuclear Program – According to a Brookings Institute study, we spent nearly eight trillion of today's dollars on nukes in the last half of the twentieth century; more than we spent on Medicare, education, social services, disaster relief, scientific research, environmental protection, food safety, highways, cops, prosecutors, judges, and prisons combined. Now we have a stockpile of aged and hard-to-upkeep nuclear weapons sitting around, deteriorating. We have been shoveling money into the Stockpile Life Extension Program, trying to keep these nukes on life support. What would you do with all those missiles? Do we really need enough nukes to blow up the entire world five times over?

7. Private Defense Contractors – Private contractors on the ground in Iraq outnumber our troops now, and each man is paid more than our soldier is. Outfits like Academi, who used to be called "Xe" and before that were called "Blackwater," enjoy a huge, undisclosed portion of our defense spending, yet hold none of the accountability and are set to no standards like our military's. Privateers wanting to cash in often die without anyone hearing about it because private companies are not obligated to report deaths of their employees. Would you curb our use of private companies for military use?

8. Drones – Drone strikes are occurring at a rate of once every four days in Pakistan. Our most cowardly method of warfare yet, drones are operated at game-like consoles from U.S. bases 7,000 miles away from human targets. In Pakistan alone, over 775 civilians were killed (called "collateral deaths") between 2004 and 2011, including 168 children. Our Air Force men who remote control these missions are having a serious backlash of emotional and psychological problems. John Brennan,

Assistant to the President for Homeland Security and Counterterrorism, lies when he says that our drones attack with "surgical precision." Obama is on the slippery slope of bringing war to areas without even officially calling it "war" and there is no end in sight to drone use. I, for one, cannot stand idly by and I am calling Obama a murderer. He and any future Presidents must be stopped from this unconscionable use of force. What is your stance on drones?

9.Why Do We Fight – Why do we fight? What are we fighting for? (See video for the rest of this question.)

10. Bush Doctrine – The Bush Doctrine insists that preemptive strikes are necessary. Would you wait for an aggressive event to happen to us before taking military action, or would you go into countries that have not asked for our help to be so-called "liberators"?

Debate 8: Healthcare, Drugs

1. Cause of Disease – It doesn't matter where the "dirty dozen" pollutants are released, because they are found long distances away and end up in the fats of animals and the people who consume animal fats. We ingest these toxins and they cause cancer, diabetes, obesity, endocrine and reproductive problems, and neurobehavioral disorders. Many companies make their profits by not cleaning up their messes. What can be done to address these issues, and thus improve the health of Americans?

2. GMOs – In California, we are voting for Proposition 37, which requires labeling of GMOs, genetically modified organisms, in our food. Right now, over 70% of supermarket foods contain GMOs without our knowledge or consent. These foods have not been extensively tested for safety on humans because Obama has appointed Michael Taylor as his FDA Deputy Commissioner for Foods. Michael Taylor was formerly Vice President of Monsanto, the biggest agriculture biotech company in the world. The animal studies that have been conducted show that GMOs cause allergies, digestive problems, inflammation, gene mutation, infertility and stunted growth, among many other things. Would you put the teeth back into the FDA and what would you tell the agricultural biotech businesses?

3. Insurance Company Conflict of Interest – Insurance companies have a problem with conflict of interest. They are in business to make money, so every time they provide money for healthcare, it comes off their bottom line. Do you see this as problematic, and what is the solution?

4. CAFOs – How do you think CAFOs (Concentrated Animal Feed Operations) should be handled, when they add antibiotic-resistant

bacteria, hormones, cleaning agents, ammonia, heavy metals, and silage to our surface water, creating algae blooms that lead to fish kills. How would you recommend re-vamping animal farm operations?

5. Affordable Care Act – Do you like the Affordable Care Act, also called Obamacare? Why or why not? If you want to repeal it, what do you say to the 35 million newly insured people?

6. Mad Cow Disease – A new case of BSE (bovine spongiform encephalopathy or Mad Cow Disease) was recently found in a dairy cow on April 23, 2012 in California during a planned Agriculture Department surveillance program. Would you ban the use of ground up animal parts being fed to cattle and do you know if our meat is being tested enough?

7. Vouchers for Medicare – Romney's running mate, Paul Ryan, proposes using a voucher program to pay for Medicare premiums. Medicare won't go away immediately; it will be offered as one of a list of companies that can provide seniors benefits. But, insurance companies don't have to provide exactly the same coverage as Medicare has in the past. To "compete" for seniors' business, they can start changing the benefits that are provided, thus attracting healthier people and discouraging those with more complex health issues. Into the future, as insurance plan premiums increase, the amount the government has to pay actually decreases as our population ages. Therefore, the burden of healthcare costs, both premiums and cost of care when you've hit insurance limits, goes up. Unfortunately, this happens whether we have Democrats or Republicans in office. How would you structure the Medicare plan and how would taxpayers pay for it?

8. Single Payer – We spend twice as much as other industrialized nations on health care, yet our outcomes are poorer in comparison. Even after enacting the ACA, 50 million Americans go without health coverage and millions more are inadequately insured. ACA has mandated that insurance companies reduce their administration costs from 31% to 20%. That means for every dollar given to a private insurance company, twenty cents goes to pushing paperwork, while Medicare administration is at only 3%. Streamlining payments through a single nonprofit payer would save more than $400 billion per year, enough to provide comprehensive, high-quality coverage for all Americans. Do you think a single payer program makes sense, and if so, would you expand the Medicare program? How would we phase out insurance companies?

9. Dirty Dozen Chemicals – There is a "dirty dozen" of the worst pollutants found to cause health problems in humans. One such chemical is dioxin. Many countries around the world, for example the Netherlands, Ireland and Belgium have all recalled foods because they tested high for

dioxin. In the USA, dioxin is conspicuously absent from the Fourth National Report on Human Exposure to Environmental Toxins, published in February 2012. Would you increase testing of foods to identify their potential hazards to our citizens?

10. Monsanto RoundUp®– One application of RoundUp® can cause a dramatic plunge in the number of beneficial soil microorganisms that provide nutrients to plants. "Studies show a reduction in the species that build humus, thus it contributes to the decline in soil organic matter," says Andre Leu, a researcher on the literature on glyphosate and its effects. In fact, RoundUp® is responsible for the increase in harmful soil pathogens, while killing beneficial soil "mycorrhizae," an important fungus that is an effective means for sequestering carbon in the soil. Carbon sequestration is an important mechanism for addressing carbon in the atmosphere. Monsanto is trying furiously to find a way to make money off of carbon sequestration, a process that would happen naturally if they weren't killing the very organisms most efficient at doing it naturally. How do we get out from under the use of RoundUp® in agriculture? Most importantly, how do we educate farmers and citizens about healthy soil versus Monsanto-treated soil?

11. Externalities – Margaret L. Williams, who lived next to two Superfund sites in Pensacola FL, Hilton Kelley, who found intense emissions from the Exxon Mobil refinery next his housing project, and Laura Ward, who found groundwater pollution from the nearby Lockheed Martin weapons plant, are just three examples of activists who stood up to the pervasive pollution put out by corporations without regard to the ill health affects it causes [to neighboring] low income populations. There are too many examples to name here of pollution caused by companies that go unreported by our media that cause hundreds of millions of dollars in health care costs. These costs are dumped on citizens rather than traced back to the companies who caused them. The "externalities" or costs of doing business have gone unregulated and unreported. What would you do to fix this problem?

12. State vs Federal Single Payer – Some people object to a single payer system, saying that it would be too unwieldy and that each individual state should administer its own policy. Any thoughts about state-run programs? And should the policy for them be written by the federal government so that protections are in place to provide a certain standard of care? Or should a single payer program be run like Medicare, as the group Physicians for a National Health Program recommends?

13. RoundUp® Ready – RoundUp®, or glyphosate, is a weed control chemical put out by Monsanto. It is a proven neurotoxin and endocrine disruptor that has been found by the United States Geological Survey in

the rainwater, air, streams, and river basins. In fact, it is found nearly everywhere, since more than one million tons of it is sprayed worldwide every year. The degradation product of glyphosate, amino methlyphosphonic acid, lasts very long and is toxic to one's liver and kidneys, and causes problems in fertility and fetal development. RoundUp® is banned in many European nations. Can you comment on its use, and how would you address this chemical when most of the USA's farmers are on a program of using Monsanto's RoundUp Ready® seeds and weed killing chemicals?

Debate 9: Foreign Policy

1. Foreign Policy on Weapons – According to classified reports given to President Obama, the majority of weapons secretly shipped to Syria at the behest of Saudi Arabia and Qatar go to hardline Islamic rebel groups rather than more secular organizations favored by the West. In any case, weapon deals are made without vetting the organizations receiving them. On Tuesday Oct 9th, 2012, Russia sold $4.2 billion worth of weapons to Iraq, making them the second next to the U.S. in arms dealings. What is Iraq doing with more than $8.5 billion worth of weapons, anyway? How do you plan to address the problem of arms dealers and so many weapons everywhere? Is there anything a President can do to stop the profit motive behind weapon building? Or are we doomed to live in a hellish world where escalated bullying is the norm?

2. Iran's Nuclear Threat – What will you do about Iran's nuclear threat? Do you have any ideas that would make nuclear disarmament a reality, regardless of who is in power?

3. Two State Solution – Do you support a two-state solution to the Palestinian-Israeli conflict? What is your position on Jerusalem?

4. Pakistan Swat Valley – Swat Valley in Pakistan is going through hell right now. Recently, 14-year-old Malala Yousafzai was shot by the imposing Taliban regime for simply asking for an education. These bullies have destroyed hundreds of schools in the region, hung beheaded bodies of policemen in the town square, cut off noses and ears of opposition figures, and continue to shell the area and punish women for going out without an escort. How would you, as President, deal with these realities going on in other countries? Specifically, how would you support women as in the film, "Half the Sky"?

5. Human Rights Violations – Human rights violations seem to be getting worse all over the world, including right here in the United States. But specifically, China's treatment of workers at FoxConn, the factory where Apple, Dell, HP, Motorola, Nintendo, Sony and Nokia products are made is just as much an American problem as it is a Chinese

problem. American companies choose to ship jobs overseas to save a few bucks at a factory where conditions are so bad, that they have to hang nets across the buildings to discourage workers from committing suicide. Can a President use foreign policy to improve worker conditions? What would you do?

6. Syria, Turkey – Syria and Turkey are in crisis. There are an estimated 32,000 Syrians dead, 145,000 refugees in Turkey and roughly 2 million internally displaced people in Syria itself. The Turkish foreign minister, Ahmet Davutoglu, said Turkey was not seeking military confrontation with the regime of President Bashar al-Assad. He wants the international community to send a "stark warning" via the United Nations security council that some of Damascus's actions constituted a "war crime," and he wants humanitarian intervention. What would you do?

7. Boys to Men – All over the world, boys who feel alienated, lost, restless, and who lack a sense of identity, too often choose gangs, violence, and extremism. Their families or communities do not provide boys a ceremony that acknowledges their passage into manhood, grounding them in their responsibilities as a member of the larger society. This causes many boys and men today to lack the vision to care for the earth or to see the effects of their choices over the long term. The result along all socioeconomic strata is a selfish and immature disregard for others. Please comment.

8. Diplomatic Experience – What is your experience, or lack thereof, in developing relationships with foreign leaders? What kind of diplomatic experience do you have? Convince the American people why you should be given arguably the highest leadership role in the world.

9. Islamic World – How do you view the Islamic world, and more specifically, Islam's influence on the United States as our Muslim population increases?

10. Tax Credits to Stimulate Economy – What tax credits would you give to stimulate the economy?

11. Consumer Financial Protection Bureau – Do you think that the Consumer Financial Protection Bureau (CFPB) is necessary? What would you do to restore fiscal responsibility, accountability, and transparency at banks and other financial institutions?

12. Middle East, North Africa Protection Bureau – The Middle East and Northern Africa are likely to get worse before things gets better. What will your policy be? To be involved or not involved: from trying to alleviate problems to becoming isolated from it? If leaders in the region request your help, will you refuse, and if not, in what ways will you help?

APPENDIX 7

Trans Pacific Partnership Information

Here is what we know so far from the leaked chapters that Oregon Representative Ron Wyden, Subcommittee Chair on International Trade, was finally able to obtain after much prodding:

1. Food Safety: According to the TPP, transnational companies can sue our states or federal government if our food safety laws stand in the way of expected future profits. Instead, lax international food standards will apply, making GMO labeling a thing of the past, even if we win labeling laws against the wishes of the giant seed and chemical companies. Currently, our laws mandate evaluating such things as pesticide levels, bacterial contamination, fecal exposure, toxic additives, and non-edible fillers. A company that proves our safety regulations to be a barrier to profits can sue our government, then only the tribunal has to decide between keeping our food safe or allowing the multinational company to sell tainted food.

2. Jobs: If the TPP passes, member corporations can enjoy the benefits of suing governments to allow for less stringent worker practices. "The corporation could skirt Vietnam's laws and demand compensation at an international tribunal for any government policy or action (such as a hike in the minimum wage) that undermined its 'expected' profits," write Jim Hightower and Phillip Fraser. The TPP would incentivize offshoring of good-paying jobs by offering special benefits to firms that relocate to low-wage nations.

3. Fracking: Under the TPP, the Department of Energy would have no authority to regulate natural gas that is produced for export. Our environmental laws will be helpless to protect our water table against fracking companies that sell to member nations.' "The TPP...could mean automatic approval of liquid natural gas (LNG) export permits—without any review or consideration—to TPP countries," writes the Sierra Club. Japan is the largest importer of LNG. This explains Obama's statement to Prime Minister Abe of Japan. Through the process of drilling wells, fracking allows cancer-causing contaminants into the water table and has caused a host of health problems for local residents. Breast Cancer Fund's website warns: "Fracking fluids can contain chemicals linked to breast cancer, including known and suspected carcinogens such as benzene and toluene, and

endocrine-disrupting compounds such as the phthalate DEHP."

4. Banking: The U.S. Business Coalition for the TPP includes banking firms such as Citi, Morgan Stanley, and Goldman Sachs. Their objective through the TPP is to prevent any regulations that would hamper the continued unregulated practices of the banking industry. The new law would:

    a. Prohibit any "Robin Hood" taxes that would discourage super-rich speculators, the kind that caused the crash of 2008

    b. Restrict firewall reforms that would mimic the Glass Steagall protections

    c. Roll back reforms that member governments adopted to fix the extreme banking deregulations that caused the 2007-2008 Wall Street crash

    d. Provide a safeguard against laws that would limit the size of "too-big-to-fail" companies.

5. Can't "Buy American": The TPP empowers corporations "to launch [their] own litigatory (sic) attack on our domestic laws in global trade courts – potentially costing municipalities millions of dollars." Instead of boosting our local economy by buying American or supporting businesses in the community with which we share common values, the new trade law would require local companies to bid against multinational companies who are TPP members. Simply the threat of a lawsuit could undermine the "buy local" movement.

6. Drug Prices: The TPP extends patents on medications to 20 years, and if pharmaceutical companies tweak the formulation of a drug, they can extend that patent another 20 years, delaying cost-saving generics from entering the market to save lives. Doctors in Japan are worried that the continual rise in costs will threaten their healthcare system.

7. Environmental Protection: The TPP allows companies to sue our government if our environmental laws stand in the way of their making a profit. Under the TPP, Monsanto could sue the United States or the State of California if our laws ban such things as GMOs, pesticide, or other cancer-causing contaminants such as MTBE (methyl tertiary butyl ether), a gasoline additive. Corporations have already begun suing governments for such things. Chapter 11 of NAFTA allows multinationals to make claims against governments, leaving taxpayers on the hook for paying out damages or loss of revenue, even if the corporation made drinking water unsafe or polluted the natives' land.

8. Internet Freedom: The TPP imposes similar restrictions to SOPA (The Stop Online Piracy Act) and PIPA (Protect IP Act). Currently, if you download a recipe from a website and print it, it's free. But if the TPP passes, then you may be assessed a fine of ten thousand dollars for violating copyright laws. The folks who are crafting the TPP say they won't do this, but they've already lifted language from the Digital Millennium Copyright Act (DCMA) that lays the groundwork for collecting data from individuals sufficient to bill and prosecute Internet users later for use of material. The Electronic Frontier Foundation states that the TPP legislation "is likely to further entrench controversial aspects of U.S. copyright law [such as the DCMA] and restrict the ability of Congress to engage in domestic law reform to meet the evolving IP needs of American citizens and the innovative technology sector." The TPP opens the door to set up policies that:

   a. Ban you from Internet use if you violate copyright, which will be set at 120 years by the TPP.
   b. Require you to have your blogs or content filtered by an Internet intermediary for possible copyright infringement.
   c. Block websites if they might be infringing on copyright.
   d. Force Internet Service Providers to hand over your identity should you infringe on someone's copyright.

Note: This information came out of only one chapter of the 29 chapter bill. One source in New Zealand said "this will be why John Key (the Prime Minister of NZ) is in a rush to sign the TPP which has little to do with trade and much more to do with state surveillance. Only four chapters in the entire document realtes (sic) to trade. After the TPP is signed Key does not care if he is re-elected."

APPENDIX 8

Request for TPP documents by Walter B. Jones
HRES 767 IH
112th CONGRESS
2d Session
H. RES. 767
Expressing the sense of the House of Representatives relating to increased transparency in the negotiations of the Trans-Pacific Partnership (TPP) Agreement, and for other purposes.
IN THE HOUSE OF REPRESENTATIVES
August 2, 2012
Mr. JONES submitted the following resolution; which was referred to the Committee on Ways and Means

---

RESOLUTION

Expressing the sense of the House of Representatives relating to increased transparency in the negotiations of the Trans-Pacific Partnership (TPP) Agreement, and for other purposes.

Whereas government officials from the United States and eight Pacific Rim nations—Australia, Brunei, Chile, Malaysia, New Zealand, Peru, Singapore, and Vietnam—have been negotiating for over three years to sign a Trans-Pacific Partnership (TPP) Agreement;

Whereas Canada and Mexico joined the negotiations in June 2012;

Whereas Members of Congress, the American public, and the press have been denied access to the negotiations and to the draft text of this lengthy international agreement;

Whereas press reports suggest that the TPP would compromise United States sovereignty by imposing a regime of global governance on the United States regarding domestic land use; control of United States natural resources and property rights; immigration and visa rights; service sector regulation; patents and copyrights; and food and product standards and labeling;

Whereas leaked text of the draft agreement reveals that the TPP would submit the United States to the jurisdiction of foreign tribunals administered by the United Nations and the World Bank that would be empowered to order unlimited payment of United States taxpayer dollars to foreign firms who claim that Federal, State, or local governments are not delivering on the new privileges and rights TPP would grant to them;

Whereas leaked TPP text suggests foreign investors and firms operating within the United States would be given greater substantive and procedural rights than United States citizens and firms are provided under the United States Constitution as interpreted by the United States Supreme Court;

Whereas press reports indicate the TPP would ban 'buy American' and 'buy local' preferences in Federal Government procurement;

Whereas leaked TPP text reveals the TPP would include special protections and incentives that promote the offshoring of United States jobs and investment;

Whereas the TPP may require the United States to import meat and other foods that do not meet United States safety standards, putting United States producers at a disadvantage and United States consumers' health at risk;

Whereas under the terms of the draft agreement, failure by the Federal, State, or local governments to conform United States domestic laws, regulations, and administrative procedures to this regime would subject the United States Government to trade sanctions imposed until United States laws are altered to conform with the TPP requirements;

Whereas the terms of this international regime of governance could only be altered by consensus of all signatory governments and the TPP has no expiration date, meaning the TPP would lock in expansive international preemption of United States laws and policies; and

Whereas every Pacific Rim nation, including China and Russia, could eventually be included in the TPP, which is being designed as a 'docking' agreement to which additional countries may join: Now, therefore, be it

Resolved, That it is the sense of the House of Representatives that—

(1) Members of Congress should be allowed to observe Trans-Pacific Partnership (TPP) Agreement negotiations on behalf of the American people they represent.

(2) Members of Congress, the American public, and the press should be allowed access to the draft text of the agreement and to the text of United States negotiating proposals.

(3) Any final TPP agreement should not undermine United States sovereignty by submitting the United States, its people, or its businesses to the jurisdiction of foreign tribunals.

(4) Any final TPP agreement should not increase United States unemployment or the United States trade deficit.

(5) Any final TPP agreement that is not a treaty approved by two-thirds of the Senate under Article II, section 2, clause 2 of the Constitution does not have the force of law.

APPENDIX 9

Article V of the Constitution

Article V.

The Congress, whenever two thirds of both Houses shall deem it necessary, shall propose Amendments to this Constitution, or, on the Application of the Legislatures of two thirds of the several States, shall call a Convention for proposing Amendments, which, in either Case, shall be valid to all Intents and Purposes, as Part of this Constitution, when ratified by the Legislatures of three fourths of the several States, or by Conventions in three fourths thereof, as the one or the other Mode of Ratification may be proposed by the Congress; Provided that no Amendment which may be made prior to the Year One thousand eight hundred and eight shall in any Manner affect the first and fourth Clauses in the Ninth Section of the first Article; and that no State, without its Consent, shall be deprived of its equal Suffrage in the Senate.

APPENDIX 10

Poll Tape Capture Instructions

To All Suspicious Citizens: Yes, someone may be tampering with your vote! Citizens can use the following method for counting at the poll station before the tapes are taken away and corrupted by officials.

Bev Harris, an activist who fights against vote-tampering, often travels to vulnerable polling sites to help locals. Join Bev on Facebook: https://www.facebook.com/groups/blackboxvoting/?fref=nf and find her at her nonprofit called Black Ballot Voting. When Georgia changed its voting to all-touchscreen, she recommended Poll Tape Capture in 2012.

Ms. Harris writes: "The state of Georgia has installed a results-reporting middleman for all Georgia counties. What this means is that all voting machine aggregations will be electronically transferred to the state before reporting them to the public. This process allows middleman alteration by persons at the state level."

Ms. Harris urges citizens to fan out, capture poll tape results, and compare it to the state-gathered results. Further, "it is crucial to take photographs or video, not just notes, because if there are discrepancies, your say-so won't prove anything."

The guidelines for Poll Tape Capture are outlined below. Garland Favorito, Elections Director of the Constitution Party, author of *"Our Nation Betrayed,"* and founder of VoterGA, made the following announcement in an email, in which he bullets the actions citizens must take to protect their votes.

CRITICAL: ELECTION DAY REPORTING
Date: Fri, 27 Jul 2012
VoterGa Supporters,
The Secretary of State has implemented a new statewide reporting system that will report election results for all counties. Each county will no longer report its own results online but will instead have their websites link to the state website that will report uploaded results for that county. The results will be uploaded from the county servers to the state server before any hard copy reports are produced at the county election office. Therefore, the county servers must utilize their remote connection to report interim results prior to producing final county results. As you can probably recognize, this exasperates a potential vulnerability where remote tampering with county election results could take place prior to county reports being produced. It represents another security risk in an

election counting and reporting system that is already riddled with security flaws.

- ❖ Have representatives present as observers at selected precincts just before 7pm when the polls close (author's note: polls close at different times throughout the country).
- ❖ Observe and record the precinct and/or machine totals for the candidate or referendum
- ❖ Visit other precincts as necessary to get more totals that will be visibly posted on the door of the precinct when the precinct workers leave
- ❖ Visit the county office(s) around 9 pm to view an election results report when the report is printed by the office
- ❖ Verify that the totals from the precincts and counties are incorporated correctly into the state totals on the county website

The county website may not be available in the county office lobby so the observer may have to use a smart phone browser to access the county site from within the lobby.

Garland, Voterga.org

For more information about Poll Tape Capture and taking video footage at the polls, refer to the following:

When activists were worried that votes wouldn't get counted correctly to pass Proposition 37, the labeling of GMOs in California, they recommended poll tape capture and videotaping, along with instructions here: https://www.organicconsumers.org/old_articles/letter-11-5.htm

Election Defense Alliance, a nonpartisan nonprofit, gives voters a comprehensive toolkit for verifying votes at your polling location here: http://electiondefensealliance.org/?q=verified_voting_transparency_proje ct_election_monitoring_checklists

To learn how to observe the polls for a measure of election integrity, watch this video prepared by the Institute for American Democracy and Election Integrity: https://www.youtube.com/watch?v=ywEcU1j2AWg

At Video the Vote dot org (http://www.videothevote.org/resources/), a grassroots organization that organizes videotaping the polls, you can learn how to document long lines, intimidation, and other obstructions to voting. John Ennis's documentary film called *Free for All* will enlighten even the most adamant denier of voting shenanigans.

APPENDIX 11

Judy's List of Solutions

1. Government of the People: Form a Citizen's Congress that includes every registered voter in the United States. Set federal educational goals to include learning how to participate in a Citizen's Congress, and add it to the curriculum of 5th, 9th, and 12th graders.
2. Election and Campaign Reforms:
   a. Clean up the ballot box by returning to paper ballots throughout the country
   b. Institute Range Voting.
   c. Limit campaigning and election ads to the two months prior to election day.
   d. Limit fundraising by candidates; run advertising on the Internet and return to in-person campaigning.
   e. Hold debates on television and post on the Internet, edited to one question per video.
   f. Get rid of the gerrymandered district lines. Change congressional districts to represent population density. Use the "shortest splitline algorithm" outlined at http://rangevoting.org/GerryExamples.html.
   g. Limit big advertising expenditures and run ads only for two months prior to election day. Advertising funds must be coordinated through a fund manager, who oversees that "pro" and "con" issue ads spend equally, so there is no greater amount of "speech" for either side.
   h. Give tax credits for campaign volunteer work.
   i. Limit campaign pro spending.
   j. Give the Federal Election Commission some real teeth for making politicians accountable and transparent in their election practices. Write a letter to the FEC: *I demand that the Federal Election Commission provide full disclosure of corporate, union and wealthy funding sources behind express advocacy ads and electioneering communications. If corporations, billionaires and labor unions want to finance broadcast messages to influence my vote, they should be required to say who they are.* See: http://sers.fec.gov/fosers/showpdf.htm?docid=312952.
   k. Allow the FEC to find their own commissioners from the general public, not from the parties, and not relying on the POTUS to appoint and Congress to confirm them.

3. Energy

    a. In your community, pass an ordinance called a "Right to Sustainable Energy Future" essentially banning the transportation, manufacture or drilling of non-sustainable energy sources. See: https://www.youtube.com/watch?v=8Prylnj4NQ8 (See also Santa Monica's ordinance to establish sustainability rights for clean water, air, soil, and food systems: http://www.smgov.net/departments/council/agendas/2013/201303 12/s2013031207-C-1.htm).

    b. Change federal policies to give sovereignty to local communities and to abolish state and federal laws that protect corporate rights over human rights.

4. Water

    a. Develop an overall plan for protecting conserving, and providing water for consumption and food production. Break that plan into smaller, locally controlled systems.

    b. Abolish "smart meter" controls and educate end-users how to conserve their own water through municipal-level training programs.

    c. Collect water from rooftops, permeable pavement, grey water systems for drought-stricken areas.

    d. Construct indoor, low water consumption agricultural systems such as aeroponics, aquaponics, and hydroponics.

5. Government Reform

Form a Citizens' Congress through an amendment to the Constitution that works in one or several of the following ways:

    a. The U.S. Congress (legislative branch of government) only counts toward 50% of a vote to pass a bill into law; the other 50% has to come from a majority of the Citizen's Congress.

    b. The U.S. Congress votes and can pass a bill, but the bill cannot become law if a majority of citizens disagrees with it. (Similar to the veto power of the Swiss.) –or–

    c. A bill may be written by the Citizen's Congress, pass a majority, then the U.S. Congress goes through their normal process without changing the wording and must do so in a timely fashion. Our representatives have an opportunity to discuss the bill with the Citizen's Congress and advise accordingly. The U.S. Congress can veto the bill, but must do so against the wishes of the majority for the reasons Madison warned against: that the new law might be "adversed to the rights of other citizens."

6. End the Welfare State.

    a. Turn welfare recipients and unemployed people into workers, first by job training and then by providing jobs. Give tax breaks to companies with paid training that leads to full-time employment.

b. Where there aren't enough jobs through the private sector, the government will develop public works projects to fix roads, bridges, hospitals, and other infrastructure that is in great need of repair.

c. Revisit all government contractors to assess their job training programs. Adjust job training for new technologies and disciplines, such as clean energy and healthy agriculture.

d. Offer entrepreneurs microloans based on merit and experience.

7. Financial/Economic Reform (see also Appendix 12)

a. Re-set the dollar and replace it with debt-free federal script. Break up the big banks and honor all accounts under one million dollars by issuing the new federal script to smaller, local banks in place of the old dollar. Require filing a claim for issuance of script on accounts greater than one million but less than one billion. Require audits on all companies and individuals with holdings greater than one billion dollars before issuing government-backed script.

b. Re-regulate derivatives and make each step of the process transparent.

c. Separate investment and securities institutions from lending institutions; break up the "too big to fail" entities (refer to economists Henry C. Simons and conservative George Stigler and the Chicago School of Economics recommendations to institute break-them-up antitrust efforts) and utilities and predatory companies such as Internet service providers and cell phone providers. All businesses must follow antitrust laws that reign in monopolistic practices allowing fair competition in the marketplace.

d. Institute rolling jubilees, where organizations buy debt for pennies on the dollar and release debtors from the impossible task of repaying student loans, etc.

e. Public banks at the local level shall give loans.

f. Make it illegal for money managers to commit arbitrage or sell dubious instruments

8. Media

Open up the media by reinstating FCC (Federal Communications Commission) regulations that existed before the Telecommunications Reform Act of 1996 and reinstating antitrust provisions.

9. Trade

Refuse to participate in bilateral or multilateral trade deals until all participating countries institute "fair labor" practices that include healthcare and respect for human rights.

10. Ecology
   a. Rewrite the laws around release of chemicals into the environment by updating the Toxic Substances Control Act. Strengthen the EPA's power to control new chemicals before they are used through a revised New Use Rule (rather than the poorly crafted SNUR, Significant New Use Rule) and to review existing chemicals through the Chemical Data Reporting Rule.
   b. Make polluting industries clean up their act or pay heavy fines, funding outside companies to help them comply with ecological standards. Businesses' externalities must be borne internally. (If companies refuse to clean up their externalities, the cost would be borne elsewhere, such as medical costs.) All industries must be open, reviewed regularly for ecological violations, and must subordinate their profit motive to the health of life on earth.

11. Agriculture
   a. Ban the use of glyphosate, 2,4-D, dicamba and other toxic chemicals.
   b. Regenerate the soil by application of organic material from animal husbandry operations
   c. Instead of irrigating by spraying water, use Netafim, Rain Bird copper shield dripline, or a similar drip system
   d. Increase the number and size of indoor, greenhouse farms. For small spaces, aeroponics, hydroponics, and aquaponics can be used. See Archi's Acres, a 1-acre hydroponic organic greenhouse that produces thrice the yield of conventional farms, yet uses approximately ten percent of the water. Their model offers creative financing and training programs for veterans.
   e. In high density populated areas, use rooftops to grow food
   f. Collect water during floods and divert to areas of drought
   g. Make it illegal for genetically modified pollen to contaminate God-given genes and hold biotech seed companies accountable for ruining organic farmers' crops.
   h. Educate farmers and gardeners about the food-soil web, using principles from Dr. Elaine Ingham.
   i. Implement aquaculture (aquafarming) and permaculture systems where applicable.

12. Business
   a. Encourage businesses to democratize wealth through ESOPs, Employee Stock Option Plans where at least 51% ownership is with the employees. Employee-owned companies often make less

expensive products because their management pay themselves reasonable salaries. Other community-based forms of democratized ownership includes neighborhood corporations, land trusts, social enterprises, local cooperatives, B Corporations. (See Alperovitz.)

b. Change bankruptcy law so that highest paid employees and board members become personally responsible for business failure and illegal acts such as money laundering for drug cartels, arbitrage, bait and switch and misleading lending practices.

c. Promote local businesses. Remove barriers to produce energy locally.

d. Urge all corporations to become "B Corps" and failing that, make consumers aware of which companies are following the B Corporation style of conducting business. Urge consumers to boycott non-B Corps that are not good global citizens. For more information, see The Shareholder Value Myth by Lynn Stout or visit: https://www.bcorporation.net/

e. Sanction businesses, including banks that fail to practice business equitably and retire vast sums of money that are hoarded for no tangible purpose.

f. Stop subsidizing and contracting with the following businesses: oil and gas, agriculture and feedlots larger than 100 acres, prisons, companies that hoard cash in the USA or overseas, pharmaceutical companies and any other companies that sell shares, private companies that do not offer the public a tangible life-supporting benefit, for-profits and non-profits that donate money to influence elections. Stop subsidizing anything where there is an agreement NOT to perform a function, unless it is to support open spaces and federal lands such as parks. For example, stop subsidizing farmers to NOT farm.

13. Education
   a. Fund public schools through states
   b. Review charter schools for violations
   c. Remove "race to the top," "no child left behind," and Common Core standards.
   d. Focus on early start, reward students for college prep, and add back music, art, and civics.
   e. Allow more flexibility for teachers to be creative, not teach to the test.
   f. Encourage each state to decide its own curriculum and standards. On the local level, educators can fine tune education for their own geographic area.

g. Double federal spending on university research and development.
h. Stop conflicts of interest between private industry and graduate institutions, for example, a pharmacology company funding research that relates to medication.
i. Extend research and development (R&D) tax credits.
j. Promote free high speed Internet nationwide, like other countries do.
k. Set federal educational goals to include learning how to participate in a Citizen's Congress, and add it to the curriculum of 5th, 9th, and 12th graders.

14. Foreign Policy
   a. Stop killing people with drones.
   b. Return to the principles of the Geneva Convention.
   c. Stop using executive privilege to start wars, stop violating the Constitution, treat others with respect, human decency and civilized neighborly behavior, shame those who do not return same respect.
   d. Use diplomacy to improve international relations.
   e. Use force as a last resort, and only in self-defense.
   f. Support on-the-ground, native-driven proven methods for peace. (See Scilla Elworthy in her TED presentation called Fighting With Non Violence.
   g. Follow the advice of the Generals with on-the-ground, at-the-front-lines experience.

15. Public Works Projects (jobs, jobs, jobs!)
   a. Build interstate high speed rail
   b. Renovate agriculture by reducing large mono-crop farms into smaller, more manageable units near smaller animal husbandry operations. Recycle animal waste into the land rather than using petrochemical fertilizers.
   c. Construct indoor farming operations with low water consumption systems.
   d. Build grey water, rainwater, and snow water catchment systems to divert that water to these farming operations and others in drought-stricken areas.
   e. Reinstate Superfund projects and fund them.
   f. Audit the financial services industry, banks, and securities.
   g. Evaluate businesses based on the B Corporation model.
   h. Install infrastructure for a hydrogen capture, storage, and transport
   i. Focus on energy production such as geothermal, hydrothermal, hydroelectric, ocean and wave-driven, wind, solar, tides, turbine, flywheel, carbon recycling, and WAMSR (Waste Annihilating

Molten Salt Reactor) nuclear power plants.

j.   Audit big polluters to account for their toll on society via their externalities. A greater savings in healthcare will offset the increase in consumer spending.

k.   Municipal and state development: municipalization of utilities and Internet service costs 14% less on the average, compared with public utilities. Establish local institutions such as land trusts and public energy facilities. States and municipalities often do better under local investment strategies. (See Alperovitz.) Educate states and consumers about Community Choice Aggregation arrangements for energy sourcing and savings.

l.   Make the Federal Emergency Management Agency (FEMA) more agile and responsive to respond to weather crises.

m.   Prepare for increasing sea level in lowland areas.

n.   Build infrastructure to respond to drought in advance of crises. Prepare routing mechanisms to bring water to communities and farming operations.

16. Increase the number of Supreme Court Justices so that one person cannot decide the fate of the entire country.

17. Improve relationships between communities and law enforcement agencies. Teach officers how to communicate with people so that simple situations do not escalate into adversarial and potentially lethal altercations. Start programs where police officers walk poor children to their schools so that they get to know the community and build trust and understanding.

18. Decrease social workers' paperwork and bureaucracy.

19. Repeal the acts that erode our democracy, such as the Telecommunications Act of 1996, and repeal the acts that violate our rights and the Constitution, such as the Patriot Act, the NDAA, among others. Repeal legislation that has dismantled the Glass Steagall Act. Break up the banking and securities behemoths. Repeal trade agreements like NAFTA, GATT, and others that have caused job loss in the USA and caused Mexican farm workers to lose their jobs in Mexico, thus causing mass illegal immigration.

20. Remove many of the presidential appointees who were top executives in industries such as: banks, finance, medicine, pharmacology, Internet Service Providers, communications, media, oil, chemical and seed companies. Replace them with scholars, scientists, and policy experts who have no conflict of interest and who will straighten out our protective agencies. Make the FDA, EPA, communication, banking and health agencies have real teeth again when regulating businesses and protecting public health and the earth's ecology.

21. Turn part of the National Security Administration (NSA) into the

Veterans Administration (VA). Re-train most NSA employees to become Veterans Administration employees who each have a caseload of specific veterans that they must take from square one to health. Turn the NSA computers that are used to collect vast unnecessary information on Americans into VA computers that keep up-to-date medical records for the military and veterans.

22. Listen to authentic whistleblowers.

23. No more anonymous companies. All corporate filings must be traceable to the responsible parties so that they can be held to standards, such as moral and ethical standards. See:
https://www.youtube.com/watch?v=LFJ9WAHowcg and
www.facebook.com/EndAnonymousCompanies

24. Healthcare: Adopt a single-payer system and abolish the insurance company model. Insurance companies have a built-in incentive to withhold care, keep their shareholders happy rather than patients, and pay executives ridiculous salaries. Their grip on our medical system jacked up costs to 20% of GDP. Medicare does the job with only 5% or less going to administrative costs, depending upon who you talk to, versus 20% for private insurers.

25. Make it unconstitutional to patent genes.

APPENDIX 12

Solutions for the Economy
By Peter Bearse and Carmine Gorga

1. Reform the tax code to:
    a. Simplify, but also increase progressivity, of the graduated income tax by including a steeply rising marginal tax on the highest earners.
    b. Levy taxes and fees to internalize the social costs of private enterprise; e.g., effluent fees on carbon emissions.
    c. Revise taxation of corporations to discourage growth by acquisition and encourage repatriation of foreign earnings.
    d. Remove incentives for short-term investment and increase incentives for long-term (more than 5 years) investment.
    e. Enact a Value-Added Tax or Consumption Tax that is also progressive.
    f. Maintain the inheritance (death) tax.
    g. Heavily tax fast-trading financial transactions.
    h. Tax costs external to (unrecognized by) the market economy, including costs of carbon emissions, large plant shutdowns involving job shifting to other countries, et al. As the Occupy Movement recognizes, this would be a move toward a true (and full) cost market regime in which the price of every product reflects the ecological cost of its production, distribution and use.
    i. Gradually eliminate all tax advantages and subsidies to established (more than 5 years old) businesses.[1]
2. Provide tax incentives and reduce regulations to enable people to invest in new and early-stage enterprises in their own communities.
3. Incentivize innovation in clean energy businesses by levying a carbon tax.
4. Break up the big banks.
5. Ensure that regulations to implement Dodd-Frank legislation require the separation of investment banking from depository banking.
6. Decentralize government: Move power and money out of Washington down to the local level via General Revenue Sharing.
7. Discourage hoarding by wealthy individuals, big businesses and big banks.
8. Revise and strengthen anti-trust laws.
9. Focus on the long-term; e.g., rates of taxation of capital gains should rise steeply the shorter the term of the investment.

10. Modernize the Federal Reserve System (a.k.a. "The Fed") by:
   a. Revising the 1913 Charter through which Congress enabled the establishment of the Federal Reserve.
   b. Auditing the Fed annually;
   c. Requiring the Fed to close its discount window to large banks and businesses and open it to entrepreneurs and small businesses.

11. Reform failed campaign finance "reforms":
   a. Set limits on outlays for political "pro's" and campaign advertising but no limits for expenditures to equip political volunteers.
   b. Recognize the value of volunteer participation by giving a tax credit for the time people spend on campaigns.
   c. Allow political campaign contributions from natural persons only, not from corporations, unions or other organizations.
   d. Do not allow PACs, "bundling" or other organizational contributions.
   e. Reduce, and do not index, limits for individual monetary contributions.
   f. Enable time to be provided at no cost by major media to enable candidates to conduct debates.
   g. Do not allow public financing of campaigns. The only public financing for political purposes should be provided on a matching grant basis to parties to help them cover the cost of voter registration, education and training for voters and activists, and outreach and informational activities to encourage people's participation in the political process.

12. Complete development of a new model that brings economic justice and concerns over the distribution of income and wealth into an integrated political-economic framework. Such a model is necessitated by the fact that the failed economic policies of the Obama Administration, like that of other governments, have been inspired by "defunct economists."[2]

13. Devise triggers and mechanisms to limit inequalities of income and wealth in the U.S. These would follow from a new Declaration of Rights and Responsibilities. For example, legal limits could be put in place, both on executive pay and unearned financial sector incomes and executive bonuses.[3] The former would address the excessive multiples that corporate executives are paid relative to their employees; the latter, excessive bonuses paid to people for taking excessive risks with other people's money or bonuses to executives of underperforming or even failing companies.

14. Introduce economic democracy into the U.S. by:
    a. Broadening and liberalizing legislation that enables Employee Stock Ownership Plans (ESOPs) to include proper representation of long-term employees in the governing boards of companies.[4]
    b. Expanding the legal rights of long-term stockholders in corporate governance and major corporate decisions, including those on the distribution of retained earnings.
    c. Legislation to limit or prohibit growth-by-purchase rather than growth-from-within; e.g., limit growth via M&A (mergers and acquisitions).
    d. Gain-sharing to distribute the returns to productivity more equitably.

15. Enact former Senator Mike Gravel's Constitutional Democracy Amendment and Democracy Act. These would enable laws to be made via national initiative and referendum (I&R).[5]

16. Convert the Earned Income Tax Credit and the welfare system into a Guaranteed Family Survival Income based upon hours worked per week in relation to family subsistence requirements. This could pertain to limited time periods to help families overcome hardships and enable better transition(s) to a sound economy.

17. Revise Gross Domestic Product to account for costs external to the market economy, such as:
    a. The costs of carbon emissions.
    b. Large plant shutdowns involving job shifting to other countries.
    c. The value of women's work in the home.
    d. The value of volunteer work, including political volunteerism.
    e. Other significant omissions identified by various analysts and reports over the years.

18. Adopt and implement a National Entrepreneurship Development program to substantially:
    a. Increase funds available for investment in new, innovative or early-stage, independent enterprises.
    b. Subsidize entrepreneurship education at all levels.
    c. Allow a portion of unemployment insurance funds to be used to finance business start-ups (by adapting past models from states and other countries).
    d. Enable more start-up funds to be obtained without SEC registration, via crowd sourcing, Joint Municipal-Private Security Offerings, micro-financing programs, Community Development Finance Institutions.

19. Amend, refine and advocate significant changes to laws that regulate

the financial sector. These should include oversight by independent citizens' committees of regulations still being written to implement Dodd-Frank, plus taxation of financial transactions, such as a Tobin Tax.[6]

20. Formulate and advocate changes to the legal framework that governs the operations of large, private, multinational and private/public corporations in the United States. Especially: A Constitutional amendment to revoke corporate personhood unless corporations introduce provisions of economic democracy into their governance.

21. Provide incentives for government agencies to save money (rather than spend the full amount of their budget).[7]

NOTES:

[1] See Gorga, Carmine (2010), *The Economic Process*. Lanham, MD: University Press of America. Dr. Gorga calls his framework "Concordian Economics." Work to put it into testable, econometric form is ongoing by Gorga and Bearse.

[2] As set forth by Gorga, op.cit., as essential prerequisites to a "Concordian Economics"

[3] "In 1980, American CEOs earned 42 times more than the average employee...that figure has sky-rocketed to more than 300 times...By way of comparison, top executives at the 30 (German) blue-chip(s) ...rarely earn over 100 times..." Shultz, Thomas (2011), "Has America Become an Oligarchy," *Spiegel Online* (10/28, translated from the German).

[4] Note that this and ESOPs serve to reduce unjustified inequalities in the distribution of returns to productivity, a problem that Robert Reich identified as one of the causes of our economic crisis in his book *AFTERSHOCK: The Next Economy and America's Future* (Vintage paperback).

[5] As proposed by former U.S. Senator Mike Gravel. See Gravel, op.cit.

[6] First advocated by Nobel Laureate economist James Tobin in his 1972 Janeway Lectures at Princeton, this tax was "originally defined as a tax on spot conversions of one currency into another." As an economist, in this author's view, such a tax should include all financial transactions and graduated to decrease with the length of time that an investment enabled by a financial transaction is held -- "to put a penalty on short-term financial excursions..." Quotes from *WIKIPEDIA* on "Tobin Tax."

[7] Farrell, Paul B. (2011), op.cit.

APPENDIX 13

Pledge Signers of the Pledge for Honest Candidates

1.	Ted Gianoutsos	Alaska	At-Large
2.	Richard Grayson	Arizona	4
3.	Joseph McCray	California	6
4.	David Hernandez	California	29
5.	Stephen Smith	California	34
6.	David Secor	California	50
7.	Michael Crimmins	California	51
8.	Doug Aden	Colorado	4
9.	Wayne Winsley	Connecticut	3
10.	William Drummond	Florida	1
11.	Floyd Patrick Miller	Florida	2
12.	Mike Nieves	Florida	9
13.	Thomas Cruz-Wiggins	Florida	27
14.	Mike McCalister	Florida	Senate
15.	Joe Ruiz	Indiana	2
16.	Joe Bowman	Indiana	4
17.	Tara Nelson	Indiana	4
18.	Bart Gadau	Indiana	8
19.	Andrew Dodge	Maine	Senate
20.	Joe Krysztoforski	Maryland	6
21.	Bill Cimbrelo	Massachusetts	Senate
22.	Cobby Williams	Mississippi	2
23.	Ron Williams	Mississippi	4
24.	Anatol Zorikova	Missouri	2
25.	Thomas Holbrook	Missouri	4
26.	Rick Vandeven	Missouri	8
27.	Russell Anderson	Nebraska	Senate
28.	Stan Vaughan	Nevada	1
29.	Floyd Fitzgibbons	Nevada	4
30.	Stephen DeLuca	New Jersey	8
31.	E. David Smith	New Jersey	9
32.	Mick Erikson	New Jersey	10
33.	Kenneth Cody	New Jersey	12
34.	David Dranikoff	New Jersey	Senate
35.	Dan Halloran	New York	6
36.	Joseph Diaferia	New York	16
37.	Donald Hassig	New York	21

38.	John Mangelli	New York	Senate
39.	Scott Noren	New York	Senate
40.	Bob Fitrakis	Ohio	3
41.	Elaine Mastromatteo	Ohio	14
42.	Michael Fulks	Oklahoma	2
43.	William Sanders	Oklahoma	3
44.	Tom Guild	Oklahoma	5
45.	Delia Lopez	Oregon	3
46.	Mike Koffenberger	Pennsylvania	4
47.	Jack Arnold	Tennessee	7
48.	Chauvin Arlin	Texas	6
49.	John Wieder	Texas	9
50.	Jim Riley	Texas	11
51.	Dave Robinson	Texas	12
52.	Benjamin Perez	Texas	15
53.	Barbara Carrasco	Texas	16
54.	Ed Scharf	Texas	23
55.	Ed Rankin	Texas	30
56.	Seth Hollist	Texas	32
57.	Andre LaFramboise	Vermont	At-Large
58.	Laurel LaFramboise	Vermont	Senate
59.	David Heaster	Wisconsin	5
60.	Joe Kallas	Wisconsin	6
61.	Dale Lehner	Wisconsin	7

APPENDIX 14

The Renew Democracy Amendment

1. The right of the individual qualified citizen voter to participate in and directly elect all officeholders by popular vote in all pertinent local, state, and federal elections shall not be denied or abridged and the right to vote is limited to individuals.

2. The right to contribute to political campaigns and political parties is held solely by individual citizens either through direct contributions and or a voter authorized public campaign funding system.

3. Political campaign and political party contributions shall not exceed an amount reasonably affordable by the average American.

4. The rights of all groups, associations and organizations to other political speech may be regulated by Congress but only as to volume and not otherwise lawful content and only to protect the right of the individual voter's voice to be heard.

5. The manner and course of lobbying and petitioning of federal, state, and local government officials by all groups and organizations and those who represent them may be regulated by Congress.

APPENDIX 15

We the People Amendment

Section 1. *[Artificial entities are not persons and can be regulated]*

The rights protected by the Constitution of the United States are the rights of natural persons only. Artificial entities established by the laws of any State, the United States, or any foreign state shall have no rights under this Constitution and are subject to regulation by the People, through Federal, State, or local law.

The privileges of artificial entities shall be determined by the People, through Federal, State, or local law, and shall not be construed to be inherent or inalienable.

Section 2. *[Money is not speech and can be regulated]*

Federal, State, and local government shall regulate, limit, or prohibit contributions and expenditures, including a candidate's own contributions and expenditures, to ensure that all citizens, regardless of their economic status, have access to the political process, and that no person gains, as a result of their money, substantially more access or ability to influence in any way the election of any candidate for public office or any ballot measure.

Federal, State, and local government shall require that any permissible contributions and expenditures be publicly disclosed.

The judiciary shall not construe the spending of money to influence elections to be speech under the 1st Amendment.

APPENDIX 16

CITIZENS AMENDMENT to the CONSTITUTION of the UNITED STATES

Section 1. The sovereign authority of the People of the United States, vested in an independent "Legislature of the People" with the power to enact, repeal and amend public policies, laws, charters and constitutions by local, state and national initiative, shall not be denied or abridged by any federal, state or local government of the United States.

Section 2. The citizens of the United States hereby sanction the national election conducted by the nonprofit corporation Philadelphia II, permitting the enactment of this fundamental law: the ratification of the Citizens Amendment and the enactment of the accompanying Citizens Legislative Procedures Act.

Section 3. A Citizens Trust is hereby created to conduct initiative elections and to administer the legislative procedures created by the Citizens Legislative Procedures Act. A Board of Trustees and a Director shall govern the Citizens Trust. The Citizens Legislative Procedures Act defines the composition of the Board of Trustees and their election, their duties and responsibilities, and the duties, responsibilities and the selection process of the Director.

Section 4. An initiative created under the authority of this Amendment that amends the Constitution of the United States or the constitution of any state or the charter of any local government becomes law when it is approved by more than one-half the registered voters of the relevant government jurisdiction in each of two successive elections. If the amendment is approved in the first election, a second ratification election shall occur no earlier than six months and no later than a year after the first election. An initiative that enacts, modifies or repeals a statute becomes the law when approved by more than one-half the registered voters of the relevant government jurisdiction who participate in the election.

Section 5. Only natural persons who are citizens of the United States may introduce legislation, contribute funds, services or property in support or in opposition to initiatives under this Amendment.

Section 6. Citizens shall have the power to enforce the provisions of this Amendment through the accompanying Citizens Legislative Procedures Act and additional appropriate legislation. No court in the United States may enjoin an initiative election except on grounds of fraud.

Source: http://www.ncid.us/amendment

BIBLIOGRAPHY

Introduction
[1] Clarke, Dave, Kate Davidson, and John Prior. "How Wall St. Got Its Way." *POLITICO*. Politico.com, 11 Dec. 2014. Web. 26 Jan. 2015. http://www.politico.com/story/2014/12/wall-street-spending-bill-congress-113525.html

[2] "1789-present National General Election Voting-eligible Population Turnout Rates." *United States Elections Project*. Electproject.org, 11 June 2014. Web. 05 Mar. 2015. http://www.electproject.org/national-1789-present

[3] Fuller, R. Buckminster. "A Candid Conversation with the Visionary Architect/inventor/philosopher R. Buckminster Fuller" *Playboy* 19.2 (1972): 15. Cesc Publications. Web. https://bfi.org/sites/default/files/attachments/pages/CandidConversation-Playboy.pdf.

Chapter 1
[4] Mangano, Joseph J., and Janette D. Sherman. "Trends in Hypothyroidism among Newborns after the Fukushima Nuclear Meltdown." *Elevated Airborne Beta Levels in Pacific/West Coast U.S. States and Trends in Hypothyroidism among Newborns after the Fukushima Nuclear Meltdown Joseph J. Mangano MPH MBA, Janette D. Sherman MD 1* (n.d.): n. pag. *SCIRP.org*. Scientific Research, Mar. 2013. Web. www.radiation.org/articles/Hypothyroid%20article%20OJPED.pdf

[5] Jeavons, John. *How to Grow More Vegetables: (and Fruits, Nuts, Berries, Grains, and Other Crops) than You Ever Thought Possible on Less Land than You Can Imagine.* Berkeley: Ten Speed, 2012. Print. http://www.amazon.com/How-Grow-More-Vegetables-Eighth/dp/160774189X/ref=sr_1_1?s=books&ie=UTF8&qid=1410919746&sr=1-1&keywords=john+jeavons

[6] "California Rare Fruit Growers." *California Rare Fruit Growers*. N.p., n.d. Web. 06 Mar. 2014. http://www.crfg.org/

[7] "How to Make a Mycorrhizae Fungi Soil Web in 3 Days & Jack the Rippers to Supersoil." *YouTube*. Socalpride619, 30 Nov. 2012. Web. 13 Jan. 2015. https://www.youtube.com/watch?v=gzbI7wAS-JM

[8] "Gallery: Study Finds Fungi Is Responsible for Majority of Carbon Seques..." *Inhabitat Sustainable Design Innovation Eco Architecture Green Building Mycorrhizal Root Tips Comments*. N.p., n.d. Web. 06 Mar. 2014. http://inhabitat.com/study-finds-fungi-is-responsible-for-majority-of-carbon-sequestration-in-northern-forests/forest-mushroom-amanita/

[9] Dekker, Anna. "The Role of Mycorrhiza for Plants in Stressed Environments." *Royal Institute of Business Architects (RIBA) Enterprises, Ltd. NBS*. NBS, n.d. Web. 06 Mar. 2014. http://www.thenbs.com/topics/DesignSpecification/articles/mycorrhiza.asp

[10] Qiangsheng, Wu, Xia Renxue, and Hu Zhengjia. *Effect of Arbuscular Mycorrhiza on the Drought Tolerance of Poncirus Trifoliata Seedlings - Springer*. N.p., 01 Jan. 2006. Web. 06 Mar. 2014. http://link.springer.com/article/10.1007%2Fs11461-005-0007-z

[11] "Mycorrhizal Fungi Can Reduce the Effects of Drought on Plants." *Turf and Landscape Fertilizers, Biological Products, Grass Seed and Control Products*. N.p., n.d. Web. 06 Mar. 2014. http://www.lebanonturf.com/education/mycorrhizal-fungi-can-reduce-the-effects-of-drought-on-plants

[12] Qiang-Shen, Wu, Zou Ying-Ning, and Huang Yong-Ming. *The Arbuscular Mycorrhizal Fungus Diversispora Spurca Ameliorates Effects of Waterlogging on Growth, Root System Architecture and Antioxidant Enzyme Activities of Citrus Seedlings - Fungal Ecology - Tom 6, Numer 1 (2013) - Biblioteka Nauki - Yadda*. Ceon Biblioteka Nauki, n.d. Web. 06 Mar. 2014. http://yadda.icm.edu.pl/yadda/element/bwmeta1.element.elsevier-61d7b4d7-daab-3bd1-a02f-dbb4b8200b2c

[13] Druille, Magdelena, Marta N. Cabello, Marina Omacini, and Rodolfo A. Golluscio. "Glyphosate Reduces Spore Viability and Root Colonization of Arbuscular Mycorrhizal Fungi." *Applied Soil Ecology*. Sciencedirect.com, 17 Dec. 2012. Web. 03 Mar. 2015. http://www.sciencedirect.com/science/article/pii/S0929139312002466

[14] Estok, D., B. Freedman, and D. Boyle. "Effects of the Herbicides 2,4-D, Glyphosate, Hexazinone, and Triclopyr on the Growth of Three Species of Ectomycorrhizal Fungi - Springer." *Effects of the Herbicides 2,4-D, Glyphosate, Hexazinone, and Triclopyr on the Growth of Three Species of Ectomycorrhizal Fungi - Springer*. Bulletin of Environmental Contamination and Toxicology, 01 June 1989. Web. 03 Mar. 2015. http://link.springer.com/article/10.1007%2FBF01701623?LI=true#page-1

[15] Zaller, Johann G., Florian Heigl, Liliane Ruess, and Andrea Grabmaier. "Glyphosate Herbicide Affects Belowground Interactions between Earthworms and Symbiotic Mycorrhizal Fungi in a Model Ecosystem." *Nature.com*. Nature Publishing Group, 9 July 2014. Web. 03 Mar. 2015. http://www.nature.com/srep/2014/140709/srep05634/full/srep05634.html

[16] Druille, M., M. N. Cabello, PA Garcia Parisi, R. A. Golluscio, and M. Omacini. "Glyphosate Vulnerability Explains Changes in Root-symbionts Propagules Viability in Pampean Grasslands." *Sciencedirect.com*. Agriculture, Ecosystems, and Environment, 8 Jan. 2015. Web. 03 Mar. 2015. http://www.sciencedirect.com/science/article/pii/S0167880914005611

[17] Solaiman, Zakaria, Lynette Abbott, and Varma Ajit. "Mycorrhizal Fungi: Use in Sustainable Agriculture and Land Restoration | Springer." *Mycorrhizal Fungi: Use in Sustainable Agriculture and Land Restoration | Springer*. Soil Biology, 2014. Web. 03 Mar. 2015. http://www.springer.com/us/book/9783662453698#

[18] Rodale, Maria. "1." *Organic Manifesto: How Organic Farming Can Heal Our Planet, Feed the World, and Keep Us Safe*. New York, NY: Rodale, 2010. 10. Print.

[19] William, Abraham. "Patent US7771736 - Glyphosate Formulations and Their Use for the Inhibition of 5-enolpyruvylshikimate-3-phosphate Synthase." *Google Books*. N.p., 30 Aug. 2002. Web. 13 Jan. 2015. https://www.google.com/patents/US7771736

[20] Ibid 17, p. ix.

[21] "Preharvest Staging Guide." *Monsanto Document* (n.d.): n. pag. Web. http://roundup.ca/_uploads/documents/MON-Preharvest%20Staging%20Guide.pdf

[22] "Glyphosate (CASRN 1071-83-6) | IRIS | U.S. EPA." *EPA*. Environmental Protection Agency, 3 Jan. 1987. Web. 13 Jan. 2015. http://www.epa.gov/ncea/iris/subst/0057.htm

[23] Ritterman, Jeff. "The Case for Banning Monsanto's RoundUp." *East Bay Express*. Eastbayexpress.com, 15 Apr. 2015. Web. http://www.eastbayexpress.com/oakland/the-case-for-banning-monsantos-roundup/Content?oid=4247612&showFullText=true

[24] Seneff, Stephanie. "Autism Explained: Synergistic Poisoning from Aluminum and Glyphosate - Stephanie Seneff." *Autism Explained: Synergistic Poisoning from Aluminum and Glyphosate*. Autism One, 28 May 2014. Web. 13 Jan. 2015. http://www.autismone.org/content/autism-explained-synergistic-poisoning-aluminum-and-glyphosate-stephanie-seneff

[25] Schrödl, Wieland, Susanne Krüger, Theodora Konstantinova-Müller, Awad A. Shehata, Ramon Rolff, and Monika Krüger. "Possible Effects of Glyphosate on Mucorales Abundance in the Rumen of." *Springer.com*. Current Microbiology, 01 Dec. 2014. Web. 03 Mar. 2015. http://link.springer.com/article/10.1007/s00284-014-0656-y#page-1

[26] Bradbury, SM, AT Proudfoot, and JA Yale. "Glyphosate Poisoning." *National Center for Biotechnology Information*. U.S. National Library of Medicine, 2004. Web. 13 Jan. 2015. http://www.ncbi.nlm.nih.gov/pubmed/15862083

Chapter 2

[27] Isaacson, John. "Presidential-Appointments.org." *Presidential-Appointments.org*. N.p., n.d. Web. 06 Mar. 2014. http://www.presidential-appointments.org/

[28] http://www.brandrepublic.com/News/874187/Obama-site-Changegov-adopts-CRM-software-facilitate-citizen-feedback/

[29] Goodman, John. "Whatever Happened to the https://www.youtube.com/watch?v=akVL7QY0S8Azen's Briefing Book?" *Health Policy Blog RSS*. National Center for Policy Analysis, 28 Sept. 2009. Web. 13 Jan. 2015. http://healthblog.ncpa.org/whatever-happened-to-the-citizen%E2%80%99s-briefing-book/

[30] "Ballot Access." *Wikipedia*. Wikimedia Foundation, 29 Nov. 2014. Web. 13 Jan. 2015. http://en.wikipedia.org/wiki/Ballot_access

[31] "Ballot Access." *Libertarian Party*. Lp.org, n.d. Web. 13 Jan. 2015. http://www.lp.org/ballot-access

[32] Winger, Richard. "Write-in Voting for President." 14 Oct. 2014. E-mail.

[33] "Candidate Write In Requirements, State Certifications." *An American Vision*. Anamericanvision.com, n.d. Web. 25 Apr. 2015. http://www.anamericanvision.com/info/state_certifications.php

[34] Candidate Write In Requirements, State Certifications." *Independent Statesman Party*. Anamericanvision.com, n.d. Web. http://www.anamericanvision.com/info/state_certifications_requirements.php

[35] "The Ins and Outs of Write-Ins." *Bloomberg Business Week*. Bloomberg, 01 Nov. 2004. Web. 13 Jan. 2015. http://www.businessweek.com/stories/2004-11-01/the-ins-and-outs-of-write-ins

[36] "About Rootstock." *Heirloom Roses*. Heirloom Roses, n.d. Web. 06 Mar. 2014. http://www.heirloomroses.com/care/rootstock/

[37] "The Antique Rose Emporium." *American Beauty*. The Antique Rose Emporium, n.d. Web. 06 Mar. 2014. https://www.antiqueroseemporium.com/roses/807/american-beauty

Chapter 3

[38] Frankel, Judy. "Change Is Scary." *Judys Homegrown Blog*. Judy's Homegrown, 11 Sept. 2011. Web. 06 Mar. 2014. http://blog.judyshomegrown.com/2013/03/11/change-is-scary/

Chapter 4

[39] Reid, Wilson. "Dr. Reid Wilson Clip - "How the Amygdala Learns"" *YouTube*. ReidWilsonPhD, 03 Jan. 2011. Web. 06 Mar. 2014. http://www.youtube.com/watch?v=0vhBkRipwis

Chapter 5

[40] Yaney, Kevin. "Will Generation Z Be the New Silent Generation?" *The Nailing Post: Marketing, Business and Life In Between.* Yaney Marketing, Inc., 20 Jan. 2011. Web. 06 Mar. 2014. http://www.yaney.net/NailingPost.aspx?pid=34

[41] Tietz, Jeff. "Middle-class Americans, Suddenly Homeless and Living in Their Cars -- Society's Child -- Sott.net." *SOTT.net.* Rolling Stone, 25 June 2012. Web. 10 Mar. 2014. http://www.sott.net/article/247382-Middle-class-Americans-Suddenly-Homeless-and-Living-in-their-Cars

[42] "United States Census Bureau." *About Poverty.* Census.gov, n.d. Web. 21 Jan. 2015. https://www.census.gov/hhes/www/poverty/about/overview/

[43] Williamson, Elizabeth. "Some Americans Lack Food, but USDA Won't Call Them Hungry." *Washington Post.* The Washington Post, 16 Nov. 2006. Web. 22 Jan. 2015. http://www.washingtonpost.com/wp-dyn/content/article/2006/11/15/AR2006111501621.html

Chapter 6

[44] Ryter, Jon Christian. "The Death of Indianapolis Baptist Temple and the Anti-Tax Movement." *Jon Christian Ryter.* Jon Christian Ryter's Conservative World Blog, n.d. Web. 10 Mar. 2014. http://www.jonchristianryter.com/2007/070228.html

[45] "Tax Protest Movement." *Anti Defamation League.* Adl.org, n.d. Web. http://archive.adl.org/learn/ext_us/tpm.html

[46] "Federal Reserve Act." *Wikipedia.* Wikimedia Foundation, 03 July 2014. Web. 09 Mar. 2015. http://en.wikipedia.org/wiki/Federal_Reserve_Act

[47] Hall, Ed. "U.S. National Debt Clock FAQ." *U.S. National Debt Clock FAQ.* N.p., 6 Feb. 2008. Web. 10 Mar. 2014. http://www.brillig.com/debt_clock/faq.html

[48] Schulz, Robert L. "We The People Features - Taxes - Philander Knox." *We The People Features - Taxes - Philander Knox.* Givemeliberty.org, n.d. Web. 22 Jan. 2015. http://www.givemeliberty.org/features/taxes/philanderknox.htm

[49] Volubrjotr. "Did Woodrow Wilson REALLY REGRET Handing AMERICA To The Rothschild BANKSTERS?" *Political Vel Craft.* Http://politicalvelcraft.org, 16 Sept. 2012. Web. 23 Jan. 2015. http://politicalvelcraft.org/2012/09/16/did-woodrow-wilson-really-regret-handing-america-to-the-rothschild-banksters/

[50] "Did Woodrow Wilson REGRET Handing AMERICA to the BANKSTERS?" *YouTube.* Unconventional Finance, 6 Sept. 2012. Web. 23 Jan. 2015. https://www.youtube.com/watch?v=7sr2DspCZig

[51] Wilson, Woodrow. "Chapter 9/Benevolence, or Justice." *The New Freedom; a Call for the Emancipation of the Generous Energies of a People.* New York and Garden City: Doubleday, Page, 1913. 201. Print.

[52] Brown, Ellen Hodgson. *Web of Debt: The Shocking Truth about Our Money System and How We Can Break Free.* Baton Rouge, LA: Third Millennium, 2008. Print. Page 102.

[53] Ibid.

[54] "Employment Situation Summary." *U.S. Bureau of Labor Statistics.* U.S. Bureau of Labor Statistics, Feb. 2015. Web. 25 Feb. 2015. http://www.bls.gov/news.release/empsit.nr0.htm

[55] "Executive Order 6102." *Wikipedia.* Wikimedia Foundation, 03 Aug. 2014. Web. 10 Mar. 2014. http://en.wikipedia.org/wiki/Executive_Order_6102

[56] Ritholtz, Barry. "A Brief History Lesson: How We Ended Glass Steagall | The Big Picture." *The Big Picture.* Ritholtz.com, 17 May 2012. Web. 23 Jan. 2015. http://www.ritholtz.com/blog/2012/05/how-we-ended-glass-steagall/

[57] Gonzalez, Sarah. "Dodd-Frank Reform Bills Move out of House Agriculture Committee | AgriPulse." *Dodd-Frank Reform Bills Move out of House Agriculture Committee | AgriPulse.* Agri-pulse.com, 20 Mar. 2013. Web. 23 Jan. 2015. http://www.agri-pulse.com/Dodd-Frank-reform-bills-move-out-of-House-Agriculture-Committee-03202013.asp

[58] Sorenson, Sally Jo. "Bluestem Prairie: Collin Peterson Regrets Vote on Glass-Steagall, Cautions about Weakening Dodd-Frank Regs." *'Bluestem Prairie'* Bluestemprairie.com, 21 May 2013. Web. 24 Jan. 2015. http://www.bluestemprairie.com/bluestemprairie/2013/03/collin-peterson-regrets-vote-on-glass-steagall-cautions-about-weakening-dodd-frank-regs.html

[59] Carter, Zach. "Wall Street Deregulation Advances As Top Democrat Warns That Vote Could 'Haunt' Congress." *The Huffington Post.* TheHuffingtonPost.com, 20 Mar. 2013. Web. 24 Jan. 2015. http://www.huffingtonpost.com/2013/03/20/wall-street-deregulation-n_2916795.html?1363804456

[60] Pendery, David. "Three Top Economists Agree 2009 Worst Financial Crisis Since Great Depression; Risks Increase If Right Steps Are Not Taken." *Reuters.* Thomson Reuters Business Wire, 27 Feb. 2009. Web. 24 Jan. 2015. http://www.reuters.com/article/2009/02/27/idUS193520+27-Feb-2009+BW20090227

[61] Weissman, Robert. "$5 Billion in Lobbying for 12 Corrupt Deals Caused the Multi-Trillion Dollar Financial Meltdown." *Multinational Monitor.* AlterNet, 8 Mar. 2009. Web. 11 Mar. 2014. http://www.alternet.org/story/130683/%245_billion_in_lobbying_for_12_corrupt_deals_caused_the_multi-trillion_dollar_financial_meltdown/?page=2

Chapter 7

[62] Cillizza, Chris. "Is the Presidential Bully Pulpit Dead?" *Washington Post.* The Washington Post, 24 June 2013. Web. 13 Jan. 2015. http://www.washingtonpost.com/blogs/the-fix/wp/2013/06/24/is-the-bully-pulpit-dead/

[63] Morss, Elliott. "Obama's Biggest Economic Mistakes." *Eliott Morss Blog.* Morssglobalfinance.com, n.d. Web. 13 Jan. 2015. http://www.morssglobalfinance.com/obama%E2%80%99s-biggest-economic-mistakes/

[64] Duray, Dan. "Peter Orszag: Obama's Budget Director - ALL YOU NEED TO KNOW." *The Huffington Post.* TheHuffingtonPost.com, 12 Dec. 2008. Web. 13 Jan. 2015. http://www.huffingtonpost.com/2008/11/18/peter-orszag-obamas-budge_n_144704.html

[65] Froomkin, Dan. "Millions of Reasons to Doubt Summers." *White House Watch.* The Washington Post, 6 Apr. 2009. Web. 13 Jan. 2015. http://voices.washingtonpost.com/white-house-watch/financial-crisis/millions-of-reasons-to-doubt-s.html

[66] Dash, Eric. "Ex-White House Budget Director Joins Citigroup." *The New York Times.* Dealb%k, 09 Dec. 2010. Web. 13 Jan. 2015. http://dealbook.nytimes.com/2010/12/09/ex-white-house-budget-director-joins-citigroup/?_php=true&_type=blogs&_r=0

[67] Shear, Michael D., and Ed O'Keefe. "Orszag to Resign as White House Budget Director, Source Says." *Washington Post.* The Washington Post, 22 June 2010. Web. 13 Jan. 2015. http://www.washingtonpost.com/wp-dyn/content/article/2010/06/21/AR2010062104882.html

[68] "Where'd the Bailout Money Go? Shhhh, It's a Secret." *Fox News.* FOX News Network, 22 Dec. 2008. Web. 13 Jan. 2015. http://www.foxnews.com/story/2008/12/22/whered-bailout-money-go-shhhh-it-secret/

[69] Reeves, Jeff. "2008 TARP Funds -- Where Are They Now? | InvestorPlace." *InvestorPlace*. InvestorPlace.com, 23 May 2012. Web. 13 Jan. 2015. http://investorplace.com/2012/05/2008-tarp-funds-where-are-they-now/#.U5cigYVdQch

[70] Rodriguez Valladares, Mayra. "Derivatives Markets Growing Again, With Few New Protections." *Dealb%k*. The New York Times, 13 May 2014. Web. 13 Jan. 2015. http://dealbook.nytimes.com/2014/05/13/derivatives-markets-growing-again-with-few-new-protections/?_php=true&_type=blogs&_php=true&_type=blogs&_r=1

[71] Snyder, Michael. "The Size Of The Derivatives Bubble Hanging Over The Global Economy Hits A Record High." *The Economic Collapse*. Theeconomiccollapseblog.com, 26 May 2014. Web. 13 Jan. 2015. http://theeconomiccollapseblog.com/archives/the-size-of-the-derivatives-bubble-hanging-over-the-global-economy-hits-a-record-high

[72] "Greenspan Makes Friedman Eat His Words." *YouTube*. Rodrigo Villela, 22 May 2009. Web. 13 Jan. 2015. https://www.youtube.com/watch?v=YzsiXsbPQY4

[73] United States. Financial Crisis Inquiry Commission. *Final Report of the National Commission on the Causes of the Financial and Economic Crisis in the U.S.* By Phil Angelides, Bill Thomas, Brooksley Born, Bob Graham, Keith Hennessey, Douglas Holtz-Eakin, John Thompson, and Peter Wallison. Washington: U.S. Govt. Printing Office, 2011. Print. Official Govt. Ed. http://www.google.com/url?sa=t&rct=j&q=&esrc=s&source=web&cd=1&ved=0CCAQF jAA&url=http%3A%2F%2Fwww.gpo.gov%2Ffdsys%2Fpkg%2FGPO-FCIC%2Fpdf%2FGPO-FCIC.pdf&ei=vq1VVJnTJoutogTGzIKoCw&usg=AFQjCNFTTGdOIGYQT8XkqcyhG NF946weng&sig2=IGDJ0PeXGHxsz0NytrjHXg&bvm=bv.78677474,d.cGU

[74] "What Is the Current Face Value of All Derivatives in the World?" Message to the author. 5 Mar. 2015. E-mail.

[75] "OTC Derivatives Market Activity in the Second Half of 2013." *Bank for International Settlements*. Bis.org, 8 May 2014. Web. 06 Mar. 2015. http://www.bis.org/publ/otc_hy1405.htm

[76] Ibid.

[77] Chance, Don M., and Robert Edwin Brooks. *An Introduction to Derivatives and Risk Management*. N.p.: n.p., n.d. Print.http://books.google.com/books?hl=en&lr=&id=b8PgBQAAQBAJ&oi=fnd&pg=PP 1&dq=face+value+of+all+derivatives&ots=dKmfzZu1A9&sig=OGSG-jzoBIwzTBrn_BK9W10LQD8#v=onepage&q=face%20value%20of%20all%20derivativ es&f=false

[78] Taibbi, Matt. "Frisk and Stop." *The Divide: American Injustice in the Age of the Wealth Gap*. New York: Spiegel & Grau, 2014. 58-63. Print.

[79] Dayen, David. "Clueless Law Firm's Out-of-touch Boasting: "Got off with Just a $5 Million Fine!" *Salon*. Salon.com, 5 Mar. 2014. Web. 13 Jan. 2015. http://www.salon.com/2014/03/05/clueless_law_firms_out_of_touch_boasting_got_off_ with_just_a_5_million_fine%E2%80%9D/

[80] Tangel, Andrew. "Mary Jo White Could Face Conflicts of Interest as SEC Chairwoman." *Los Angeles Times*. Los Angeles Times, 18 Feb. 2013. Web. 13 Jan. 2015. http://articles.latimes.com/2013/feb/18/business/la-fi-white-conflicts-20130218

[81] "Dylan Ratigan Audit Exposes Secrets ~ Corruption of Federal Reserve.flv." *YouTube*. ProtectAmericasDream, 13 Apr. 2012. Web. 13 Jan. 2015. https://www.youtube.com/watch?v=ugz4DFzdUOY

[82] "Audit of the Federal Reserve Reveals $16 Trillion in Secret Bailouts -- Sott.net." *SOTT.net*. SOTT.net, n.d. Web. 13 Jan. 2015. http://www.sott.net/article/250592-Audit-of-the-Federal-Reserve-Reveals-16-Trillion-in-Secret-Bailouts

[83] United States. Government Accountability Office. GAO. *Opportunities Exist to Strengthen Policies and Processes for Managing Emergency Assistance.* Vol. 11-696. N.p.: GAO, July 2011. Print. http://www.google.com/url?sa=t&rct=j&q=&esrc=s&source=web&cd=1&ved=0CCsQFj AA&url=http%3A%2F%2Fwww.gao.gov%2Fnew.items%2Fd11696.pdf&ei=ZjyGU4T0 CpWqyASX44HYBA&usg=AFQjCNGBZrchDuhAVC8CiFI846EdgutHOw&sig2=2Gu a8sz8cNRcRha5Pc9SNA&bvm=bv.67720277,d.aWw&cad=rja

[84] Ivry, Bob, Bradley Keoun, and Phil Kuntz. "Secret Fed Loans Gave Banks $13 Billion Undisclosed to Congress." *Bloomberg.com.* Bloomberg, 27 Nov. 2011. Web. 13 Jan. 2015. http://www.bloomberg.com/news/2011-11-28/secret-fed-loans-undisclosed-to-congress-gave-banks-13-billion-in-income.html

[85] "Michael R. Taylor." *Wikipedia.* Wikimedia Foundation, 5 Dec. 2014. Web. 13 Jan. 2015. http://en.wikipedia.org/wiki/Michael_R._Taylor

[86] "Is It Possible to Escape Genetic Engineering at the Grocery Store?" *Farmaid.org.* Farm Aid, n.d. Web. 13 Jan. 2015. http://www.farmaid.org/site/apps/nlnet/content2.aspx?c=qlI5IhNVJsE&b=6281749&ct=9 141885

[87] Gunnar, Ulson. "Geopolitics of Organic Food: Russia, China and France Ban GMOs." *Global Research.* GlobalResearch.ca, 2 May 2014. Web. 13 Jan. 2015. http://www.globalresearch.ca/geopolitics-of-organic-food-russia-china-and-france-ban-gmos/5380228

[88] Baker, Brandon. "Chinese Army Bans All GMO Grains and Oils » EcoWatch." *EcoWatch.com.* EcoWatch, 15 May 2014. Web. 13 Jan. 2015. http://ecowatch.com/2014/05/15/chinese-army-gmo/

[89] NSNBC International. "China's GMO Ban Costs U.S. Corn Traders $ 427 Million in Sales - Russia Banned Import of GMO Food." *Nsnbc.me.* Nsnbc International, 12 Apr. 2014. Web. 14 Jan. 2015. http://nsnbc.me/2014/04/12/chinas-gmo-ban-costs-us-corn-traders-427-million-in-sales-russia-banned-import-of-gmo-food/

[90] "What Countries Have Banned GMO Crops?" *Examiner.com.* Examiner, 18 June 2011. Web. 14 Jan. 2015. http://www.examiner.com/article/what-countries-have-banned-gmo-crops

[91] Barrett, Mike. "Breakdown of GMO Labeling Laws in Each Country (Global Map)." *Natural Society.* NaturalSociety.com, 30 July 2013. Web. 14 Jan. 2015. http://naturalsociety.com/breakdown-of-gmo-labeling-laws-by-country-global-map/

[92] "Monsanto Protection Act." *Snopes.com.* Snopes.com, 13 Sept. 2013. Web. 14 Jan. 2015. http://www.snopes.com/politics/business/mpa.asp

[93] "Obama Signs 'Monsanto Protection Act' Written by Monsanto-sponsored Senator." *RT USA.* Rt.com, 28 Mar. 2013. Web. 14 Jan. 2015. http://rt.com/usa/monsanto-bill-blunt-agriculture-006/

[94] Painter, Sally. "Monsanto Protection Act Sneaks through Senate during Sequestration." *Top Secret Writers.* Topsecretwriters.com, 13 Apr. 2013. Web. 14 Jan. 2015. http://www.topsecretwriters.com/2013/04/monsanto-protection-act-sneaks-through-senate-during-sequestration/

[95] Boerma, Lindsey. "Critics Slam Obama for "protecting" Monsanto." *CBSNews.* CBS Interactive, 28 Mar. 2013. Web. 14 Jan. 2015. http://www.cbsnews.com/news/critics-slam-obama-for-protecting-monsanto/

[96] Fredrix, Emily. "Goodbye High Fructose Corn Syrup, Hello Corn Sugar (Signed, Corn Industry)." *The Huffington Post.* TheHuffingtonPost.com, 14 Sept. 2010. Web. 14 Jan. 2015. http://www.huffingtonpost.com/2010/09/14/corn-sugar-high-fructose-corn-syrup_n_716007.html

[97] "Obama Signs Farm Bill That Continues Subsidies, Trims Food Stamps." *Fox News.* FOX News Network, 07 Feb. 2014. Web. 14 Jan. 2015. http://www.foxnews.com/politics/2014/02/07/obama-signs-farm-bill-that-trims-food-stamps/

[98] "High Fructose Corn Syrup: Guess What's Lurking in Your Food." *High Fructose Corn Syrup: Guess What's Lurking in Your Food.* Highfructosecornsyrup.org, 23 Feb. 2009. Web. 14 Jan. 2015. http://www.highfructosecornsyrup.org/2009/02/guess-whats-lurking-in-your-food.html

[99] Hagstrom, Jerry. "Vilsack Thanks Farm Bureau, Asks Support for Biotech Plan." *The Hagstrom Report: Agriculture News as It Happens.* Hagstromreport.com, 11 Jan. 2011. Web. http://www.hagstromreport.com/2011news_files/011111_vilsack.html

[100] "USDA Secretary Vilsack Challenges Seed Industry." - *Crop Biotech Update.* International Service for the Aquisition of Agri-Biotech Applications, 22 June 2012. Web. 14 Jan. 2015. http://www.isaaa.org/kc/cropbiotechupdate/article/default.asp?ID=9762

[101] Cohen-Cole, Linn. "OpEdNews Article: Vilsack Is Not Just Totally Pro-biotech, He Is Committedly Anti-democracy." *OpEdNews.* Opednews.com, 18 Dec. 2008. Web. 02 Feb. 2015. http://www.opednews.com/articles/Vilsack-is-not-just-totall-by-Linn-Cohen-Cole-081218-394.html

[102] Bright, Peter. "We Don't Need Net Neutrality; We Need Competition." *Ars Technica.* Arstechnica.com, 26 June 2014. Web. 01 Mar. 2015. http://arstechnica.com/tech-policy/2014/06/we-dont-need-net-neutrality-we-need-competition/

[103] Anders, George. "Five Loopholes That Could Undermine Net Neutrality." *MIT Technology Review.* Technologyreview.com, 24 Feb. 2015. Web. 01 Mar. 2015. http://www.technologyreview.com/news/535371/five-loopholes-that-could-undermine-net-neutrality/

[104] Van Schewick, Barbara. "Analysis of Proposed Network Neutrality Rules." (n.d.): n. pag. Cyberlaw.stanford.edu, 18 Feb. 2015. Web. http://cyberlaw.stanford.edu/downloads/vanSchewick2015AnalysisofProposedNetworkN eutralityRules.pdf

[105] Turner, S. Derek, and Matt Wood. "Wonkblog Gets It Wrong: The FCC's Shrinking Authority Isn't Enough to Save Net Neutrality." *Free Press.* Savetheinternet.com, n.d. Web. 14 Jan. 2015. http://www.savetheinternet.com/blog/2014/01/16/wonkblog-gets-it-wrong-fcc%E2%80%99s-shrinking-authority-isn%E2%80%99t-enough-save-net-neutrality

[106] "Faculty on Point | Barbara Van Schewick on Network Neutrality." *YouTube.* Stanfordlawschool, 3 Feb. 2015. Web. 01 Mar. 2015. https://www.youtube.com/watch?v=E0cGw72pZRw#t=95

[107] Crawford, Susan. "Furious About Your Cable Bill? Go Tell City Hall | BillMoyers.com." *BillMoyers.com.* BillMoyers.com, 01 May 2014. Web. 14 Jan. 2015. http://billmoyers.com/2014/05/01/the-wire-next-time/

[108] Lee, Timothy B. "Obama Calls for Cities to Build Government-run High-speed Internet." *Vox.* Vox.com, 14 Jan. 2015. Web. 09 Apr. 2015. http://www.vox.com/2015/1/14/7546865/obama-municipal-broadband-fcc

[109] Silver, Josh. "How Lobbyists Killed Net Neutrality." *YouTube.* Represent.us, 16 Jan. 2014. Web. 14 Jan. 2015. https://www.youtube.com/watch?v=oemQxYSHKgA

[110] Sokolove, Michael. "Comcast's Real Repairman." *The New York Times.* The New York Times, 19 Apr. 2014. Web. 14 Jan. 2015. http://www.nytimes.com/2014/04/20/business/media/comcasts-real-repairman.html?_r=0

[111] Shields, Todd, Stephanie Green, and Laura Litvan. "Time Warner Cable Deal Sets Comcast's D.C. Lobbying Machine in Motion." *Bloomberg Business Week*. Bloomberg, 06 Mar. 2014. Web. 14 Jan. 2015. http://www.businessweek.com/articles/2014-03-06/time-warner-cable-deal-sets-comcast-lobbying-machine-in-motion

[112] "David L. Cohen." *David L. Cohen*. Corporatecomcast.com, n.d. Web. 14 Jan. 2015. http://corporate.comcast.com/news-information/leadership-overview/david-l-cohen

[113] "Fore! Obama Playing Golf with World Bank President, Comcast CEO." *CBS DC*. Washingtoncbslocal.com, 14 Aug. 2013. Web. 14 Jan. 2015. http://washington.cbslocal.com/2013/08/14/fore-obama-playing-golf-with-world-bank-president-comcast-ceo/

[114] "Comcast Corp." *Opensecrets*. OpenSecrets.org, n.d. Web. 14 Jan. 2015. https://www.opensecrets.org/orgs/summary.php?id=D000000461&cycle=2012

[115] Ruiz, Rebecca R., and Steve Lohr. "In Net Neutrality Victory, F.C.C. Classifies Broadband Internet Service as a Public Utility." *The New York Times*. The New York Times, 26 Feb. 2015. Web. 26 Feb. 2015.http://www.nytimes.com/2015/02/27/technology/net-neutrality-fcc-vote-internet-utility.html?_r=0

[116] Wyatt, Edward. "Obama Asks F.C.C. to Adopt Tough Net Neutrality Rules." *The New York Times*. The New York Times, 10 Nov. 2014. Web. 14 Jan. 2015. http://www.nytimes.com/2014/11/11/technology/obama-net-neutrality-fcc.html?_r=0

[117] Tichenor, Jordan. "County Action Coming On NDAA Detention?" *County Action Coming On NDAA Detention?* EugeneWeekly.com, 14 Nov. 2013. Web. 14 Jan. 2015. http://www.eugeneweekly.com/20131114/news-briefs/county-action-coming-ndaa-detention

[118] Nies, Yunji De. "With Reservations, Obama Signs Act to Allow Detention of Citizens." *ABC News*. ABC News Network, 31 Dec. 2011. Web. 14 Jan. 2015. http://abcnews.go.com/blogs/politics/2011/12/with-reservations-obama-signs-act-to-allow-detention-of-citizens/

[119] "Federal Court Rules Obama NDAA in Violation of 1st and 5th Amendments." *SelectSmart.com Forums*. Selectsmart.com, 17 May 2012. Web. 14 Jan. 2015. http://www.selectsmart.com/DISCUSS/read.php?16,896051

[120] Jewell, Jessica. "NDAA Violates American Rights." *The Sundial*. California State University Northridge, 23 Jan. 2012. Web. 14 Jan. 2015. http://sundial.csun.edu/2012/01/ndaa-violates-american-rights/

[121] "America Under Siege: Fighting the NDAA." *Understanding The National Defense Authorization Act* (n.d.): n. pag. Pandaunite.org. Web. https://www.google.com/url?sa=t&rct=j&q=&esrc=s&source=web&cd=4&ved=0CDoQFjAD&url=https%3A%2F%2Fpandaunite.org%2Fdownloads%2FActionKit%2FColorflyer.pdf&ei=yDWaU634Lc2uyATbjoCACQ&usg=AFQjCNHhj9ttjESoof4MdfVtZbP_uDFgkA&sig2=RW8z0l4VM9rlbQ4CLv1j_w&bvm=bv.68911936,d.aWw&cad=rja

[122] Johnson, D. "Six Down: Another City Unanimously Votes to Block NDAA Detention Provisions." *Jobs Not Wars RSS*. Jobs-not-wars.org, 03 June 2014. Web. 14 Jan. 2015. http://www.jobs-not-wars.org/six-down-another-city-unanimously-votes-to-block-ndaa-detention-provisions/

[123] "How You Can Stop the NDAA's Indefinite Detention In Your City | Think Tank." *YouTube*. Breakingtheset, 23 May 2014. Web. 16 Jan. 2015. https://www.youtube.com/watch?v=QFjUtaHbJUU#t=360

[124] "Washington, George." "Americans Have Lost VIRTUALLY ALL of Our Constitutional Rights." *Zero Hedge*. Zerohedge.com, 17 Oct. 2013. Web. 16 Jan. 2015.

http://www.zerohedge.com/contributed/2013-10-17/americans-have-lost-virtually-all-our-constitutional-rights

[125] Mariner, Joanne. "The NDAA Explained: Part One in a Two-Part Series of Columns on the National Defense Authorization Act." *Verdict: Legal Analysis and Commentary.* Justia.com, 20 Dec. 2011. Web. 16 Jan. 2015. http://verdict.justia.com/2011/12/21/the-national-defense-authorization-act-explained

[126] "Buck McKeon - Administration's Terrorist Detention Policy." *YouTube.* HASC Republicans, 24 July 2009. Web. 16 Jan. 2015. https://www.youtube.com/watch?v=kMJnTmbHFZc

[127] "61 Senators Betrayed You Today." *YouTube.* Tony Brown18, 18 May 2014. Web. 16 Jan. 2015. https://www.youtube.com/watch?v=1OkcSP3XZH0

[128] Obama, Barack. "Statement by the President on H.R. 4310." *The White House.* Whitehouse.gov, 3 Jan. 2013. Web. 16 Jan. 2015. http://www.whitehouse.gov/the-press-office/2013/01/03/statement-president-hr-4310

[129] "National Defense Authorization Act for FY 2012." *U.S. Government Printing Office.* Gpo.gov, 31 Dec. 2011. Web. 16 Jan. 2015. http://www.gpo.gov/fdsys/pkg/PLAW-112publ81/html/PLAW-112publ81.htm

[130] Grayson, Rep. Alan. "Cut Off One Head, and 50 More Spring Up." *The Huffington Post.* TheHuffingtonPost.com, 2 Dec. 2013. Web. 16 Jan. 2015. http://www.huffingtonpost.com/rep-alan-grayson/cut-off-one-head-and-50-m_b_4373882.html

[131] Dao, James. "Drone Pilots Are Found to Get Stress Disorders Much as Those in Combat Do." *The New York Times.* Nytimes.com, 22 Feb. 2013. Web. 16 Jan. 2015. http://www.nytimes.com/2013/02/23/us/drone-pilots-found-to-get-stress-disorders-much-as-those-in-combat-do.html?_r=0

[132] Kaag, John. "Drones, Ethics and the Armchair Soldier." *The New York Times Opinionator.* Opinionator.blogs.nytimes.com, 17 Mar. 2013. Web. 16 Jan. 2015. http://opinionator.blogs.nytimes.com/2013/03/17/drones-ethics-and-the-armchair-soldier/

[133] Chamberlain, Jacob. "Colonel West: 'Obama Is a War Criminal'" *Black Agenda Report.* Blackagendareport.com, 14 May 2013. Web. http://blackagendareport.com/content/cornel-west-obama-%E2%80%9C-war-criminal%E2%80%9D

[134] Swire, Peter. "Legal FAQs on NSA Wiretaps." *PeterSwire.net.* Peterswire.net, n.d. Web. 16 Jan. 2015. http://www.peterswire.net/nsa_full_faq.htm

[135] Dinan, Stephen. "Federal Judge Says NSA Phone Program Violates Fourth Amendment." *Washington Times.* The Washington Times, 16 Dec. 2013. Web. 15 Jan. 2015. http://www.washingtontimes.com/news/2013/dec/16/federal-judge-says-nsa-phone-program-violates-four/?page=all

[136] "Reform the Patriot Act | Section 215." *American Civil Liberties Union.* Aclu.org, n.d. Web. 14 Jan. 2015. https://www.aclu.org/free-speech-national-security-technology-and-liberty/reform-patriot-act-section-215

[137] Brown, Jamie E. "Letter to F. James Sensenbrenner Jr." *U.S. Department of Justice* (2003): n. pag. Justice.gov. Web. http://www.google.com/url?sa=t&rct=j&q=&esrc=s&source=web&cd=8&ved=0CFQQFjAH&url=http%3A%2F%2Fwww.justice.gov%2Farchive%2Fll%2Fsubs%2Fcongress%2Fhjcpatriotwcover051303final.pdf&ei=3RlEVNanAcXy8QHI3oDgCQ&usg=AFQjCNEb8b7ckXnTE69kyi6ORsGjM4XMyw&sig2=6FF-MULWcmGx2B0dk6ldew&bvm=bv.77648437,d.b2U&cad=rja

[138] "Trans-Pacific Partnership Agreement." *Electronic Frontier Foundation.* Eff.org, n.d. Web. 10 Apr. 2015. https://www.eff.org/issues/tpp

[139] Freeman, Joshua, Gay Keating, Rhys Jones, George Laking, Marilyn Head, and Alexandra Macmillan. "The Impact of the Trans-Pacific Partnership on Health: Why an Independent, Comprehensive Health Impact Assessment Is Crucial Prior to Signing." *Un-Doctored: Un-edited Statements from the Health Care Sector and beyond.* NZDoctor.co.nx, 28 Oct. 2014. Web. http://www.nzdoctor.co.nz/un-doctored/2014/october-2014/28/the-impact-of-the-trans-pacific-partnership-on-health-why-an-independent,-comprehensive-health-impact-assessment-is-crucial-prior-to-signing.aspx

[140] "Updated Secret Trans-Pacific Partnership Agreement (TPP) - Freedom of Information, Civil Liberties and Access to Medicines at Stake." *Global Research.* GlobalResearch.ca, 18 Oct. 2014. Web. 16 Jan. 2015. http://www.globalresearch.ca/updated-secret-trans-pacific-partnership-agreement-tpp-freedom-of-information-civil-liberties-and-access-to-medicines-at-stake/5408730

[141] "Obama and Problems in the Prison System." *YouTube.* TheLipTV, 27 Feb. 2014. Web. 19 Jan. 2015. https://www.youtube.com/watch?v=HrdSc1eFn9c

[142] Klein, Ezra, and Evan Soltas. "Wonkbook: 11 Facts about America's Prison Population." *Washington Post.* The Washington Post, 13 Aug. 2103. Web. 18 Jan. 2015. http://www.washingtonpost.com/blogs/wonkblog/wp/2013/08/13/wonkbook-11-facts-about-americas-prison-population/

[143] "Interview with Bryan Stevenson." *Jon Stewart/The Daily Show.* Thedailyshow.cc.com, 17 Oct. 2014. Web. 19 Jan. 2015. http://thedailyshow.cc.com/guests/bryan-stevenson/d9wrvk/bryan-stevenson

[144] "Banking on Bondage: Private Prisons and Mass Incarceration." *American Civil Liberties Union.* Aclu.org, 2 Nov. 2011. Web. 19 Jan. 2015. https://www.aclu.org/prisoners-rights/banking-bondage-private-prisons-and-mass-incarceration

[145] Pelaez, Vicky. "The Prison Industry in the United States: Big Business or a New Form of Slavery?" *Global Research.* GlobalResearch.ca, 31 Mar. 2008. Web. 19 Jan. 2015. http://www.globalresearch.ca/the-prison-industry-in-the-united-states-big-business-or-a-new-form-of-slavery/8289

[146] Seandel, Caitlin. "Prison Labor: Three Strikes and You're Hired." *Ella Baker Center.* Ellabakercenter.org, 27 June 2013. Web. 19 Jan. 2015. http://ellabakercenter.org/blog/2013/06/prison-labor-is-the-new-slave-labor

[147] Flounders, Sara. "The Pentagon and Slave Labor in U.S. Prisons." *Global Research.* GlobalResearch.ca, 4 Feb. 2013. Web. 19 Jan. 2015. http://www.globalresearch.ca/the-pentagon-and-slave-labor-in-u-s-prisons/25376

[148] "Choiforsenate2014." *Choiforsenate2014.* Choiforsenate2014.com, n.d. Web. 19 Jan. 2015. http://www.choiforsenate2014.com/#!prison-reform/c1a8s

[149] Downs, Ray. "Who's Getting Rich off the Prison-Industrial Complex? | VICE | United States." *VICE.* Vice.com, 17 May 2013. Web. 19 Jan. 2015. http://www.vice.com/read/whos-getting-rich-off-the-prison-industrial-complex

[150] Schiller, Ben. "The World's Most Energy-Efficient Countries." *Fast Company Exist.* Fastcoexist.com, 23 July 2014. Web. 19 Jan. 2015. http://www.fastcoexist.com/3033186/the-worlds-most-energy-efficient-countries

[151] Koronowski, Ryan. "Why Obama Just Named Sweden As A Model For Energy Policy." *ThinkProgress RSS.* Thinkprogress.org, 4 Sept. 2013. Web. 19 Jan. 2015. http://thinkprogress.org/climate/2013/09/04/2568981/obama-sweden-energy/

[152] Holdren, John P. "The Energy Challenge and How to Meet It." Goldman Sachs Conference on Energy, Environment and the Financial Markets. London. Lecture. 27 Mar. 2007.

s3.amazonaws.com/zanran_storage/www2.goldmansachs.com/ContentPages/21852847.pdf

[153] Maessen, Jurriaan. "Climate Crazies: Geo-Engineering Schemes Risky But Necessary, Will Only Cost Taxpayer $ 1 Billion... Annually." *ExplosiveReports.Com.* Explosivereports.com, 18 Aug. 2012. Web. 19 Jan. 2015. http://explosivereports.com/2012/08/18/climate-crazies-geo-engineering-schemes-risky-but-necessary-will-only-cost-taxpayer-1-billion-annually/

[154] Hamilton, Clive. "Geoengineering Is Not a Solution to Climate Change." *Scientific American Global RSS.* Scientificamerican.com, 10 Mar. 2015. Web. 12 May 2015. http://www.scientificamerican.com/article/geoengineering-is-not-a-solution-to-climate-change/

[155] "Pilots, Doctors & Scientists Tell Truth about Chemtrails [Excerpts]." *YouTube.* John Kuhles, 2 Oct. 2014. Web. 19 Jan. 2015. https://www.youtube.com/watch?v=DPnWaBsMYnY

[156] "Geoengineering Whistleblower ~ Ex-Military ~ Kristen Meghan, Hauppauge, NY, January 18th, 2014." *YouTube.* DianeDi, 27 Jan. 2014. Web. 19 Jan. 2015. https://www.youtube.com/watch?v=jHm0XhtDyZA

[157] Cockerham, Sean. "Obama Position on Fracking Leaves Both Sides Grumbling." *Obama Position on Fracking Leaves Both Sides Grumbling.* McClatchydc.com, 23 Apr. 2013. Web. 19 Jan. 2015. http://www.mcclatchydc.com/2013/08/23/200205/obama-position-on-fracking-leaves.html

[158] Goldenberg, Suzanne. "2013 in Review: Obama Talks Climate Change – but Pushes Fracking." *The Guardian.* Theguardian.com, 20 Dec. 2013. Web. http://www.theguardian.com/environment/2013/dec/20/2013-climate-change-review-obama-fracking

[159] Frankel, Judy. "Leave It to an Oil Company." *Writeindependentorg Blog.* Judyshomegrown.com, 13 Apr. 2013. Web. http://blog.judyshomegrown.com/2013/04/29/leave-it-to-an-oil-company/

[160] Frankel, Judy. "Those Frackin' Chemicals." *Writeindependentorg Blog.* Judyshomegrown.com, 30 Apr. 2013. Web. 19 Jan. 2015. http://blog.judyshomegrown.com/2013/04/30/those-frackin-chemicals/

[161] Frankel, Judy. "Fracking in California." *Writeindependentorg Blog.* Judyshomegrown.com, 14 Oct. 2013. Web. 19 Jan. 2015. http://blog.judyshomegrown.com/2013/10/14/fracking-in-california/

[162] Cockerham, Sean. "McClatchy DC." *Obama Position on Fracking Leaves Both Sides Grumbling.* Mcclatchydc.com, 23 Aug. 2013. Web. 20 Jan. 2015. http://www.mcclatchydc.com/2013/08/23/200205_obama-position-on-fracking-leaves.html?rh=1

[163] Amico, Chris, Danny DeBelius, Scott Detrow, and Matt Stiles. "Natural Gas Drilling in Pennsylvania." *State Impact Pennsylvania Shale Play.* Stateimpact.npr.org, n.d. Web. http://stateimpact.npr.org/pennsylvania/drilling/

[164] Grenoble, Ryan. "Fracking Waste Linked To City's Toxic Drinking Water, Class-Action Suit Alleges." *The Huffington Post.* TheHuffingtonPost.com, 14 Nov. 2013. Web. 20 Jan. 2015. http://www.huffingtonpost.com/2013/11/14/bokoshe-fracking-waste-disposal-class-action-suit_n_4268732.html

[165] "Pennsylvania Alliance for Clean Water and Air List of the Harmed." *PA Alliance for Clean Water and Air.* Pennsylvaniaallianceforcleanwaterandair.wordpress, 19 Dec. 2012. Web. http://pennsylvaniaallianceforcleanwaterandair.wordpress.com/the-list/

[166] Jackson, Robert B., Brooks Rainey Pearson, Stephen G. Osborn, Nathaniel R. Warner, and Avner Vengosh. *Research and Policy Recommendations for Hydraulic Fracturing*

and Shale-Gas Extraction. Tech. Durham, NC: Center on Global Change, Duke U, 2011. Print. https://nicholas.duke.edu/cgc/HydraulicFracturingWhitepaper2011.pdf

[167] Gorder, Pam F. "Gas Leaks from Faulty Wells Linked to Contamination in Some Groundwater." *Gas Leaks from Faulty Wells Linked to Contamination in Some Groundwater.* Phys.org, 15 Sept. 2014. Web. 22 Jan. 2015. http://phys.org/news/2014-09-gas-leaks-faulty-wells-linked.html

[168] Darrah, Thomas H., Avner Vengosh, Robert B. Jackson, Nathaniel R. Warner, and Robert J. Poreda. *Noble Gases Identify the Mechanisms of Fugitive Gas Contamination in Drinking-water Wells Overlying the Marcellus and Barnett Shales* (n.d.): n. pag. *Proceedings of the National Academy of Sciences.* PNAS, 29 July 2014. Web. 2 Dec. 2014. http://sites.biology.duke.edu/jackson/pnas2014a.pdf

[169] New York State Department of Environmental Conservation. "Review of Selected Non-Routine Incidents in Pennsylvania." *Revised Draft SG Environmental Impact Statement Well Permit Issuance for Horizontal Drilling and High-Volume Hydraulic Fracturing* (2011): n. pag. Dec.ny.gov. Web. http://www.dec.ny.gov/docs/materials_minerals_pdf/rdsgeisch100911.pdf

[170] Sadasivam, Naveena. "New York State of Fracking: A ProPublica Explainer." *Pro Publica.* Propublica.org, 22 July 2014. Web. 20 Jan. 2015. http://www.propublica.org/article/new-york-state-of-fracking-a-propublica-explainer

[171] Kelly, Sharon. "Banks Reluctant to Lend in Shale Plays as Evidence Mounts on Harm to Property Values Near Fracking." *DeSmogBlog.* Desmogblog.com, 25 Nov. 2013. Web. 20 Jan. 2015. http://www.desmogblog.com/2013/11/25/new-evidence-fracking-s-property-value-impacts-banks-growing-reluctant-lend-near-gas-wells

[172] Conlin, Michelle. "Analysis: U.S. Drilling Boom Leaves Some Homeowners in a Big Hole." *Reuters.* Thomson Reuters, 12 Dec. 2013. Web. 20 Jan. 2015. http://www.reuters.com/article/2013/12/12/us-fracking-homeowners-analysis-idUSBRE9BB0GS20131212

[173] "James Dahlgren, MD on the Health Hazards of Fracking Chemicals." *YouTube.* Transition Culver City, 26 Apr. 2013. Web. 20 Jan. 2015. https://www.youtube.com/watch?v=Cb_SHtyINp0

[174] Tibbets, Peggy. "Study Shows Unsafe Air Quality at Oil and Gas Facilities." *From the Styx by Peggy Tibbetts.* Fromthestyx.wordpress.com, 30 Oct. 2014. Web. 20 Jan. 2015. https://fromthestyx.wordpress.com/2014/10/30/study-shows-unsafe-air-quality-at-oil-and-gas-facilities/

[175] Macey, Gregg P., Ruth Breech, Mark Chernaik, Caroline Cox, Denny Larson, Deb Thomas, and David O. Carpenter. "Air Concentrations of Volatile Compounds near Oil and Gas Production: A Community-based Exploratory Study." *Environmental Health.* Environmental Health, 30 Oct. 2014. Web. 03 Dec. 2014. http://www.ehjournal.net/content/13/1/82

[176] Ibid.

[177] "Chevron's Pa. Wild Gas Well UPDATE: 2 Big Unknowns: Why Propane Tank Near Well, How To Stop Blazing Gas. Local Describes Event (Fire Video) | Energy." *Before It's News.* Http://beforeitsnews.com, 11 Feb. 2014. Web. 21 Jan. 2015. http://beforeitsnews.com/energy/2014/02/chevron-massive-gas-well-explosion-fire-1-injured-1-missing-2453172.html

[178] "How Oil and Gas Disposal Wells Can Cause Earthquakes." *Energy and Environment Reporting for Texas.* Http://stateimpact.npr.org, n.d. Web. 20 Jan. 2015. http://stateimpact.npr.org/texas/tag/earthquake/

[179] Zelman, Joanna, and Justin Juozapavicius. "States With Fracking See Surge In Earthquake Activity." *The Huffington Post.* TheHuffingtonPost.com, 14 July 2014. Web.

21 Jan. 2015. http://www.huffingtonpost.com/2014/07/14/fracking-earthquake_n_5585892.html

[180] "The Halliburton Loophole." *The New York Times.* nytimes.com, 02 Nov. 2009. Web. 21 Jan. 2015. http://www.nytimes.com/2009/11/03/opinion/03tue3.html?_r=0

[181] "U.S. Energy Information Administration - EIA - Independent Statistics and Analysis." *How Much Carbon Dioxide Is Produced When Different Fuels Are Burned?* Eia.gov, 4 June 2014. Web. 21 Jan. 2015. http://www.eia.gov/tools/faqs/faq.cfm?id=73&t=11

[182] Eilperin, Juliet, and Steven Mufson. "EPA Proposes Cutting Carbon Dioxide Emissions from Coal Plants 30% by 2030." *Washington Post.* The Washington Post, 2 June 2014. Web. 22 Jan. 2015. http://www.washingtonpost.com/national/health-science/epa-to-propose-cutting-carbon-dioxide-emissions-from-coal-plants-30percent-by-2030/2014/06/01/f5055d94-e9a8-11e3-9f5c-9075d5508f0a_story.html

[183] Frankel, Judy. "G8 Energy Policy." *Writeindependentorg Blog.* Judyshomegrown.com, 22 Oct. 2013. Web. 22 Jan. 2015. http://blog.judyshomegrown.com/2013/10/22/g8-energy-policy/

[184] Klein, Naomi. *This Changes Everything: Capitalism vs. the Climate.* New York (N.Y.): Simon & Schuster, 2014. 6. Print.

Chapter 11

[185] Lowell, Amy. "The Congressional Library [excerpt]." *Poets.org.* Academy of American Poets, n.d. Web. 11 Mar. 2014. http://www.poets.org/viewmedia.php/prmMID/16510

[186] Nocera, Joe. "Boycott Campaign Donations!" *The New York Times.* The New York Times, 12 Aug. 2011. Web. 11 Mar. 2014. http://www.nytimes.com/2011/08/13/opinion/nocera-boycott-campaign-donations.html?_r=0

[187] Patton, Leslie. "Starbucks' Schultz Urges Fellow CEOs to Halt Campaign Giving." *Bloomberg.com.* Bloomberg, 15 Aug. 2011. Web. 24 Jan. 2015. http://www.bloomberg.com/news/2011-08-15/starbucks-schultz-urges-fellow-ceos-to-boycott-campaign-giving.html

Chapter 12

[188] "The Colbert Bump." *Wikiality.* Wikia, n.d. Web. 11 Mar. 2014. http://wikiality.wikia.com/The_Colbert_Bump

Chapter 13

[189] "Dylan Ratigan (rightfully) Loses It on Air." *YouTube.* Nyankee2003, 9 Aug. 2011. Web. 24 Jan. 2015. https://www.youtube.com/watch?v=gIcqb9hHQ3E

[190] Lessig, Lawrence. "Big Campaign Spending: Government by the 1%." *The Atlantic.* Atlantic Media Company, 10 July 2012. Web. 11 Mar. 2014. http://www.theatlantic.com/politics/archive/2012/07/big-campaign-spending-government-by-the-1/259599/

[191] Lessig, Lawrence. "Lawrence Lessig: We the People, and the Republic We Must Reclaim." *YouTube.* YouTube, 03 Apr. 2013. Web. 11 Mar. 2014. http://www.youtube.com/watch?v=mw2z9lV3W1g

[192] Domhoff, G. William. "Who Rules America: Wealth, Income, and Power." *Who Rules America: Wealth, Income, and Power.* 2.ucsc.edu, Feb. 2013. Web. 22 Jan. 2015. http://www2.ucsc.edu/whorulesamerica/power/wealth.html

[193] Stiglitz, Joseph E. "Of the 1%, by the 1%, for the 1%." *Vanity Fair*. Vanityfair.com, May 2011. Web. 22 Jan. 2015. http://www.vanityfair.com/society/features/2011/05/top-one-percent-201105

[194] 23 Year Old Female. "We Are the 99 Percent." *We Are the 99 Percent*. Wearethe99percent.tumblr.com, 14 Oct. 2013. Web. 24 Jan. 2015. http://wearethe99percent.tumblr.com/

[195] Roos, Dave. "Is It True That 1 Percent of Americans Control a Third of the Wealth? - HowStuffWorks." *HowStuffWorks*. Money.howstuffworks.com, n.d. Web. 24 Jan. 2015. http://money.howstuffworks.com/one-percent-control-third-of-wealth.htm

[196] Gebeloff, Robert, and Shaila Dewan. "Measuring the Top 1% by Wealth, Not Income." *Economix Measuring the Top 1 by Wealth Not Income Comments*. The New York Times, 17 Jan. 2012. Web. 11 Mar. 2014. http://economix.blogs.nytimes.com/2012/01/17/measuring-the-top-1-by-wealth-not-income/

[197] Lee, Danny. "Occupy L.A. Targets Home Auctions, Banks In Anti-Foreclosure March." *Occupy L.A. Targets Home Auctions, Banks In Anti-Foreclosure March*. Neontommy.com, 13 Jan. 2012. Web. 24 Jan. 2015. http://www.neontommy.com/news/2012/01/occupy-la-targets-home-auctions-banks-anti-foreclosure-march

[198] "Occupy Foreclosures Press Conference Jan 13th 2012." *YouTube*. Lenago111 Channel, 13 Jan. 2012. Web. 01 Apr. 2014. http://www.youtube.com/watch?v=If0OBn6FjFA

[199] "Bailout Increases by $800 Billion." *Washington Times*. The Washington Times, 26 Nov. 2008. Web. 24 Jan. 2015. http://www.washingtontimes.com/news/2008/nov/26/bailout-increases-by-800-billion/?page=all

[200] O'Keeffe, Suzanne. "The Great Swindle: How to Stomach Knowing the Banks Are Stealing a Nation's Worth of Homes, One Home at a Time." *The Huffington Post*. TheHuffingtonPost.com, 5 Mar. 2012. Web. 24 Jan. 2015. http://www.huffingtonpost.com/suzanne-okeeffe/bertha-herrera-foreclosure_b_1309170.html

[201] Coscarelli, Joe. "Occupy Wall Street, Julian Assange, and the Advantages of a Leaderless Movement." *Daily Intelligencer*. New York Magazine, 29 Nov. 2011. Web. 12 Mar. 2014. http://nymag.com/daily/intelligencer/2011/11/advantages-of-a-leaderless-movement.html

Chapter 14

[202] "Presidential Candidate Harry Braun." *Writein Dependent Channel*. YouTube, 08 Feb. 2012. Web. 14 Mar. 2014. http://www.youtube.com/watch?v=Hu_Z1aa448I

[203] "League of Women Voters." *Wikipedia*. Wikimedia Foundation, 13 Mar. 2014. Web. 14 Mar. 2014. http://en.wikipedia.org/wiki/League_of_Women_Voters

[204] "Andre Barnett For President 2012." *ABarnett2012 Channel*. YouTube, 11 July 2011. Web. 14 Mar. 2014. http://www.youtube.com/watch?v=rPFQATYbGSs

[205] "Debate 1 Price of Oil." *YouTube*. Writein Dependent Channel, 14 Feb. 2012. Web. 19 Mar. 2014. https://www.youtube.com/watch?v=gEwAZLwJMM8

Chapter 15

[206] "Take the Money and Run for Office | This American Life." *This American Life*. Http://content.time.com/time, n.d. Web. 25 Jan. 2015.

http://content.time.com/time/specials/packages/article/0,28804,1877351_1877350_18773 30,00.html

[207] Lessig, Lawrence. "Chapter 7/Why Isn't Our Financial System Safe?" *Republic, Lost: How Money Corrupts Congress -- and a Plan to Stop It.* New York, NY: Twelve Hachette Book Group, 2011. 76. Print.

[208] "Jeffrey Sachs (Columbia University Professor) Supports Occupy Wall Street." *YouTube.* Arman Rousta, 7 Oct. 2011. Web. 26 Jan. 2015. https://www.youtube.com/watch?v=H8svbm4WYmU

[209] Slaughter, Nathan. "ConocoPhillips: Warren Buffett's Largest Energy Holding." *Street Authority.* Seeking Alpha, 21 Dec. 2011. Web. 12 Mar. 2014. http://seekingalpha.com/article/315196-conocophillips-warren-buffetts-largest-energy-holding

[210] "ConocoPhillips: Betting Against Buffett." *[Phillips 66, Berkshire Hathaway Inc., Marathon Oil Corporation, Marathon Petroleum Corp].* Seeking Alpha, 18 July 2012. Web. 12 Mar. 2014. http://seekingalpha.com/article/728061-conocophillips-betting-against-buffett

[211] Ogg, John C. "Warren Buffett and Berkshire Hathaway New Stock Holdings: Value, Dividends, Growth." *247wallst.com.* 24/7 Wall St., 15 May 2013. Web. 12 Mar. 2014. http://247wallst.com/industrials/2013/05/15/warren-buffett-and-berkshire-hathaway-stock-holdings-bring-value-dividends-and-growth/

[212] "Warren Buffett Buys Plenty Of NOV In Fourth Quarter." *Warren Buffett Buys Plenty Of NOV In Fourth Quarter.* WarrenBuffett.com, 22 Feb. 2013. Web. 12 Mar. 2014. http://www.warrenbuffett.com/warren-buffett-buys-plenty-of-nov-in-fourth-quarter/

[213] Schaefer, Steve. "Goldman Sachs Reworks $5B In Warrants Held By Buffett's Berkshire." *Forbes.* Forbes Magazine, 26 Mar. 2013. Web. 12 Mar. 2014. http://www.forbes.com/sites/steveschaefer/2013/03/26/goldman-sachs-reworks-warrants-held-by-buffetts-berkshire/

[214] Kass, David. "Notes from 2013 Berkshire Hathaway Meeting." *» Notes From 2013 Berkshire Hathaway Annual Meeting.* Dr. David Kass Blog, 31 May 2013. Web. 12 Mar. 2014. http://blogs.rhsmith.umd.edu/davidkass/uncategorized/notes-from-2013-berkshire-hathaway-annual-meeting/

[215] McWhinnie, Eric. "Warren Buffett Checks in on His Coke Investment." *USA Today.* Gannett, 29 Apr. 2013. Web. 12 Mar. 2014. http://www.usatoday.com/story/money/business/2013/04/27/wall-st-cheat-sheet-warren-buffett-coca-cola-ceo/2116309/

[216] Ro, Sam. "Warren Buffett Raised His Bets On Wal-Mart And Wells Fargo." *Business Insider.* Business Insider, Inc, 15 May 2013. Web. 12 Mar. 2014. http://www.businessinsider.com/warren-buffett-berkshire-hathaway-13f-2013-5

[217] Stevenson, Heidi. "Gates, Monsanto, and Monopoly: Foundation Keeps Wealth in the Club." *Gates, Monsanto, and Monopoly: Foundation Keeps Wealth in the Club.* RSN: Reader Supported News, 26 Jan. 2011. Web. 12 Mar. 2014. http://www.gaia-health.com/articles351/000375-foundations-keep-wealth-in-the-club.shtml

[218] Logan, John. "Walmart's Poor Labor Record." *SFGate.* SF Gate, 29 Nov. 2012. Web. 13 Mar. 2014. http://www.sfgate.com/opinion/openforum/article/Walmart-s-poor-labor-record-4078901.php

[219] "Turkey: Coca-Cola and Coca-Cola Icecek Fail Critical Test over Key Supplier's Ongoing Human Rights Abuses." *IUF UITA IUL.* The International Union of Food, Agricultural, Hotel, Restaurant, Catering, Tobacco and Allied Workers' Associations, 17 July 2013. Web. 13 Mar. 2014. http://cms.iuf.org/?q=node/2607

[220] Nielsen, Robert. "Boycott Coca-Cola." *Robert Nielsen Blog*. Robert Nielsen, 10 Jan. 2013. Web. 13 Mar. 2014. http://robertnielsen21.wordpress.com/2013/01/10/boycott-coca-cola/

[221] "Wal-Mart's Offence Against Human Rights" StudyMode.com., Feb. 2013. http://www.studymode.com/essays/Wal-Mart-s-Offence-Against-Human-Rights-1465409.html

[222] "High-Impact Entrepreneurship | Endeavor Global." *High-Impact Entrepreneurship | Endeavor Global*. N.p., n.d. Web. 14 Mar. 2014. http://www.endeavor.org/

[223] Peter Ackerman." *Wikipedia*. Wikimedia Foundation, 15 Mar. 2014. Web. 18 Mar. 2014. http://en.wikipedia.org/wiki/Peter_Ackerman

[224] Yandek, Chris. "AmericansElect.org's Elliot Ackerman Shares His Organization's Mission With CYInterview; In Short, Break Free of the Political Duopoly and Put Power in the Hands of the People." *CYInterview RSS*. Http://www.cyinterview.com, 26 Jan. 2015. Web. 26 Jan. 2015. http://www.cyinterview.com/2011/09/americanselect-org%E2%80%99s-elliot-ackerman-shares-his-organization%E2%80%99s-mission-with-cyinterview-in-short-break-free-of-the-political-duopoly-and-put-power-in-the-hands-of-the-people/

[225] Cook, Jim. "Americans Elect COO Elliot Ackerman Fibs Twice on National Television." *Irregular Times*. Http://irregulartimes.com, 01 Dec. 2011. Web. 26 Jan. 2015. http://irregulartimes.com/2011/12/01/americans-elect-coo-elliot-ackerman-fibs-twice-on-national-television/

Chapter 16

[226] "Colbert Super PAC." *Wikipedia*. Wikimedia Foundation, 14 Mar. 2014. Web. 18 Mar. 2014. http://en.wikipedia.org/wiki/Colbert_Super_PAC

[227] "Americans for Tax Reform." *Opensecrets RSS*. Center for Responsive Politics, 30 May 2012. Web. 18 Mar. 2014. https://www.opensecrets.org/pacs/indexpend.php?cycle=2010&cmte=C90011289

[228] Aboud, Paul. "Nonprofit Profile: Americans for Tax Reform." *Center for Public Integrity*. Publicintegrity.org, 21 June 2012. Web. 26 Jan. 2015. http://www.publicintegrity.org/2012/06/21/9169/nonprofit-profile-americans-tax-reform

[229] Ratigan, Dylan. "VIDEO: Announcing United Republic & Get Money Out." *Dylan Ratigan*. N.p., n.d. Web. 09 Mar. 2014. http://www.dylanratigan.com/2011/11/15/video-announcing-united-republic-get-money-out/

Chapter 17

[230] Sheehan, Cindy. "Good Riddance Attention Whore." *Common Dreams*. CommonDreams.org, 29 May 2007. Web. 18 Mar. 2014. http://www.commondreams.org/archive/2007/05/29/1495

[231] MacArthur, John R. *You Can't Be President: The Outrageous Barriers to Democracy in America*. Brooklyn, NY: Melville House Pub., 2008. Print. p. 38.

[232] Frankel, Judy. "I Want All Three." *Judys Homegrown Blog*. Judy's Homegrown, 27 Feb. 2012. Web. 14 Mar. 2014. http://blog.judyshomegrown.com/2013/08/29/i-want-all-three/

[233] Sheehan, Cindy. " Robert Fisk: From Washington This Looks like Syria's 'Benghazi Moment'. But Not from Here." *Cindy Sheehan's Soapbox: February 2012*. Http://cindysheehanssoapbox.blogspot.com, 27 Feb. 2012. Web. 26 Jan. 2015. http://cindysheehanssoapbox.blogspot.com/2012_02_01_archive.html

[234] Knutson, Susan. "BOOK REVIEW: "Damn Interesting in Its Own Right"" *Mind, Culture, and Activity* 11.3 (2004): 241-48. *Economist.com*. John Wiley & Sons, 2004.

Web. http://www.google.com/url?sa=t&rct=j&q=&esrc=s&source=web&cd=2&ved=
0CCgQFjAB&url=http%3A%2F%2Fwww.economist.com%2Fmedia%2Fglobalexecutiv
e%2Fdamn_right_e_02.pdf&ei=jXrAU-_6HIbL8wGjmYHQDg&usg=AFQjCNEU8eX
XKNPfdIr4SoaAh81imdyj4A&sig2=tlGMk_N3as6PKdEf355H5Q&bvm=bv.70810081,
d.b2U

Chapter 18
[235] "Apple - Think Different Commercial." *YouTube*. ReclamenNL Channel, 25 Mar.
2013. Web. 18 Mar. 2014.
http://www.youtube.com/watch?v=9jZi2waofq8&list=PLtyv6mh-
Y0csX3BKmLhAC3_gkIZhugWuA&index=4
[236] "Lack of Civic Education Does Not Bode Well for Nation." *DALLAS, Oct. 3, 2013
/PRNewswire-USNewswire/*. American Board of Trial Advocates, 3 Oct. 2013. Web. 18
Mar. 2014. http://www.prnewswire.com/news-releases/lack-of-civic-education-does-not-
bode-well-for-nation-226352691.html
[237] Kuczynski-Brown, Alex. "Civics Education Testing Only Required In 9 States For
High School Graduation: CIRCLE Study." *The Huffington Post*. TheHuffingtonPost.com,
12 Oct. 2012. Web. 17 Mar. 2014. http://www.huffingtonpost.com/2012/10/12/circle-
study-finds-most-s_n_1959522.html
[238] Léon, Aline. *Hydrogen Technology: Mobile and Portable Applications ; with 50
Tables*. Berlin: Springer, 2008. 131. Print.
http://books.google.com/books?id=JuGJHXj_jcwC&pg=PA131&lpg=PA131&dq=Germ
any+hydrogen+pipeline&source=bl&ots=OHBXTuDSuv&sig=KnfLgxHWi0tB8HIvVgP
G_yfSs7s&hl=en&sa=X&ei=F5WAUeiJN4Wh2AWYkYDIBA&ved=0CE0Q6AEwAg#
v=onepage&q=Germany%20hydrogen%20pipeline&f=false
[239] "Energy and Environmental Security." *Energy and Environmental Security*. Lawrence
Livermore National Laboratory, n.d. Web. 18 Mar. 2014.
https://energy.llnl.gov/hydrogen.php

Chapter 19
[240] Baptiste, Sally. "Blog Talk Radio with Sally Baptiste." *American Statesman*.
Blogtalkradio.com/americanstatesman, 9 Feb. 2012. Web.
http://www.blogtalkradio.com/americanstatesman
[241] Naughton, Pete. "The Best Internet Radio Stations." *The Telegraph*. Telegraph Media
Group, 3 Dec. 2014. Web. 28 Jan. 2015.
http://www.telegraph.co.uk/culture/tvandradio/10409420/The-best-internet-radio-
stations.html
[242] Johnson, Edith. "Speaking out - Judy Frankel's Non-partisan Website Aims to Give
American Voters a Voice." *Easy Reader News*. Peninsula People Magazine, 30 Apr.
2012. Web. 19 Mar. 2014. http://www.easyreadernews.com/50387/judy-frankel/
[243] "Deepsea Challenge." *Deepsea Challenge*. National Geographic, 26 Mar. 2012. Web.
18 Mar. 2014. http://deepseachallenge.com/the-team/james-cameron/
[244] Curry, Neil, and Sheena McKenzie. "James Cameron: 'Deep Sea Exploration Could
Help Predict Tsunamis'" *CNN*. Cable News Network, 01 Jan. 1970. Web. 18 Mar. 2014.
http://www.cnn.com/2013/06/06/tech/james-cameron-deep-sea-exploration
[245] Keegan, Rebecca. "James Cameron's Oil-Spill Brainstorming Session: "It Was Time
to Sound the Horn"." *Vanity Fair*. Vanity Fair, 3 June 2010. Web. 18 Mar. 2014.
http://www.vanityfair.com/online/oscars/2010/06/james-camerons-oil-spill-
brainstorming-session-it-was-time-to-sound-the-horn

[246] "About PewDiePie" *YouTube*. PewDiePie, n.d. Web. 29 Jan. 2015.
https://www.youtube.com/user/PewDiePie/about
[247] "LETS START AN ADVENTURE BROS! - Shadow of the Colossus: 1st Colossus
(The Minotaur)." *YouTube*. PewDiePie, 1 Nov. 2012. Web. 29 Jan. 2015.
http://www.youtube.com/watch?v=0KS1TFg1Rx8
[248] Tech2 News Staff. "24-year Old Gamer Has More YouTube Subscribers than Justin
Bieber and Rihanna - Tech2." *Tech2*. Tech.firstpost.com, 17 Mar. 2014. Web. 29 Jan.
2015. http://tech.firstpost.com/news-analysis/gamer-felix-kjellberg-2-5-million-youtube-
subscribers-justin-bieber-rihanna-219981.html
[249] Westlund, Donna. "Felix Kjellberg A/K/A PewDiePie Makes Excellent Living
Playing Video Games." *Guardian Liberty Voice*. Http://guardianlv.com, 22 Mar. 2014.
Web. 29 Jan. 2015. http://guardianlv.com/2014/03/felix-kjellberg-aka-pewdiepie-makes-
excellent-living-playing-video-games/
[250] Farrell, Bryan. "You Only Need 10 Percent: The Science behind Tipping Points and
Their Impact on Climate Activism - Waging Nonviolence." *Waging Nonviolence You
Only Need 10 Percent The Science behind Tipping Points and Their Impact on Climate
Activism Comments*. Http://wagingnonviolence.org, 2 Jan. 2012. Web. 29 Jan. 2015.
http://wagingnonviolence.org/feature/you-only-need-10-percent-the-science-behind-
tipping-points/

Chapter 20
[251] Jochnick, Chris. "The Politics of Poverty." *The Politics of Poverty*.
Http://politicsofpoverty.oxfamamerica.org, 1 Aug. 2013. Web. 29 Jan. 2015.
http://politicsofpoverty.oxfamamerica.org/2013/08/buffett-challenges-philanthropic-
peers/
[252] Brown, Brené. "The Power of Vulnerability." *Brené Brown: The Power of
Vulnerability*. TED, June 2010. Web. 04 Feb. 2015.
http://www.ted.com/talks/brene_brown_on_vulnerability?language=en
[253] Otis, Bobbi. "Businessman Runs for President." *Gcsunade.com*. The Colonnade, 10
Nov. 2011. Web. 18 Mar. 2014. http://www.gcsunade.com/2011/11/10/businessman-
runs-for-president/
[254] "Rape & Abuse in Africa: Michaelene Risley at TEDxCMU 2011." *YouTube*. TEDx
Talks Channel, 29 Apr. 2011. Web. 18 Mar. 2014.
http://www.youtube.com/watch?v=5tW4qpMHwI4
[255] Evans, Will. "Group Promoting Third-party Candidates Faces Rebellion." *California
Watch*. Californiawatch.org, 24 May 2012. Web. 29 Jan. 2015.
http://californiawatch.org/dailyreport/group-promoting-third-party-candidates-faces-
rebellion-16307
[256] Appleman, Eric M. "Americans Elect Nomination." *2012 Third Party and
Independent Candidates, Democracy in Action*. P2012.org, 2012. Web. 29 Jan. 2015.
http://www.p2012.org/candidates/candsamelect.html
[257] Freeman, Josh. "Medicine and Social Justice." *: Medicare for All: Moran's Logic, Not
the Idea, Is Flawed*. Medical and Social Justice Blog, 9 Sept. 2009. Web. 18 Mar. 2014.
http://medicinesocialjustice.blogspot.com/2009/09/medicare-for-all-morans-logic-not-
idea.html
[258] Howell Jr., Tom. "Obamacare and Birth Control: Religious Ties Split Coverage."
Washington Times. The Washington Times, 18 Feb. 2013. Web. 18 Mar. 2014.
http://www.washingtontimes.com/news/2013/feb/18/religious-ties-split-coverage-for-
birth-control/?page=all

[259] "Wisconsin Governor Scott Walker Signs Abortion Bill Requiring Ultrasound." *Politico*. Associated Press, 5 July 2013. Web. 18 Mar. 2014. http://www.politico.com/story/2013/07/wisconsin-governor-signs-abortion-bill-requiring-ultrasound-93762.html

[260] Melich, Tanya. "The Republican War Against Women." *Kirkus Reviews*. Kirkus Reviews, 20 May 2010. Web. 19 Mar. 2014. https://www.kirkusreviews.com/book-reviews/tanya-melich/the-republican-war-against-women/

[261] Claus, Santa. "Santa Claus | Facebook." *Santa Claus | Facebook*. Facebook Profile, n.d. Web. 19 Mar. 2014. https://www.facebook.com/santaclaus1

[262] Claus, Santa. "Santa Claus | Facebook." *Santa Claus | Facebook*. The Santa Claus Page, n.d. Web. Jan 30. 2015. https://www.facebook.com/TheSantaClaus

[263] "Debate 3 RFID Chip." *YouTube*. Writein Dependent, 9 Apr. 2012. Web. 04 Feb. 2015. https://www.youtube.com/watch?v=gAeIUU756_4

Chapter 23
[264] "Billboard Power 100: John Frankenheimer." *Billboard*. Billboard Website, 26 Jan. 2012. Web. 19 Mar. 2014. http://www.billboard.com/biz/articles/news/1099243/billboard-power-100-john-frankenheimer

[265] Frankel, Judy. "The Easiest Way to Fix Our Government!" *YouTube*. Writein Dependent Channel, 14 July 2012. Web. 19 Mar. 2014. http://www.youtube.com/watch?v=-48pqH77AR0

Chapter 24
[266] Stephan, Maria J., and Erica Chenoweth. "Why Civil Resistance Works: The Strategic Logic of Nonviolent Conflict." *International Security* 33.1 (2008): 7-44. Print.

[267] "Vlad, 99% Spring Presenter." Telephone interview. 8 Aug. 2013.

[268] Young, Charles M. "Yes, the 99% Spring Is a Fraud." *» CounterPunch: Tells the Facts, Names the Names*. Counterpunch.org, 15 Apr. 2012. Web. 29 Jan. 2015. http://www.counterpunch.org/2012/04/13/yes-the-99-spring-is-a-fraud/

Chapter 25
[269] Barnes, Robert. "'Hillary: The Movie' to Get Supreme Court Screening." *Washington Post*. The Washington Post, 15 Mar. 2009. Web. 29 Jan. 2015. http://www.washingtonpost.com/wp-dyn/content/article/2009/03/14/AR2009031401603.html

[270] "Who-We-Are." *Who-We-Are*. Citizensunited.org/who-we-are, 2014. Web. 29 Jan. 2015. http://www.citizensunited.org/who-we-are.aspx

[271] The Bureau of National Affairs. "Bloomberg Law - Document - Citizens United v. Fed. Election Comm'n, 558 U.S. 310, 130 S. Ct. 876, 175 L. Ed. 2d 753, 187 LRRM 2961 (2010), Court Opinion." *Bloomberg Law - Document - Citizens United v. Fed. Election Comm'n, 558 U.S. 310, 130 S. Ct. 876, 175 L. Ed. 2d 753, 187 LRRM 2961 (2010), Court Opinion*. Http://www2.bloomberglaw.com, n.d. Web. 29 Jan. 2015. http://www2.bloomberglaw.com/public/desktop/document/Citizens_United_v_Federal_Election_Commission_130_S_Ct_876_175_L_

[272] ManfromMiddletown. "This Is How Citizens United Dies." *This Is How Citizens United Dies*. Dailykos.com, 13 Feb. 2014. Web. 29 Jan. 2015. http://www.dailykos.com/story/2014/02/13/1277252/-This-is-How-Citizens-United-Dies#

[273] "PACs." *Opensecrets RSS*. Opensecrets.org, n.d. Web. 29 Jan. 2015.
https://www.opensecrets.org/pacs/foreign.php
[274] "2012 Election Will Be Costliest Yet, With Outside Spending a Wild Card."
Opensecrets. OpenSecrets.org, 01 Aug. 2012. Web. 29 Jan. 2015.
http://www.opensecrets.org/news/2012/08/2012-election-will-be-costliest-yet/
[275] Bentley, Nick. "What Is Citizens United? | An Introduction." *Reclaim Democracy*.
Reclaimdemocracy.org, 17 Dec. 2012. Web. 29 Jan. 2015.
http://reclaimdemocracy.org/who-are-citizens-united/
[276] Liu, L. Larry. "Citizens United v. FEC and Corporations in America: A History of
Political Economy." *Citizens United v. FEC and Corporations in America: A History of
Political Economy*. Academia.edu, 4 May 2013. Web. 29 Jan. 2015.
http://www.academia.edu/3562736/Citizens_United_v._FEC_and_Corporations_in_Ame
rica_A_History_of_Political_Economy
[277] Trott, Bill, and Peter Cooney. "Koch Brothers Political Network Planning $889
Million of Spending in 2016." *Reuters*. Thomson Reuters, 26 Jan. 2015. Web. 04 Feb.
2015. http://www.reuters.com/article/2015/01/26/us-usa-politics-kochs-
idUSKBN0KZ2JQ20150126
[278] "The Money Behind the Elections." *Opensecrets RSS*. OpenSecrets.org, n.d. Web. 28
Jan. 2015. https://www.opensecrets.org/bigpicture/
[279] "Represent.Us: A Movement for the People." *YouTube*. Represent.us, 14 Feb. 2014.
Web. 29 Jan. 2015. https://www.youtube.com/watch?v=BlbV8BO06-0

Chapter 26
[280] Qvortrup, Matt. "The 'Neverendum'? A History of Referendums and Independence."
The 'Neverendum'? A History of Referendums and Independence. Psa.ac.uk, n.d. Web. 29
Jan. 2015. http://www.psa.ac.uk/political-
insight/%E2%80%98neverendum%E2%80%99-history-referendums-and-independence
[281] "Peoples Congress With John Mulkins." *BlogTalkRadio RSS Main*.
hosts.blogtalkradio.com, 15 June 2012. Web. 29 Jan. 2015.
http://hosts.blogtalkradio.com/sfpiradio/2012/06/15/peoples-congress-with-john-mulkins
[282] Pietrowski, Alex. "Iceland's Hörður Torfason – How to Beat the Banksters." *Waking
Times*. Waking Times, 11 Dec. 2012. Web. 21 Mar. 2014.
http://www.wakingtimes.com/2012/12/11/icelands-hordur-torfason-how-to-beat-the-
banksters/
[283] "2009 Icelandic Financial Crisis Protests." *Wikipedia*. Wikimedia Foundation, 18 Mar.
2014. Web. 21 Mar. 2014.
http://en.wikipedia.org/wiki/2009_Icelandic_financial_crisis_protests
[284] "Iceland's Pots and Pans Revolution." *YouTube*. Marie-Danielle Smith, 14 Dec. 2012.
Web. 09 Mar. 2015. https://www.youtube.com/watch?v=g8EC6yb4zVk
[285] "Heart Link Women's Network for Women Entrepreneurs." *Women's Network,
Women Networking Entrepreneurs, Professional Networking*. Heart Link Website, n.d.
Web. 21 Mar. 2014. http://www.theheartlinknetwork.com/
[286] "Commercial and Web Video Production - Klein Creative Media."
Kleincreativemedia.com. N.p., n.d. Web. 09 Mar. 2015.
http://www.kleincreativemedia.com/

Chapter 27
[287] McLuhan, Marshall, and Barrington Nevitt. *Take Today; the Executive as Dropout*.
New York: Harcourt Brace Jovanovich, 1972. 92. Print.

[288] Hickey, Roger. "Economist Jeffrey Sachs Says NO to the TPP and the TAFTA Trade Treaties." *Campaign For America's Future*. Ourfuture.org, 15 Sept. 2014. Web. 08 Feb. 2015. http://ourfuture.org/20140915/economist-jeffrey-sachs-says-no-to-the-tpp-and-the-ttip-trade-treaties

[289] "Public Citizen, Inc. and Public Citizen Foundation." *Public Citizen Home Page*. Public Citizen Website, n.d. Web. 21 Mar. 2014. http://www.citizen.org/Page.aspx?pid=183

[290] Wolverton II, Joe. "SOPA: Dead in Congress, Alive in Trans-Pacific Partnership." *SOPA: Dead in Congress, Alive in Trans-Pacific Partnership*. Thenewamerican.com, 17 Mar. 2014. Web. 29 Jan. 2015. http://www.thenewamerican.com/economy/item/17861-sopa-dead-in-congress-alive-in-trans-pacific-partnership

[291] "'A Corporate Trojan Horse': Obama Pushes Secretive TPP Trade Pact, Would Rewrite Swath of U.S. Laws." *YouTube*. Democracynow, 4 Oct. 2013. Web. 29 Jan. 2015. https://www.youtube.com/watch?v=CS-x5SlcPPM

[292] "How the Trans Pacific Partnership Would Impact Corporate Power." *Expose the TPP*. Exposethetpp.org, n.d. Web. http://www.exposethetpp.org/TPPImpacts_CorpPowerAttacks.html

[293] Common Dreams Staff. "Corporation Uses NAFTA to Sue Canada for $250 Million Over Fracking Ban." *Common Dreams*. Commondreams.org, 27 Nov. 2012. Web. 29 Jan. 2015. http://www.commondreams.org/headline/2012/11/27-8

[294] Archibold, Randal C. "First a Gold Rush, Then the Lawyers." *The New York Times*. The New York Times, 25 June 2011. Web. 29 Jan. 2015. http://www.nytimes.com/2011/06/26/world/americas/26mine.html?pagewanted=all&_r=0

[295] Swenson, Michele. "TPP: Prescription for Galloping Corporatism." *The Huffington Post*. TheHuffingtonPost.com, 28 June 2013. Web. 29 Jan. 2015. http://www.huffingtonpost.com/michele-swenson/trans-pacific-partnership-corporatism_b_3819197.html

[296] "Wyden Statement Introduction of Congressional Oversight Over Trade Negotiations Act." *Scribd*. Senator Ron Wyden, 23 May 2012. Web. 22 Mar. 2014. http://www.scribd.com/doc/94584236/Wyden-Statement-Introduction-of-Congressional-Oversight-Over-Trade-Negotiations-Act

[297] Fang, Lee. "Obama Admin's TPP Trade Officials Received Hefty Bonuses From Big Banks." *Republic Report Obama Admins TPP Trade Officials Received Hefty Bonuses From Big Banks*. Republicreport.org, 17 Feb. 2014. Web. 29 Jan. 2015. http://www.republicreport.org/2014/big-banks-tpp/

[298] Citizens Trade Campaign. "Next on Wall Street's Policy Agenda: The Trans Pacific Partnership." *The Trans-Pacific Partnership (TPP)* (n.d.): n. pag. *Citizenstrade.org*. Law.washington.edu. Web. http://www.google.com/url?sa=t&rct=j&q=&esrc=s&source=web&cd=2&ved=0CCYQFjAB&url=http%3A%2F%2Fwww.law.washington.edu%2FAsianLaw%2FHumanTrafficking%2FTransPacificFactsheet.pdf&ei=8DlkVJu8CpfUoATcyoLYDg&usg=AFQjCNFlkr-HlYJiu5qgdrug9noA442QUw&sig2=yb_UfA6S48brBfb59IAu9A&bvm=bv.79400599,d.cGU

[299] Ellis, Curtis. "Will Obama Trade American Jobs for His War on Syria?" *The Huffington Post*. TheHuffingtonPost.com, 09 Sept. 2013. Web. 21 Mar. 2014. http://www.huffingtonpost.com/curtis-ellis/will-obama-trade-american_b_3881366.html

[300] Palmer, Doug. "President Obama Speaks Out on Trade Promotion Authority." *Politico*. Politico Website, 19 Sept. 2013. Web. 21 Mar. 2014. http://www.politico.com/story/2013/09/obama-trade-promotion-authority-97073.html

[301] Depillis, Lydia. "How Congress Might Have Already Tied Obama's Hands In Trade Negotiations." *Wonk Blog*. The Washington Post, 17 July 2013. Web. 21 Mar. 2014.

http://www.washingtonpost.com/blogs/wonkblog/wp/2013/07/17/how-congress-might-have-already-tied-obamas-hands-in-trade-negotiations/

[302] Klein, Aaron. "Obama Secretly Signing Away U.S. Sovereignty." *WND Politics.* WorldNetDaily Website, 15 Oct. 2013. Web. 21 Mar. 2014. http://www.wnd.com/2013/10/obama-secretly-signing-away-u-s-sovereignty/

[303] "Obama Pledges Completion of Trans-Pacific Trade Deal." *VOA.* Voices of America Website, 5 Sept. 2013. Web. 21 Mar. 2014. http://www.voanews.com/content/obama-pledges-completion-of-transpacific-trade-deal/1743801.html

[304] "Trans-Pacific Partnership (TPP): Job Loss, Lower Wages and Higher Drug Prices." *Trans-Pacific Partnership.* Public Citizen Website, n.d. Web. 21 Mar. 2014. http://www.citizen.org/TPP

[305] U.S. Department of Agriculture. "Members Named to Seven Agricultural Trade Advisory Committees Additional Applicants Sought | USDA Newsroom." *Members Named to Seven Agricultural Trade Advisory Committees Additional Applicants Sought.* U.S.D.A, 8 Sept. 2011. Web. 26 Mar. 2014. http://www.usda.gov/wps/portal/usda/usdamediafb?contentid=2011/09/0394.xml&printable=true&contentidonly=true

[306] Rogers, David. "Big Agriculture Flexes Its Muscle." *Politico.* Politico Website, 25 Mar. 2013. Web. 26 Mar. 2014. http://www.politico.com/story/2013/03/big-agriculture-tom-vilsack-monsanto-89268_Page2.html

[307] Palmberg, Elizabeth. "The Insider List." *Sojourners.* God's Politics: A Blog by Jim Wallis and Friends, 29 June 2012. Web. 26 Mar. 2014. http://www.flushthetpp.org/tpp-corporate-insiders/

[308] "Tools for Organizing Creative Actions 4." *Flush the TPP.* FlushtheTPP.org, n.d. Web. 08 Feb. 2015. http://www.flushthetpp.org/tools/

[309] "Members Named to Seven Agricultural Trade Advisory Committees Additional Applicants Sought | USDA Newsroom." *USDA Newsroom.* USDA.gov, 8 Sept. 2011. Web. 08 Feb. 2015. http://www.usda.gov/wps/portal/usda/usdamediafb?contentid=2011/09/0394.xml&printable=true&contentidonly=true

[310] Devaney, Jacob. "Here's Why Neil Young Is Right to Boycott Starbucks." *The Huffington Post.* TheHuffingtonPost.com, 17 Nov. 2014. Web. 08 Feb. 2015. http://www.huffingtonpost.com/jacob-devaney/heres-why-neil-young-is-r_b_6169102.html

[311] "An Open Door for GMOs? – Take Action on the EU-US Free Trade Agreement." *Corporate Europe Observatory.* Corporate Europe Observatory Website, 22 May 2013. Web. 26 Mar. 2014. http://corporateeurope.org/trade/2013/05/open-door-gmos-take-action-eu-us-free-trade-agreement

[312] Fang, Lee. "Media Companies Lobby for Trans-Pacific Partnership." *Republic Report Media Companies Lobby for TransPacific Partnership Comments.* Republicreport.org, 19 Feb. 2014. Web. 29 Jan. 2015. http://www.republicreport.org/2014/tpp-media-companies/

Chapter 28

[313] McArdle, Megan. "Why I Think the GOP Will Have Control in 2017." *Megan McArdle Blog.* Meganmcardle.com, 12 July 2013. Web. 29 Jan. 2015. http://meganmcardle.com/2013/07/12/why-i-think-the-gop-will-have-control-in-2017/

[314] Saez, Emmanuel. Striking It Richer: The Evolution of Top Incomes in the United States, updated with 2012 preliminary estimates, September 3, 2013. elsa.berkeley.edu/~saez/saez-UStopincomes-2012.pdf

[315] "Sly's Office." *93.7 FM*. Sly Website, n.d. Web. http://www.slysoffice.com/

Chapter 29
[316] Gannett Washington Bureau. "Why Is the Economy a Significant Issue in This Election?" *USATODAY.COM*. USA Today Website, n.d. Web. 27 Mar. 2014. http://usatoday30.usatoday.com/news/politics/issues/economy
[317] CBS News Poll. "Problems and Priorities." *PollingReport.com*. Polling Report Website, 23 Mar. 2014. Web. 27 Mar. 2014. http://www.pollingreport.com/prioriti.htm
[318] "Fix Congress: Get Money out of Politics - Original Version." *YouTube*. Writein Dependent Channel, 11 Sept. 2012. Web. 28 Mar. 2014. http://www.youtube.com/watch?v=PmlN6eYhJ4k&feature=plcp

Chapter 30
[319] Stableford, Dylan. "Voter Turnout for 2014 Midterms Worst in 72 Years." *Yahoo! News*. Yahoo!, 12 Nov. 2014. Web. 26 Jan. 2015. http://news.yahoo.com/voter-turnout-2014-midterms-worst-in-72-years-143406756.html
[320] Cooper, Michael. "After Ruling, States Rush to Enact Voting Laws." *The New York Times*. The New York Times, 05 July 2013. Web. 04 May 2015. http://www.nytimes.com/2013/07/06/us/politics/after-Supreme-Court-ruling-states-rush-to-enact-voting-laws.html?pagewanted=all
[321] Bingham, Amy. "Voter Fraud: Non-Existent Problem or Election-Threatening Epidemic?" *ABC News*. ABC News Network, 12 Sept. 2012. Web. 29 Jan. 2015. http://abcnews.go.com/Politics/OTUS/voter-fraud-real-rare/story?id=17213376
[322] National Conference of State Legislatures. "Online Voter Registration." *Online Voter Registration*. Ncsl.org10, 10 Dec. 2014. Web. 29 Jan. 2015. http://www.ncsl.org/research/elections-and-campaigns/electronic-or-online-voter-registration.aspx
[323] Fuller, Jaime. "How Has Voting Changed since Shelby County v. Holder?" *Washington Post*. The Washington Post, 7 July 2014. Web. 28 Jan. 2015. http://www.washingtonpost.com/blogs/the-fix/wp/2014/07/07/how-has-voting-changed-since-shelby-county-v-holder/
[324] "The Truth About Voter Fraud." *The Journal of World Investment & Trade* 12.2 (2011): 197-223. *The Brennan Center for Justice*. Brennancenter.org, Sept. 2006. Web. www.brennancenter.org/page/-/d/download_file_38347.pdf
[325] Mikulich, Alex. "Loyola University New Orleans." *The Real Fraud in "Voter Fraud"* Loyola University, Aug. 2012. Web. 29 Jan. 2015. http://www.loyno.edu/jsri/real-fraud-%E2%80%9Cvoter-fraud%E2%80%9D
[326] Lipton, Eric, and Ian Urbina. "In 5-Year Effort, Scant Evidence of Voter Fraud." *The New York Times*. The New York Times, 11 Apr. 2007. Web. 29 Jan. 2015. http://www.nytimes.com/2007/04/12/washington/12fraud.html?pagewanted=all&_r=0
[327] Carney, Eliza Newlin. "The Risk of Voter Suppression." *Www.nationaljournal.com*. Nationaljournal.com, n.d. Web. 29 Jan. 2015. http://www.nationaljournal.com/columns/rules-of-the-game/the-risk-of-voter-suppression-20101018
[328] "Chicken Little in the Voting Booth: The Non-Existent Problem of Non-Citizen "Voter Fraud"" *Chicken Little in the Voting Booth: The Non-Existent Problem of Non-Citizen "Voter Fraud"* Immigrationpolicy.org, 13 July 2012. Web. 30 Jan. 2015. http://www.immigrationpolicy.org/just-facts/chicken-little-voting-booth-non-existent-problem-non-citizen-%E2%80%9Cvoter-fraud%E2%80%9D

[329] Beadle, Amanda Peterson. "Non-Citizen Voter Fraud Is Not Swaying Elections." *Immigration Impact*. Immigrationimpact.com, 27 Oct. 2014. Web. 30 Jan. 2015. http://immigrationimpact.com/2014/10/27/non-citizen-voter-fraud-swaying-elections/

[330] Kahn, Natasha, and Corbin Carson. "New Database of U.S. Voter Fraud Finds No Evidence That Photo ID Laws Are Needed." *NBC News*. Investigations.nbcnews.com, 11 Aug. 2012. Web. 28 Jan. 2015. http://investigations.nbcnews.com/_news/2012/08/11/13236464-new-database-of-us-voter-fraud-finds-no-evidence-that-photo-id-laws-are-needed

[331] Gandy, Imani. "Well Actually, It's Pretty Hard for Some People to Get a Photo ID So They Can Vote #ABLC." *RH Reality Check*. Rhrealitycheck.org, 16 Oct. 2014. Web. 30 Jan. 2015. http://rhrealitycheck.org/ablc/2014/10/16/well-actually-pretty-hard-people-get-photo-id-just-vote/

[332] Gaskins, Keesha, and Sundeep Iyer. "The Challenge of Obtaining Voter Identification | Brennan Center for Justice." *The Challenge of Obtaining Voter Identification*. Brennancenter.org, 18 July 2012. Web. 30 Jan. 2015. http://www.brennancenter.org/publication/challenge-obtaining-voter-identification

[333] Riestenberg, Jay, and Allegra Chapman. "President Obama's Comments on Voter ID Don't Line Up With The Facts." *Common Cause*. Commoncause.org, 22 Oct. 2014. Web. 30 Jan. 2015. http://www.commoncause.org/democracy-wire/president-obama-voter-id.html

[334] Weiser, Wendy R. "How Much of a Difference Did New Voting Restrictions Make in Yesterday's Close Races? | Brennan Center for Justice." *How Much of a Difference Did New Voting Restrictions Make in Yesterday's Close Races?* Brennancenter.org/blog, 5 Nov. 2014. Web. 30 Jan. 2015. http://www.brennancenter.org/blog/how-much-difference-did-new-voting-restrictions-make-yesterdays-close-races

[335] Baxley, Perry, and T. Williams. "Senate Bill 1355." *The Florida Senate*. Flsenate.gov, 19 May 2011. Web. http://www.flsenate.gov/session/Bill/2011/1355

[336] Weiser, Wendy R., and Lawrence Norden. *Voting Law Changes in 2012*. Rep. New York: Brennan Center for Justice, 2011. Print. www.brennancenter.org/sites/default/files/legacy/Democracy/VRE/Brennan_Voting_Law_V10.pdf#page=28

[337] "Third Party Voter Registration Organization Registration Agent's Sworn Statement." *Section 97.0575, Florida Statutes* (2011): n. pag. *Rule 1SER11-02, F.A.C.* Election.dos.state.fl.us, June 2011. Web. election.dos.state.fl.us/rules/emergency-rules/pdf/dsde120_06-11.pdf

[338] "The New Face of Jim Crow: Voter Suppression in America." *People for the American Way*. Pfaw.org, n.d. Web. 30 Jan. 2015. http://www.pfaw.org/media-center/publications/new-face-jim-crow-voter-suppression-america

[339] Wells, Jr., Michael. "Minority Voter Suppression In North Carolina Witnessed Firsthand." *PoliticusUSA*. Politicususa.com, 1 Nov. 2014. Web. 30 Jan. 2015. http://www.politicususa.com/2014/11/01/minority-voter-suppression-north-carolina-witnessed-firsthand.html

[340] Lee, Trymaine. "Democrat Kay Hagan Loses Her Seat to GOP Challenger Thom Tillis." *Msnbc.com*. NBC News Digital, 05 Nov. 2014. Web. 30 Jan. 2015. http://www.msnbc.com/msnbc/north-carolina-results-kay-hagan-loses-thom-tillis

[341] "If We Ever Needed to Vote! | Rev. Dr. William J. Barber." *YouTube*. NC Forward Together Moral Movement Channel, 15 Oct. 2012. Web. 30 Jan. 2015. https://www.youtube.com/watch?v=2FG98NusLEA#t=42

[342] Ose, Erik. "GOP Voter Intimidation Efforts Are in Full Swing." *The Huffington Post*. TheHuffingtonPost.com, 4 Nov. 2014. Web. 30 Jan. 2015. http://www.huffingtonpost.com/erik-ose/gop-voter-intimidation-ef_b_6087280.html

[343] Jones, Sarah. "Mitch McConnell May Have Committed Two Felonies With Illegal Voter Intimidation Tactics." *PoliticusUSA*. Politicususa.com, 1 Nov. 2014. Web. 30 Jan. 2015. http://www.politicususa.com/2014/11/01/felonies-mitch-mcconnell-republican-lawmaker-lawbreaker.html

[344] Elbow, Steven. "'Wisconsin Poll Watcher Militia' Plans to Confront Scott Walker Recall Petition Signers at Polls : Ct." *Madison.com*. The Capital Times, 20 Sept. 2014. Web. 30 Jan. 2015. http://host.madison.com/news/local/writers/steven_elbow/wisconsin-poll-watcher-militia-plans-to-confront-scott-walker-recall/article_062df082-5fea-5363-b498-c0c51aa5fa30.html

[345] "Watching the "Wisconsin Poll Watcher Militia"" *Facebook*. N.p., n.d. Web. 30 Jan. 2015. https://www.facebook.com/pages/Watching-the-Wisconsin-Poll-Watcher-Militia/353533321481630

[346] Turque, Bill. "Angst in Ohio about Bain, Romney Donors Links to Voting Machine Company." *Washington Post*. The Washington Post, 23 Oct. 2012. Web. 30 Jan. 2015. http://www.washingtonpost.com/blogs/post-politics/wp/2012/10/23/angst-about-counting-the-votes-in-ohio/

[347] Tobin, Maryann. "Romney Family Buys Voting Machines through Bain Capital Investment." *Romney Family Buys Voting Machines through Bain Capital Investment*. Allvoices.com, 19 Oct. 2012. Web. 30 Jan. 2015. http://www.allvoices.com/contributed-news/13221476-romney-family-buys-voting-machines-through-bain-capital-investment

[348] Levine, Art. "Ohio, Facing Vote-Rigging Lawsuit, Adds Voter-Purging Software: Are Dems, Liberals, Election Officials Ready to Safeguard Votes?" *The Huffington Post*. TheHuffingtonPost.com, 11 Nov. 2012. Web. 30 Jan. 2015. http://www.huffingtonpost.com/art-levine/mia-in-voting-machine-war_b_2054411.html

[349] Pollack, Peter. "Diebold Voting Machines Hacked in Florida." *Ars Technica*. Arstechnica.com, 22 Dec. 2005. Web. 30 Jan. 2015. http://arstechnica.com/uncategorized/2005/12/5821-2/

[350] Collier, Victoria. "How to Rig an Election." *Harpers Magazine*. Harpers.org, Nov. 2012. Web. 30 Jan. 2015. http://harpers.org/archive/2012/11/how-to-rig-an-election/

[351] "Hacking Democracy." *YouTube*. Cinedigm, 3 June 2011. Web. 30 Jan. 2015. http://www.youtube.com/watch?v=vx1vxPFXIiw

[352] Klimas, Liz. "More Electronic Voting Machines Changing Romney Votes to Obama: We Looked Into It and Here's What a Vendor Told Us." *The Blaze*. Theblaze.com, 31 Oct. 2012. Web. 30 Jan. 2015. http://www.theblaze.com/stories/2012/10/31/more-electronic-voting-machines-changing-romney-votes-to-obama-we-looked-into-it-and-heres-what-a-vendor-told-us/

[353] Carrasco, Ed. "Election Day Rigging? Voting Machine Changes Obama Votes to Romney [VIDEO]." *NMR*. Newmediarockstars.com, 6 Nov. 2012. Web. http://newmediarockstars.com/2012/11/election-day-rigging-voting-machine-changes-obama-votes-to-romney-video/

[354] "Rigged USA Elections Exposed." *YouTube*. Truthstream, 2 Mar. 2006. Web. 30 Jan. 2015. http://www.youtube.com/watch?v=JEzY2tnwExs

[355] "Center for Information Technology Policy » Voting Videos." *Center for Information Technology Policy » Voting Videos*. Princeton University, n.d. Web. 30 Jan. 2015. http://citpsite.s3-website-us-east-1.amazonaws.com/oldsite-htdocs/voting/videos.html

[356] Feldman, Halderman, Felten; Security Analysis of the Diebold AccuVote-TS Voting Machine, Princeton University, September 13, 2006.

[357] MacArthur, John R. "Problem #2/Parties You're Not Invited To." *You Can't Be President: The Outrageous Barriers to Democracy in America*. Brooklyn, NY: Melville House Pub., 2008. 44. Print.

[358] "Voting by Mail." *The New York Times*. The New York Times, 05 Oct. 2012. Web. 30 Jan. 2015. http://www.nytimes.com/interactive/2012/10/07/us/voting-by-mail.html?_r=0

[359] Schmidt, Katie. "Washington to Shift to All Vote-by-mail Elections - Political Buzz." *Tacoma News Tribune*. Blog.thenewstribune.com, 5 Apr. 2011. Web. 30 Jan. 2015. http://blog.thenewstribune.com/politics/2011/04/05/washington-to-shift-to-all-vote-by-mail-elections/

[360] "Vote by Mail." *Washington Secretary of State*. Wei.sos.wa.gov, n.d. Web. 30 Jan. 2015. https://wei.sos.wa.gov/agency/osos/en/voters/Pages/vote_by_mail.aspx

[361] Marley, Patrick. "Voters Who Returned Absentee Ballots Must Send ID Copies." *Journal Sentinel*. Jsonline.com, 30 Jan. 2015. Web. 30 Jan. 2015. http://www.jsonline.com/news/statepolitics/ballot-fight-is-brewing-as-state-scrambled-on-voter-id-b99352576z1-275311521.html

[362] "Election Administration and Voting Survey." *Election Administration and Voting Survey | The U.S. Election Assistance Commission (EAC)*. Eac.gov, n.d. Web. 30 Jan. 2015. http://www.eac.gov/research/election_administration_and_voting_survey.aspx

[363] Liptak, Adam. "Error and Fraud at Issue as Absentee Voting Rises." *The New York Times*. The New York Times, 06 Oct. 2012. Web. 30 Jan. 2015. http://www.nytimes.com/2012/10/07/us/politics/as-more-vote-by-mail-faulty-ballots-could-impact-elections.html?pagewanted=all

[364] "Why Are Provisional Ballots Not Being Counted?" *Provisional Voting*. Projectvote.org, n.d. Web. 30 Jan. 2015. http://projectvote.org/provisional-voting.html

[365] Lovelace, Ryan. "Election Day Shocker: There Are Ballot Irregularities in Chicago, by Ryan Lovelace, National Review." *National Review Online*. Nationalreview.com, 4 Nov. 2014. Web. 30 Jan. 2015. http://www.nationalreview.com/corner/391916/election-day-shocker-there-are-ballot-irregularities-chicago-ryan-lovelace

[366] "Black Box Voting." *Wikipedia*. Wikimedia Foundation, 29 Apr. 2013. Web. 30 Jan. 2015. http://en.wikipedia.org/wiki/Black_box_voting

[367] "Conversation with Judy Alter." Telephone interview. 1 Aug. 2013.

[368] "The Trouble with the Electoral College." *YouTube*. CGP Grey, 7 Nov. 2011. Web. 30 Jan. 2015. https://www.youtube.com/watch?v=7wC42HgLA4k

[369] Neale, Thomas H. "Election of the President and Vice President by Congress: Contingent Election." *Election of the President and Vice President by Congress: Contingent Election*. Electoralcollegehistory.com, 16 Aug. 1999. Web. 30 Jan. 2015. http://electoralcollegehistory.com/electoral/crs-congress.asp

[370] "Election of the President and Vice President by Congress: Contingent Election, Policy Archive, January 2001." *UNZ.org*. UNZ.org, Jan. 2001. Web. 30 Jan. 2015. http://www.unz.org/Pub/PolicyArchive-2001jan-00140

[371] Neale, Thomas H. "The Electoral College: Reform Proposals in the 107th Congress." *The Electoral College: Reform Proposals in the 107th Congress* (n.d.): n. pag. Law.umaryland.edu, 7 Feb. 2003. Web. http://www.law.umaryland.edu/marshall/crs reports/crsdocuments/RL30844_02072003.pdf

[372] DelReal, Jose A. "National Roundup: Midterm Voter Turnout Lowest since World War II." *Washington Post*. The Washington Post, 10 Nov. 2014. Web. 30 Jan. 2015. http://www.washingtonpost.com/politics/national-roundup-midterm-voter-turnout-lowest-since-world-war-ii/2014/11/10/40558a7e-6917-11e4-9fb4-a622dae742a2_story.html

[373] Grey, CGP. "The Alternative Vote Explained." *YouTube*. CGP Grey, 6 Apr. 2011. Web. 30 Jan. 2015. https://www.youtube.com/watch?v=3Y3jE3B8 HsE&index=3&list=PLqs5ohhass_TF9mg-mqLie7Fqq1-FzOQc

[374] Poundstone, William. "Chapter 9/Instant Runoff." *Gaming the Vote: Why Elections Aren't Fair (and What We Can Do about It)*. New York: Hill and Wang, 2008. 171. Print.

[375] Poundstone, William. "Chapter 14/Hot or Not?" *Gaming the Vote: Why Elections Aren't Fair (and What We Can Do about It)*. New York: Hill and Wang, 2008. 234. Print.

[376] *Redrawing the Map on Redistricting 2012*. Rep. Philadelphia: Azavea, 2012. Print. https://s3.amazonaws.com/s3.azavea.com/com.redistrictingthenation/pdfs/Redistricting_ The_Nation_Addendum.pdf

[377] "Gerrymandering Analysis - Read about Our Ongoing Gerrymandering and Redistricting Research and Analysis Studies | Cicero." *Gerrymandering Analysis*. Azavea.com, n.d. Web. 30 Jan. 2015. http://www.azavea.com/products/cicero/services/political-and-elections-projects/gerrymandering-analysis/

[378] Maciag, Mike. "Which States, Districts Are Most Gerrymandered?" *Which States, Districts Are Most Gerrymandered?* Governing.com, 25 Oct. 2012. Web. 30 Jan. 2015. http://www.governing.com/blogs/by-the-numbers/most-gerrymandered-congressional-districts-states.html

[379] Ingraham, Christopher. "America's Most Gerrymandered Congressional Districts." *Washington Post*. The Washington Post, 15 May 2014. Web. 29 Jan. 2015. http://www.washingtonpost.com/blogs/wonkblog/wp/2014/05/15/americas-most-gerrymandered-congressional-districts/

[380] "RangeVoting.org - Proportional Representation." *RangeVoting.org - Proportional Representation*. Rangevoting.org, n.d. Web. 30 Jan. 2015. http://rangevoting.org/PropRep.html

[381] Stephanopoulos, Nicholas. "New Research: The Part of the Voting Rights Act the Supreme Court Left Alone Works Better Than Expected." *Slate*. Slate.com, 23 Oct. 2013. Web. 30 Jan. 2015. http://www.slate.com/articles/news_and_politics/jurisprudence/2013/10/section_2_of_the_voting_rights_act_is_more_effective_than_expected_new_research.html

[382] Ennis, John. "FREE FOR ALL! One Dude's Quest to Save Our Elections." FREE FOR ALL! Freeforall.tv, n.d. Web. 05 Apr. 2015. http://www.freeforall.tv/

Chapter 31

[383] Da Silva, Tekoa. "World Bank Whistle-blower: "Precious Metals To Serve As An Underpinning For Paper Currencies"." *Bull Market Thinking*. Http://bullmarketthinking.com, 6 May 2013. Web. 30 Jan. 2015. http://bullmarketthinking.com/world-bank-whistle-blower-precious-metals-to-serve-as-an-underpinning-for-paper-currencies/

[384] Poor, Jack. "Drum Roll: The Biggest Media Impact Maker on the 2012 Presidential Elections Was…Local Market Broadcast Television. (again!)." *PowerPoint Presentation*. TVB Local Media Marketing Solutions, 2012. Web. http://www.tvb.org/media/file/Drum-Roll-Political-2013.pdf

[385] "Deregulation." *SUNY Levin Institute*. Globalization101.org, n.d. Web. 01 Feb. 2015. http://www.globalization101.org/deregulation

[386] "FCC - Telecommunications Act of 1996." *FCC - Telecommunications Act of 1996*. FCC.gov, n.d. Web. 23 July 2014. http://transition.fcc.gov/telecom.html

[387] "The Public Interest Standard in Television Broadcasting." *Currentorg For People in Public Media*. Current.org, 18 Dec. 1998. Web. 30 Jan. 2015.
http://www.current.org/1998/12/the-public-interest-standard-in-television-broadcasting/
[388] "Red Lion v Federal Communications Commission." *Red Lion v Federal Communications Commission*. Http://law2.umkc.edu, 9 June 1969. Web. 30 Jan. 2015.
http://law2.umkc.edu/faculty/projects/ftrials/conlaw/redlion.html
[389] "Take Back the Airwaves Pt 2 (Pete and Duane's Window - Show 3)." *YouTube*. Pete and Duane's Window, 19 Jan. 2011. Web. 30 Jan. 2015.
http://www.youtube.com/watch?v=a53hL5Z1WHE&feature=youtu.be
[390] Elgin, Duane. "The Power of a ' Community Voice' Movement." *The Huffington Post*. TheHuffingtonPost.com, 18 Nov. 2011. Web. 30 Jan. 2015.
http://www.huffingtonpost.com/duane-elgin/future-occupy-movement_b_1100549.html
[391] Elgin, Duane, Ted Becker, and Richard J. Varn. "Electronic Democracy." *Spectrum: The Journal of State Government* 2nd ser. 66.Spring (1993): n. pag. Duaneelgin.com.
Web. http://www.google.com/url?sa=t&rct=j&q=&esrc
=s&source=web&cd=1&ved=0CC4QFjAA&url=http%3A%2F%2Fduaneelgin.com%2F
wp-content%2Fuploads%2F1993%2F12%2FETMs-Spectrum-
Journal.pdf&ei=W8BIUvK5Ee7q2wWr9ICwCw&usg=AFQjCNH-
rHLZD3mi3FKhlQqZK5AxBM9kJg&sig2=_Vl7SY8rXVlItdtqSbs2jw&bvm=bv.532177
64,d.b2I
[392] Froman, Michael. "U.S. Trade Rep. Talks Trans-Pacific Partnership, China Trade." *Fox Business*. Http://video.foxbusiness.com, 20 Feb. 2014. Web. 30 Jan. 2015.
http://video.foxbusiness.com/v/3231939472001/us-trade-rep-talks-trans-pacific-
partnership-china-trade/?#sp=show-clips
[393] "U.S., China Reach 'understanding' to Scrap Tariffs on Some High-tech Goods, Obama Says." *Fox News*. Foxnews.com, 11 Nov. 2014. Web.
http://www.foxnews.com/politics/2014/11/11/us-china-reach-understanding-to-scrap-
tariffs-on-high-tech-goods-obama-says/

Chapter 32
[394] Clark, Josh. "Commission on Presidential Debates - HowStuffWorks." *HowStuffWorks*. People.howstuffworks.com, 13 Oct. 2000. Web. 30 Jan. 2015.
http://people.howstuffworks.com/debate4.htm
[395] "Open Debates | What Is the CPD?" *Open Debates | What Is the CPD?* Opendebates.org, n.d. Web. 30 Jan. 2015
http://www.opendebates.org/theissue/whatisthecdp.html
[396] Tuccille, J.D. "Presidential Debates Lose Sponsors Over Exclusion of Third-Party Candidates." *Reason.com*. Reason.com, 01 Oct. 2012. Web. 30 Jan. 2015.
http://reason.com/blog/2012/10/01/presidential-debates-lose-sponsors-over
[397] "President Obama and Governor Romney, Vice President Biden and Rep. Paul Ryan Invited to CPD's Debates." *Commission on Presidential Debates*. Debates.org, 21 Sept. 2012. Web. 30 Jan. 2015.
http://www.debates.org/index.php?mact=News,cntnt01,detail,0&cntnt01articleid=42&cnt
nt01origid=27&cntnt01detailtemplate=newspage&cntnt01returnid=80
[398] Broder, John M. "Both Romney and Obama Avoid Talk of Climate Change." *The New York Times*. The New York Times, 25 Oct. 2012. Web. 30 Jan. 2015.
http://www.nytimes.com/2012/10/26/us/politics/climate-change-nearly-absent-in-the-
campaign.html?pagewanted=all&_r=0
[399] Fullwood III, Sam. "Opinion: Why Won't Either Presidential Candidate Talk About Race and Poverty?" *Www.nationaljournal.com*. Nationaljournal.com, 29 Oct. 2012. Web.

30 Jan. 2015. http://www.nationaljournal.com/thenextamerica/politics/why-won-t-either-presidential-candidate-talk-about-race-and-poverty--20121029

[400] Matthews, Dylan. "Millions of Americans Live in Extreme Poverty. Here's How They Get By." *Washington Post*. The Washington Post, 13 May 2013. Web. 30 Jan. 2015. http://www.washingtonpost.com/blogs/wonkblog/wp/2013/05/13/millions-of-americans-live-in-extreme-poverty-heres-how-they-get-by/

[401] "2012 Third Party Presidential Debate | 2012 Third Party Presidential Debate | Ora TV." *YouTube*. Ora TV, 23 Oct. 2012. Web. 30 Jan. 2015. https://www.youtube.com/watch?v=e0vE5CTTSFI

[402] "About Free and Equal Elections Foundation." *Free Equal*. Freeandequal.org, n.d. Web. 30 Jan. 2015. https://www.freeandequal.org/about/

[403] "Phone Message from Christina Tobin." Telephone interview. 27 Dec. 2014.

[404] "Interview with Christina Tobin." Telephone interview. 26 Dec. 2013.

[405] "Free & Equal's Open 2012 Presidential Debate between Gary Johnson & Jill Stein." *YouTube*. Freeandequal.org, 5 Apr. 2013. Web. 30 Jan. 2015. https://www.youtube.com/watch?v=xVfTNtoB4bY

Chapter 33

[406] "Code Pink: About." *CODEPINK*. Codepink.org, n.d. Web. 29 Jan. 2015. http://www.codepink4peace.org/article.php?list=type&type=3

[407] Black, Louis. "Keynsian Economics Made Easy - Lewis Black." *YouTube*. P Carr, 29 Nov. 2011. Web. 30 Jan. 2015. https://www.youtube.com/watch?v=YgXCw2eYUaU

[408] "Talk: Henry Kissinger." *Wikiquote*. En.wikiquote.org, 24 Aug. 2014. Web. 30 Jan. 2015. http://en.wikiquote.org/wiki/Talk:Henry_Kissinger

[409] "Organic Matter - Spring 2013." *Organic Matter - Spring 2013*. Mofga.org, 2013. Web. 30 Jan. 2015. http://www.mofga.org/Publications/MaineOrganicFarmerGardener/Spring2013/OrganicMatter/tabid/2575/Default.aspx

[410] "Monsanto Co." *MON Annual Income Statement*. Marketwatch.com, n.d. Web. 13 Feb. 2015. http://www.marketwatch.com/investing/stock/mon/financials

[411] "Contamination of Crops." *GM Education*. Gmeducation.org, n.d. Web. 30 Jan. 2015. http://www.gmeducation.org/environment/p149075-contamination%20of%20crops%20.html

[412] Duprey, Rich. "Monsanto's Next Conquest for GMO Dominance." *The Motley Fool*. Fool.com, 14 Sept. 2013. Web. 30 Jan. 2015. http://www.fool.com/investing/general/2013/09/14/why-you-should-invest-in-monsanto.aspx

[413] Dupont, Veronique. "GMO Corn, Soybeans Dominate U.S. Market." *GMO Corn, Soybeans Dominate U.S. Market*. Phys.org, 4 June 2013. Web. 30 Jan. 2015. http://phys.org/news/2013-06-gmo-corn-soybeans-dominate.html

[414] Kelly, Margie. "Top 7 Genetically Modified Crops." *The Huffington Post*. TheHuffingtonPost.com, 30 Oct. 2012. Web. 30 Jan. 2015. http://www.huffingtonpost.com/margie-kelly/genetically-modified-food_b_2039455.html

[415] "Meet Michael R. Taylor, J.D., Deputy Commissioner for Foods and Veterinary Medicine." *U.S. Food and Drug Administration*. Fda.gov, 7 July 2014. Web. 30 Jan. 2015. http://www.fda.gov/aboutfda/centersoffices/officeoffoods/ucm196721.htm

[416] Lipman, Frank. "Q and A's About The Safety Issues Regarding GMO'S Are They Safe?" *Dr Frank Lipman*. Drfranklipman.com, n.d. Web. 30 Jan. 2015. http://www.drfranklipman.com/q-and-as-about-the-safety-issues-regarding-gmos/

[417] Smith, Jeffrey M. "Doctors Warn: Avoid Genetically Modified Food." *Mercola.com*. Articles.mercola.com, 25 Mar. 2010. Web. 31 Jan. 2015. http://articles.mercola.com/sites/articles/archive/2010/03/25/doctors-warn-avoid-genetically-modified-food.aspx

[418] Bashshur, Romona. "FDA and Regulation of GMOs." *FDA and Regulation of GMOs*. Americanbar.org, Feb. 2013. Web. 31 Jan. 2015. http://www.americanbar.org/content/newsletter/publications/aba_health_esource_home/a ba_health_law_esource_1302_bashshur.html

[419] "Commonly Asked Questions about the Food Safety of GMOs." *Monsanto*. Monsanto.com, n.d. Web. 29 Jan. 2015. http://www.monsanto.com/newsviews/pages/food-safety.aspx#q7

[420] "Stop the Pipeline of New GE Seeds!" *Pesticide Action Network*. Action.panna.org, n.d. Web. 14 Mar. 2015. http://action.panna.org/p/dia/action/public/?action_KEY=11896

[421] Cox, Caroline. "Herbicide Dicamba." *Journal of Pesticide Reform*. Pesticide.org, Spring 1994. Web. http://www.pesticide.org/get-the-facts/pesticide-factsheets/factsheets/dicamba

[422] Antoniou, M., M.E.E. Mostafa. H.C. Vyvyan, HC. Jennings, C. Leifert Rubens, O. Nodari, C. Robinson, and J. Fagan. 2001. Roundup and birth defects Is the public being kept in the dark? Earth Open Source. June 2011. 52 pp. 03 May. 2015. http://www.google.com/url?sa=t&rct=j&q=&esrc=s&source=web&cd=1&ved=0CC4QFj AA&url=http%3A%2F%2Fresponsibletechnology.org%2Fdocs%2FRoundupHealth2011 .pdf&ei=Hd9FUpjrHsfp2AX5y4GwCQ&usg=AFQjCNHnK2eut-0-wgf1QhIAG0CbOrAFAg&sig2=gxr2SpmwGf-8JkSUD7dMBA&bvm=bv.53217764,d.b2I

[423] Engdahl, F. William. "Study Shows Monsanto Roundup Herbicide Link to Birth Defects." *Global Research*. Globalresearch.ca, 30 Sept. 2010. Web. 31 Jan. 2015. http://www.globalresearch.ca/study-shows-monsanto-Roundup-herbicide-link-to-birth-defects/21251

[424] Paganelli, Alejandra, Victoria Gnazzo, Helena Acosta, Silvia L. Lopez, and Andreas E. Carrasco. "Glyphosate-Based Herbicides Produce Teratogenic Effects on Vertebrates by Impairing Retinoic Acid Signaling." *Chemical Research in Toxicology*. Acs.org, 9 Aug. 2010. Web. 31 Jan. 2015. http://pubs.acs.org/doi/abs/10.1021/tx1001749

[425] Govindarajulu, Purnima P. "Literature Review of Impacts of Glyphosate Herbicide on Amphibians: What Risks Can the Silvicultural Use of This Herbicide Pose for Amphibians in B.C.?" June (2008): n. pag. Stopthespraybc.com. Web. http://www.google.com/url?sa=t&rct=j&q=&esrc=s&source=web&cd=2&ved=0CDcQFj AB&url=http%3A%2F%2Fstopthespraybc.com%2Fwp-content%2Fuploads%2F2011%2F07%2FLiterature-Review-of-Impacts-of-Glyphosate-Herbicide1.pdf&ei=nBBGUrCBLojJrQGSq4DwAQ&usg=AFQjCNHBHDQ8ATtS9p3G IXTMGCLijpwDTQ&sig2=dLeTppnhrs5NREN4CCy0bw&bvm=bv.53217764,d.aWM& cad=rja

[426] Leu, Andre. "The Myths of Safe Pesticides." *Biodynamic Agriculture Australia*. Biodynamics.net.au, 10 Jan. 2011. Web. 01 Feb. 2015. http://www.biodynamics.net.au/articles/myths_of_safe_pesticides.htm

[427] Gammon, Chrystal. "Weed-Whacking Herbicide Proves Deadly to Human Cells." *Scientific American Global RSS*. Environmental Health News, 23 June 2009. Web. 30 Jan. 2015. http://www.scientificamerican.com/article/weed-whacking-herbicide-p/

[428] Capel, Paul, and Kara Capelli. "Widely Used Herbicide Commonly Found in Rain and Streams in the Mississippi River Basin." *USGS Release:*. U.S. Geological Service, 29 Aug. 2011. Web. 01 Feb. 2015. http://www.usgs.gov/newsroom/article.asp?ID=2909

[429] "Glyphosate Found in Wastewater Discharged to Streams." *U.S. Geological Survey.* toxics.usgs.gov, 19 Dec. 2014. Web. 01 Feb. 2015. http://toxics.usgs.gov/highlights/glyphosate_wastewater.html

[430] U.S. EPA, Office Of Pesticide Programs. *USGS Usage Map for Glyphosate* (n.d.): n. pag. Epa.gov, 17 Sept. 2004. Web. http://www.google.com/url?sa=t&rct=j&q=&esrc=s&source=web&cd=7&ved=0CGMQ FjAG&url=http%3A%2F%2Fwww.epa.gov%2Fespp%2Flitstatus%2Feffects%2Fusgs-usagemap.pdf&ei=WP9FUsfIIsWyygG3pIDwDQ&usg=AFQjCNEBdssqc9BNwNcqkoO PU7ZZdAZFJg&sig2=IX-6eThVMVdGK8J24FsHEQ&bvm=bv.53217764,d.aWc

Chapter 36

[431] Guyton, Kathryn Z. et al. *Carcinogenicity of Tetrachlorvinphos, Parathion, Malathion, Diazinon, and Glyphosate.* Rep. The Lancet Oncology, 20 Mar. 2015. Web. 11 Apr. 2015. http://www.thelancet.com/journals/lanonc/article/PIIS1470-2045%2815%2970134-8/abstract

[432] World Health Organization, IARC. "IARC Monographs Volume 112: Evaluation of Five Organophosphate Insecticides and Herbicides." *IARC Monographs Volume 112: Evaluation of* (2015): n. pag. *Iarc.fr.* World Health Organization, 20 Mar. 2015. Web. 11 Apr. 2015. http://www.iarc.fr/en/media-centre/iarcnews/pdf/MonographVolume112.pdf

[433] Walton, Alice G. "WHO Says Monsanto Roundup Ingredient Is 'Probably Carcinogenic.' Are They Right?" *Forbes.* Forbes Magazine, 21 Mar. 2015. Web. 11 Apr. 2015. http://www.forbes.com/sites/alicegwalton/2015/03/21/monsanto-herbicide-dubbed-probably-carcinogenic-by-world-health-organization-are-they-right/

[434] Fine, Allison H., and Esther Dyson. "Professional Politicians Beware!" *Rebooting America: Ideas for Redesigning American Democracy for the Internet Age.* San Francisco, CA: Creative Commons, 2008. 100. Print.

[435] "The American Anti-Corruption Act." *The American AntiCorruption Act Home Comments.* Anticorruptionact.org/, n.d. Web. 31 Jan. 2015. http://anticorruptionact.org/

[436] "@DylanRatigan." Message to the author @judyshomegrown. 28 Dec. 2014. Twitter.

[437] Frankel, Judy. "Call Your Candidate: Get Money out of Politics Today!" *YouTube.* Writein Dependent, 26 Sept. 2012. Web. 01 Feb. 2015. http://www.youtube.com/watch?v=_bRsXWsmRpE

[438] "Americans for Tax Reform." *Wikipedia.* Wikimedia Foundation, 21 Jan. 2015. Web. 01 Feb. 2015. http://en.wikipedia.org/wiki/Americans_for_Tax_Reform

Chapter 37

[439] Whyte, David. "Everything Is Waiting for You." *Everything Is Waiting for You: Poems.* Langley, WA: Many Rivers, 2003. 6. Print.

[440] Miles, Kathleen. "Move To Amend LA: City Council To Vote On Amending U.S. Constitution To Say Corporations Are Not People (VIDEO)." *The Huffington Post.* TheHuffingtonPost.com, 5 Dec. 2011. Web. 01 Feb. 2015. http://www.huffingtonpost.com/2011/12/05/move-to-amend-la_n_1129725.html

[441] "Move to Amend." *Frequently Asked Questions.* Movetoamend.org, n.d. Web. 01 Feb. 2015. https://movetoamend.org/frequently-asked-questions#5

[442] "The Problem With Money in Politics - Lawrence Lessig, Harvard Law." *YouTube.* The Young Turks, 23 Nov. 2012. Web. 01 Feb. 2015. http://www.youtube.com/watch?v=3xzVBe3hmOk&list=PLvGgnmsqvzeyE3AIh74_7Xg Zd6VTuPC_c

[443] "Center for Food Safety | Issues | GE Food Labeling | About GE Labeling." *Center for Food Safety*. Center for Food Safety Website, n.d. Web. 26 Mar. 2014.
http://www.centerforfoodsafety.org/issues/976/ge-food-labeling/about-ge-labeling#
[444] Langer, Gary. "Poll: Skepticism of Genetically Modified Foods." *ABC News*. ABC News Network, 19 June 2014. Web. 24 Mar. 2014.
http://abcnews.go.com/Technology/story?id=97567&page=1
[445] Kopicki, Allison. "Strong Support for Labeling Modified Foods." *The New York Times*. The New York Times, 27 July 2013. Web. 26 Mar. 2014.
http://www.nytimes.com/2013/07/28/science/strong-support-for-labeling-modified-foods.html?smid=tw-share&_r=4&
[446] "One Mom's Story |." *Just Label It*. Just Label It Website, n.d. Web. 26 Mar. 2014.
http://justlabelit.org/right-to-know/why-labels-matter-to-moms/
[447] Simon, Michele. "Lies, Dirty Tricks and $45 Million Kill GMO Labeling in California." *The Huffington Post*. TheHuffingtonPost.com, 08 Nov. 2012. Web. 27 Mar. 2014. http://www.huffingtonpost.com/michele-simon/prop-37-defeated_b_2087782.html
[448] "AB 583, California Clean Money and Fair Elections Act: California Clean Money Campaign." *California Clean Money Campaign*. Caclean.org, n.d. Web. 01 Feb. 2015. http://www.caclean.org/progress/ab583.php
[449] "A Brief History of Fair Elections Victories." *Public Campaign*. Publicampaign.org, n.d. Web. 01 Feb. 2015. http://www.publicampaign.org/briefhistory
[450] "The Young Turks." *YouTube*. The Young Turks: About, 7 Feb. 2015. Web. 07 Feb. 2015. https://www.youtube.com/user/TheYoungTurks/about
[451] "Cenk's Speech - Money Out of Politics (Money Out Voters In Conference)." *YouTube*. The Young Turks, 23 Nov. 2012. Web. 01 Feb. 2015.
https://www.youtube.com/watch?v=OsTm8qaaGDI
[452] "Vermont Becomes The First State To Pass Wolf PAC Resolution." *YouTube*. The Young Turks, 2 May 2014. Web. 01 Feb. 2015.
https://www.youtube.com/watch?v=CiiOUp-V6-4
[453] "These Americans Are Getting Money Out Of Politics & It's Time For You To Join." *YouTube*. The Young Turks, 12 June 2012. Web. 01 Feb. 2015.
https://www.youtube.com/watch?v=L5WlfvjRFio
[454] "Illinois Passes Historic Measure To Fight Money In Politics." *YouTube*. The Young Turks, 4 Dec. 2014. Web. 01 Feb. 2015.
https://www.youtube.com/watch?v=qGh6qE4UZfQ
[455] "They Marched 500 Miles To Save Democracy, Now It's Your Turn." *YouTube*. The Young Turks, 20 June 2014. Web. 01 Feb. 2015.
https://www.youtube.com/watch?v=1MrJWz4aG7Q
[456] Egelko, Bob. "California Seeks Constitutional Convention over Citizens United." *SFGate*. Sfgate.com, 26 June 2014. Web. 01 Feb. 2015.
http://www.sfgate.com/politics/article/California-seeks-constitutional-convention-over-5579322.php
[457] Gatto, Mike. "California AJR1 | 2013-2014 | Regular Session." *LegiScan*. Legiscan.com, 27 June 2014. Web. 01 Feb. 2015. http://legiscan.com/CA/bill/AJR1/2013
[458] "Illinois Passes Historic Measure To Fight Money In Politics." *YouTube*. The Young Turks, 4 Dec. 2014. Web. 01 Feb. 2015.
https://www.youtube.com/watch?v=qGh6qE4UZfQ#t=849
[459] "Wolf PAC Resolution Passes New Jersey Senate." *YouTube*. The Young Turks, 24 Dec. 2014. Web. 01 Feb. 2015. https://www.youtube.com/watch?v=Uvx4UcBz73c

Chapter 38

[460] "Exploring an Article V Convention for Proposing Amendments." *YouTube.* IIonKBDI, 27 Mar. 2014. Web. 01 Feb. 2015. https://www.youtube.com/watch?v=1Y7llGNd8bc

[461] Long, David. "Amending the Constitution by State-led Convention." *Indiana's Model Legislation* (n.d.): n. pag. *Presented by Indiana Senate President Pro Tempore David LongU.S. Constitution, Article V:.* Ncsl.org/. Web. http://www.ncsl.org/documents/summit/summit2013/online-resources/SenLongArticleV.pdf

[462] Rothberg, Daniel. "Retired Justice John Paul Stevens Tells Congress 'money Is Not Speech'" *Los Angeles Times.* Latimes.com, 30 Apr. 2013. Web. 01 Feb. 2015. http://www.latimes.com/nation/politics/politicsnow/la-pn-supreme-court-stevens-congress-money-speech-20140430,0,4630203.story#axzz30b6bwhwS

[463] Greenley, Larry. "Levin's Risky Proposal: A Constitutional Convention." *The New American.* Thenewamerican.com, 20 Sept. 2013. Web. 01 Feb. 2015. http://www.thenewamerican.com/reviews/books/item/16578-levin-s-risky-proposal-a-constitutional-convention

[464] Ibid.

[465] May, Kate Torgovnick. "Larry Lessig Completes 185-mile Walk across New Hampshire, Spreading the Word That the U.S. Electoral System Can Be Fixed." *TED Blog.* Blog.ted.com, 24 Jan. 2014. Web. 10 Mar. 2015. http://blog.ted.com/larry-lessig-completes-185-mile-walk-across-new-hampshire/

[466] "New Hampshire HCR 2 Floor Vote." *YouTube.* Noah Neumark, 4 Mar. 2015. Web. 09 Mar. 2015. https://www.youtube.com/watch?v=e8ff3WVUj0Y

[467] Deutch, Theodore. "H.J.Res.119 - Proposing an Amendment to the Constitution of the United States Relating to Contributions and Expenditures Intended to Affect Elections.113th Congress (2013-2014)." *Congress.gov.* Congress.gov, 2 Sept. 2014. Web. 01 Feb. 2015. https://beta.congress.gov/bill/113th-congress/house-joint-resolution/119/text

[468] Gaines, Jim. "A Constitutional Amendment to Take Big Money out of Politics Dies Quietly." *Reuters.* Blogs.reuters.com, 12 Sept. 2014. Web. 01 Feb. 2015. http://blogs.reuters.com/jamesrgaines/2014/09/12/nearly-80-percent-of-americans-want-it-but-their-chance-of-getting-it-just-took-another-hit/

[469] Citizens for Self-Governance, Mark Meckler, Michael Farris, and Eric O'Keefe. *USA Convention of the States: A Handbook for Legislators and Citizens.* Rep. 3rd ed. N.p.: ConventionofStates.com, n.d. Print. https://d3n8a8pro7vhmx.cloudfront.net/conventionofstates/pages/142/attachments/original/1416248525/COS_Handbook.pdf?1416248525

[470] "Do We Need a New Constitutional Convention." *- Constitutional Rights Foundation.* Crf-usa.org, n.d. Web. 01 Feb. 2015. http://www.crf-usa.org/america-responds-to-terrorism/do-we-need-a-new-constitutional-convention.html

[471] "Craig Clevidence Explains the Renew Democracy Amendment." Telephone interview. 7 Jan. 2015.

[472] Madison, James. *Federalist Paper No. 10 (1787-11-22).*

[473] Email from Mike Gravel, May 25, 2014.

[474] "Democracy Symposium Panelists." *Democracy Symposium.* Demofound.org, n.d. Web. 01 Feb. 2015. http://demofound.org/symposium/panelists.htm

[475] "Citizens Amendment | The National Citizens Initiative for Democracy." *The National Citizens Initiative for Democracy.* Ncid.us, n.d. Web. 01 Feb. 2015. http://www.ncid.us/amendment

[476] Soltz, Jon. "Senate Republicans About to Screw Veterans -- All for a Campaign Ad." *The Huffington Post*. TheHuffingtonPost.com, 27 Feb. 2014. Web. 21 Mar. 2014. http://www.huffingtonpost.com/jon-soltz/senate-republicans-about_b_4867343.html
[477] Associated Press. "Senate Approaches Showdown Vote on a Veterans Bill Entangled in Push for Iran Sanctions." *Fox News*. FOX News Network, 27 Feb. 2014. Web. 21 Mar. 2014. http://www.foxnews.com/us/2014/02/27/senate-approaches-showdown-vote-on-veterans-bill-entangled-in-push-for-iran/

[479] "Mission and Goals." *E-Democracy.org*. Forums.e-democracy.org, n.d. Web. 01 Feb. 2015. http://forums.e-democracy.org/about/mission
[480] "Interview with Wolf-PAC Leaders - Money Out, Voters In!" *YouTube*. TYT Interviews, 16 July 2013. Web. 01 Feb. 2015. https://www.youtube.com/watch?v=WV51yfkm1Rg
[481] Josh. "The POPVOX Blog." *Latest Blog Articles RSS*. The Popvox Blog, 17 Aug. 2011. Web. 21 Mar. 2014. http://www.popvox.com/blog/2011/how-many-laws-does-congress-make-every-year/
[482] O'Connor, Karen J., Larry J. Sabato, Stefan Haag, and Gary A. Keith. *American Government: Roots & Reform, 2009 Texas Edition*. 5th ed. N.p.: Longman, 2009. Print.

Chapter 40
[483] Winfrey, Oprah. "Oprah Winfrey Quote." *BrainyQuote*. Brainyquote.com, n.d. Web. 01 Feb. 2015. http://www.brainyquote.com/quotes/quotes/o/oprahwinfr402113.html

Author's Note:
The preceding bibliography was formatted according to Modern Language Association (MLA) guidelines using the EasyBib online resource.

Made in the USA
Middletown, DE
25 May 2015